# THE LAWUDO LAMA

# THE
# LAWUDO LAMA

*Stories of Reincarnation*
*from the Mount Everest Region*

Jamyang Wangmo
(Helly Pelaez Bozzi)

WISDOM PUBLICATIONS • BOSTON

Wisdom Publications, Inc.
199 Elm Street
Somerville MA 02144 USA
www.wisdompubs.org

*Library of Congress Cataloging-in-Publication Data*
Wangmo, Jamyang, 1945–
  The Lawudo Lama : stories of reincarnation from the Mt. Everest
region / Jamyang Wangmo.
      p. cm.
  Includes bibliographical references and indexes.
  ISBN 0-86171-183-1 (pbk. : alk. paper)
  1. Lamas—Nepal—Biography. 2. Thubten Zopa, Rinpoche, 1946–
3. Kunzang Yeshe, 1865–1946. I. Title.
  BQ7920.W36 2004
  294.3'923'09225496—dc22

                                                        2004022914

First printing.
08  07  06  05  04
5    4    3    2    1

Cover design by Suszanne Heiser
Interior design by Gopa & Ted2, Inc.
Set in Adobe Garamond, 10.5/13.5.

Cover photos: Landscape by author (Lawudo Gompa is visible under the
    word "Reincarnation"), Lawudo Lama Kunzang Yeshe by Frances
    Howland, and Lama Zopa Rinpoche by Roger Kunsang.

*To the Primordial Wisdom Lama and*
*the Khumbu Sherpas*

*Om Svasti.*
*From the uncompounded and unfabricated natural radiance*
*Arises the supreme, magical emanation of the infinite buddhas' compassion,*
*Showing an illusory body for the sake of those to be subdued:*
*I supplicate the emanation of the playful dance of great compassion.*

*The totally perfect Buddha has completed the good qualities of relinquishing*
*and realization;*
*The holy Dharma protects without delay from the fears of existence;*
*The eminent Sangha possesses all the good qualities of a liberated mind:*
*I offer respect to the magnificent Lama, essence of the Three Precious Ones.*

—Ngawang Chöphel Gyatso

# Contents

PART ONE: THE LIFE STORY OF
THE FIRST LAWUDO LAMA, KUNZANG YESHE

# Foreword

THE DALAI LAMA

Sᴛᴏʀɪᴇs ᴏғ ᴛʜᴇ ʟɪᴠᴇs ᴏғ sᴀɪɴᴛs, great practitioners, and realized beings have been a source of inspiration in all religious traditions down the ages. In the Buddhist tradition, the story of our precious teacher, Buddha Shakyamuni, continues to have a great deal to tell us, even though it is two and a half thousand years after he lived and taught in India. The Buddha showed that enlightenment is possible, that the mind can be purified, and that ignorance and suffering can be overcome. However, he did not find enlightenment because he was a prince or because he had the help of some higher force, but because he was clear about his goal, steady in his effort, and never gave up. Similarly, the great Tibetan meditator and poet Milarepa is celebrated for attaining enlightenment in one lifetime, not because he practiced an especially quick path or found a shortcut, but because he did the necessary hard work.

This book focuses on the story of two individuals, the first Lawudo Lama, Kunzang Yeshe, and his successor, Thubten Zopa Rinpoche. It is also to some extent the story of the development of the Sherpa community living in the region of the border between Nepal and Tibet, a place where even the conditions for ordinary life are very hard. Food is sparse, the climate is harsh, and although the people have great faith, they traditionally have had little education. Under the circumstances it is remarkable that an individual like Kunzang Yeshe could seek out the Dharma, receiving teachings when the opportunity arose, but even more important that he would retire to his cave to put them steadily into practice. As a result he was able to bring real benefit to the community in which he lived and in turn commanded great respect.

His reincarnation, Thubten Zopa Rinpoche, has continued his predecessor's work in a similar spirit. This book tells how difficult it was for him to receive the education and training he sought, first in his home region, then in Tibet as it succumbed to Chinese occupation. This was followed by many years in which, despite being a Nepalese citizen, he shared the hardships experienced by many Tibetan refugee monks. In due course he has been able to return to his native region and establish a monastery and other facilities that will make it much easier than it was for him for the young to engage in spiritual study and training. He has also, of course, played a pivotal role in the growth of the Foundation for the Preservation of the Mahayana Tradition, with its branches all over the world contributing to the spread of the Buddha's teachings.

I have no doubt that readers of this book will find here encouraging evidence that, even in this day and age, where there is real faith, good motivation, and a great deal of hard work, the Dharma will flourish and grow.

July 31, 2002

# Preface

[W]hoever…demonstrates the Bodhisattvas' qualities attains
   all the virtue of Buddhas and Bodhisattvas.
[W]hoever…writes the biography of a Bodhisattva receives
   the same reward as the writers of the entire Buddhist Canon.
—THE LEGEND OF THE GREAT STUPA[1]

IN OCTOBER 1972, I was staying in a Nepali farmhouse (Ram's house) on Kopan hill near Kathmandu, waiting for the third Kopan meditation course to take place. The assembly hall of the new Kopan Monastery was being quickly finished under the supervision of Lama Thubten Yeshe and Ani Ann McNeil, but the lama who would teach the course was not in Kopan. I was told that he was still in Khumbu in the Mount Everest region at a place called Lawudo, where he had a cave and a small *gompa,* or monastery. The Lawudo Lama Thubten Zopa Rinpoche was expected to come down at any time in the next few days.

I was very curious to meet the lama. Someone who had a cave in the Himalayas sounded very exciting and just the type of lama I wanted to meet. Actually, I had already spent two months in Manali, India, wandering all over the mountains looking for "my cave," the place where I could sit down to meditate for the rest of my life! Perhaps I was now getting closer to finding it.

On the day that Lama Zopa was due to fly back from Lawudo, I went to receive him at the airport with other Westerners who were staying at Kopan. We found Lama Zopa having tea in the restaurant with his attendant Lozang Nyima and a lama from Sera Monastery called Geshe Tashi. He was a thin, handsome young man, with unfathomable deep black eyes that seemed to mirror the whole world. I greeted him shyly, while surreptitiously dropping on the floor the small bunch of wildflowers I had collected on the way; my humble flower offering seemed ridiculous compared to the nice incense bundles, flowers, and so forth that the other

Westerners offered. That evening, when Lama Zopa Rinpoche was performing his first ritual ceremony in the new Kopan Gompa, one of my housemates gave me a bundle of incense and a silk scarf and taught me how to perform prostrations. Together with her, I went into the temple and made offerings to the lama.

The one-month Kopan meditation course had a great impact on my life, and I decided to become a nun. After spending two months in Bodh Gaya making prostrations and then attending another monthlong meditation course with Lama Zopa in March, I took novice vows in Dharamsala, India. I returned to Nepal at the end of May in order to go to Lawudo for the summer. I flew to Lukla with some of Lama Zopa's little monks, walked to Namche Bazaar with them, and a few days later, after meeting Trulzhig Rinpoche at Tengboche Monastery, I walked alone toward Lawudo.

The path went through a beautiful fir and rhododendron forest surrounded by enormous snow mountains. Then, at a turning of the path, I saw the Lawudo Hermitage right in front of me in the middle of the mountain. I had never seen a picture of Lawudo; there was nobody around to tell me that this was Lawudo, but I knew the place. That was Lawudo, and it was my home. I had not the slightest doubt about it. I felt that an image dormant in my mind had finally come to light. And from that day onward, I just wanted to stay at Lawudo.

I spent months in retreat in a hut at the Charog Hermitage, built a small house under the Dragkarma (White Cliff) above Lawudo, stayed in the Sanyerpa Cave, and finally moved to the house next to the Lawudo Cave. Over the next few years I helped Lama Zopa by organizing group retreats at Lawudo, cleaning and painting the old statues, the cave, and the gompa, and putting the English books and the Tibetan texts of the previous Lawudo Lama in order.

One day, while looking through papers and books, I came across a few handwritten pages that happened to be the biography of the previous Lawudo Lama. I then asked permission from Lama Zopa to translate it into English with the help of the Sherpa monk Thubten Tsering, and I published it as a small booklet. During that time I met the author of the biography, the Maratika Lama Ngawang Chöphel Gyatso, who had been a close disciple of the Lawudo Lama and was the only one present when the lama passed away. Ngawang Chöphel had been requested by Lama Thubten Yeshe to write the life story of the Lawudo Lama, and I talked to him a few times in order to enlarge and clarify some of the information therein. The biography, entitled *A Garland of Devotion: The Life Story of the Supreme Liberator Kunzang Yeshe,*[2] was written in traditional Tibetan style, that is, with a long list of the teachings he had received but not much information concerning his life. I became very interested in finding more information about the Lawudo Lama Kunzang Yeshe and decided to rewrite and enlarge his biography.

1. Lama Thubten Zopa Rinpoche (left) and Ngawang Chöphel Gyatso; Kathmandu, 1986

Then, when I heard Lama Zopa telling stories about his childhood and youth, it became obvious that the early part of his life had to be included in my research. Again I spoke with Ngawang Chöphel, who eagerly agreed to write an account of Lama Zopa's recognition as the reincarnation of Lama Kunzang Yeshe. Finally, the story of Lama Zopa's return to Nepal, of the creation of Mount Everest Center for Buddhist Studies, and of life in and around Lawudo provided the logical continuation of the Lawudo Lama's story.

During my long sojourns in Khumbu I became acquainted with many aspects of Sherpa life that aroused my curiosity, and I was able to find a wealth of interesting stories about the Sherpa lamas. When the idea of writing the biographies of the Lawudo lamas began to materialize, I decided to use the lives of these two Sherpa lamas as the basis for presenting a wider account of Sherpa religious life. Many books have been written about the Sherpas by mountaineers and anthropologists, but those accounts do not provide detailed and reliable information about the lives of the lamas or the Sherpas of Khumbu.

For the benefit of those who are not acquainted with them, I have begun this book with an introduction to the Buddhist theories of reincarnation and the *tulku* (reincarnated lamas) system. Then, in order to set the stage for the stories of the lamas and in accordance with the traditional Tibetan biographies, I include a description of the land of the Sherpas and a brief historical sketch of the Sherpa people, their culture, and their religion.

Part I is based upon the very short biographical sketch of the first Lawudo Lama Kunzang Yeshe written by Lama Ngawang Chöphel, which is divided into three parts: The Birthplace of the Lawudo Lama, How the Lawudo Lama Kunzang Yeshe Relied upon Different Masters and Performed His Dharma Practice, and How the Lawudo Lama Dissolved His Body into the Dharmadhatu. Upon my request, the original text was enlarged in 1997 by Ngawang Chöphel himself with the account of how the reincarnation of the Lawudo Lama was found.

The first part of Ngawang Chöphel's work seems to have been inspired by the autobiography of the founder of Tengboche Monastery, Lama Gulo or Chatang Chötar, and contains a series of prophecies about Khumbu and a brief mention of the countries situated at its four cardinal points. The second part follows a very traditional Tibetan pattern of sacred biographies, with an account of all the lamas that Kunzang Yeshe had met and the teachings he had received, as well as a short account of how he found the Lawudo Cave. I have enlarged this part with details about Kunzang Yeshe's teachers, most of whom had a great impact on Sherpa religious and cultural life. In the third part, Ngawang Chöphel gives a detailed and heartfelt account of Kunzang Yeshe's death, which I have reproduced almost literally.

In order to give a portrait of the Lawudo Lama Kunzang Yeshe as lively and accurately as possible, I spent several years collecting information from elderly Sherpas and Tibetans who had met the lama or heard stories about him. I verified the information whenever possible in order to get a clear picture of his life and the society in which he lived. Details such as the actual year of the lama's birth, dates, and the sequence of events have been difficult to clarify; it was necessary to piece together the story on the basis of other, well-documented events. Extremely useful were the accounts I obtained from the Charog Lama Kusho Mangde, Lama Ngawang of Genupa Hermitage, the relatives of Lama Kunzang Yeshe, and Lama Zopa's mother. I have presented the life story of the first Lawudo Lama as a tale about his own life and of Sherpa society during the late nineteenth century and the first half of the twentieth. In addition to the stories narrated by the Sherpas and my own experience of the Sherpa mind and lifestyle, I have used a large number of Tibetan sources in order to document the religious life of the Khumbu Sherpas.

In part 2, the second Lawudo Lama Thubten Zopa Rinpoche describes his early life and his activities related to Lawudo and the Sherpas, including the creation of Kopan Gompa in the Kathmandu Valley and his early meditation courses for Westerners. Although I have relied heavily on Lama Zopa's own words (transcripts of his teachings and personal communications), a large amount of additional information comes from other sources. In order to ensure that all the information, even that given by Rinpoche himself, is accurate, I have tried to gather information from practically everyone—relatives, disciples, benefactors, acquaintances, and friends—who could shed any light upon his life. I have kept this part as a narrative in first person because my writing style cannot compare with Lama Zopa's lively and characteristic way of telling stories.

Some of Lama Zopa's students have expressed disappointment at the fact that the present book does not contain the full biography of Lama Zopa. But, except in the cases when lamas themselves write their own autobiographies, it is not auspicious to write their life stories until their work in this world has been completed. Therefore, in accordance with the wishes of Lama Zopa himself, the latter part of his life will be presented in a future book.

Finally, the epilogue reflects my own thoughts about the present and future of Khumbu, as well as an account of the whereabouts of the main personalities of the book. It is followed by a series of appendixes and a "visual journey" as an indispensable help to penetrate the stories and places described in the book.

The biographies of holy beings can be written from different points of view. "Outer" biographies are basically accounts of outer events and the activities such individuals perform for the benefit of others. "Inner" or "secret" biographies emphasize instead the teachings these beings have received, as well as their spiritual practices and inner development. In most cases, however, both the outer and inner aspects are combined into just one biography with an emphasis on the spiritual side.

Biographies of Tibetan or Sherpa lamas written by their disciples tend to present the life of their teacher in accordance with the pure perception of seeing the teacher as Buddha. The lama's achievements and activities tend to be idealized and glorified in order to inspire faith and devotion. But when a master writes his own autobiography, he tends to present his life from a more pragmatic point of view. The truly accomplished masters are usually very humble and do not like to talk about their own powers and achievements, although they may mention them occasionally in order to benefit and inspire readers.

In the present volume, the life of Kunzang Yeshe has been presented as an account of both his outer and inner achievements in accordance with the pure perception of his disciple Ngawang Chöphel, the elderly Sherpas who met the lama, and my own. The life of Lama Zopa Rinpoche is an autobiography; he tends to present himself as an ordinary person with many shortcomings. The emphasis is on his external activities, with some references now and then to his spiritual life. Nevertheless, just by listening to his words we can have a glimpse of the inner wealth of spiritual treasures present within his mind; we may not be able to look at the sun directly with bare eyes, but we can certainly benefit from its light and warmth.

According to Lama Zopa Rinpoche, the main purpose of writing the biography of holy beings is to inspire others to follow their example. When our mind is weak and invaded by desire for worldly life, reading how great beings past and present have practiced Dharma helps to revive our courage, inspiration, and devotion. By developing faith and admiration toward them, we will be inspired to practice the Dharma as they have done. Just by hearing about the wondrous deeds of the buddhas and bodhisattvas, we purify negative imprints within our mind and develop a strong wish to devote our life to following their example to the best of our ability. Therefore, it is extremely important to hear, read, and reflect upon the lives of highly realized beings. Particularly for Westerners, for whom role models for spiritual practice are difficult to find, it is very important to know how the great beings of the past and present lived their lives and put into practice the Buddha's teachings. From these life stories we can understand how they were able to use their own cultural background and the prejudices and social conventions of their countries to further their spiritual practice and benefit beings. Their cultural and social background may be different from ours, but the basic facts of life are similar. They encountered family problems, economic difficulties, social stigmas, frustrations, obstacles to finding spiritual friends and studying the Dharma, and many other situations that we are also familiar with.

Besides acquainting readers with Sherpa history and religion, I hope that the present book will inspire them to engage in serious meditation retreats and thus continue the valuable tradition of the Sherpa and Tibetan lamas. And I beg forgiveness for not being able to convey their marvelous stories in an even more inspiring manner.

# Acknowledgments

M Y DEEPEST GRATITUDE goes to the relatives of the Lawudo Lama
Kunzang Yeshe, the relatives of Lama Zopa Rinpoche, and the
Sherpas Lama Lhagpa Dorje, the late Charog Lama Kusho Mangde and
his daughter Pema Chöden, Kusho Tulku, Maratika Lama Ngawang
Chöphel Gyatso and his son Lopön Karma Wangchug, Acharya Ngawang
Özer, Ngawang Sherab (Tesho and Pharping), Lama Ngawang Tenzin
Trinle Gyatso (Genupa) and his son Lama Zangpo, the Tengboche Rin-
poche Ngawang Tenzin Zangpo, Ngawang Tharpa and his son Thubten
Jinpa (Rolwaling), the Thangme Rinpoche Ngawang Tsedrub Tenpe
Gyaltsen, the Kyabrog Lama Ngawang Tsultrim, Lama Ngawang Tsultrim
(Tolu Gompa), Ngawang Yonten (Rolwaling), Au Palden, Pemba Gyalt-
sen (Dunde) and his son Thubten Tsering, Sonam Puntsog (Tesho and
Pharping), and Thubten Lama.

Among the non-Sherpa Nepalis, I should mention the Drakar Taso
Tulku, Lama Gyani Bazra, Professors Pandey and Prem Khatri from the
Archaeology and Culture Department of Tribhuvan University, the staff
of the National Archives, the Central Library of Tribhuvan University,
and the Nepal Research Center.

Among the Tibetans, I must thank Bu Norbu (Thubten Chöling), the
nuns Tsultrim Dolma and Donma Pande of Khari Gompa, Dorje-la of Kuye
Labrang, Emi Thubten (Manali), Jampa Gyaltsen Mutuksang, Changling
Tulku, Khorchag Rinpoche, Lama Lhundub Rigsel, Lozang Nyima,
Trulzhig Rinpoche Ngawang Chökyi Lodro, the late Kochag Drogonpa
Ngawang Pema Rigzin and his nephew Buchung, Dzatul Rinpoche
Ngawang Rigzin Kunzang Chökyi Gyaltsen, Khumtul Ngawang Tenzin Jig-
dral Wangchug Chökyi Gyaltsen, Ralo Rinpoche, the Khari Lama Tenzin
Yonten and his attendants, Tenzin Zangpo and his wife Chöden (Khumde
Tsamkhang), Thubten Tsering ("T.T.-la"), Aja Tsering Kyipa, Pangboche
Geshe Urgyen Dorje, Zang Zang Tulku, the library staff at the Library of
Tibetan Works and Archives in Dharamsala, and countless others.

Among the Westerners, I have to make special mention of Hubert Decleer, who offered me countless photocopied texts and manuscripts, read through a few versions of my manuscript, and gave me invaluable advice and help. Gene Smith has been extremely helpful and kind and provided interesting information about various texts and lamas. Franz Karl Ehrhard clarified many obscure points. Merry Colony kindly gave me her notes about Kusho Mangde's life and Lama Zopa's childhood. Nick Ribush and Ailsa Cameron provided most of the transcripts of Lama Zopa's words, while Adele Husle shared her information with me. Mathew Akester read twice through the whole manuscript, corrected the Tibetan spellings, and made valuable suggestions. The mountaineer Tom Weir offered all his old photos and slides of Rolwaling and the child Lama Zopa. Sherry Ortner sent me some copies of her articles about Sherpas. H. Diemberger, Thubten Yeshe (Australia), Gary McCue, and Frances Klatzel provided wonderful photographs, most of them scanned and edited by Nick Dawson. Janice Sacherer offered additional information about Rolwaling. Philip Pierce translated a few articles from the German, and Michael Mühlich made useful comments. Information for the life of Lama Zopa was provided by Lozang Yeshe, Ann McNeil, Chip Cobalt, Judy Weitzner, Sister Max, Paula de Wijs, Steve Malasky, Chris Kolb, Lise Kolb, Thubten Pemo, Tenzin Palmo, Massimo Corona, Peter Nelson, Jackie Keeley, Jampa Zangpo, Ron Brooks, and many others.

I must not forget the help I received from the staff of the International Office of the Foundation for the Preservation of the Mahayana Tradition, and from Lama Zopa's attendants Roger Kunsang and Holly Ansett. I'd like to thank Tim McNeill and David Kittelstrom of Wisdom Publications, Venerable Connie Miller for her first editing of the manuscript, Bidur Dangol of Vajra Books, and Madhu Cannon, who did the final editing.

Many years ago, Lama Thubten Yeshe, in his usual forceful and enigmatic way, ordered me to write a book and encouraged me to communicate my experiences through writing and painting. Without Lama Thubten Zopa Rinpoche's inspiration, blessings, and collaboration, obviously this book could not have been written. And finally, His Holiness the Dalai Lama has given me the self-confidence I needed to undertake this project, and much more. For these Three Precious Lamas, the Jewels upon my head, whose kindness is impossible to repay, I feel an immense and deep gratitude.

Jamyang Wangmo
Bouddha
Saka Dawa, 2004

# List of Illustrations

PART TWO

133. Ngawang Jangchub Rigzin, the tulku of Diu Rinpoche
(courtesy of Kusho Yonten-la)

134. Ngawang Rigzin Tenpa, the tulku of Gomchen
Gampa-la

135. Tenzin Chögyal, the tulku of Ngawang Chöphel Gyatso
(courtesy of Lopon Karma Wangchug)

136. Lama Zopa Rinpoche with Charog Lama Ngawang Rigzin
Tenzin Gyatso, the tulku of Kusho Mangde (Roger Kunsang)

MAPS

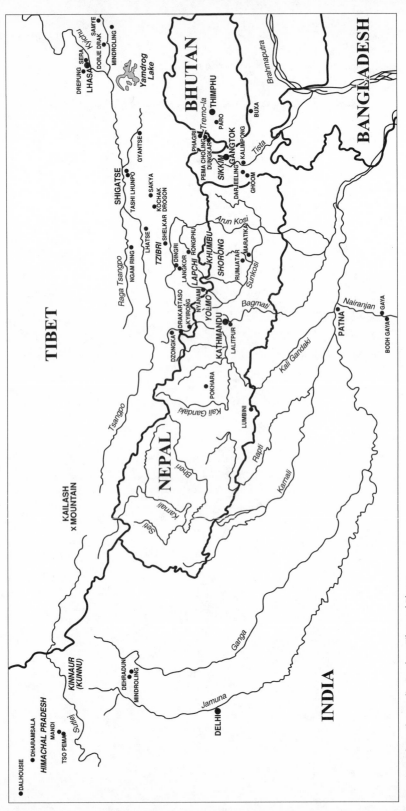

Map 1. Nepal, Northern India, Southern Tibet, and Bhutan

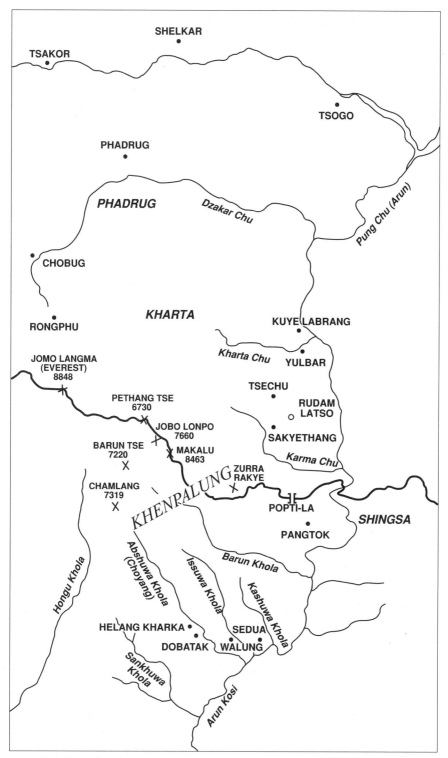

Map 2. Khenpalung and Southern Latö

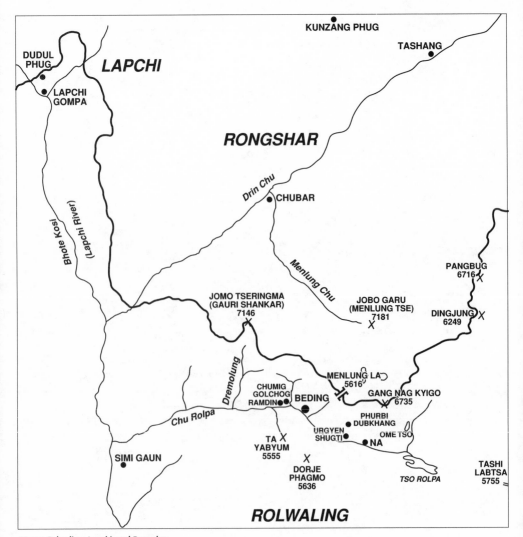

Map 3. Rolwaling, Lapchi, and Rongshar

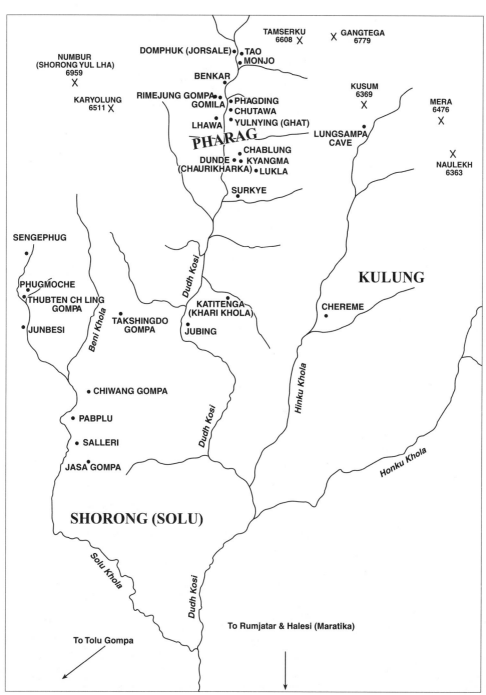

Map 4. Shorong, Kulung, and Pharag

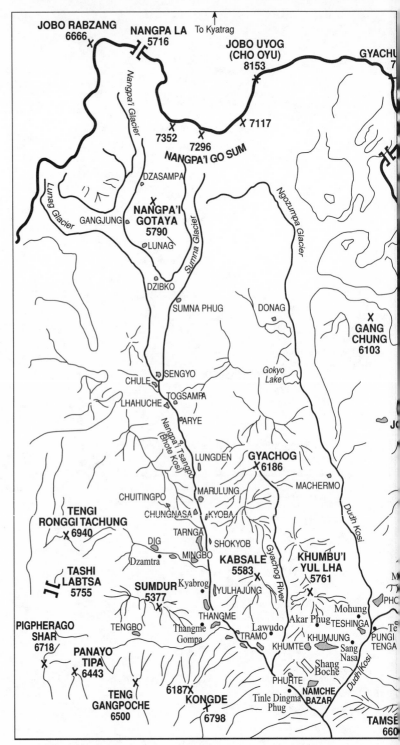

**Map 5. Khumbu**

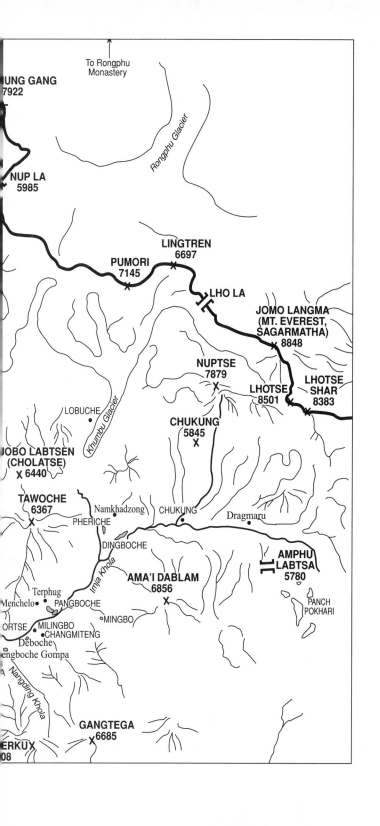

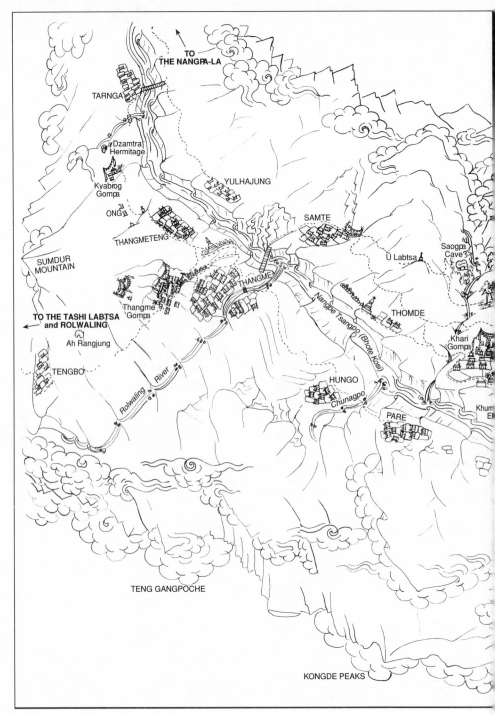

Map 6. Thangme Valley

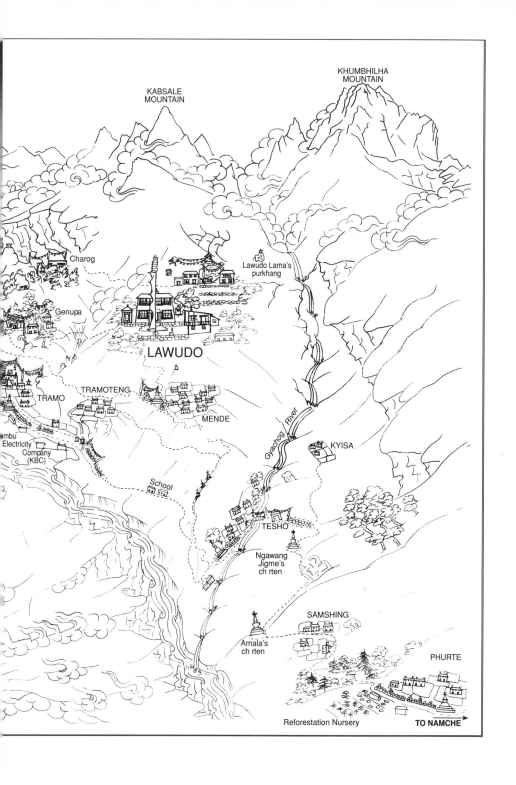

KHUMBHILHA MOUNTAIN

KABSALE MOUNTAIN

Charog

Genupa

Lawudo Lama's purkhang

LAWUDO

TRAMOTENG

TRAMO

MENDE

...mbu Electricity Company (KBC)

Gyachog River

KYISA

School

TESHO

Ngawang Jigme's ch rten

SAMSHING

Amala's ch rten

PHURTE

Reforestation Nursery

**TO NAMCHE**

# INTRODUCTION

*Geographical, Social, and Cultural Background
of the Sherpa People*

# 1. Reincarnation and the Tradition of Reincarnate Lamas *(Tulkus)*

## On Past and Future Lives

THE FOLLOWING is an excerpt from a lecture given by Lama Thubten Zopa Rinpoche at Kopan Monastery during the November 2000 meditation course:

There are many people in the West, both young and old, who remember past lives. Because their minds are clearer and less polluted than the minds of average people, they are able to remember their life in the womb and even their own past lives and those of others. But Western society accepts only what the majority of common people remember, which is just this one life, and even though it is their real experience, people who can remember past lives are afraid to talk about it in public because others will think that they are strange. On the other hand, there is nowadays a steadily growing interest to learn about karma and reincarnation. Westerners are becoming more familiar with such topics and developing a better and deeper knowledge of the mind.

Just as in a country where most of the people have goiter, someone who does not have one looks very strange, if the culture of a particular society does not include the belief in reincarnation, a person who has a real and clear experience of past lives appears to be abnormal. Generally speaking, our beliefs depend on the place and situation where we are born. We are born fresh into a new life and receive from those around us the accepted ideas and opinions of our parents and society. But those ideas and opinions are not necessarily correct. It is important that we analyze whether those beliefs accord with reality or not.

In order to understand rebirth it is very important to define what is death. At the time of death twenty-five different forms of dissolution take place,[3] following which the mind becomes extremely subtle, and three different visions occur. In the last stage of the death process all the gross minds absorb at the heart chakra and only the extremely subtle, clear light mind is left. All the heat and sensations disappear and the body appears to be dead, although the consciousness is still there. Finally, the extremely subtle mind and wind leave from the indestructible seed at the heart. Afterward, if the being is going to be reborn in the desire realm or the form realm, the gross wind and mind manifest again, and the body of the intermediate state *(bardo)* being arises.

The type of body that the reincarnated being obtains depends on the door or part of the body from where the consciousness leaves. If the consciousness leaves from the crown of the head, the being is reborn in one of the pure lands—such as Shambhala, Dagpa Khachö, or Dewachen, where the person will definitely become enlightened—or else the being will be reborn in the formless realm. If the consciousness leaves from the mouth, one will be reborn as a hungry spirit; if from the anus, one will be reborn as a hell being; if from the sex organ, as an animal; or if it leaves from the heart, as a human being.

According to the teachings of the Buddha, the extremely subtle mind is located at the heart. Because of this, the negative emotions such as anger, desire, jealousy, pride, and so forth arise from the heart and not from the brain. So we can see that our ordinary daily experience is in harmony with what the Buddha taught.

The yogis who practice the meditations of the completion stage of tantra undergo experiences similar to those that take place during the death process. Using the methods of the highest tantras, they are able to achieve the unification of the clear light and illusory body and use this realization as a weapon to purify ordinary death, intermediate state, and rebirth and actualize the resultant *dharmakaya, sambhogakaya,* and *nirmanakaya.* These meditators are able to use the subtle body to visit pure lands, make offerings to the buddhas, and receive teachings; they can then reenter their old body and perform ordinary activities just as before.

It is very important to have discussions on reincarnation and karma. In one of the early Kopan meditation courses I guided the meditation of going back to one's childhood, then to the mother's womb, and to the moment of conception. Some people who had stable concentration tried to go back even further. One person had a very strong feeling of having been a Tibetan in his previous life and was able to see clearly a house in Tibet with all the kitchen utensils, such as the churn to make Tibetan tea. If there is no reincarnation, it becomes very difficult to explain such experiences.

One can analyze by using the logical reasons found in the philosophical texts and also by considering the large number of people, both young and old, who can remember their previous lives. Besides the *tulkus,* or reincarnated lamas, there are many cases of ordinary people who can remember their past lives.

In the Eastern countries—India, Nepal, Tibet, and so forth—where Buddhism is alive, reincarnation is commonly accepted, but in the West the belief in reincarnation is not part of the culture. Only this present life is accepted. Nevertheless, even though many people profess to follow the ideas of their society, when they question deeply in their own hearts, they are not so sure that there is only one life.

If there is no continuity of life, why do people who have done many evil deeds have so much fear at the time of death? If there are no past and future lives, why does fear arise? That fear is a sign that one is going to be reborn in the lower realms. The Buddhist texts explain that at the time of death, beings are tortured by their own past actions and experience all kinds of terrifying visions. For instance, those who have killed many humans or animals have the experience of being attacked by the beings they have killed and they die with great fear. In Dharamsala, a Tibetan man who had been a butcher could see sheep and goats attacking him, but those around him could do nothing to help. Actually, no external beings are attacking the dying persons, but their own negative karma creates all those terrifying mental projections. And these are just the visions before death; the actual experience of being reborn in the lower realms is far more frightening.

Even though intellectually you do not believe in future lives, at the time of death you have the intuitive feeling that you may have wasted your life and that some very heavy things are going to happen. So, if you sincerely check your heart, the answer about reincarnation is: not sure.

These questions are very important. You may not accept reincarnation because it is not your experience to remember past lives, but that is just fooling yourself. If that were the case, what about the things that you did in this life that you don't remember? Would you say that you did not do those things? As a child you did many things that you do not remember now. You do not remember coming out of your mother's womb, but you have been told that you were born from her and you believe it. Using the same logic, you should not believe that either.

Some people argue that since the body disappears after death, reincarnation is not possible. This is a misunderstanding based on the lack of differentiation between body and mind. The body has form— color and shape—whereas the mind is a formless phenomenon that has the ability to know objects and whose nature is clarity. The body is a substantial phenomenon, while the mind is not. What goes on to the next life is the mind, not the body; the body does not reincarnate.

In short, not a single person has realized that there is no such thing as reincarnation. Some people have such an assumption, but they have no direct realization. On the other hand, there are numberless persons, even just ordinary beings, who have definitely realized the certainty of reincarnation.

## *Tulkus*

The recognition of tulkus (literally, "emanation bodies") seems to be a special feature of Tibetan Buddhism. The first official recognition and enthronement of a tulku took place in Tibet in 1288, when the Third Karmapa Rangjung Dorje (1284–1339) was recognized and enthroned as the reincarnation of Karma Pakshi (1204–83), who in turn was the tulku of Dusum Khyenpa (1110–93). There had been cases of reincarnated lamas before the thirteenth century, but they had not been officially recognized as the reincarnation of their predecessor.[4] Soon all the schools of Tibetan Buddhism adopted the tulku system, and enthronements became elaborate ceremonies, during which the monastery and property of his (or in very few cases, her) predecessor were handed over to the newly recognized incarnation. Although the tulku system has many shortcomings, it also has many advantages. In a society where proper education, even in the monasteries, was restricted to those who had sufficient means and social status, recognized tulkus were assured the thorough education and training that for an ordinary boy would be difficult to obtain.

A tulku can be defined as a being who has achieved a certain level of spiritual development and power and has consciously chosen to take rebirth in order to benefit beings. Despite their presumed spiritual achievements, tulkus have to undergo their education all over again. Most of them are able to learn much faster than ordinary children, and they usually show a certain maturity of character and a kindness and concern for others that are absent in most children.

Generally speaking, tulkus are born after the death of their predecessor, but according to Lama Zopa Rinpoche, "reincarnation does not always depend on the person being dead. Bodhisattvas can manifest everywhere." (A bodhisattva is a being who has developed the wish to achieve enlightenment in order to benefit others.) According to Chökyi Nyima Rinpoche, highly realized beings are endowed with power, wisdom, and compassion, and are able to transmit their wisdom to others. According to the Buddhist scriptures, bodhisattvas on the first level have attained the ability to manifest hundreds of versions of their own bodies. It can happen that a bodhisattva emanates another being to continue his or her work even before passing away. In such circumstances, according to Denma Locho Rinpoche, it is very important that others be informed about the appointed successor. This is a difficult topic that even learned Tibetan lamas find hard to understand. They all agree, however, that highly realized bodhisattvas have the power to do almost anything they wish, and that their actions can be beyond the comprehension of ordinary beings.

There are many examples of holy beings manifesting more than one emanation simultaneously. For instance, shortly before his death, the great yogi Milarepa (1040–1123) manifested various bodies in different places. Thangtong Gyalpo (1361–1464) appointed his close disciple Tenzin Chöje Nyima Zangpo as his tulku, and the Sixth Dalai Lama (1683–1706 [–1746?]) is believed to have been alive while the Seventh Dalai Lama (1708–57) was already occupying the throne.⁵ Jamyang Khyentse Wangpo (1820–92) manifested five different tulkus, Dudjom Rinpoche (1904–87) was born before the death of his predecessor (Dudjom Lingpa, 1835–1904), and Lama Thubten Zopa Rinpoche was born two and a half months before the Lawudo Lama Kunzang Yeshe passed away.

2. Khumbilha Mountain and Khumde village (Thubten Yeshe)

# 2. The Sacred, Hidden Khumbu Valley

Lama kunzang yeshe and Lama Thubten Zopa Rinpoche were both born in Upper Khumbu, the highest area of the Shar Khumbu or Solu Khumbu district, the northeastern region of Nepal bordering Upper Tsang (Tsang Latö) in southern Tibet.

According to the Sherpa scholar Lama Sangye Tenzin, "beyond the snow mountains, in the direction of India, there was an empty and unpopulated country known for being *khumpa,* or rugged. When the first migrants from Kham arrived into that area, they found it not only rugged but frightening and inhospitable *(khums).* Therefore, the place became known as *khums pa'i gnas,* the Fearful Place. Then, because the children or descendants *(bu)* of the people from Kham, which is situated in the eastern *(shar)* part of Tibet, settled in that frightening area, the region became known as Shar Khumbu."

Notwithstanding the efforts of the Sherpas to find an explanation for the name of their country in accordance with the Tibetan language, there is historical evidence that the area known nowadays as Solu Khumbu was included in the Khombu or Khombuwan province of the Kirat country of the Eastern Himalayas. Very likely the Tibetan migrants mispronounced Khombu and transformed it into "Khumbu."[6]

Khumbu is an extremely beautiful and fascinating region. In fact, it is considered to be a "hidden valley" or *beyul,* a special country blessed by Guru Rinpoche (Padmasambhava). According to the scriptures, Guru Rinpoche concealed texts and precious objects as treasures, or *termas,*[7] in certain remote and inaccessible valleys and sealed them with a very subtle mental barrier, transforming them into places of refuge for the people of future generations.

When the world becomes so corrupt that spiritual practice is practically impossible and our planet is on the verge of destruction, some fortunate beings will be able to reach these *beyuls,* or hidden valleys, and settle there. Such valleys can only be opened at a specific time and by a specific person who has been prophesized in the texts. Those who try to force their way into the valleys will only encounter obstacles and meet with failure or even death.

According to some scriptures, there are one hundred and eight hidden valleys in Tibet and the Himalayan regions, while other texts mention only seven, eight, or eleven.[8] Beyuls are said to have three levels—outer, inner, and secret. Some of the outer and inner levels have already been opened, as in the case of Khumbu, Rolwaling, Pemakö[9] in southeast Tibet, Dremojong (Sikkim), Khenpalung, Kyimolung, and Namgo Dakam.[10] The secret levels, however, still remain closed.

Padmasambhava concealed guidebooks with detailed descriptions of the different beyuls, the adjacent valleys that constitute their "doors," or entrances, their characteristics, and the benefits obtained by those fortunate ones who reach them. The *Guidebook to the Hidden Valleys of Dremoshong and Khenpalung* discovered by Pema Lingpa[11] describes the qualities of the hidden valleys in this manner:

> At that place there will be no frost or hail, heat or famine. Harvest and livestock will always be good. There will be no harm caused by epidemics, infectious diseases, poison, weapons, lords of the ground, or elemental spirits...By practicing there for one year, one will receive accomplishments equal to those received by practicing one hundred years somewhere else...Just being in that country purifies pollution and afflictive emotions. Everyone living there generates love and compassion, great wisdom, and a bright intellect...All beings will prosper in that country.

Khumbu is located between the hidden valleys of Rolwaling and Khenpalung and is considered to be the western door of Beyul Khenpalung. Like many other Himalayan valleys, Khumbu abounds in self-created syllables as well as footprints, handprints, and so forth, of various holy beings. The country is said to resemble a horse, and many of its mountains, caves, and boulders are the abodes of gods and goddesses and contain hidden spiritual treasures. *The Lamp of Clear Meaning: The Profound Instruction of [Dorje] Phagmo* says:

> Southwest of the holy place of Shri is the Khumbu Snow Wall. If one walks for half a month, one will reach that supreme hidden valley. If virtuous ones are lead and reach there, 30,000 hamlets will be established.[12]

In *The Great Catalogue of Prophecies* it is said:

At the entrance of the Khumbu Valley there is a treasure. When it becomes known, Tibet and Kham will know seven years of happiness.[13]

And in *List of the Six Categories of Close Transmissions of the Unobstructed Primordial Mind of the Great Completion:*

Seven people from the highlands and seven people from the lowlands of the seven southern valleys of Bud, Khumbu, Nyanang, and Kyirong, those karmically related, will come together. At the time of discovering the hidden valley, there will be a group of seven faithful followers.[14]

Tibetan and Sherpa lamas affirm that these and other quotations are definitive proofs of the sacredness of Khumbu.[15] In any case, the region is endowed with many of the wonderful qualities attributed to the hidden valleys. The fact that a large number of people nowadays feel drawn to Khumbu and Mount Everest may have deeper causes than we think. Even though their external purpose may be to climb the mountains or to trek around, they seem to be unconsciously attracted by some unknown, over-powering force that brings about a psychological and spiritual regeneration, very much in accordance with the powerful forces at play in the *beyuls.*

## The Four Gates of the Khumbu Snow Wall

Tibetan guidebooks depict sacred places as a *mandala,* or divine mansion, that can be entered through four gateways situated in the four cardinal directions. These are entrances not only in a physical sense, but they are also somehow related to the social and religious life of that particular place. Ngawang Chöphel Gyatso's *Garland of Devotion* mentions eight impor-tant sacred places that have particular relevance for the religious life of the Sherpas as the gateways to Khumbu.

*To the east of this hidden valley endowed with such boundless qualities*
*is the renowned, supreme Dremojong [Sikkim].*

Situated at the foot of the Snow Mountain of Five Treasures, or Kangchenjunga, Dremojong, which can be translated as the Valley of Rice or Valley of Crops, is called *dremo* (crops or rice) because it is blessed with an infinite variety of flowers, fruits, trees, crops, and medicinal herbs. It is called *shong* (vessel) because it is a broad and large valley. In its innermost part, which looks like a golden vessel filled with melted butter, is the White Cliff of the Auspicious Plain and the Cave of Great Bliss, where Padmasambhava meditated.[16]

*Closer by is the hidden valley of Khenpalung.*

The *Guidebook to Khenpalung Meaningful to Behold* discovered by Rigzin Godem-chen[17] says,

The hidden valley of Khenpalung lies to the west of the [Ama] Drime Snow Mountain and to the east of the Khumbu Snow Wall.

*Khenpa* is a kind of fragrant herb endowed with medicinal properties (*Artemisia vulgaris* or *Artemisia sieversiana,* mugwort), and *lung* means "valley" or "country." The *Guidebook to the Hidden Valley of Khenpajong*[18] retrieved by Pema Lingpa relates how Padmasambhava transformed Khenpalung into a beyul. One of the queens of the Tibetan king Trisong Detsen (790–844), Margyen of Tsepong, had caused the great translator Vairochana to be exiled, and the king was displeased with her. To satisfy her sexual desire she had intercourse with a dog and a goat, as a result of which she bore a child with the face of a dog and the skull of a goat who became known as Kyikha Ratho (Dog's Face Goat's Skull). When the king discovered this, he exiled both the child and his mother to a very remote southern valley called Khenpalung. Because of his evil disposition, Kyikha Ratho later wanted to conquer the throne of Tibet for himself, but Padmasambhava managed to send him across the Himalayas to the low hills, where Kyikha Ratho finally died of the heat. Padmasambhava then concealed Kyikha Ratho's riches as termas and sealed the borders and doors of Khenpalung, transforming it into a hidden valley.[19]

The southern part of Khenpalung comprises the upper valleys of the Barun, Issuwa, Abshuwa or Choyang, and Sankhuwa rivers in the Sankhuwasabha district of east Nepal, all of them tributaries of the Arun.[20] The northern section of Khenpalung is situated in the Karma Valley in Tibet, in the area adjacent to Mount Everest and the Makalu Range. The

Langma Pass connecting the Kharta and Karma valleys is regarded as the northern gate to the inner Beyul Khenpalung. In the Karma Valley is Gangla, where Kyikha Ratho is said to have built his palace. In an adjacent valley above a lake is a cave sacred to Guru Rinpoche containing the water of life *(tsechu)*. Behind a pass on the ridge between Makalu and Everest is the Sershong Lake, which is considered to be the center of Khenpalung. Here the northern route meets the western route coming from Chukhung in Khumbu and the southern route from the Barun Valley. In the lower Karma Valley is Sakeding, situated at the foot of the mountain where the wrathful mountain deity Zurra Rakye, the main protector of Khenpalung, abides. The innermost, secret level of Beyul Khenpalung remains still hidden.

According to the Sherpas, the key to the western door of Khenpalung is hidden inside the Dragmaru (Red Rock), a large, square boulder close to Chukhung between Ama Dablam and Lhotse mountains. Many types of grains are said to be hidden together with the key in order to allow people to sow crops again when the world is destroyed.

*In the south is the place renowned as the very center of this world: the Diamond Seat, or Vajrasana [Bodh Gaya].*

The Diamond, or Indestructible, Seat at Bodh Gaya in Bihar, India, is described in the scriptures as the spot where all the buddhas of the past, present, and future attain enlightenment. It is known as the Indestructible Seat because it does not undergo the process of creation or destruction.[21]

*Closer by is the Maratika Treasury Cave.*

The Maratika Cave is situated at Halesi in the Khotang district of Nepal, east of Kathmandu and south of Khumbu. The Maratika Cave is mentioned in various texts as the place where Padmasambhava attained the accomplishment of longevity with his consort Mandarava. In his *Short Guide to the Sacred Place Called Liberating from Death (Maratika) or Astonishing (Haleshe),*[22] Ngawang Chöphel Gyatso writes,

Once, Amitabha, lord of lineages and perfect teacher, in his sambhogakaya aspect, was residing in a perfect place, the Western Pure Land of Great Bliss, surrounded by a perfect retinue that included Amitayus, the lord of life of the five lineages, as well as countless male and female bodhisattvas. On that occasion, at the request of the bodhisattva Avalokiteshvara, Amitabha taught the *Eighteen Longevity Tantras*. The dakinis wrote them down in their symbolic script, using melted lapis lazuli on golden paper. They were deposited in a box made of the five precious jewels and concealed in the secret Maratika Cave.

*In the west is the Lapchi Snow Wall.*

Located between Rongshar and Nyanam (or Nyalam) on the border between Tibet and Nepal, the Lapchi Range is one of the most important pilgrimage places in south Tibet. Lapchi is considered equal to Godavari, one of the twenty-four power places associated with both the Hindu god Shiva and the Buddhist deity Chakrasamvara. Gang Rinpoche (Kailash) in western Tibet is related to the deity's body, Lapchi to his speech, and Tsari in eastern Tibet to his mind. The great Tibetan yogi Milarepa spent many years meditating in the Lapchi area and was the first to open the place for ordinary people by subduing the local gods and demons.[23]

*Closer by is one of Guru Rinpoche's hermitages, the Playground of the Dakinis [Rolwaling or Rolpa Khandroling].*

Beyul Rolwaling is a very high, narrow valley located west of Khumbu and south of Rongshar. Tseringma or Gauri Shankar (7,145 m) and Jobo Garu (Menlung Tse, 7,181 m) form a natural border between Tibet and Nepal. According to the *Abbreviated Chronicle,* Guru Rinpoche performed the Phurba, or Vajrakilaya, practice in a cave that became known as the Phurbi Drubkhang. The door to the innermost hidden valley is a cliff situated across the river in front of the Phurbi Drubkhang. Another entrance is said to be a boulder engraved with self-created syllables situated in Beding, Rolwaling's main settlement.[24]

*To the north is the celebrated Magnificent Mountain (Shri Ri) of Gyal [Tsibri].*

Shri Ri, also known as Tsibri, the Ribs Mountain, is located immediately northeast of Dingri and west of Shelkar in Latö. Padmasambhava, Milarepa, and Phadampa Sangye visited that area; it later became an important meditation place for the followers of the Drukpa Kagyu tradition.[25]

*Closer by is the Rongphu Snow Wall.*

Situated south of Dingri in the Upper Phadrug district, Rongphu, or Dza Rongphu, is the upper valley of the Dza River, which has its source in the northern slopes of the Jomo Langma Mountain (Everest). In his *Pleasant Sound of the Summer Drum*, Dzatul Ngawang Tenzin Norbu, the tulku of Dza Rongphu, says,

> Because it is the northern gate to Beyul Khenpalung and because many holy beings have blessed the place, Rongphu is renowned as a supreme, sacred spot that brings liberation by hearing about, seeing, remembering, or touching it.[26]

Padmasambhava spent seven months at Rongphu meditating in a small, dark cave known as the Damp Cave (Sadug Phug) or the Marvelous Blessed Cave, where he achieved supreme realizations and left his footprint. He was able to subdue the local spirits and gods, particularly the goddess Miyo Langzangma, one of the Five Sisters of Long Life who resides in the high snow mountain that bears her name.

Since early times, many hermits, both male and female, came to meditate at Rongphu attracted by its majestic beauty and isolation. Some used the existing caves and others built simple stone huts and locked themselves into long periods of solitary meditation.[27] In the late nineteenth century, Ngawang Tenzin Norbu spent long periods in solitary retreat at Rongphu and in 1901 built the Do-ngag Zungjug Ling Monastery, which at 4,980 meters is considered to be the highest monastery on earth.

## Sherpa Land

Shar Khumbu is divided into three parts. Upper Khumbu, or Khumbu proper, is compared to a lotus bud, Lower Khumbu, or Pharag, to the stem, and Solu, or Shorong, to a fully opened lotus flower. In *The Key to the Western Door* [of the hidden valley of Khenpalung] it is said:

> At half a month's walk from Shri of Gyal in Latö, there is a country called the Khumbu Snow Wall, which is shaped like a horse. The head

of the horse lies on the western side, and its tail lies in the east. This country is divided into two or three different regions. Toward the west is the valley called Khandro Rolwaling. East of the horse-shaped Khumbu Valley is a mountain *(gangs)* that looks like the saddle *(ga)* of a horse *(ta)* [Gangtega]. If you go past the neck of this mountain, in the upper part of the valley is the Healing Lady, Queen Miyul Lobzangma [*sic*].[28]

The Khumbu Snow Wall certainly deserves its name. Most of the highest mountains on our planet are in Khumbu: Mount Everest, or Jomo Langma or Sagarmatha, the Crown of the Head (8,848 m), Lhotse (8,501 m), Cho Oyu (Jobo Uyug, 8,201 m), Nubtse (7,879 m), Ngozumgang (7,846 m), Nangpe Gosum (7,352 m), Chamlang (7,290 m), Pumori (7,145 m), Ama Dablam (6,856 m), Tamserku (6,608 m), Gangtega (6,685 m), and many others.

3. The Nangpa La (Manuel Bauer)

The *Khum bhu'i yul lha,* or Khumbilha Mountain, where the local protector god of Khumbu resides, divides the region into two main areas. The valley of the Imja Khola runs in a southwestern direction from the Everest Range and joins the Dudh Kosi (Milk River) below Phortse. In this area are situated Pangboche, Dingboche, the Tengboche Monastery, and Phortse. Through the western, or Thangme, valley flows the Bhote Kosi

(Tibetan River), known as the Nangpe Tsangpo to the Sherpas because it has its source in the Nangpe Gosum Range on the Tibetan border. Here are situated Thangme, Tramo, and Lawudo. The Bhote and the Dudh Kosi meet below Namche Bazaar and flow south as the Dudh Kosi. At the foot of the Khumbilha Mountain are Khumde and Khumjung, the oldest Sherpa villages.

Khumbu is accessible from Tibet through the Nangpa La (5,716 m) in the north. There used to be another pass east of Jomo Langma, but it became blocked by avalanches some 200 years ago.[29] From the west, Khumbu can be reached through the Tashi Labtsa Pass (5,856 or 5,755 m), while in the east the Amphu Labtsa Pass (5,780 m) connects Khumbu with the Kulung Valley and the Arun Basin through a very high and difficult route. The easiest way into Khumbu is from the south, following the Dudh Kosi through the Pharag region.

The lower mountain slopes of Khumbu and Pharag are covered with lush forests of pines, silver fir, juniper, rhododendron, oak, and birch. In Pharag can be found a large variety of edible plants and roots, berries and strawberries, wild grapes, beans and asparagus, and a profusion of *erma* trees, the fruit of which is widely used as a spice in Sherpa food.[30] In the early spring the blue lily makes its appearance on the Khumbu mountains, followed by the blossoming of rhododendrons. Deep or pale pink, pale violet, white, or yellow, the rhododendron flowers transform the forests into a magical, fairy-tale landscape. Soon after, the yellow flowers of the berberry bushes *(Berberis angulosa)* begin to blossom, and primroses, buttercups, wild roses, and primulas cover the mountainside. Edelweiss grows profusely during the monsoon, followed by the blue gentian in early autumn. In the higher areas grow the blue Himalayan poppy and the dwarf rhododendron *(Rhododendron anthopogon)*, known to the Sherpas as *masur*. It has a very sweet and fragrant scent and is widely used as incense. Wild mushrooms and *toa*, an edible root found in the potato fields, used to be a welcome supplement to the Sherpa diet before green vegetables began to be cultivated all over Khumbu and Pharag.

Pharag and Khumbu abound in wildlife—wild goats *(tahr)*, goral, black bear, musk deer, antelope, fox, wolf, marmot, marten, and snow leopard. Impeyan pheasants *(danphe)*, the national bird of Nepal, can often be seen digging the ground for small roots and flying downward with a sharp cry when disturbed. Snow cocks, vultures, lammergeier, pigeons, and many other species of birds abound in Khumbu.[31] And it is said that high up in the rocky recesses between the snow and ice, the yetis have their abode.

## Yeti Country

The yeti has been described as a large, hairy, brown-colored, human-like or ape-like creature, with a pointed head and long arms. The search for definite proof of its existence has given rise to many "yeti expeditions."[32]

The Sherpas, though, are not interested in the scientific or zoological classification of the yeti. For them, the yetis are manifestations of local spirits from the retinue of Khumbilha, whose task is to protect the sacred mountain where the god resides and all the adjacent mountains and valleys as well. They are neither ordinary animals nor humans, but an intermediate species endowed with supernatural powers. The Sherpas affirm that yetis are not just ethereal spirits because they can be seen and heard.[33] They know that yetis feed on young bamboo and wild plants, and that there is one type, the *chugti,* that feeds on animals. Every year the herders find the remains of yaks that have been split into two by some creature of extraordinary strength; the flesh of the yaks has been eaten, and the bare bones are neatly arranged together. There seems to be another type of yeti, the *miti,* who is fond of dogs and human flesh, although there are very few instances of yetis directly harming humans. Instead, there are many stories relating how yetis have helped meditators living in remote caves by bringing them edible roots, wild fruits, water, and fuel.

According to the Sherpas, yetis like to walk their own particular paths and do not deviate from them. They look straight ahead while walking, and humans only get hurt if they happen to be in their way. In the Thangme Valley, some yetis spend the warm season eating bamboo shoots in the forests of the Kongde Mountain and return for the winter to the upper Gyachog Valley by crossing the river between Tesho and Samshing and climbing the very steep, rocky ridge of the mountain. Other yetis cross the river near Tramo and walk toward Kabsale Peak through the Genupa and Charog hermitages; the lamas living in those hermitages have had many encounters with the yeti. And there is believed to be a "yeti path" near the Mugsum Zampa on the way to Tarnga.

Besides their enormous physical strength, yetis emanate a very strong odor and a powerful energy, so terrifying that people and animals become paralyzed with fear when a yeti comes near. Some Khumbu Sherpas have seen the yeti, and many people, including myself, have heard its frightening cry. As well, there are some well-known yeti episodes, such as the one about a lady from Khumjung who was flung into the river by a yeti[34] and the folk story describing how the Sherpas got rid of a large number of yetis.[35]

4. The upper Gyachog valley (Andrea Antonietti)

Although the following story may bring a skeptical smile to the lips of some readers, I would like to relate my own experience with yetis. In December 1981, I was in retreat at Lawudo. One night I was awakened by a strange sound. At first I thought it was the scream of a drunkard or a crazy woman from Mende, the village right below Lawudo. But these shrieks did not seem to be human. I found them frightening, but at the same time I was intrigued. Was it a crazy person or an animal? Or...could that be the famous yeti? After a while the sound could be heard again, getting closer and closer to the Lawudo Cave. I am a curious person, but I don't like to take unnecessary risks. Besides, my flashlight was very small, and I could not see very far into the darkness, so I convinced myself to stay in the warmth of the cave instead of going out into the cold to try to find out who was responsible for those frightening shrieks.

The next morning I told Lama Zopa's sister about the funny sounds. She shrugged and did not want to talk about it. I found that strange, but there are so many things one may find strange in that country....

At that time a new house was being built at Lawudo, and some villagers were breaking stones and building walls. Every day Ritha Tsering, a man from Mende, would pass through Lawudo on his way to the high pastures of the Gyachog Valley, where his yaks and *naks* (female yaks) were grazing, and he would stop for a chat with the workers. On that particular day he came running down the mountain much earlier than usual, and I saw him talking very excitedly with the builders. It seems that he had gone up the mountain as usual, milked the naks, and sat down to make tea and eat *tsampa* (roasted barley flour). While he was eating, he looked up along the ridge above him; there, at a great distance, he saw a man. "Strange," he thought. "There are no other animals around except mine, and there is no path over there. I wonder where that man is going." Then he noticed that the "man" was very hairy and had a brownish color. The Mende Sherpa immediately forgot about his tea, his tsampa, his milk, and his animals, and ran down the mountain as fast as he could.

The following day was a Saturday, market day in Namche, when the Khumbu population meets in the market—or rather in the *chang* (beer) houses near the market—and exchanges all the gossip while getting nicely drunk. Then they fall asleep in the chang house or by the side of the trail, and their more sober friends or relatives have to take them home. Anyhow, that evening we heard the missing link of our story. It seems that on Thursday a monk from Kyabrog Gompa called Ngawang Loden had been invited to Tesho, right below Mende, to read a religious text for the benefit of a sick person. The monk finished the reading quite late, but his family home was in Phurte not far away, so he started to walk in the twilight. When he reached the turn in the road just before Samshing, he had a strange feeling. He looked down toward the river at his right and saw a strange creature walking up toward him. The monk was petrified with fear, but he managed to walk backward for a few meters and finally ran back to the house where he had been reading the scriptures, and he spent the night there. It was that same night that I had heard those terrifying shrieks coming up from the foot of the mountain and going toward the upper Gyachog Valley.

To conclude, I have to assert that, no matter what the beliefs of the scientific community might be, yetis do exist. At least in Khumbu.

# 3. The People of Khumbu: Their History and Culture

THE FOLLOWING INFORMATION on Sherpa history is based upon currently available sources—a few records of the clans' ancestry, which are of dubious historical authenticity, the prayers to the lineage lamas of the different religious transmissions, and the oral tradition of folk stories. Although Sherpa history cannot be considered academically accurate from a historian's point of view at the present time, there is certainly a considerable amount of interesting information in the folk legends of the Sherpas. As with all folk legends and oral traditions, there are several versions of the same story, so I have chosen those versions that seem the most plausible.[36]

## The Opening of Khumbu

Many centuries ago, glaciers and lakes covered most of the Khumbu region, while the lower mountain slopes were clothed with dense lush forests. Yetis and wild animals roamed undisturbed, and no human being had ever set foot upon that country. It was a wondrously beautiful area, although cold, wild, inhospitable, and inaccessible. Gradually, as the earth's climate warmed up, the snow line and the glaciers started to recede. The large lake below the Khumbilha Mountain filled up with silt, earth, and rocks from the continuous mountain erosion, and large platforms of fertile land began to appear.

One day, a Tibetan hunter whose mythical name is Kyirawa Gonpo Dorje[37] lost his way in the mountains while pursuing a mountain sheep. After crossing over a high pass, he descended into a wild and beautiful valley. Gigantic mountains covered with snow and ice towered over deep narrow valleys lush with trees and flowers. The scent of the dwarf rhododendron filled the air, while rainbowlike clouds danced around the rocky slopes, sometimes hiding and then suddenly revealing the snow-covered peaks. Gonpo Dorje loved the place. Because it was a rugged, wild country inspiring awe and fear, he called it Khumpa.

Gonpo Dorje spent sometime in the Khumpa region hunting the wild sheep, goats, and deer. He used to cut the meat of his prey into strips that he hung on tree branches to dry before carrying them home (Gonpo Dorje's tree is said to be in Charog, near Lawudo). Back in Tibet, he spoke to others about the beautiful valley he had accidentally chanced upon.

## Who Are the Sherpas?

The *shar pa,* "Sherpas" or easterners, were originally members of the nineteen clans or tribes living in the Zalmogang area of Kham in eastern Tibet.[38] Dongkha Ringmo, the leader of the Chagpa clan, had two sons. Sangye Paljor, the youngest, received religious education from the terton Ratna Lingpa (1403–79) in Central Tibet and became a famous teacher of *dzogchen* (the Great Completion system). He had two sons, Nyida Dorje and Dudjom Dorje. After some years, Sangye Paljor went back to Kham and taught dzogchen to his father, who was able to attain a great level of accomplishment.

At that time the situation in Kham was deteriorating,[39] so Dongkha Ringmo and Sangye Paljor decided to leave for good. The elders of the Minyag, Thimmi, and Lama clans joined them, and together with their families, the Khampa chieftains made their way toward Central Tibet. They crossed the grasslands of the Jangthang and eventually reached the Latö area of Tsang, close to the Himalayas and the border with Nepal.[40]

The Khampas had come to Latö fleeing the turmoil and violence in their homeland, but their hope for a peaceful life devoted to religion and trade was to be shattered once again. The unstable political situation in Central Tibet and Tsang, as well as fear of Nepali or Muslim armed incursions,[41] added to the problems of coexistence with the local population, and life for the migrants was not easy.

Sangye Paljor then remembered a prophecy of Guru Padmasambhava stating that Beyul Khenpalung would be opened when the world was totally overcome by wars and violence. For Sangye Paljor, as for most Tibetans, "the world" meant Tibet, Nepal, India, China, Bhutan, and Mongolia in general, and more specifically the valley where they lived. And so, Sangye Paljor thought that the time had come to search for a peaceful life in the sacred Khenpalung or its adjacent regions. Accordingly, he summoned his son Dudjom Dorje and his main disciple

Ngagchang Gyagarba Chenpo[42] and instructed them to go to Khumbu, the inaccessible country directly behind Jomo Langma and Dza Rongphu.

Dudjom Dorje and Gyagarba Chenpo crossed the mountain ranges and reached Khumbu together with their families and disciples.[43] Dudjom Dorje chose Pangboche and Gyagarba Chenpo Dingboche as their hermitages. They brought with them a substantial number of yaks, naks, sheep, and goats, as well as religious objects, carpets, jewelry, tsampa, Chinese tea, and so forth. At the beginning they stayed in caves that they made habitable by closing the entrances with stone walls, and after some time they built simple stone huts covered with slate roofs. They survived on a diet of meat, milk, wild plants, mushrooms, and roots until they started to cultivate the land and were able to produce crops of barley, buckwheat, and radishes.

After a few years in Khumbu, Dudjom Dorje dreamt of a blue-colored lady who instructed him to leave Khumbu with Gyagarba Chenpo and go to a lower, warmer valley. She told him that there they would have many disciples and benefit many beings. Following the prophetic dream, the two lamas with their families and domestic animals walked toward the south until they reached warmer and wider valleys. They called this area *Shorong,* the Lower Valleys. They were able to buy some fertile land from the local Kiranti Rai population and took over the wild and uninhabited areas. They settled in different parts of this area and built temples and hermitages.

Soon other Khampas started to move into Khumbu. One of these was Phachen of the Thimmi clan, a very powerful lama. Once, when he was staying in a cave known as Dilbu Dingma Phug on the eastern slopes of the Kongde Mountain, a group of spirits or ghosts came to disturb him and lit a large fire at the entrance of the cave. Phachen entered into deep meditation upon the unobstructed, intrinsic purity of material phenomena and was able to come out through the rock. He then flew to a spot across the river and left his footprint on a stone. That place became known as Phurte (from *phur,* to fly).[44] Phachen founded Khumde, believed by some to be the first Khumbu village, at the foot of the Khumbilha Mountain.

Gradually, many more Khampas settled in Khumbu.[45] Their social structure was based on the four original clans, subclans, and new clans, and their life was spent in cultivating the land, herding yaks, cows, and sheep, and trading.

## Lama Sangwa Dorje and His Brothers

Lama Sangwa Dorje is the most important figure in Sherpa history. He is considered the fifth in a line of reincarnations that goes back to Tsang Legdrub and Yudra Nyingpo in the ninth century. Although there is some controversy regarding his birthplace (some believe he was born in Tibet), the most widely accepted version is that Lama Sangwa Dorje was born either at the Kongmoche or the Mong hermitage on the eastern slope of Khumbilha above Teshinga, sometime in the late sixteenth or early seventeenth century. His father was the tantric practitioner Lama Buddha Tsenchen of the Thimmi clan.[46]

Buddha Tsenchen was on very good terms with the protector of Khumbu, the Khumbilha, who used to come often to visit the lama. Buddha Tsenchen was trying to extract from him information about the location of a salty lake somewhere in the valley of the Nangpe Tsangpo that would spare Sherpas the long journey to Tibet to buy salt. One day, when the god was about to reveal the exact location of the lake, Buddha Tsenchen's wife heard voices in her husband's room and went to see who was there. As she entered the room, the god vanished and never returned, and so the salty lake could not be located. Later, however, it was found near the Tashi Labtsa and is known as Tsamoche Tsho, or Salty Lake.

When still very young, Sangwa Dorje was sent to Kochag in south Tibet to study with the Drogonpa Rigzin Jigdral Zangpo, the eighth blood descendant of Terton Ratna Lingpa,[47] from whom he received the empowerments, oral transmissions, and commentaries of the works of Ratna Lingpa and Rigzin Godem-chen. Sangwa Dorje also received teachings from the Third Yolmo Tulku Tobden Pawo Tenzin Norbu[48] and from other outstanding masters.

Sangwa Dorje was said to possess an exceptional learning ability; just by glancing once at the texts, he was able to understand their meaning. By the time he had completed his studies, Lama Sangwa Dorje had become a skilled physician and had control over the four elements. Thus, on his journey back to Khumbu he did not use ordinary means but held up his shawl and flew in space. He first alighted on a large boulder close to the Mugsum Zampa bridge at the confluence of the Langmoche and Nangpe rivers, where the imprint of his head, hands, and feet, as well as his "toilet" and his resting chair can still be seen. From that spot, Lama Sangwa Dorje flew down along the valley of the Nangpe Tsangpo and turned east toward Tsangasa in the valley of the Dudh Kosi, where he left his footprint on a large boulder. He then flew toward a hill just below the Gangtega Mountain, where he left the imprints of his feet and his eating bowl on a rock. Sangwa Dorje named the place Tengboche and made strong prayers to be able to build a large monastery on that spot in a future lifetime. He then continued farther east toward Pangboche, and it is said that even his dog left its pawprints on a boulder along the way.

Lama Sangwa Dorje meditated in many remote caves and hermitages of Khumbu and Shorong[49] where, according to the local legends, yetis brought him food, water, and fuel. When one of the yetis died, the lama kept its scalp. As a sign of his accomplishments, Lama Sangwa Dorje was able to hang his shawl upon the sun's rays. Later, he was requested by the local people to build a temple, or *gompa*, at Pangboche. Just at that time, a statue of the protector Mahakala (Gonpo Nagpo Chenpo) flew from India into his hermitage, gave instructions about the location where the temple should be built, and promised to protect Dharma practitioners. The statue became known as the Gonpo Sungjonma, the "Talking Protector." The new Pangboche temple was consecrated in 1667 and named Pal Ribo Gompa, the Magnificent Mountain Temple, where the Gonpo Sungjonma and the yeti scalp were the prominent objects of worship and awe. Sangwa Dorje then cut his hair and scattered it around the area, causing juniper trees to grow.

During that time, in Tarnga lived a powerful Tibetan known as the Dzongnangpa, who had fled from Shelkar Dzong to Khumbu after committing a crime. This Tibetan became jealous of Lama Sangwa Dorje and sent two men to murder him, but the lama created the magical forms of a tiger and a leopard and sent them down the mountain to kill the prospective murderers. After that incident, Lama Sangwa Dorje appointed his disciple Thutob Wangpo as head of Pangboche Gompa and went back to Tibet, where he passed away at Chöbug in the lower Dza Valley. The six syllables *Om ma ni pad me hum* appeared spontaneously on a black stone at the spot where his corpse had been cremated. His heart, tongue, and eyes did not burn in the funeral pyre and were enshrined in a small reliquary, or *chörten*. The Pangboche people went to Tibet and tried to obtain the relics of their lama, but the Tibetans refused to give them the chörten. The Sherpas then managed to get the caretaker drunk and escaped back to Khumbu with the relics, which are still kept in Pangboche Gompa.

Lama Sangwa Dorje transmitted his lineage to Norbu Wangyal, the son of Rigzin Jigdral Zangpo, and to the Shorong Sherpas Phagtse and Michen Tsunchung Tashi. He had two highly accomplished brothers.

Ralpa Dorje, who was able to twist and knot a spear, founded the Thangme Gompa at a small cave under a rocky cliff on the southern slope of Sumdur Mountain. Khenpa Dorje was able to pile up seven grains of barley and stand a statue of Shakyamuni Buddha upon them. He founded Rimejung Gompa above Gomila in the Pharag area.[50]

It seems that at some point the followers of the lama of the Dzamtra Hermitage near Tarnga, who had been murdered by the Dzongnangpa, were able to kill the murderer and his friends. Some relatives of the Dzong-nangpa fled Khumbu and requested help from the Kiranti Rais and their Sena ruler, who were able to invade and conquer Khumbu. From that time onward, the Sherpas were considered to be subjects of the Sena kings of Makwanpur.[51]

In Tibet, the eighteenth century witnessed a fierce persecution of Padmasambhava's followers, the Nyingmapas, by some fanatic followers of the Gelug tradition.[52] During those years of unrest, a few Khampa families left their homeland and migrated to Latö. In 1788 the Nepali army again invaded Tibet, capturing Dingri and Shelkar and plundering the wealth of Tashi Lhunpo Monastery in Shigatse. A strong earthquake had hit the Latö area in 1709 causing widespread destruction. It is probable that those events prompted a new wave of Tibetans to migrate to Khumbu. Most of the new migrants settled in the Thangme Valley and Khumjung, while some went to Kulung, Shorong, and Rolwaling.

Nepal had already been unified under the Gorkha king Prithvi Narayan Shah, who in 1769 conquered the Kathmandu Valley and later brought under his control the Kiranti and Limbu areas east of the Arun Kosi. Thus, as subjects of the Makwanpur kings, by the end of the eighteenth century the Sherpas became integrated into the newly born kingdom of Nepal.

## Economic Development

Because of the rugged terrain, the Khumbu Sherpas could grow only meager crops of buckwheat and radishes. Barley, the staple Tibetan food, could only be grown successfully at Dingboche and Tarnga. The cold climate and high pastures were favorable for rearing yaks and *zobgyos* (the crossbreed between yaks and cows), but since the early days of the first settlers, the main source of income for the Sherpas was trade. In the eighteenth and nineteenth centuries, the commerce between Tibet and Nepal through Khumbu increased substantially, and in the late eighteenth or early nineteenth century a new town was founded at Nagboche (pronounced Nawuche by the Sherpas and Namche by everyone else), a strategic point on the road to Tibet. The Nepali government gave monopoly of the trade with Tibet through Khumbu to the Nawuche, or Namche, merchants. Shorong Sherpas and other ethnic groups were thus effectively barred from engaging in the trade with Tibet, while the Sherpa traders of Khumbu became extremely wealthy and powerful.[53]

Potato cultivation was introduced in Khumbu and Shorong during the late eighteenth or early nineteenth century. The Sherpa farmers eagerly adopted the new crop, and soon potatoes became the staple food and the pride of Sherpa cuisine.[54]

With the development of trade and potato cultivation, Khumbu became a prosperous region, and Nepalis from other ethnic groups migrated to Namche in search of work. Economic prosperity gave the Sherpas leisure time for religious activities, with the result that the nineteenth and early twentieth centuries witnessed a surge of spiritual development and the creation of new gompas and hermitages throughout Khumbu. Temples, chörtens, mani walls, and prayer wheels were built, and religious practitioners found ample sponsorship for their Dharma practice.

The British economic expansion in northern India had a lasting impact upon the life of the Sherpas.[55] Some of them would walk to Darjeeling to work on road and railway construction and would return home for the potato harvest. In this way, some Sherpas were able to amass considerable wealth. In 1907 Sherpas were hired as porters for the first time for a climbing expedition led by A. M. Kellas; Sherpas later became famous as the world's best trekking and mountaineering guides and porters.

During the nineteenth century, Nepal and Tibet were on the brink of war on a number of occasions.[56] Together with the prospects of the new economic development of Khumbu, this instability in southern Tibet may have served to lure some Tibetan families to cross the Nangpa La and settle in Khumbu.

## Cultural and Religious Development

So far, no clear information has emerged about the early history of the gompa built by Ralpa Dorje above Thangme. We do know, however, that sometime in the eighteenth century, Tenpa Sangye of the Lhugpa clan[57] settled in Thangme or Thangteng. Tenpa Sangye's son Rigzin Pema Longyang,[58] who lived in Pangboche and in various hermitages in

Khumbu, became a well-known teacher. His son Tulku Ngawang Dorje[59] settled in the Yib Golchag, or Lock-shaped Cave, above Thangteng and gave a new impetus to Thangme Gompa. He was a skillful artist; the three large statues of Amitabha, Padmasambhava, and Avalokiteshvara now in Thangme Gompa are said to have been made by him.

Tulku Ngawang Dorje's son Chatang Chöying Rangdrol[60] was to play a very important role in Sherpa religious life. From Drakar Taso Chökyi Wangchug (1775–1837)[61] he received all the main lineages of the Nyingma tradition and was able to pass them to his own Sherpa and Tibetan disciples. After his father's death, Chöying Rangdrol assumed the leadership of Thangme Gompa. He built a new hermitage across the Nangpe Tsangpo at a secluded spot known as Charog ("raven"), where the shape of a bird-print is clearly visible on the cliff, and named it Tashi Nyi-öd Khyilba Enpe Ritö, the Secluded Hermitage of the Auspicious Whirl of Sunlight.

Chatang Chöying Rangdrol stayed at Charog for a while and then moved to a cave farther down the mountain where there is a water spring among tall juniper trees. He named the new hermitage Ngodrub Chöling Palgyi Drubkhang, the Magnificent Meditation House Dharma Island of Accomplishments. The place became popularly known as Gaphugpa, the Joyful Cave, which the locals pronounce as Genupa.

Chatang Chöying Rangdrol gathered many disciples and left his footprint on a rock and his fingerprints on a small stone. His descendants became known as the Charog lamas and continued to assume the leadership of Thangme Gompa (see appendix 4). After his passing away around 1865, the spiritual leadership of the gompa fell to his son Ngawang Trinle Lhundrub.[62]

In 1831, a new gompa was founded in Khumjung,[63] while Rigzin Chökyi Gyaltsen[64] built the Drag-ri, or Rocky Mountain, Gompa at Phortse. His main disciple, Dreltse Donden Jamyang Chökyi Rigzin, a direct descendant of Phachen, built a gompa and a large mani wall at Lukla in Pharag. According to popular tradition, Dreltse Donden flew from the gompa to a large flat rock and left his footprint there.[65] He passed away at Lukla, where his ashes are kept in a small *purkhang*, or funerary house, near the gompa.

The Sherpas tell the following story about Dreltse Donden's death. One day, the lama told his wife: "I am going upstairs to do some practice. Do not let anyone come into the room and do not touch my body until the *phurba* (ritual dagger) I am holding falls down." His wife could hear the steps of the lama performing a dance, but after a while the sound ceased, and she went to have a look. Dreltse Donden was standing still with his right hand outstretched holding the phurba. The lady forgot the lama's advice and touched his body; at that moment the phurba fell from the lama's hand and he passed away.

# 4. The Religion of the Sherpas

*The Sherpas work hard, they live peaceably,*
*and they are happy and content; and it seems to me*
*now that this in itself is a simple tribute to God.*
—A VISIT TO THE SHERPAS, by Jennifer Bourdillon

## Tibetan Buddhism

IN KHUMBU, as in Tibet where the Sherpas originally came from, the relationship between man and nature has a deep significance. The external, physical landscape is closely related to the psychological or mental activities of man and plays an essential role in society. Mountains, lakes, trees, rocks, and particular features of the landscape are the abode of spirits or forces that can be benevolent or harmful for the individual and the whole community, and need to be tamed and propitiated by rituals and offerings.

When the Tibetan king Trisong Detsen decided to build the first Buddhist monastery of Tibet, he was unable to do so because of the power of the spirits associated with the land who were opposed to the project. Finally, the king invited Guru Padmasambhava, a great tantric master from India endowed with amazing powers, to come to Tibet and assist in the taming of local forces. On his way to Tibet through Nepal and the Himalayas, Padmasambhava was able to tame and bind the worldly spirits under an oath not to harm the population but instead to protect the teachings of the Buddha. Having successfully controlled the forces that were obstructing the construction of Samye Monastery, Guru Padmasambhava, or Guru Rinpoche (the Precious Teacher) as he became known, spent the rest of his life on earth disseminating the Buddha's Doctrine among Tibetans.

Padmasambhava became a legendary personage, a kind of spiritual superman with full control over all natural forces, both internal and external. He was able to leave imprints of his hands, feet, or body upon boulders and rocky cliffs and could cause springs of water to appear out of rocks, fly in space, assume different forms, and conceal texts and objects in the earth, rocks, trees, temples, water, space, or mind. Many of his Tibetan disciples, both male and female, obtained similar powers.

As Buddhism spread in Tibet over the centuries, various different schools arose. The followers of Guru Rinpoche, who based their practice upon the early translations of Sanskrit texts, became known as the Nyingmapas, members of the Old Tradition of Early Translations *(Ngagyur Nyingma)*. The followers of the Later Translations *(Sarma)* include the three main schools known as the Sakya, Kagyu, and Kadampa (Old Kadampa and New Kadampa, or Gelug). The Nyingma tradition in turn consists of two different types of lineages, the Kahma, or Oral, Tradition of teachings passed from master to disciple, and the Terma, or Treasures, the tradition of teachings concealed by Padmasambhava and revealed by his prophesied disciples, or *tertons*.

With the exception of a few men and women who received religious training in Sakya and Gelug institutions in Tibet, and more recently in India and the Kathmandu Valley, the majority of the Sherpas are Nyingmapas. Although most Sherpas do not understand the philosophical principles of Buddhism and do not practice meditation, they do have a very strong faith in Guru Rinpoche and the Three Jewels of Refuge (the Buddha, his Doctrine, or Dharma, and his Followers, or Sangha). They firmly believe in karma (every action we perform brings about a corresponding result, good for virtuous actions and bad for nonvirtuous actions) and in past and future lives. The more complicated aspects of Buddhism are the domain of the lamas and monks, who can read the scriptures, engage in meditation retreats, and are experts in performing rituals.

The religious practice of ordinary Sherpas is limited to the recitation of a few mantras, turning prayer wheels filled with many thousands of mantras, and walking clockwise around temples, large prayer wheels, carved stones, and so forth. Attending and sponsoring communal religious gatherings (Mani Rimdu, Dumche, and Nyungne), performing offerings to the local gods and goddesses, and donating food, tea, and money to the lamas and monks are religious activities that prevent or minimize the negative results of "bad karma" and increase one's stock of merit, or "good karma." Besides praying to Guru Rinpoche, Sherpas have particular devotion to Phagpa Chenrezig (Arya Avalokiteshvara), also known as

Thugje Chenpo (Karunamaya, the Great Compassionate One) and pray to be reborn in the Pure Realm of Buddha Amitabha or Öpagme.

Sherpa monks and married lamas practice in accordance with the traditions of Rigzin Chenpo Godem-chen, Jatson Nyingpo, Ratna Lingpa, Karma Lingpa, and Minling Terchen Terdag Lingpa, among others. Mahakala in his aspect as Gonpo Maning and Magon Chamdrel or Ekajati are the principal Dharma protectors propitiated by the Khumbu lamas.

## The Cult of the Worldly Gods and Goddesses

### THE FIVE SISTERS OF LONG LIFE

In contrast to deities who embody different aspects of the enlightened mind, gods and goddesses abiding in mountains, lakes, and so forth are worldly beings subject to the same changes of mind as humans. They can help practitioners but can just as easily be offended, and have to be regularly propitiated and pacified by different means.

Among the worldly gods and goddesses inhabiting the Himalayas, the Five Sisters of Long Life play a very important role in Sherpa religious life. They are worldly *khandromas,* dakinis or "sky-goers," who live in the Himalayas on the border between Tibet and Nepal. They were very mischievous, and although they vowed in front of Padmasambhava to refrain from harming people, it was only when Milarepa meditated at Lapchi near their abode that the five sisters were finally subdued. Since that time, they have protected and helped anyone who invokes them with sincere devotion.

When the five dakinis asked Milarepa to give them the bodhisattva vows, he told them, "First, each of you should offer me your individual worldly accomplishments and tell me your real names." Thereupon, the principal lady of the group said: "I am their leader. My name is the Auspicious Lady of Long Life (Tashi Tseringma), and I offer you the accomplishment of protecting life and increasing one's lineage."

The girl sitting at the right side of the principal lady said: "My name is Blue-Faced Fair Lady (Thingi Shalzangma), and I offer you the accomplishment of divining with a mirror." The girl sitting at her right said: "My name is Fair-Throat Diadem Lady (Chopen Dinzangma), and I offer you the accomplishment of obtaining a treasury of jewels." The girl sitting at the left of the principal lady said: "My name is Immutable Elephant Fair Lady (Miyo Langzangma), and I offer you the accomplishment of beauty, prosperity, and food." Finally, the girl sitting at her left said: "My name is White Magician Fair Lady (Tekar Drozangma), and I offer you the accomplishment of increasing the four-footed animals."[66]

Tseringma is described as white in color, youthful and beautiful, riding a lion and holding a golden *vajra,* or *dorje* (a ritual implement sometimes translated as "thunderbolt"), in her right hand and a vase with the nectar of immortality in her left. Thingi Shalzangma is blue, rides a wild ass, and holds a mirror and divination flag. Miyo Langzangma is yellow, rides a tigress, and her right hand is in the gesture of giving, while her left holds a vessel full of divine foods. Chopen Dinzangma is red, rides on a deer, and holds a chest full of jewels. Tekar Drozangma is green, rides on a turquoise dragon, and holds a bundle of grass in her right hand and a snake lasso in her left.[67]

5. The Five Sisters of Long Life (illustration from the *Rinjung Gyatsa*) (L-R Immutable Elephant Fair Lady, Blue-Faced Fair Lady, Auspicious Lady of Long Life, White Magician Fair Lady, Fair-Throat Diadem Lady)

Regarding their places of residence, Tseringma resides in the mountain bearing her name situated between Rolwaling and Rongshar, and Miyo Langzangma in the mountain known nowadays as Mount Everest. They are also said to abide in five lakes that can be seen from the Tashi Labtsa Pass between Khumbu and Rolwaling.[68]

### THE "COUNTRY GODS": KHUMBILHA AND HIS RETINUE

The chief "god of the country" *(yul lha)* of the Khumbu region, Khumbilha, is one of the twenty-one mountain gods of Tibet subdued by Padmasambhava and resides in the rocky mountain named after him. No one is allowed to climb the Khumbilha Mountain, and people have to be extremely careful not to disturb the god or his entourage.

Country gods belong to a group of five ancient deities known as the Five Deities of the Individual, the other four being the "goddess of females" *(mo lha),* the "god of life" *(srog lha),* the "god of males" *(pho lha),* and the "god of enemies" *(dgra lha).* These five deities are closely associated with the internal physical elements of a person and with the external elements. They have a strong influence on the health, wealth, and fortune of people and animals.[69]

According to a text used by the Khumbu Sherpas entitled *Golden Garland of Clouds of Offerings to the Country Deities*,[70] Khumbilha's maternal uncle is Lui Tsabo, his father is Yabje Gyalpo, and his mother Lusin Phungchema. Khumbilha is the mountain spirit known as Je-gyal Tritsen Nyen, white and radiant, his body dressed in white silks and his head adorned with a white silk turban. He holds a lance adorned with red silk ribbons in his right hand and a red lasso in his left. His mount is a mare with a red muzzle, identified by the local lamas as a mountain with two peaks resembling a horse's ears on the northern side of Khumbilha Mountain. The god is accompanied by a tiger on his right and a leopard on his left, as well as his wife, children, ministers, and a great army of *tsen* spirits. According to the Tengboche Rinpoche, his wife is the goddess Tamo Sermo, the Yellow Mare, who abides in Tamserku Mountain (6,608 m) on the opposite bank of the Dudh Kosi.

The text goes on to describe the mountain where the god resides and its surroundings. At his right, in the upper part of a valley resembling a basket, is a snow peak with a white silk turban. At his left is the black rock tsen with a black turban. When looking at the principal god from the eastern side, it looks like a golden stupa *(chörten)* adorned with many jewels. If one looks at it from the south, it resembles a king's throne. If one looks from the west, it seems to have a turquoise hanging from the neck. His friends are the five healing goddesses. His wife is surrounded by 1,090 healing goddesses. His daughter is Zurmo Chagmo and his son is Gangmar Jobo. His "inner minister" is Lhatsen Taga, who resides in Gangtega Mountain. The "outer minister" is Sego, or Lhatsen Marpo, who lives near the Nangpa La.

Khumbilha is said to belong to the retinue of Zurra Rakye, the guardian god of all hidden valleys in general and of Beyul Khenpalung in particular, who resides in a sharp pointed snow mountain named after him situated east of Makalu (8,475 m) and visible from the Thangme area.[71]

## OTHER WORLDLY BEINGS

Khumbu and its adjacent areas are populated by a vast number of country gods, "lords of the ground," "door guardians," *nagas,* or water gods, ghosts *(srindi),* and mountain spirits *(telma).*

According to some informants, the country god Yarlha Karpo resides in a pointed mountain across the Nangpe Tsangpo in front of Thangme, while in the valleys of the Dudh Kosi and the Imja Khola some other country gods from Khumbilha's retinue are said to reside.

6. The Ome Tso in Rolwaling (Gary McCue)

In the central part of every Sherpa village is the shrine to the local "owner of the ground," while each house has its own smaller shrine dedicated to the owner of the ground and the family gods. Naga shrines are found near water springs and large trees. Srindi are said to roam around abandoned houses and caves and to be quite mischievous; telma seem to be inhabitants of the forests that are fond of playing drums.

RITUALS

The main rituals for the propitiation of Khumbilha take place during the fifth Tibetan month at the start of the Dumche festival and seem to present slight variations according to each particular village. Namche people perform incense offering *(lhasang)* and "golden drink" offering *(serkyem)* at the Khumbilha shrine above the village or in their own houses. These are performed during the first half of the first, fourth, sixth, and ninth lunar months, each family choosing the day of the week that corresponds to the birthday of the head of the household. The offerings are accompanied by the hanging of prayer flags on the roofs of their homes in Namche or at the family god's shrine in other villages, followed by a party.

Sherpas believe that making offerings to Khumbilha and the gods of their ancestors helps to have a long life, good health, and prosperity. Not performing the rituals and not taking part in the Dumche festival will cause problems and the family lineage to become extinguished.

The monks and villagers of the Thangme area perform elaborate offerings to the Five Sisters of Long Life and to Sharlungdrag, the local protector of Dza Rongphu. Zurra Rakye is propitiated during the Mani Rimdu and Dumche festivals at Tengboche.

The people from Pharag perform offerings to the local gods at the Kusum Gang Garu Mountain[72] and the Lungsampa Cave, an important pilgrimage place connected with Khenpalung situated on the Dranag Tsen Mountain, on the eastern side of Kusum. The cave is two-storied and has a large number of crystals. Sometime in the early nineteenth century a temple was built there and later abandoned. When the local people tried to bring the three statues (of Amitayus, Avalokiteshvara, and Tara) housed there to Junbesi in Solu, they became too heavy and had to be left in the cave. Nearby are some rocks shaped with auspicious forms, and it is said that somewhere below there is a *terma* hidden in a boulder.

According to local informants, people used to go to the cave to ask the mountain god for money, and money would appear. They could take it but had to promise to repay the money after a certain time; if they failed to do so, they would die. These days, Sherpas who pass by the Lungsampa Cave on mountain expeditions never fail to leave an offering.

The Rolwaling Sherpas perform elaborate incense offerings to Tseringma at the Ome Tsho, or Milk Lake, and request her protection against avalanches, landslides, and other natural calamities.

# PART ONE

*The Life Story of the First Lawudo Lama,*
*Kunzang Yeshe*

*Although from the very beginning he had discarded the seeds of birth and death and their imprints and was abiding in the safe haven of the immortal, primordial clear light, he appeared in this world as a perfect, powerful protector and unsurpassable refuge for those rough-minded migrators of this present time of the five increasing degenerations. He was the pervading lord of an ocean of lineages and mandalas, being in essence a great vajra-holder gone beyond the tenth bodhisattva ground.*

*Even though in reality his mind is inseparable and of one taste with the mind of Kunzang Pema Jungne, the All-Good Lotus-Born One, in order to guide all those worthy ones who could be subdued, he purposely appeared as a knowledge-holder accomplished in the playful dance of magical emanations. He had secretly realized the essence of emptiness and compassion, but externally he took the aspect of an ordinary house-holder. Such was the ascetic whose mind was totally free of elaborations, known as Kunzang Yeshe, or the Lawudo Lama Yeshe, renowned like a banner fluttering on the very peak of cyclic existence.*

*In order to share the extensive and deep ocean of his life and deeds with fortunate ordinary, childish beings like myself, what I am presenting here is like a mere drop of water on the tip of a hair.*

—Ngawang Chöphel Gyatso

7. The Lawudo Lama Kunzang Yeshe

# 5. Who Was Kunzang Yeshe?

A SMALL FIGURE in brightly colored felt boots with soft, pleated leather soles under a dark red woolen coat, a yellow hat, and on his back a cone-shaped basket held by a leather band around his forehead steadily climbs the stony path leading toward Thangme Gompa. On top of the ridge high above the village, the man stops to take a rest, leaning his load on a rock. To the north, the Nangpe Tsangpo—the river that flows south from the Nangpa glacier—disappears among the maze of snow peaks. On a flat, sandy spot above the riverbank, the eight buddha eyes of a large chörten watch peacefully over the four cardinal directions. Close to the chörten is a large group of houses and potato fields. That is Thangteng, or Upper Thangme. A path winds its way through the fields and hills toward the north. The young man on the ridge knows that path very well. He has trod it many times on his marches toward the wide and deep snowfields of the Nangpa La and on into Tibet.

After a short rest, he continues to climb past a small chörten and a long row of stones carved with the mantra *Om mani padme hum hrih.* Farther up, the path goes through a gate, or *kani,* that marks the entrance to the gompa's territory. As one approaches the gompa, there are more and more mani stones, and hundreds of prayer flags hanging from the tall juniper trees dance in the wind.

The main building of Thangme Gompa is the *lhakhang,* or "house of the deities," where the lamas assemble periodically to perform religious ceremonies. Below the lhakhang is the residence of the head lama. His name is Ngawang Trinle Lhundrub, and he is a highly realized tantric lama who lives most of the time in his hermitage at Charog, a secluded, mysterious, and romantic spot under a high cliff on the opposite side of the river. Only on certain occasions does the Thangme Lama come up to the gompa to perform ceremonies and give teachings to the married tantric practitioners, the *ngagpas*[73] who form the gompa's community.

The houses of the lamas are scattered on the steep mountainside surrounding the lhakhang. Some are large houses surrounded by potato fields, and some are meditators' huts big enough only for a square meditation box, a shrine, and a fireplace. Kunzang Yeshe walks along the fields and houses until he reaches a medium-sized stone house with a massive door set on a beautifully carved threshold. This is Kunzang Yeshe's home.

**8. Thangteng chörten**

Kunzang Yeshe's ancestors came from a gompa of married lamas situated near Sakya Monastery in Tibet. In the late eighteenth or early nineteenth century, some lamas from the four tantric communities known as the Four Corners *(zurshi)* in the Sakya district moved into Khumbu and became known to the Sherpas as Sakya Khampas. One of them settled in Thangme, married a Sherpa woman, and had three sons.[74] Ang Norbu, the eldest, built a house for his family in the lower Gyachog Valley and named it Kyisa, the Land of Happiness. The second son, Ang Nami, stayed in Thangteng, while the youngest inherited the family house in Mende and became the father of a girl whom they called Da Lhakyi and of a boy, Kunzang Yeshe.

At the sound of the approaching footsteps, the face of a young woman with red cheeks and shiny eyes appears at the window. Kunzang Yeshe enters the house and climbs the steep wooden stairs to the first floor. Tsamchi helps her husband to put down his load, and she takes out the three bags made of coarse yak wool. One of them contains millet, part of which will be used to make chang. Another bag contains rice, and the third bag, rock sugar and chilies. Some of the rice, sugar, and chilies will be kept for the family's consumption, but the main portion will soon be taken to Kyatrag in Tibet to be exchanged for salt, wool, and dry meat.

Kunzang Yeshe sits in his usual seat by the fireplace and drinks a few bowls of chang, the white fermented drink that helps to keep one warm and cheerful when exhausted from walking the steep mountain paths or from digging the potato fields. Tsamchi takes off the lid from a copper pot resting on an iron tripod above the fire; she fills a large brass plate with boiled potatoes and places it on the table in front of her husband, together with a small bowl containing salt, ground erma, and chili. She then sits on the floor next to the fire and waits for news of his trading journey and the world beyond Thangme. Next to her, inside a rectangular basket, is a baby girl fast asleep.

Kunzang Yeshe talks about his journey to Katitenga (Khari Khola for Nepalis) two days' walk south of Thangme, where he had bartered a good quantity of salt for grain. He describes the people he met on the road, the families in whose houses he spent the night, and the incidents of the journey, all of it interspersed with jokes and laughter. Like most Sherpas, Kunzang Yeshe and Tsamchi thoroughly enjoy joking, gossiping, and drinking chang.

The sun had gone beyond the snow peaks long ago, and Kunzang Yeshe goes out to bring home the cattle—a couple of cows and a zobgyo. Tsamchi revives the fire by adding a few juniper branches and chips of dried yak dung, and places another pot on the hearth. She peels and cuts some potatoes and radishes, washes them carefully, and throws them into the pot together with some buckwheat flour and animal fat to be cooked into *shagpa,* the Sherpa evening stew.

After securing the door with a wooden pole, Kunzang Yeshe returns upstairs, lights a butter lamp in front of the image of Guru Rinpoche, and sits again near the fireplace with a text in front of him. Unwrapping it, he begins to recite loudly and melodiously the prayers and ritual invocations of various tantric deities.

Although he was a married man who loved his family and did not hesitate to undertake trading journeys to improve their material welfare, Kunzang Yeshe's main interest was the practice of Dharma. Being a young and sturdy Sherpa, he was able to make the difficult journey to Tibet as many as thirteen times each year, and he never missed an opportunity to visit holy places and meet the most renowned religious masters of the area.

Since childhood, Kunzang Yeshe had seen and experienced for himself the hardships of Sherpa life and how people's lives revolved continuously around the question of survival. Like other Sherpa children, he had been expected to help at home with the animals and the potato fields and to bring water from the spring in a heavy wooden container. Fuel, either juniper and rhododendron branches or yak dung, had to be brought from the distant forests or from the high pastures. The fields had to be tilled, manure had to be spread on them, potatoes and radishes had to be planted and then collected a few months later. Barley for making tsampa, millet for *sen* and chang, rice for special occasions, flour, salt, tea, chilies, and sugar—all had to be brought from very long distances. The soil at Thangme would yield only potatoes and buckwheat, and even the much-needed barley could be grown only at nearby Tarnga and at Dingboche, on the southern slopes of Jomo Langma.

Kunzang Yeshe had seen how people were mean to each other because of jealousy, greed to acquire material possessions, or miserliness to part with even a small amount of their hard-won foodstuffs. He saw how pride transformed the wealthy and powerful into ruthless despots. He saw men getting drunk and beating their wives and children, or engaging in brawls with other drunkards. He saw people earning substantial amounts of money in far-away Kathmandu or Darjeeling or in business expeditions and wasting it by gambling and drinking. He also saw lamas heavily drunk with chang and *arak,* sleeping through the rituals they had been invited to perform in people's houses and reading through pages and pages of holy scriptures without understanding a single word of what they had read.

Kunzang Yeshe watched the yaks and zobgyos overloaded with goods and forced to tramp through the deep snow of the Nangpa La. He saw sheep and small cattle preyed upon by wolves and *serkang* (snow leopards), and yaks split in two and eaten by yetis. And then he saw people, young and old alike, becoming ill, suffering accidents, and dying.

There was something else, however, that Kunzang Yeshe perceived around him. Some lamas, and even some ordinary people, had devoted their lives to true Dharma practice. Most of them lived in remote hermitages far away from villages and had achieved control over their minds. Greed, hatred, ignorance, jealousy, pride, and miserliness did not have sway over them. They were at ease and radiated loving-kindness and compassion toward men and animals alike. Some of them were very learned and knew the meaning of the texts and rituals very well, and a few, so Kunzang Yeshe had heard, had realized the true nature of the primordial mind through the practice of *atiyoga* or *dzogpa chenpo,* the highest vehicle of the Nyingma tradition.[75]

## How Kunzang Yeshe Began His Spiritual Journey

While still a child, Kunzang Yeshe had been introduced to *ka kha ga nga* (the Tibetan "alphabet") by his father. When he was able to read, he learned a few prayers by heart, such as those for taking refuge in the Three Jewels and developing a kind heart. Kunzang Yeshe loved to recite the seven-line prayer to Guru Rinpoche[76] and was convinced that by repeating the prayer loudly enough and with great devotion, the Precious Guru would hear it and come to Thangme from above the Tashi Labtsa, riding upon the last rays of the setting sun. Another of his favorite prayers was the one known as *Spontaneous Fulfillment of One's Wishes.*[77] He used to recite it fervently whenever he was told to carry water or to perform some other task and could not get free time to play with the other boys of his age. As he grew up, Kunzang Yeshe's father took him to receive religious instruction from eminent and holy Sherpa lamas.

Together with a group of Thangme lamas, Kunzang Yeshe received his first formal teachings from Kagyu Chökyi Lodro,[78] an old Sherpa lama reputed to have achieved a good understanding of the real nature of the mind and to be capable of imparting the most secret instructions of dzogchen practice. He stayed either in Pangboche or in Phortse at the recently built Drag-ri Gompa, where many ascetic practitioners lived in caves and huts on the surrounding mountainside.

The Thangme Sherpas carried their blankets, provisions, religious texts, and gifts for the lama secured on a bamboo frame or in baskets. Below Thangme, the path descended steeply toward the river and crossed a well-built bridge festooned with hundreds of prayer flags, the little rectangular pieces of cloth printed with the "wind horse" *(lung ta),*[79] Guru Rinpoche's mantra, and so forth. The Sherpas would always hang prayer flags at dangerous spots to counteract the negative forces or spirits that could cause accidents. Close to the river could be seen some large white boulders entirely carved with *Ah a sha sa ma ha,* the six syllables that have the power to purify sentient beings of the six realms and are believed to prevent floods and landslides.[80]

Leaving behind Tomde and Tramo, Kunzang Yeshe and his companions crossed the Gyachog Stream at Tesho, passed through Samshing and Phurte, and took a steep and narrow trail up the mountain. The Nangpe

Tsangpo was now a long way down to their right, and the little path climbed steadily toward Khumde and Khumjung, two large villages nestled at the foot of the holy Khumbilha Mountain. The travelers continued toward Tsangasa, set in a forest of rhododendron, fir, and juniper trees below the impressive slopes of the Khumbilha. It was here that Lama Sangwa Dorje had left one of his footprints impressed on the surface of a large boulder when he flew back from Tibet to Khumbu. The Thangme lamas burnt a few fragrant branches of *shugpa* (juniper)[81] as an offering to their great saint and went on their way.

9. Phortse (F. Klatzel)

It was late afternoon when they reached Phortse and Drag-ri Gompa. Kunzang Yeshe and his companions went to offer respect to Kagyu Chökyi Lodro, prostrating three times before the lama and presenting him with white scarves *(khatag)* and the sugar, rice, and potatoes they had brought as offerings. The lama draped the khatags around their necks in blessing and invited them to sit down. After inquiring about Chökyi Lodro's health, the conversation turned toward gentle gossip about different matters relevant to Sherpa society. The lama's wife brought butter tea and filled the porcelain cups set upon the long low tables in front of them. A short while later, large brass plates of steaming hot boiled potatoes were placed on the tables, and the Thangme lamas plunged themselves into the important task of eating and drinking. Afterward, they politely excused themselves and went to find accommodation in the houses of relatives or friends.

The next day, Kagyu Chökyi Lodro gave the empowerment of the *Self-Created and Self-Luminous Primordial Purity*[82] using a mandala of colored sand. This was followed by the oral transmission of the text explaining the preliminary practices to be undertaken before being able to meditate on the primordial purity of the mind. Then the lama began to expound the three essential points of dzogchen, the great perfection:

> The dzogchen path includes three main aspects: view, meditation, and conduct. "View" means identifying the primordially pure essence of the mind and its natural, spontaneous manifestations. The essence of the mind is stainless, uncompounded, vast like space, without boundaries, and free from mental elaborations. It is known as the essence of all those gone beyond [suffering], or tathagatas.
>
> "Meditation" means sustaining the view that understands the essence of mind, while radiating love and compassion toward all sentient beings. "Conduct" is to engage in the altruistic deeds of a bodhisattva. Bodhisattvas will give to others whatever they ask, even their own bodies. Bodhisattvas will never steal, cheat, or harm others in any way whatsoever. They do not retaliate when hurt or abused, do not indulge in sleep or gossip, are always ready to help others, and continuously abide in the blissful, empty clarity of the primordial mind.

Kunzang Yeshe's heart opened like a lotus flower touched by the rays of the sun, and he clearly saw the path that had been laid out before him. He understood the impermanence of life and the absurdity of worldly pursuits. Right there and then, Kunzang Yeshe resolved to become a bodhisattva in that very lifetime.

Kagyu Chökyi Lodro also gave the *Excellent Secret Slaying of the Ego*,[83] a special and quick method to cut attachment to one's physical body by offering it as food to all beings, particularly to the harmful spirits. Finally, to celebrate the completion of the teachings and to show their gratitude to the lama, the disciples offered a thanksgiving sacred feast *(tsog)* and returned to their homes.

### Kunzang Yeshe Goes into Retreat

Around 1883, the Phortse Lama Kagyu Rangdrol[84] gave the empowerment, oral transmission, and commentary of *The Unobstructed Primordial Mind of the Great Perfection*[85] and the fire empowerment of the *Wind Practice of the Profound Seal of [Dorje] Phagmo.*[86] Kunzang Yeshe attended the teachings and took the *Unobstructed Primordial Mind* as his main practice. Sometime later, Kunzang Yeshe received teachings from Rechen Drogon Urgyen Chöphel[87] in the Akar Phug Hermitage, on the slopes of Khumbilha above Khumjung.

The Akar Phug, or Cave of the White *Ah,* is a very special place. A white syllable *Ah* had appeared spontaneously on its rocky walls, and in one of Guru Rinpoche's biographies it is said that the Precious Guru flew from Maratika to Akar Cave with his consort Mandarava and left his footprint on a rock. In fact, from a hill many miles to the south just above Maratika Cave, the Khumbilha Mountain can be seen towering like a jeweled crown above the valleys, with the Dudh Kosi flowing between rows of mountains that look like thick plaits of hair.

Lama Urgyen Chöphel gave teachings on *The Profound Essential Meaning of the Great Perfection*[88] and the preliminary practices relating to it, instructions about meditation on the nature of the mind, the commentary of Gampopa's *Jewel Ornament of Liberation,*[89] and the empowerments and instructions of the *Heart Drop of the Dakinis*[90] and *The Guru Yoga of the Great Perfection.*[91]

Well equipped with the empowerments and instructions, Kunzang Yeshe went into retreat to complete the preliminary practices for purification of negative deeds and accumulation of merit.[92] Kunzang Yeshe was very diligent and energetic and was able to complete the preliminaries in a short time. He used to wake up around three in the morning and meditate until sunrise, then he would revive the fire, make tea, and eat a bowl of tsampa before continuing his practice. At noon, after eating a few boiled potatoes, he would go to fetch water from the spring and sit outside in the sun reading scriptures. When the sun disappeared behind the mountains, he would go back inside the hut and continue his practice late into the night.

When he was in his early twenties, Kunzang Yeshe married Tsamchi, a girl from Namche of the Lhabushingtog clan who was a couple of years older than him. The families of Kunzang Yeshe and Tsamchi had arranged their children's wedding after consulting some Sherpa lamas well versed in astrological calculations. The preliminary steps of engagement had already taken place some years before, and after the final ceremony, the couple were officially married. Tsamchi moved into the house that her husband had built at Thangme Gompa.[93] Kunzang Yeshe then had to assume the new responsibilities of supporting his wife and children and was compelled to combine his spiritual practice with worldly, practical matters. Thus, like many of his countrymen, he became a trader, an occupation that took him on journeys to different parts of Khumbu, Shorong, and Tibet and gave him the opportunity to meet many eminent lamas and practitioners.

# 6. Kunzang Yeshe Learns to Combine Religious Practice and Worldly Matters

## A Trading Journey

I T WAS NOW the third month according to the Tibetan lunar calendar, and the trading season was at its peak. Kunzang Yeshe spent some days at home with his family cutting wood in the forests of the Kongde Mountain and fixing large bamboo mats to the roof of the house as an extra protection from the heavy rains. Tsamchi planted potatoes helped by other women, first at their field in Mende, then at Thangme, and finally at Tarnga, one hour's walk farther up the valley of the Nangpe Tsangpo.

Before the fourth lunar month, when the lamas and villagers of Khumbu would be busy commemorating the enlightenment of the Buddha with a two-week fasting retreat known as *nyungne,* Kunzang Yeshe planned another trip to Tibet. He searched the calendar for an auspicious date to start the journey and began his preparations by carefully packing into thick yak-wool sacks some of the rice, sugar, and chilies he had brought from Katitenga, as well as some dried potatoes.[94]

The morning of his departure, Kunzang Yeshe performed the *Mountain Incense Offering*[95] and burnt some branches of fragrant juniper and masur with a bit of tsampa, butter, sugar, and milk outside the house. He made prayers to the buddhas and bodhisattvas of the ten directions, to the Dharma protectors, to Khumbilha, and to other local gods. Tsamchi prepared a few *kur* (potato pancakes) for her husband and packed some tsampa and butter in small leather bags. She placed the provisions into a bamboo basket together with a large *kara* (wooden container) full of chang, some dry grass, and a blanket.

When the ritual was over, Kunzang Yeshe ate kur and drank butter tea, placed his wooden cup into the folds of his cloak, took the loads downstairs, and secured them onto the zobgyo. Waving goodbye to his wife and their baby Karzang, he went on his way. At Thangteng he met his traveling companions, and together they walked toward Tibet.

Their path went through very high mountains, bare but for a few dwarf rhododendrons, willows, and black junipers that could never grow tall because of the cold, strong wind. They passed the summer settlements of Tarnga and Marulung and soon entered an uninhabited area where only a few scattered shepherd's huts and caves could be found. The travelers gathered dry shrubs and yak dung to make a fire and spent their first night at Lungnag in a herder's hut, under the icy slopes of the Nangpe Gotaya.

Early the next morning they climbed a steep cliff and reached the Nangpa La, an immense extension of empty snowfields surrounded by gigantic snow peaks. To their right was the Jobo Uyug (Cho Oyu) and to their left the Jobo Rabzang,[96] like two sentinels keeping watch over the sacred land of Tibet. For mile after mile, only snow and ice could be seen. Sometimes the snow was very deep, making the crossing extremely difficult; at other times sudden blizzards had been known to freeze both people and animals to death. Sherpa traders knew the dangers, but they were always confident that strong devotion to the Three Jewels and the recitation of the mantras of the Great Compassionate One and the Precious Guru would provide indisputable protection for crossing the pass safely.

On this particular occasion, Kunzang Yeshe and his companions had an easy journey. Like every other traveler before them, they added a few stones and prayer flags to the cairn marking the top of the pass as an offering to the local gods, and shouted, "Lha gyaloooo!" ("The gods have wooooon!") at the top of their voices. Then they hurried down the glacier and into Kyatrag.

A small nomadic community of only three families, Kyatrag was nonetheless an important trading center. Kunzang Yeshe and his friends were only engaged in small-scale business, but the Namche traders who traveled with large caravans of yaks and zobgyos had warehouses at Kyatrag and houses at Dingri Gangar, where they conducted their business.

At Kyatrag, Kunzang Yeshe exchanged his rice and sugar for salt, a dried leg of mutton, woolen cloth, aprons, tsampa, and dried apricots and returned quickly to Thangme with his companions.

## Nyungne

In the early morning hours of the first day of the Saka Dawa, the fourth Tibetan lunar month, the sound of a conch shell reverberated across the valley, awakening the sleepy Thangme lamas and villagers. Pushing aside

10. Eight-arm Chenrezig
(Tibetan woodblock print)

the thick woolen blanket, Kunzang Yeshe jumped out of bed, washed his face and hands, grabbed his religious text and ritual implements, and walked toward the gompa. The sound of the conch was replaced by the deep tone of the *dungchens,* the long Tibetan horns, followed by the gleeful melody of the *gyalings* (oboes) sending their invocations in the four directions. The Thangme Lama made his entrance into the temple and the ritual began.

Every day for the next two weeks, the nyungne practitioners would take the eight Mahayana vows, promising to abstain from killing, stealing, lying, sexual intercourse, taking intoxicants, wearing jewelry, singing and dancing, and eating after midday. In addition, every two days they would observe a complete fast, abstaining from taking even a drop of water, and would keep total silence.

The nyungne ritual includes the recitation of mantras and performance of numerous full-length prostrations to Chenrezig, the Great Compassionate One.[97] Although a physically demanding practice, no one seemed to think of the nyungne as a kind of somber penance; quite the contrary, everyone was very cheerful. The elderly people, the "mothers" *(ama)* and "uncles" *(au)* who were too old to prostrate and could not read the texts, sat at the back of the temple or in the courtyard, spinning their prayer wheels and reciting *Om mani padme hum hrih* interspersed with bits of gossip.

Every two days, tea was served almost without interruption to make up for the lack of solid food. Before midday a substantial meal of rice, potatoes, tsampa, and *pagril* was served to the nyungne practitioners and to those who came to make offerings. Pagril is a special Sherpa and Tibetan delicacy consisting of boiled dough balls served with melted butter, powdered cheese, and sugar. Tibetans and Sherpas love to eat pagril during nyungne because they are so hard to digest that one's stomach stays full for at least the next two days!

Tsamchi also came to the gompa carrying her baby in a basket and a bag of potatoes as a contribution toward the nyungne expenses. She sat in the kitchen with the other ladies and helped in the preparation of the countless teas and the daily meal. On the last day of the nyungne, the participants offered an elaborate *tsog* ceremony, or sacred feast. Large trays and tables were stacked with conical tsampa cakes made with lots of butter, dried cheese, and lumps of brown sugar, fried sweet pastries *(kabse),* boiled potatoes, popcorn, dried meat, chang, rock sugar, dried apricots, roasted beans, and so forth. Everyone ate and drank and enjoyed and took home a large quantity of tsog offerings imbued with the blessings of the Great Compassionate One.

## *The Rainy Season*

The monsoon rains had already set in. Thick clouds advanced through the valley toward Thangme, enveloping the mountains in mist and fog. Only during the early morning and in the evening would the clouds part, and at those times the snow peaks could be seen for a few moments to remind people that they were still there.

Kunzang Yeshe made another journey to Katitenga to sell the Tibetan salt, and in the fifth month, after taking part in the Dumche festival, he went back to Akar Hermitage to receive teachings from Lama Urgyen Chöphel. On this particular occasion, Urgyen Chöphel taught *The Perfection of Wisdom in Eight Thousand Verses,*[98] the volume of *Many Sutras,*[99] the *Stainless Confession Tantra,*[100] the *Confession of Oaths Sutra,*[101] the three types of *kurim,*[102] and *The Confession Prayer.*[103] The lama also gave teachings on the *Liberation through Hearing in the Intermediate State,*[104] which contains a detailed explanation on how to lead to a good rebirth the consciousness of dying people and of those already dead.

The Buddhist teachings explain that after death the consciousness wanders about in the *bardo,* or intermediate state, between death and rebirth. Every seven days the bardo being experiences a kind of death or change of status, until by the end of the seventh week at the latest it has found a new body in one of the six realms of existence. The duty of the lamas who perform rites for the deceased is to guide the consciousness through the terrifying visions of the bardo toward a rebirth among humans or gods, where they will have the opportunity to progress along the spiritual path. Kunzang Yeshe was not interested in performing rituals in the homes of villagers, but he had a very compassionate heart and was always ready to help those in need. Years later, whenever he heard that someone had passed away, he would grab his dorje and bell and join the ritual for the deceased, whether he had been invited or not.

When the teachings at the Akar Hermitage were over, Kunzang Yeshe returned to Thangme and spent some time at home reciting scriptures. Tsamchi spent the rainy months spinning wool and weaving it into strips of material to be used for making new clothes for the family. Another set of eight nyungnes took place at Thangme Gompa during the sixth lunar month. A couple of weeks later, grass had to be cut on the high mountain slopes and then brought home as fodder for the cattle during the cold winter months. Flowers were also picked and left to dry, to be sold later to Tibetan doctors for the preparation of medicinal pills. Soon the potato crop was ready for collection at Mende, and then at Thangme and Thangteng. The villagers helped each other dig the potatoes, working as a team and enjoying themselves by drinking chang and singing.

During the autumn, the Himalayan golden season of clear skies and whitest moons, Kunzang Yeshe went back to Tibet and Katitenga a few times. The winter was spent in retreat at Thangme, while Tsamchi and little Karzang stayed at Mende with Kunzang Yeshe's parents. After the New Year celebrations, when the snow began to melt in the high passes, Kunzang Yeshe resumed his trading journeys across the Nangpa La.

A few years went by in this way. In the year of the dragon 1892, Tsamchi gave birth to a boy whom they named Wangyal. To create auspicious conditions for the survival of his son, Kunzang Yeshe built a prayer wheel at the end of the long mani wall on the path leading to Thangme Gompa.[105] Karzang was now a grown-up little girl who helped her mother by carrying small loads of wood and yak dung, watching the fire, and keeping an eye on her little brother. Her father taught her the *ka kha ga nga,* and soon she was able to recite some basic prayers.

# 7. Kunzang Yeshe's Teachers

## The Kochag Drogonpa and the Dumche Festival

WHEN HIS ACTIVITIES in the Land of Snows had been completed, Padmasambhava rose into the sky in a body of light gone beyond the gross elements. The Precious Guru now resides in a palace on Copper-Colored Mountain in the southwestern continent, surrounded by knowledge-holders, *dakas,* and dakinis.

Before leaving Tibet, Guru Rinpoche had promised that on the tenth day of the waxing moon he would appear in person to those who prayed to him with strong faith and devotion.[106] Thus, on the *tsechu,* the tenth day of each lunar month, or the Guru's Day, his disciples perform extensive offerings to Guru Rinpoche and request his compassionate help. Particularly on the tenth day of the fifth month, Tibetan Buddhists commemorate the miraculous birth of the Precious Guru upon a lotus flower in Dhanakosa Lake in the land of Oddiyana.

When Lama Sangwa Dorje built the Pangboche temple, he gave special importance to the religious celebrations of the tsechu of the fifth month as a village festival and an occasion for the whole community to accumulate merit. The celebrations, which became known as the Drubchö (locally pronounced "Dumche"),[107] took place just before the herders were to take all the cattle from the villages to the higher pastures.

In the early days of Lama Sangwa Dorje, all the Sherpas from Khumbu and Pharag would go to Pangboche for Dumche. After the death of the lama, his disciple Thutob Wangpo took care of Pangboche Gompa, but the official leadership rested with the Kusho Drogonpa[108] from Kochag in Tibet, where Lama Sangwa Dorje had received religious instructions under the Drogonpa Jigdral Zangpo.

The Dumche celebrations continued under the auspices of the Kochag lamas as a commemoration of Lama Sangwa Dorje's death. The shawl that Lama Sangwa Dorje used to hang on the sun's rays, the scalp of his yeti disciple, and the statue of the Gonpo Sungjonma were taken out of their cases by the Drogonpa lama and carried in procession around the village with great pomp and ceremony in order to bless the people, animals, houses, and fields. After the rituals were over, the Drogonpa would again seal the holy objects in their cases. The statue of the Gonpo was considered to be extremely sacred and powerful, and only the Drogon lamas, reputed for their great powers to control spirits, were able to display it without harmful consequences. The villagers believed that if any other lama tried to open the case and show the statue, many calamities would befall the community, such as earthquakes, floods, and avalanches.

Every year the Kochag Drogonpa came to Khumbu for the Dumche celebrations and stayed a few months giving teachings to his Sherpa disciples. Thus, from the Kochag Drogonpa Tenzin Dorje, Kunzang Yeshe, Lama Gulo from Khumjung, and other Sherpa lamas received the empowerments of *The Longevity Practice of the Iron-Faced Goddess*[109] and the *Secret Hayagriva*.[110]

### The Thangme Lama Ngawang Trinle Lhundrub

During his youth, Ngawang Trinle Lhundrub spent long periods of time in solitary retreat in a hut that he himself built on the ledge of an almost inaccessible cliff above his family home at Charog. At that place he completed eight sets of preliminary practices and practiced the *Union of the Three Precious Ones*.[111] He was regarded as a very holy lama, and there were many stories about his spiritual power. The climb to his hut was quite steep, and once he started retreat he would not come down under any circumstances. During one of his strict retreats, he ran out of salt and was having a hard time swallowing his tsampa and potatoes. One day, a small animal that Sherpas call *temo* (a kind of marmot) came into the hut through a hole on the ground, looked at the lama, and went back into the hole. After the temo repeated the same action several times, the lama had a look into the hole and found a small leather bag full of salt.

On another occasion, the fire in Ngawang Trinle Lhundrub's hearth died out, and he was unable to cook or make tea. (In those days, matches and lighters were not available and people used to keep the hot embers to avoid having to light a new fire every day.) After some days, a cat appeared at his hut. The lama then wrote a note saying that he had no fire and tied it to the cat's neck. The animal went away, and a few hours later a villager from Mende brought him some embers.

After becoming the head of Thangme Gompa, Ngawang Trinle

Lhundrub built a new, larger temple and started the Dumche celebrations in the large plain at Thangteng. He alternated his solitary retreats with performing rituals in Thangme Gompa and teaching an increasingly large number of disciples.

The fame of the Thangme Lama as a realized master spread far and wide throughout Khumbu and Shorong, and stories about his fantastic achievements multiplied. On one occasion, when Ngawang Trinle Lhundrub and some of his disciples were performing funeral ceremonies for a man from Khumjung, the corpse suddenly stood up. The touch of a resurrected corpse, or *rolang,* is said to be deadly, and everyone in the room ran away closing the door behind them. Unperturbed, the lama meditated on compassion and recited the ritual mantras and words to control the rolang and guide his consciousness through the bardo and toward a good rebirth. After a while, the corpse fell down and the lama called the people back.

Ngawang Trinle Lhundrub was also a very skillful artist, credited with the carving of a large number of images on stones. But his masterpiece is a large stone at Zamte carved with the images of Guru Rinpoche, the Wrathful Guru, and the Lion-Faced Dakini. Ngawang Trinle Lhundrub carved and painted it for the benefit of the deceased Tragtho Sangye Dorje as a protective measure against floods and landslides. Together with a long mani wall, the beautifully carved stone became an object of devotion for many people, and the Precious Guru has indeed protected his devotees for many years.[112]

Together with other Sherpa lamas, Kunzang Yeshe received many teachings from Ngawang Trinle Lhundrub, such as the empowerment and oral transmission of the *Three Cycles of Rituals of the Northern Treasure,*[113] the *Prayer in Seven Chapters,*[114] the *Union of the Three Precious Ones,* the *Essential Actual Meaning of the Peaceful and Wrathful Deities,*[115] the *Wisdom Liberating by Seeing of the Great Completion,*[116] and the oral transmission and empowerment of *The Glorious Treasure of Immortality.*[117]

In 1895, Ngawang Trinle Lhundrub became very sick.[118] His son and heir Lama Ngawang Chöphel, also known as Kunzang Dechen Gyalpo,[119] asked Kunzang Yeshe to go to Khumjung and invite Lama Gulo, a well-respected lama and disciple of Ngawang Trinle Lhundrub, to come to Charog and perform rituals on behalf of the lama. A day after Lama Gulo's arrival, however, the Charog Lama Ngawang Trinle Lhundrub passed away. His body was kept in the shrine room for three days while he was engaged in the meditation of the clear light of death, or *thugdam.*

11. Purkhang of Ngawang Trinle
Lhundrub at Charog

The Phortse Lama Kyabje Kagyu Rangdrol was invited to perform the cremation rituals, during which time many amazing sounds could be heard in the sky. Three of the lama's teeth did not burn in the fire and took the shape of flowers. They were enshrined in a silver reliquary commissioned by his daughter Ani Kyipal. His ashes were mixed with clay and molded into statues of Amitayus, then placed into a purkhang in front of the hermitage.

After the rituals were over, Kyabje Kagyu Rangdrol, Kunzang Yeshe, and other lamas went to the Genupa Hermitage, and while they were performing prayers in the cave, a large amount of nectar began to drip from the rock.

## The Dzamtra Lama Kunzang Trinle Gyatso

Not far from Thangme, in the narrow valley where Mingbo, Drig, and Langmoche are situated, there was once a secluded hermitage known as Dzamtra, consisting of a cave and a few huts. In the late nineteenth century, Lama Kunzang Trinle Gyatso, the son of a wealthy Thangme headman of the Shangkhug clan,[120] moved to the Dzamtra Hermitage to practice meditation. The Dzamtra Lama, as he became known, had taken the vows of a fully ordained monk in Tibet and did extensive meditation practice in Khenpalung. He gradually gathered many disciples, including four young Sherpas who took monastic vows with Dzatul Ngawang Tenzin Norbu at Rongphu.

In 1905, the Dzamtra Lama sponsored the building of a *mani tunchur* (a large prayer wheel) on the northern slopes above Namche. He contributed substantial amounts to the renovation of the Khumjung temple and was the main sponsor of the new gompa in Namche. Stories also abounded about Kunzang Trinle Gyatso. It was said that once he saw a large flat stone by the river and asked his disciples to bring it up to the cave to be used as a table. The stone proved to be too heavy even for the strong Sherpas and they had to leave it where it was, but the following morning the stone was found outside the cave. It was concluded that a yeti had carried it up for the lama.

Sometime after 1919, Kunzang Trinle Gyatso's four monks joined the new Tengboche Monastery. The lama himself left for Tibet and Sikkim, where he became the teacher of the Sikkimese royal family.

From the Dzamtra Lama, Kunzang Yeshe received the empowerment, oral transmission, and commentary of *The Vajra Garland of Longevity,*[121] the oral transmission of the *Mani Kabum,*[122] and the *Hundred Protecting Wheels.*[123]

## Other Sherpa Lamas

From the Sherpa yogi Mipham Tashi Chögyal,[124] a disciple of Trulzhig Kunzang Thongdrol, Kunzang Yeshe received the oral transmission of the *Life and Songs of Milarepa,*[125] the *Jewel Ornament of Liberation, The Precious Sublime Path,*[126] and *The Golden Garland of the Kagyu Tradition.*[127]

From the Phortse Lama Phurdrub Tenzin,[128] he received the empowerment and oral transmission of the *Collected Treasures* of Ratna Lingpa,[129] the *Condensed Secret Longevity Practice,*[130] and *Hayagriva with Iron Hair Locks.*[131] From Lama Sangye Tenzin, Kunzang Yeshe received the empowerment, oral transmission, and commentary of *Vajrapani Subduing All the Haughty Spirits.*[132]

From the holy lama Rinchen Dorje, he received the complete empowerments and oral transmissions of Vajrayogini in the tradition of the Indian *mahasiddha* Naropa[133] and the *Secret Hayagriva*. From Lama Ngodrub of Charog,[134] Kunzang Yeshe again received the empowerment, oral transmission, and commentary of *The Essential Actual Meaning of the Peaceful and Wrathful Deities,* the *Three Cycles of Rituals of the Northern Treasure,* and the commentary of *The Union of the Three Precious Ones.*

## Kunzang Yeshe Meets His Tsawe Lama

It was rumored that Lama Yonten Gyatso, the Precious Hermit of the Excellent Cave, or Kunzang Phug, was more than one hundred years old. Originally from Kham, he had been a hunter in his youth until he met the outstanding master Dza Paltul Rinpoche, at which point his whole life was changed; he gave up killing animals and devoted himself to meditation. Following in the footsteps of the great yogi Milarepa, Yonten Gyatso left his native country and spent many years in Lapchi and Rongshar, living in remote caves without possessions or food and surviving by eating his own excrement and whatever faithful yetis brought to him.[135]

A few years later, the villagers heard about him and began to bring offerings of food and clothing. At the people's request, he moved to the Kunzang Cave near Tagshang in Rongshar[136] and later took a yogini as consort. Following the example of Paltul Rinpoche, Yonten Gyatso used the offerings he received to sponsor the carving of mantras on stones and arranged them into mani walls along the paths.

The reputation of the precious hermit of Rongshar as a saintly man endowed with boundless love toward all beings had reached Khumbu. Together with Lama Gulo and the Charog Lama Kunzang Dechen Gyalpo, Kunzang Yeshe undertook the journey to Rongshar to request teachings and instructions from the hermit Yonten Gyatso. After crossing the Nangpa La, they passed Kyatrag and turned west toward Rongshar. Young and agile, Kunzang Yeshe walked briskly like a sixteen-year-old youth, but Lama Gulo was already an elderly, corpulent lama. Streams of perspiration ran down his face as he struggled through the mountain passes carrying his luggage on his back. On that occasion, the journey had been undertaken as a pilgrimage, and no attendants or relatives were accompanying them.

After a turn in the path, the Secluded Hermitage of the Excellent Cave came into sight. To their surprise, the lama was waiting for them. In front of the cave was a throne-like, freshly built platform of stones and mud covered with a sheepskin. Yonten Gyatso greeted the Sherpas and invited Lama Gulo to sit on the throne. Although Lama Gulo was meeting the Precious Hermit for the first time and no one had been sent ahead to announce the visit of such an eminent lama, Yonten Gyatso seemed to have known about their coming and made the proper arrangements. As a result, deep faith and devotion toward the Precious Hermit arose in the minds of the Sherpa lamas.

Lama Yonten Gyatso was a humble, unassuming man, as is often the case with those who have attained true spiritual heights. His person radiated loving-kindness and compassion. Kunzang Yeshe felt a strong bond with him, as if he had been reunited with an old friend of many lifetimes. He made extensive offerings to the lama, including his whole body, speech, and mind, and regarded the Precious Hermit as His *Tsawe* Lama, his "root," or main, teacher.

The Sherpa lamas returned in subsequent years, four in total, for the continuation of the teachings. During those years, Kunzang Yeshe received the Father and Mother sections of the *Heart Drop of the Great Expanse,* the *Seven Great Treasures* of Longchen Rabjampa,[137] *The Words of My Perfect*

*Teacher,*[138] the two volumes of Longchenpa's *Miscellaneous Writings,*[139] and many other empowerments and instructions.

## Pema Kunzang Gyatso

The wealthy traders from Namche, Khumjung, and Khumde had built large houses with beautiful shrine rooms furnished with intricately carved wooden shrines and decorated with murals painted by the artists of the Khapa family from Khumjung. From Tibet or from Lalitpur in the Kathmandu Valley, they brought costly statues gilded and studded with precious stones, woolen carpets, Chinese brocade, and religious ritual instruments made of copper, silver, and gold. The printing of the hundreds of volumes of the Buddha's Words (Kangyur), the commentaries on them (Tengyur), and *The Perfection of Wisdom Sutra in One Hundred Thousand Verses* (*Prajnaparamita,* or *Bum*) was commissioned in the large Tibetan monasteries such as Tashi Lhunpo and brought to Khumbu on the back of zobgyos and yaks.

When Dorje Chang Pema Kunzang Gyatso, a well-known tulku from Kham,[140] passed through Khumbu on his way to the sacred pilgrimage places of Nepal and India, the wealthy Namche trader Nyima Gyaltsen of the Tragtho clan requested him to teach in the large shrine room of his house. Over the following month, Kunzang Yeshe received from Pema Kunzang Gyatso the empowerment and oral transmission of Karma Lingpa's *Peaceful and Wrathful Deities: The Self-Liberated Mind, The Words of My Perfect Teacher,* the twelve volumes of *The Perfection of Wisdom Sutra in One Hundred Thousand Verses,* the *Collection of Nyingma Tantras,*[141] the volume of *Many Sutras,* and the empowerment and oral transmission of *Rahu Poisonous Razor.*[142]

## Trulzhig Kunzang Thongdrol

Trulzhig Kunzang Thongdrol was the tulku of Chingkarwa Donyo Dorje,[143] a highly accomplished lama and treasure discoverer. Kunzang Thongdrol studied at Mindroling and received teachings from many great masters of all traditions. Following a prophecy of Chogyur Dechen Lingpa, he settled in the Yamdrog Lake region, at the Dechen Chöling Gompa. In 1902, on his return from a pilgrimage to the Kathmandu Valley with Dzatul Ngawang Tenzin Norbu, he discovered the *Guru Sadhana* that he had concealed in his previous life at Dzongka in Kyirong.

In the fourth month of the water tiger year 1902, Kunzang Yeshe, Lama Gulo, Au Yeshe of Khumjung, and many other Sherpa lamas went to Rongphu to receive teachings from Trulzhig Kunzang Thongdrol. To a very large gathering of Tibetan and Sherpa disciples, the lama gave the empowerment and oral transmission of the *Great Compassionate Lord*,[144] *The Guru Yoga of Milarepa*,[145] *The Profound Drop of Tara*,[146] *The Union of the Three Precious Ones,* and other instructions.

### Togden Shakya Shri

12. Togden Shakya Shri (unknown)

Shakya Shri (1853–1919) was a Drukpa Kagyu treasure discoverer who had received teachings from all four traditions of Tibetan Buddhism. He spent most of his time in retreat and became famous for his achievements and great powers. It is said that on one occasion, when he was giving the empowerment of *The Lineage of Knowledge-Holders* of the Northern Treasure, something very special took place. During a long invocation of the lamas of the lineage, when the cymbals, drums, dungchens, and gyalings were played for a long time, Shakya Shri's body began to rise in space until he was sitting in mid-air above the throne. Then, slowly, as the music died out, he descended back to his seat and resumed the prayers.[147]

Shakya Shri visited Lapchi twice and had a large number of followers from Tibet and the Himalayan regions, including Khumbu and the Kathmandu Valley. At the Crystal Cave Bamboo Castle, Kunzang Yeshe received from Togden Shakya Shri the empowerment, oral transmission, and commentary of the *Goddess Chandali*[148] and *The Union of the Three Roots.*[149] From the cycle of *The Heart Drop of the Great Expanse*,[150] the lama gave the empowerment, oral transmission, and commentary of *The Gathering of Knowledge-Holders* and of *The Queen of Great Bliss.*[151] To those serious practitioners who had completed the preliminary practices, Shakya Shri gave detailed explanations about the two stages of dzogchen meditation, *tregchö* (cutting through) and *thögal* (leap over),[152] and the practices for differentiating between samsara and nirvana[153] in accordance with the *Unobstructed Primordial Mind* cycle. Kunzang Yeshe adopted the *Goddess Chandali* cycle as one of his main practices and was eventually able to achieve great realizations through it.

The Lapchi area was populated with hermits intent on following the example of the great yogi Milarepa. Among them was Kyabje Rangjung Lagchog,[154] who meditated in the Cave of Subduing Evil Beings where Milarepa had subdued the outer, local evil spirits and achieved complete control over the inner evil spirits—the negative emotions that cause the appearance of what ignorant people call evil spirits. In that blessed cave, Kunzang Yeshe received the empowerment of Chakrasamvara,[155] as well as the oral transmission and commentary of a text related to the practice of mahamudra, which is the highest meditation technique according to the tradition of Milarepa's followers.

## On Pilgrimage with Artsa Lama

The Artsa Lama Thubten Namgyal Palden was one of the foremost disciples of Togden Shakya Shri. Born in the region of Artsa Lake in Kham, he became renowned for his achievements in meditation and his supernatural powers.[156] In the earth bird year 1909, when Artsa Lama arrived in Khumbu on his way to the holy places of India and Nepal, the Thangme Lama Kunzang Dechen Gyalpo invited him to stay at the Charog and Genupa hermitages.

A few months earlier, in the fourth month of the earth bird year, the new Namche Kangyur Lhakhang had been consecrated by the Dzamtra Lama, who also wrote the *chayig,* or gompa regulations. Over the years, the Khumjung and Namche people had been quarreling about the management of the Dumche festival, until the Namche traders finally decided to build their own temple and establish their own Dumche celebrations. The Thangme Lama and the Dzamtra Lama Kunzang Trinle Gyatso, together with the most influential Namche traders, requested permission from the Kochag Drogonpa to build a new gompa and also celebrate the Dumche at Namche. In the following month, the Dumche took place at Namche for the first time, and the chayig, which included a long list of sponsors, was read aloud for everyone to rejoice in their merits.[157]

Artsa Lama was requested to teach in the new Kangyur Lhakhang at Namche. There, to a small group of select disciples that included the Dzamtra

Lama, the Thangme Lama Kunzang Dechen Gyalpo, Lama Gulo, and Kunzang Yeshe, the Artsa Lama gave the empowerment of the elaborate aspect of *The Unobstructed Primordial Mind* relating to the "cutting through" practice.

For many years, Kunzang Yeshe had had a strong wish to visit the holy Vajra Seat at Bodh Gaya, where Shakyamuni Buddha attained enlightenment, and now he decided to join Artsa Lama in his pilgrimage through India and Nepal. Before continuing the journey, Artsa Lama and his Tibetan disciples spent some time in the Pharag region at the Kyongma Go Hermitage not far from Lukla, while Lama Kunzang Yeshe and other Sherpas made preparations for the journey. They packed dried potatoes and tsampa for their meals and a bag of salt for trading along the way, and left home.

The road took them south through the Dudh Kosi Valley toward the Maratika Cave at Halesi, situated in a predominantly Hindu area where Buddhist pilgrims were tolerated but not welcomed. Many Tibetans and Sherpas used to make the pilgrimage to the cave where, according to tradition, Padmasambhava and Mandarava had attained control over life and death. In one of Padmasambhava's biographies it is said:

> Then, Padmasambhava went to the country of Zahor. Arshadhara, the king of that country, had a sixteen-year-old daughter called Mandarava Flower, worthy and qualified, and Padmasambhava took her as his *mudra,* or consort for mantrayana practice.
>
> South of the Potala, where Avalokiteshvara's palace is situated, there is a cave called Maratika, facing toward the south. Rainfalls of flowers occur at that place. It is surrounded by a subtle rainbow canopy, permeated with the scent of incense, and adorned with a grove of sandal trees. That great place has been blessed by the protectors of the three lineages [Mañjushri, Avalokiteshvara, and Vajrapani]. Having gone there, Padmasambhava and Mandarava opened the mandala of the protector Amitayus and performed the practice of the longevity knowledge-holders. After three months they beheld the face of Amitayus, the Buddha of Boundless Radiance and Infinite Life, who placed a vase full of the nectar of immortality upon their crowns. As they drank from it, their bodies became like diamonds, vajra bodies beyond birth and death, and they achieved the *siddhi* of a longevity knowledge-holder.[158]

At the sacred Maratika Cave, Artsa Lama gave the empowerment and oral transmission of the *Goddess Chandali* cycle, and the group spent some time performing longevity practices.

From Halesi they walked to Bihar in India, where Kunzang Yeshe and his Sherpa companions experienced for the first time the pleasures and pains of modern transport. After reaching the holy town of Gaya, they took horse carts and approached the sacred Bodh Gaya stupa riding slowly along the banks of the Nairanjana River, between rows of tall palm trees. To the left they could see the dark mass of hills where the mahasiddha Savari had experienced a vision of the protector Mahakala, while to their right were lush fields of mustard and wheat. As they neared the holy shrine, silence fell upon the pilgrims. Everyone could feel the powerful, peaceful energy emanating from the holiest place of the Buddhist world. The physical form of Shakyamuni was not present any longer, but his inexhaustible wisdom and compassion were clearly still alive at Bodh Gaya.

With long silk khatags in their hands, Artsa Lama and his followers offered plates of rice and fruit, butter lamps, and incense, and prostrated themselves before the wondrous Buddha image and the Bodhi Tree. During the following days they visited the place where the Buddha had spent six years performing ascetic practices and the spot where he had received a bowl of sweet rice from the girl Sujata. They also went to the Mahakala Cave and the Cool Grove Cemetery,[159] to Vultures' Peak near Rajgir (or Rajagriha, as it was known in the past), where the Buddha had preached the Perfection of Wisdom sutras, and to the ruins of Nalanda Monastic University. In each place they performed extensive offerings.

Kunzang Yeshe circumambulated the Bodh Gaya temple many times and made extensive prayers under the Bodhi Tree to be able to benefit many beings. Sitting in that hallowed spot under the shade of the sacred tree, an inexpressible sense of peace enveloped him. Mental conceptuality subsided, and the world with its problems and joys disappeared. Only clear light and boundless compassion were present in his mind.

At Bodh Gaya, Artsa Lama gave the empowerment of the display of primordial awareness, the aspect without elaborations of the *Unobstructed Primordial Mind* related to the practice of thögal. He also organized the building of a stone path around the main temple. The pilgrims then made their way to the holy city of Benares (Varanasi) and to Sarnath, where Shakyamuni Buddha had set in motion the wheel of Dharma for the first time, and continued toward Mandi, the home of Padmasambhava's consort,

Princess Mandarava, and the Lotus Lake in nearby Rewalsar, which had been miraculously created by Padmasambhava.[160]

At that time there was a severe drought in the area. No rain had fallen for many months, and the villagers were unable to grow any crops. Although the local Hindu priests had performed many *pujas* (ritual ceremonies), these had brought no result. Artsa Lama told the local people to recite the prayer of taking refuge in the Three Jewels, as well as the mani and Vajra Guru mantras. Everyone, including the Hindu priests, joined in the recitation, and before long there was a heavy downpour of rain. The people were overjoyed and promised to abandon sinful actions and practice virtue.

Afterward, Artsa Lama and his disciples engaged in a long retreat in Kunnu, in the Sutlej Valley, and then crossed into Tibet, where they visited the holy places of Kyirong and Dingri. At Langkor, the place sacred to the Indian Phadampa Sangye,[161] Artsa Lama gave the *Elaborate Golden Vase Empowerment of the Unobstructed Primordial Mind*[162] and the oral transmission, empowerments, and commentaries of *The Great Compassionate One Dredging the Depths of Cyclic Existence*[163] and *The Guru of Great Bliss.*[164]

From Langkor the party proceeded to Tsibri, where they circled the holy mountain, visited the hermitages and temples, and performed the practice of "slaying the ego" *(chöd)* in the cemeteries. Unfortunately, Artsa Lama's health had deteriorated during the strenuous journey, and to the great distress of his disciples, he passed away in Tsibri. After performing the funeral ceremonies and before returning to Khumbu, Kunzang Yeshe and the Sherpa lamas went to Zapulung,[165] where they received commentaries on the *Lankavatara Sutra*[166] and the *Great Deliverance Sutra*,[167] and to Dza Rongphu to meet Dzatul Ngawang Tenzin Norbu.

# 8. Kunzang Yeshe's Hermitage

## *The Thangme Gompa Retreat House*

WHEN HE RETURNED from his extensive pilgrimage with Artsa Lama, Kunzang Yeshe reflected thus: "I am almost fifty years old and probably will not be around for much longer. I have already obtained all the teachings and instructions I need for my own practice. Since I have received the transmissions of many lineages, after performing the corresponding retreats I will be able to pass them to my disciples and thus benefit many beings. Regarding material needs, I have enough resources for my family and myself. We have potatoes from the fields and milk from the cows, and my son can help with trading ventures. Now I have the possibility to stay in retreat for a few years and fulfill the commitments received from my lamas by performing all the various retreats and practices."

Kunzang Yeshe's house at Thangme Gompa was too small to accommodate a meditator and a family. Although his wife and children spent long periods of time at Mende, it was not possible to ensure enough privacy for serious retreats. Therefore, Kunzang Yeshe decided to build an adjacent new shrine room where he could practice meditation undisturbed. Before beginning to build, he carefully checked the astrological and geomantic conditions, keeping in mind various texts that describe the characteristics of places conducive for meditation. For instance, Longchen Rabjam said:

> Since our mind changes and our virtuous practices can either develop or decline depending on the place where we are dwelling, it has been said that it is extremely important to examine well the place and environment.[168]

According to the *Ornament of Clear Comprehension*,[169] one should perform meditation in a good location where food, water, and other necessities can be easily obtained. Kunzang Yeshe felt that his house at Thangme fulfilled these requirements, but there were other factors to be taken into consideration, such as the shape of the mountains and other external conditions relating to the elements (earth, water, fire, air, and space). There is continuous interaction between the body and the external world. If the gross and subtle elements of the outer environment are not in accordance with the gross and subtle elements of the body, a person can easily become sick and may even go crazy. For someone who practices tantric meditation involving the subtle channels, winds, and drops, the external elements can be either a great help or a great obstacle. Only highly realized yogis who have achieved control over the inner elements are able to meditate undisturbed by the external environment.

Kunzang Yeshe examined the external conditions of his house carefully and concluded that the fire, water, and air elements were conducive for meditation. Regarding the earth element, however, there were some obstacles. It is said in the scriptures that a triangular-shaped, sharply pointed mountain is not favorable for meditation, and the Sumdur Mountain where Thangme Gompa is located has a perfect pyramidal shape. "Well," Kunzang Yeshe concluded, "it is practically impossible to find a perfect place for meditation. After all, the mere shape of a mountain should not be such a great obstacle for my practice." So he proceeded with building and his preparations for retreat.

But still, there was some kind of uneasiness in his mind. The Dechen Chökhor, or Thangme Gompa, is built under a cliff, on top of which is a large boulder standing precariously on the edge. The local people call it the Crooked Horse Body *(Takugug)* because its shape is vaguely similar to the body of a horse. That particular boulder is said to be the abode of a *za,* a type of local god or spirit connected with planetary influences from the retinue of the Dharma protector Rahula.[170] Kunzang Yeshe's house was situated right below the steep mountain slope leading to the Takugug.

Again Kunzang Yeshe pondered, "In case there is too much rain, I wonder whether stones and mud will come down from the mountain. And if there is an earthquake, it is almost sure that the Takugug will fall down and hit my retreat house." When such misgivings arose in his mind, he went up to have a look. He inspected the site and concluded that building a stone wall below the Takugug could solve part of the problem. Accordingly, he sent his son Wangyal to construct a strong, solid stone wall.

Kunzang Yeshe relaxed and decided to start his retreat, but suddenly half his body became paralyzed and he was unable to move or to speak. He then realized that he had made a mistake: when the place where the *za* reside is disturbed by digging the earth, cutting trees, breaking rocks, or polluting the environment in any way, they become angry and react by bringing sickness, especially paralysis, upon those responsible for the disturbance.

The Thangme lamas were invited to perform exorcising rituals and prayers for Kunzang Yeshe's recovery, and after a while the sickness receded and he recovered his health.

## The Kusho Tulku

The Charog Lama Kunzang Dechen Gyalpo had three sons. Since the time when he was a baby, the middle son Ngawang Yonten Norbu had shown signs of being a reincarnated lama. He used to talk continuously about his home at Jasa and about a mountain with tall trees and large barley fields, a landscape utterly different from the rugged Thangme Valley. The Rongphu Sangye confirmed that the boy was the tulku of Lama Ratna Tsewang Norbu of the Rainbow Land (Jasa) Hermitage[171] in Shorong. The boy began his studies with his father and, when he grew up, went to study with the Rongphu Sangye.

The Tashi Nyi-öd Khyilba Hermitage at Charog consisted of a large, one-storied house with a large kitchen/sleeping room and a small shrine room. During his stay at Charog, Artsa Lama had seen a vision of Guru Rinpoche above the shrine room and the syllable *Hum* in the rocky cliff next to the house, and he had suggested that it would be good to build a new shrine room right at that spot. Kunzang Dechen Gyalpo followed his advice, and with the help of his sons, relatives, and disciples, the new shrine room was completed in one year. But Kunzang Dechen Gyalpo's precarious health had further deteriorated in the course of the work, and he passed away in 1915, four days after the completion of the building.

During that period, an identity crisis was slowly brewing among the Sherpas in general, and at Thangme Gompa in particular. With the increasing economic development, the structure of Sherpa society was experiencing deep changes and a religious revival. Wealthy families sponsored the building of large prayer wheels, chörtens, *kani* (gates), prayer wheels turned by water, and so forth. The mani walls swelled in size, and the lamas were extremely busy performing religious ceremonies in the houses of the wealthy for the removal of obstacles and the increase of their fortune.

The influence of the Rongphu Sangye, a *gelong*, or fully ordained monk, was growing among the Sherpas. Another influential figure, the Dzamtra Lama, was also a gelong, as were some of his disciples. Even Lama Gulo, although aged, had taken vows at Rongphu. Thus, as the next step, the Khumbu Sherpas aspired to adopt the most outstanding, idiosyncratic features of Tibetan Buddhism: the tulku system and celibate monasteries as centers of practice and learning. There were no schools or proper monasteries in Khumbu, and the only option for Sherpa families was to send their sons to Tibet to study in one of the large monasteries. As for the girls, they would only get an education if they happened to be relatives of a lama.

The Sherpas were moving toward seeing fully ordained monks and tulkus as objects of the highest respect and veneration, and when the time came to elect the new spiritual head of the Thangme Gompa, opinions were divided. The married lamas wanted to follow their tradition and nominate Lama Ngawang Tsering Dondrub, the eldest son of Kunzang Dechen Gyalpo, who was a married lama and the heir of his father's lineage. On the other hand, the Kusho Tulku Ngawang Yonten Norbu had the double advantage of being a reincarnated lama and a monk. To join the ranks of truly civilized Buddhist countries like Tibet, Sherpa society needed someone with both of these qualities. Therefore, the spirit of innovation and progress prevailed over tradition, and the fully ordained monk Kusho Tulku became the head of the Dechen Chökhor Gompa, whose inmates were mainly married lamas.

Although the Thangme *ngagpas* (married lamas) accepted the leadership of a fully ordained tulku, the situation was not easy. Some Sherpa monks became very proud of their status and behaved arrogantly toward the married lamas, ridiculing their long pigtails and their chang-drinking habit. Soon it became obvious that the Kusho Tulku had the intention of transforming the gompa into a celibate monastery on the model of Do-ngag Zungjug Ling at Rongphu. The ngagpas were not happy, quarrels arose frequently between the two groups of practitioners, and the atmosphere at Thangme Gompa was far from peaceful or conducive to a long spell of meditation.

Kunzang Yeshe was already a well-respected lama with a reputation as a learned, kind, and compassionate practitioner. Sometimes, however, his friends would tease him because he refused to take part in village rituals, and when he did, he would often close his eyes and go into what ordinary people thought was slumber but was in reality a deep meditative state. Only during the rituals for the deceased did Lama Kunzang Yeshe seem fully awake and concentrating on performing the transference of consciousness. The other Sherpa lamas used to ask him jokingly, "Kunzang Yeshe, what kind of 'lama' are you?"

Kunzang Yeshe found himself at odds with Kusho Tulku. There was no open hostility, but there was no good understanding either, and although Kunzang Yeshe wanted to do his retreats undisturbed, obstacles kept arising. He then remembered the words of Atisha[172] and other saintly lamas of the past who advised against practicing meditation or even staying in a place where there is disharmony among practitioners. In such spiritually polluted places, they said, it is not possible to obtain realizations for at least thirteen years. Such a place feels burned and without any positive energy because all the dakas and dakinis who help practitioners to progress along the path avoid going there. In these places one cannot develop concentration, and one's meditation practice becomes more like chopped wood—in small bits and pieces. Therefore, the masters emphasize the importance of meditating in a place that is not only physically suitable but also free from spiritual pollution.

Having considered all the obstacles that were hampering his meditation practice, Kunzang Yeshe sadly concluded, "It seems that I have exhausted my *karmic* connection with this place. It might be time to look for a hermitage elsewhere."

### Kunzang Yeshe Finds the Lawudo Cave

The Tashi Nyi-öd Khyilba and the Ngodrub Chöling hermitages of the Charog and Genupa lamas are situated on the southwestern slopes of Kabsale Mountain, close to the northern side of the sacred Khumbilha. The path from Thangme goes across the Nangpe Tsangpo and straight up to Zamte, a temporary settlement for the Thangme and Thangteng people. A wide path leads to Tramoteng and Mende, while a smaller trail rises steadily toward the U Labtsa, where Kunzang Dechen Gyalpo had built a chörten in memory of his mother. The path continues toward Genupa and Mende, while a short distance past the chörten a small trail leads to Charog.

After Kunzang Dechen Gyalpo's death, his youngest son Ngawang Sherab Zangpo[173] stayed in the Charog Hermitage with his mother, while the eldest brother Lama Dondrub was living in Genupa with his family. Over time, people built small meditation huts at Genupa, and it became a busy hermitage. Water was always a problem at Charog, particularly during the spring, but Genupa had a continuous and abundant water supply from a source right below the caves.

Kunzang Yeshe visited Lama Dondrub and discussed the possibility of building a meditation house at Genupa or using one of the caves at Charog, but he could not make up his mind. Both hermitages were, without doubt, beautiful and blessed spots, but although a place can be very conducive for some people, others may feel unhappy there and unable to concentrate on their Dharma practice.

From Genupa, Kunzang Yeshe crossed a large, dangerous landslide and went toward his family house at Mende. Suddenly, he remembered that somewhere on the mountainside, halfway between Mende and the pass leading to the Gyachog Valley, there was a small cave. The cave faced south and was surrounded by tall juniper trees, while a small spring nearby provided water for the cattle grazing in the vicinity. Wild goats used the cave as their home, and shepherds and woodcutters used it as a shelter from the wind and rain. The villagers called it Rawudo, the Rock of the Goats. Because of its shape it was also known as Labudo, the Radish Rock, and also as Laogdo ("Lawudo"), the Rock Below the Pass.

Kunzang Yeshe went to have a look at the cave and sat for a while in the sun. He beheld a magnificent view. In front of him he could see the Kusum peaks and a row of mountains descending toward the lower hills of Shorong. To his left, the mighty Khumbilha towered across the Gyachog Stream. Behind the ridge that hid Khumde village, he could see the Tamserku and Gangtega peaks. To his right was the Kongde Range. Below were the fields and houses of Mende in a flat and almost circular plain. Behind were the three peaks known as the Gyabumche Mountain, while the mountain ridge descended toward Lawudo and Mende like an elephant trunk, with the cave at the elephant's forehead. Kunzang Yeshe then remembered that according to the scriptures, an elephant-shaped mountain is considered to be very auspicious and conducive for meditation.

That evening, Kunzang Yeshe slept at his house in Mende. In the early morning hours he had a vivid dream in which he saw a page of scripture on which was written a verse:

A massive rock *(do)* on the upper mountain slope,
   below a pass *(la og);*
Above is a three-pointed rocky summit shaped like a tripod of
   human heads.[174]

[In regards to spiritual power,] it is equal to the Cool Grove
  Cemetery.

Upon waking, Kunzang Yeshe remembered that he had seen that verse
in a copy of the *Zanglingma* text belonging to Lama Kunzang Pema
Gyatso from Mindroling Monastery. Now he was fully convinced that
the Rawudo, or Laogdo, or Lawudo Cave was the best place for him.

**13. The Lawudo Cave**

The cave was very small; one could not stand upright in it, and there
was almost no space inside, but Kunzang Yeshe knew what to do. He took
with him a spade to dig with and a jar of chang for refreshment and started
to dig out the earth from inside the cave. His family and some of the villagers went to have a look. "You are mad," they remarked. "If you keep on
digging, the boulder is going to fall down on your head!" But Kunzang
Yeshe paid no attention to them and kept on digging, until eventually the
Lawudo cave became a large, beautiful, deep cave. "Well, Tibet, Nepal,
and India are full of self-created statues, footprints, and so forth. So here
is my self-created cave!" he exclaimed triumphantly.

The next step was to build a wall across the mouth of the cave and
install a door and a window. With the help of his children Wangyal and

Karzang, Kunzang Yeshe hauled stones, mixed the mortar, and built a thick wall with a tiny window and a rough wooden door. At the back of the cave he built a low wall surmounted by wooden shelves to serve as a shrine and bookshelf, and he set up his *maldom* (wooden meditation box) facing west. From the artist at Khumjung, Kunzang Yeshe ordered large clay statues of Guru Rinpoche and his two main female disciples, the Indian princess Mandarava and the Tibetan queen Yeshe Tsogyal. When all the arrangements had been completed, he moved to the Lawudo Cave.

Because of his previous bad experience when he built the wall below the Takugug, before digging out his cave Kunzang Yeshe had not forgotten to appease the local spirits with elaborate incense offerings. And after completing the work, he performed many rituals inside the cave in order to subdue the local spirits and transform them into helpers for his Dharma practice. One evening, while he was performing the dance of the chöd practice and offering his body in charity to the spirits, he saw a large red bull with sharp horns and a fierce look rushing toward him. Lama Kunzang Yeshe's mind was firmly established in the realization of the ultimate nature of reality, the absence of inherent existence. Calmly, he looked at the bull and smiled, and the bull disappeared. The words of Milarepa then came to his mind:

> If you take spirits as spirits, they will harm you.
> If you understand their empty nature, they just go away.
> If you consider the ultimate reality of spirits, they are liberated.
> If you understand spirits to be your parents, that's the end of them.
> If you understand spirits to be mental creations,
> They become an ornament for your practice.[175]

"This is a sign of having completely subdued the local spirit, the owner of this place," Kunzang Yeshe thought.

For some time, Kunzang Yeshe built his fire and cooked his food inside the cave. But the smoke was blackening the walls, the statues, the scriptures, and even his face and hands, so he decided to build a small kitchen next to the cave where his daughter Ani Karzang could stay and look after him.

# 9. The Consecration of Tengboche Monastery

## Dzatul Ngawang Tenzin Norbu and Rongphu Monastery

A T THE BEGINNING of the twentieth century, Dzatul Ngawang Tenzin Norbu (1867–1940), the fifth incarnation of Lama Sangwa Dorje, built a monastery at Dza Rongphu on the northern slopes of the Jomo Langma Mountain. Born in Kharta Og in the Phadrug district, he had been recognized as the tulku of Lama Urgyen Tenphel, who had spent most of his life meditating in Rongphu.

After completing the preliminary practices and receiving extensive teachings from Gyurme Trinle Namgyal of Kuye Labrang in Kharta,[176] Ngawang Tenzin Norbu entered into a long retreat at Rongphu in Padmasambhava's cave, during which he had to endure many hardships. Afterward, he went to Mindroling Monastery[177] to continue his studies. The rules of the monastery allowed visiting monks to obtain lodging on the monastery premises, but only incarnate lamas were entitled to receive food and a share of the offerings from benefactors. Ngawang Tenzin Norbu did not tell the monastery management that he was a tulku, and when his provisions were exhausted, he survived by begging a little tea and tsampa from his friends. Fortunately, his identity was soon discovered and he did not have to fast for too long.

Around 1895, after completing a three-year retreat at Rongphu, he undertook an extensive pilgrimage and then returned to Mindroling to receive more teachings. There he met his root teacher Trulzhig Kunzang Thongdrol, who advised him to build a monastery at Rongphu. Following his teacher's advice, he built the Do-ngag Zungjug Ling (Island of the Union of Sutra and Tantra) Monastery, which was consecrated by Trulzhig Kunzang Thongdrol in the year of the female iron bull 1901.

Ngawang Tenzin Norbu emphasized both the practice of meditation and very strict moral discipline. He gave individual instructions to each

14. Dzatul Ngawang Tenzin Norbu
(courtesy of Khumtul Rinpoche)

15. Lama Ngawang Norbu Zangpo
(Lama Gulo)(courtesy of Tengboche
Rinpoche)

disciple, and each one would practice in their own small cell, never lying down to sleep but spending the night sitting upright in their meditation box. Following the instructions of the *Vinaya Sutra,* before drinking hot water or tea in the morning, they would take a spoonful of dry tsampa so that the worms inside their intestines would get nourishment and not be burnt by the hot liquid. In short, the Dzatul Lama and his disciples were renowned as excellent, dedicated ascetic practitioners. In 1936, the members of the Everest British Expedition visited Rongphu for a second time and made some interesting observations about the Rongphu hermits:

[In] the last 4 miles to the Base Camp past the nunnery, [there are] little caves in the hillsides or excavations in the tumbled heaps of old moraine boulders, where hermits spend a life of what is called meditation but most closely resembles hibernation. One is forced to admire the strength which can keep them alive in those bitter solitudes where the rock faces are grooved by sand blast from the driving wind. We think ourselves hardy when we approach those regions in the spring, with tents and windproof clothing and swansdown sleeping bags and pressure cookers. What have these men in the depths of winter but perhaps an old woollen rug and a smouldering branch of juniper with a pittance of food just sufficient to ward off starvation? "Our religion," they would probably reply, and the answer must suffice. The most wonderful thing is that they retain mental normality; I have conversed with a hermit who had just emerged after 15 years incarceration, and could observe no difference between him and an ordinary lama. We do not know everything in the West; is it possible that we have everything to learn?[178]

The Dzatul Lama became known to Tibetans and Sherpas alike as the Rongphu Sangye, the Buddha of Rongphu, and the Khumbu Sherpas regarded him as their foremost religious teacher. People flocked to him continuously in search of religious guidance or with requests to transfer the consciousness of a deceased person to a pure land.

In the seventh month of the wood tiger year 1914, Lama Gulo, Lama Karma, Gen Tsepel, Tragtho Jampa,[179] and some monks from the Dzamtra Hermitage went to Rongphu to receive teachings from the Rongphu Sangye. One day the lama told them, "It is difficult for the Sherpas to come here whenever they need instructions. In previous times, Lama Sangwa Dorje brought the holy Dharma to Khumbu and performed many good activities, but he was unable to spread the doctrine extensively. However, he developed bodhichitta and made the vow to be able to spread the Dharma in the future. Now this vow has ripened, and it is the right time to build a monastery in Khumbu that will benefit many beings."

The Khumbu people decided to follow the lama's advice. Lama Karma, Gen Tsepel, and Tragtho Jampa accepted the responsibility to sponsor the monastery, and the Rongphu Sangye appointed Lama Gulo as abbot. But there was some disagreement among them regarding the location. Lama Gulo favored a place called Pholsa Tongpa, Gen Tsepel thought that the best place would be the Tashigang Ridge above Namche, while Tragtho Jampa and others thought it would be better to build it on the mountainside above Khumjung, near Akar Hermitage. At some point, Lama Karma mentioned a place called Tengboche. When the Rongphu Sangye heard that name, he was overwhelmed by joy. Gradually, the imprints from a past life arose in his mind, and he remembered having made a vow to build a gompa at that place.

Since the Sherpas disagreed about the location, the Rongphu Sangye decided to check carefully before making a decision. The following morning before dawn, he had a very clear vision of the place called Tengboche. It was a delightful meadow facing south on top of a mountain resembling heaps of barley grains, where Lama Sangwa Dorje had left his footprint. The place was surrounded by thick forests and had abundant water. Right in front were Gangtega and other mountains mentioned in the prophecies of Padmasambhava.

In the morning he summoned the Sherpa disciples and sponsors and explained to them his vision and why Tengboche seemed to be the right choice. They were all delighted and developed even greater faith and devotion toward the Rongphu Sangye. After that, the Sherpas returned to Khumbu and began felling trees for the construction. Lama Gulo went to Shorong to collect donations in the form of valuable objects of veneration, material goods, and money.

The construction of the first Sherpa monastery progressed rapidly thanks to the efforts of Lama Gulo and the Sherpa benefactors. The villagers offered free labor and food for the workers, while sponsors paid the wages of the skilled workers, such as carpenters and painters. The ritual objects, statues, books, and so forth were financed with the donations that Lama Gulo had collected in Shorong and Khumbu.

During the summer of the earth sheep year 1919, Lama Gulo sent his nephew Pu Gyaltsen, Gen Yeshe, Gen Tsultrim, and other monks to Tibet to buy statues and ritual objects in Kyatrag and to commission the printing of texts in Central Tibet.[180] On their way back to Khumbu, the Tengboche monks requested the Rongphu Sangye to perform the consecration of the new monastery. Ngawang Tenzin Norbu accepted and left for Khumbu with seven disciples on the twenty-ninth day of the eighth month of the earth sheep year (September–October 1919).

The lama's party went through Chöbug and Kyatrag and was welcomed before the Nangpa La by a group of Sherpas. Eight meditators carried the lama through the pass in a sedan chair because it was not possible to ride horses through the deep snows. They crossed the Nangpa La in excellent weather and were received on the Khumbu side by the Sherpa lama Urgyen Tenzin, known also as Guyang Rinpoche,[181] and a large number of disciples and sponsors. The Sherpas brought horses, and the lama rode to Lungnag, where he stayed the night.

The next day, the Kusho Tulku Ngawang Yonten Norbu, the headman of Thangme Lozang Dorje, and other disciples met the lama at the Red Chörten of Marulung. The Rongphu Sangye rested for three days at Marulung in Lozang Dorje's house. During those days a bright rainbow could be seen above the distant Dechen Chökhor Gompa at Thangme, while the house where the lama was staying was encircled by another tent-like rainbow.

The lama and his party proceeded to Khumjung, where the Rongphu Sangye was invited to spend the night at the Kangyur Lhakhang built by the Tragtho family. The next day the lama performed a tsog offering ceremony, and a large crowd gathered in the village, setting up large tents and enjoying picnics. That night, Ngawang Tenzin Norbu had a strange dream. In it he saw a broken and dilapidated chörten out of which poured many silver coins. The lama thought that it was not a good sign and decided to perform an incense offering ritual before continuing the journey, but somehow he was unable to do it. Then, when they reached the bridge over the Dudh Kosi at Phungi Dranga, one of the horses that had been sent ahead carrying a leather bag with medicines fell from the cliff into the water. They managed to retrieve the medicines, but the horse died.

A large welcoming party was waiting for the lama at Bedur Pass below Tengboche. On the right side were the sponsors and all the men dressed in their best clothes, wearing hats with fur and holding silk scarves and incense sticks. On the left side were the women, all elegantly dressed with golden earrings and ornaments, holding flowers, incense sticks, and silver prayer wheels. In the center were the main disciples of the lama and the monks, forming a procession and playing various musical instruments. Lama Gulo and Lama Karma came on horseback and offered scarves to the Rongphu Sangye. Together they rode toward the top of the ridge, where a large chörten had been built. At that point they all dismounted and walked slowly to the gompa. The lama sat on a high throne, and Lama Gulo offered him the auspicious representations of the universe and of the body, speech, and mind of the buddhas.

The next morning at daybreak, the Rongphu Sangye performed an incense-offering ceremony. Just as he was concluding the ritual, he was amazed to see the sun, moon, and stars all at the same time. Just as in his vision, he beheld a solid mass of mountains before him. The large green meadow was covered with young bushes and flowers. There were large colorful birds like peacocks and many other birds whose songs brought about renunciation in one's mind. A stream of clear water seemed to be singing with the sound of *Hum*. Wild animals, such as deer, played there, and the sweet scent of juniper filled the air. In short, it was a delightful and wondrous place. At that moment, the recollection of having been there long before came into the lama's mind, and an experience of the natural clear light of primordial awareness as a release from all boundaries was born in him.

After a few days, the Rongphu Sangye conferred the five vows of Buddhist lay practitioners and the vows of novice monks. After the ceremony, he explained in detail *The Ritual of the Three Grounds*,[182] and from that time onward the monks began to perform the confession ceremony twice each month. The lama also wrote a small text, *All-Clear Mirror,* containing the official regulations and rules of behavior of the new monastery.[183]

To fulfill the prophecy that the profound termas of Terdag Lingpa would spread in the southern border areas, the Rongphu Sangye gave the commentary and oral transmission of the preliminary practices of *The Great Compassionate One Embodiment of All the Blissful Ones*[184] and explained how to perform the ritual. He then gave the commentary on the actual practice of the nature of the mind, the *Red Wrathful Guru,*[185] the *Condensed Essential Longevity Practices,*[186] *The Playful Ocean of Accomplishments,*[187] the Northern Treasure, *The Great Compassionate Lord,* the volume of ritual daily prayers and ceremonies, and other instructions. In that way, the monastic community at Tengboche received the blessings of all the practices from a pure source.

In accordance with the tradition of the mother monastery at Rongphu, Ngawang Tenzin Norbu advised them to perform every year the extensive ritual of *The Embodiment of All the Blissful Ones* for the consecration of mani pills *(mani rildrub).*[188] The Tengboche community agreed to perform this ritual for two weeks every year starting on the first day of the tenth lunar month. The lama gave them the empowerment for the ritual dances and a large offering of 3,133 *tam* (Tibetan currency) for the costumes and masks.

Then, on the first day of the tenth month, when the stars and planets were in an auspicious conjunction, the Rongphu Sangye performed the actual consecration of the new Sang-ngag Thegchog Chöling (Dharma Island of the Supreme Vehicle of Secret Mantra) Monastery in accordance with the elaborate mandala of *The Embodiment of All the Blissful Ones.* The lamas and monks went in procession around the place scattering flowers and rice and invoking the blessings of all the buddhas.

On that day, a large crowd gathered at Tengboche. The whole sky was filled with rainbow clouds, and the rays of the sun enveloped everything with their warmth. Many auspicious signs could be seen, and some people had visions of holy beings and so forth. After the consecration, the lama performed a fire offering to pacify obstacles followed by an extensive tsog offering. The Sherpas organized a show with horse races, competitions, and a play about the Nepalis and the *inji* (British) soldiers. Some people, including the lama, sang melodious poems. The lamas, monks, and common Sherpa folk enjoyed themselves for three days with singing and dancing.

The village headmen and the common folk from Khumbu and Pharag who were assembled at Tengboche agreed to place under the protection of the monastery the land extending from the bridge at Phungi Dranga in the west to the stream below Deboche in the east. From then on, no one would be allowed to cut trees or hunt wild animals within that area, and any problems that arose there would be dealt with according to the rules set by the lama and monks of Tengboche Gompa.

In order to revive the lineage of Ratna Lingpa introduced in Khumbu by Lama Sangwa Dorje, Lama Gulo requested the empowerment of the *Cycle of the Three Roots.*[189] Then, as the last ceremony, the lama performed the *Ribo Sangchö* incense offering to the Khumbilha while a large prayer flag was being installed in the center of the courtyard. At that time, a group of men that no one seemed to recognize carried the heavy pole with the prayer flag and installed it. The Rongphu Sangye thought that they were the local Khumbilha god and his retinue.

On that same day, many Sherpas, Rais, and Limbus came to meet the lama. The people from the lower valleys, who were not Buddhists and did not speak Tibetan, paid respect in accordance with their own tradition by offering flowers and prostrating before the lama. The Rongphu Sangye conferred on them the vows of refuge in the Three Jewels as well as the oral transmission of the mantra *Om mani padme hum,* and gave them protection strings and blessed pills, praying that in the future they would meet the precious teachings of the Buddha.

The Lawudo Lama Yeshe, as Kunzang Yeshe came to be known, participated in the consecration ceremonies at Tengboche and received all the teachings and empowerments from the Rongphu Sangye. He enjoyed spending time with his Dharma friends and, like everyone else, rejoiced at the creation of a monastic establishment in Khumbu.

Kunzang Yeshe then pondered about the life of the monks. The Buddha had said that keeping monastic vows is a source of great benefit for both present and future lives. Monks and nuns constitute the Sangha Jewel and as such, are objects of veneration, irrespective of their personal virtues or faults. They keep the vow of celibacy, are supposed to abstain from drinking chang and arak, and they spend their time studying, meditating, and performing rituals. Kunzang Yeshe had a deep respect for monks and nuns. But, he reflected, the teachings of the Buddha can be practiced by everyone, whether ordained or lay, as long as they use their lives to develop loving-kindness and compassion and to deepen their awareness of the ultimate nature of the mind. Therefore, he put aside any thought about becoming a monk himself in that lifetime.

As it was already late in the year and there was too much snow on the Nangpa La, the benefactors and disciples urged the Rongphu Sangye to perform his usual winter retreat at Tengboche, but the lama did not want to delay his departure. He gave them his last instructions, and on the eleventh day of the eleventh month, he set off for Rongphu. The farewell party assembled at the Chagtsel Gang, the Ridge of Prostration. The elderly people were particularly sad, and tears were streaming from their eyes because they knew that they were unable to make the long journey to Rongphu and would not meet the lama again. The Rongphu Sangye told them that there was no need to feel sorrow; he reminded them that all composite things are devoid of real substance and that whatever comes together must separate in the end.

From Tengboche, the lama went to Khumjung and Khumde and then to Namche. He stayed three days in the Kangyur Lhakhang performing tsog offerings and purification rites, consecrating wealth vases, giving empowerments, and so forth. From Namche he proceeded to Thangme, where he stayed at the house of his disciple Lozang Dorje and gave the empowerment of *The Great Compassionate Lord*. The next day the lama visited the Thangme Gompa. The Thangme monks also pledged to perform the Mani Rildrub (which the Sherpas pronounce *mani rimdu*) for two weeks every year, starting on the first day of the fourth lunar month. The Rongphu Sangye gave them a donation for the costumes and masks of the Mani Rimdu dances.

The lama then proceeded to Marulung and Lungnag, where the lamas, disciples, sponsors, and devotees who were not going any farther offered silk scarves to the lama, their eyes full of tears. The lama returned the scarves to them together with knotted silk strings as a blessing and protection, and offered a song of spiritual advice to the Khumbu Sherpas. Before the final ascent to the Nangpa La, the Rongphu Sangye exchanged his horse for the sedan chair and was carried across the pass. At the resting huts of Palhung, where his manager Ngawang Tenzin was waiting, he left the sedan chair and rode by horse to Kyatrag. There he gave a lavish banquet, gifts, and protection strings to the Tengboche monks and those who had carried him across the pass, and then resumed his journey back to Rongphu with his attendants.

From Lungnag, once the sedan chair carrying the Rongphu Sangye was out of sight, Lama Kunzang Yeshe returned to his house in Thangme Gompa and soon resumed his meditation at the Lawudo cave.

## 10. Life in Khumbu

*Life at Lawudo*

For some years, Kunzang Yeshe's wife Tsamchi split her time among Thangme, Mende, and Lawudo. Their son Wangyal was now a tall, bright young man, although he had a birth defect and could not speak well. He too traveled to Tibet and engaged in small trading ventures just as his father had done. Around 1924 or 1925, Wangyal married Peni, a Namche girl from the Chuserwa clan, and settled with her in his father's house at Thangme Gompa. In 1926, the year of the tiger, a son was born to Peni and Wangyal, and they called him Karma Tenzin. The next year, a daughter was born to them, and they named her Pemba Dekyi.

The villagers had agreed to give the land between the water spring in the west and the steep rocky cliffs in the east to the Lawudo Lama, so that only the lama's family was allowed to cut wood in that area. Because of the high altitude, strong winds, and scarcity of water, trees grew slowly and with much difficulty in Khumbu. Kunzang Yeshe was aware of the precarious environmental situation and encouraged people to respect the young trees and to be content with cutting only the dry branches. Unfortunately, the Sherpas did not always listen to his advice and the mountain slopes of Khumbu were becoming bare at an alarming rate.

To benefit the simple, illiterate villagers who could not practice meditation or perform rituals, Kunzang Yeshe requested Dargye, a stone carver from Kyabrog, to cover a large boulder near Lawudo with mantras. Thus, those who came along the path from Zamte or Mende could circle the boulder while reciting mantras and accumulate at least a tiny bit of merit.[190]

On special occasions, such as Sherpa New Year, the Lawudo Lama would go to Charog or Genupa to visit Lama Dondrub. While the two of them shared stories, cracked jokes, laughed, and sang beautiful songs, Lama Dondrub's wife plied them with chang and arak. "Shey, shey!" ("Drink, drink!") she would press them, and as soon as they had taken a few sips, she would again fill their bowls. Although neither Kunzang Yeshe nor Lama Dondrub were particularly rich, they certainly honored the Tibetan saying, "A rich man's lips are always moist with tea or chang."

16. Carved boulder at Lawudo

The milky beverage passed swiftly and easily down their throats, and soon their tongues would lose all shyness. Kunzang Yeshe spoke Tibetan very well, and after a few bowls of chang, he could speak even better and more quickly. He could spend hours and hours giving wonderful Dharma talks or telling delightful stories that made everyone roar with laughter. Then, when the visit was over, he would stand up and walk straight to Lawudo across the dangerous landslide and over the steep mountain path without tripping or falling over or ever showing any signs of being drunk.

Kunzang Yeshe's fondness for chang was well known, and stories about him began to circulate in Khumbu. It was said that on one occasion Ama Tsamchi had refused to serve chang to her husband because she was worried about his health. Kunzang Yeshe did not say anything. After a few days, people noticed that the grass and the potato crops around Lawudo were becoming dry and withered, even though it was the height of the rainy season. When Tsamchi reported the matter to Kunzang Yeshe, he replied, "The fields are thirsty, just like me. Bring me some chang." Reluctantly, Tsamchi served chang to her husband, and as soon as he had drunk to his heart's content, the mountain slopes and fields became as green and lush as before.

Kunzang Yeshe did not like to visit the villages, but sometimes he was compelled to do so. Ang Dawa of the Tragtho clan and Lama Lozang Dorje, who was a Sakya Khampa like Kunzang Yeshe, used to invite him to their houses at Zamte to give long-life empowerments and perform rituals when a member of one of their families was sick. The Lawudo Lama also went a few times to Namche to perform the ritual of the *Peaceful and Wrathful Deities* on behalf of the deceased. On these rare occasions he used to stay in the house of a Khampa man called Au Palden, who lived close to the Kangyur Lhakhang.

As the heir of his father's lineage, Lama Wangyal was to receive all the empowerments and transmissions that Kunzang Yeshe himself had received. Around 1930, Wangyal built a small, one-storied house at Lawudo next to the cave and spent the winters there with his family. The Lawudo kitchen was enlarged with a cowshed to accommodate the family's five cows and one *dzomo,* and Ama Tsamchi also moved to Lawudo. Thus, Kunzang Yeshe once again found himself surrounded by his family. He taught the different rituals to his son and daughter, and they helped arrange the altar for the retreats, ceremonies, and empowerments.

Every morning, Kunzang Yeshe practiced the meditation of the *Goddess Chandali* and, after completing the required number of mantras, began to give long-life empowerments. During the rainy season, water used to drip copiously from a few spots inside the cave. Kunzang Yeshe collected the water, consecrated it, and distributed it as the "water of life" *(tsechu).* After a while, the Lawudo Lama Yeshe became famous for his long-life empowerments. Sometimes a group of up to five or six families would gather at Lawudo and squeeze themselves inside the cave and in the small courtyard outside to receive the empowerment. Ama Tsamchi and Ani Karzang prepared food, tea, and chang for the visitors, while Lama Wangyal helped his father with the ritual.

The Sherpas brought offerings of potatoes, corn, tsampa, butter, tea, salt, and so forth, and sometimes they also brought fresh meat. Kunzang Yeshe always inquired about the origins of the meat and only accepted meat from an animal that had died a natural death, proceeding to give lengthy explanations about the terrible consequences of taking the life of any living being.

One villager from Mende called Gonpo regularly offered loads of firewood, dry yak dung, and juniper branches to the Lawudo Lama. The loads used to be carried to Lawudo by Shangkhug Kalden, a brother of the Dzamtra Lama. Kalden was a very good Dharma practitioner and had an interesting peculiarity: there was a hole in the left side of his belly, which he kept closed with a wooden bowl and a bandage to keep his intestines from coming out.[191]

Every year, the Lawudo Lama performed the nyungne ritual with the Charog lamas, either at Charog or at Lawudo itself in the house built by Wangyal next to the cave.

### How the Lawudo Lama Kunzang Yeshe Completed His Dharma Practice

One morning, Kunzang Yeshe woke up to the realization that he could not move. Just as had happened before, his body was paralyzed and his tongue could not articulate any sound. For about six months he could not go anywhere, and even to attend to the calls of nature he needed the help of Karzang. Forced into silence and immobility, the Lawudo Lama placed his mind in primordial awareness, in a meditation beyond words or rituals. Slowly, he was able to recover from his sickness and resume his normal life, but the soles of his feet were very painful, and he was unable to walk. Because of this, for about thirteen years Kunzang Yeshe did not move from Lawudo. Sitting continuously on the same cushion and concentrating on his meditation practice, he was able to complete a large number of retreats and attain a high level of spiritual development. Although others pitied him on account of his sickness, Kunzang Yeshe himself did not mind. In fact, he used to say that it was due to these seemingly unfavorable circumstances that he had been able to perform his practice without disturbances. "This sickness actually means that the protectors of the secret mantra path are supporting what I am doing," he used to say cheerfully. Then he would quote a few lines from the abbreviated offering to the secret mantra protector Magon Chamdrel (Ekajati)[192] from the *Unobstructed Primordial Mind:*

> When the view of the self-created primordial awareness arises,
> Guard us from hindrances, O protector.
> When we are perceiving the manifest wisdom,
> Guard us from hectic activities, O protector.

"These words are very true," Lama Kunzang Yeshe used to say.

During those thirteen years, the Lawudo Lama meditated continuously, day and night, without interruption. Sitting cross-legged in his meditation box, he performed rituals, recited mantras, and kept his mind steadily concentrated upon the nature of the primordial mind. He never lay down to sleep but contented himself with dozing on and off. Sometimes he would sit in the sunshine to read scriptures, copy manuscripts, or illustrate the texts with colorful drawings. Before dusk, sitting outside the cave, Kunzang Yeshe made offerings to the buddhas, local spirits, and beings in the intermediate state by burning some tsampa mixed with the three white substances (milk, butter, curd) and the three sweets (sugar, molasses, honey). In the evenings he used to perform the fulfilling ritual of the Dharma protector Magon Chamdrel.

In this way, the Lawudo Lama completed the retreats of all the tantric empowerments he had received, such as the practices related to the lama, the dzogchen practices, and those of the Great Compassionate One according to Ratna Lingpa's termas.[193] Particularly, he put great effort into the practice of meditation on the direct manifestation of reality[194] according to the *Unobstructed Primordial Mind* and the *Heart Drop* tradition.

In early autumn, when the Hindus in Nepal celebrate the Dasain festival by sacrificing an extremely large number of goats, ducks, and buffaloes to the Hindu goddess Durga, Kunzang Yeshe would perform many practices for the good rebirth of the animals killed and for the purification of those who performed the killing.

### The Dharma Flourishes among the Sherpas

After Kusho Tulku took over the leadership in 1915, things began to change at the Thangme Gompa. Following the visit of the Rongphu Sangye, the Mani Rimdu began to be performed yearly during the fourth lunar month,[195] while nyungnes took place during the sixth month only. Ngawang Sherab Zangpo, the younger brother of Kusho Tulku, spent three years at Tengboche Monastery learning the rituals and dances of the Mani Rimdu from the senior monks who had learned them in Rongphu. Local artists made the masks for the dancers using clay mixed with paper and glue, while the elaborate brocade costumes were commissioned in Tibet. Soon the Mani Rimdu became the Sherpas' main religious and social event because of its elaborate dances and comic features, which appealed very much to the ordinary villagers. All this work kept the Khumbu monks quite busy and satisfied.

In contrast, the local married lamas were not happy. Among many other problems, most of the ritual dances of the Mani Rimdu could not be performed by laymen but only by monks, and the families that had lived at Thangme Gompa for much longer than the monks resented being relegated to second place. The situation was not easy for Kusho Tulku, and the pressure against him from the married lamas became increasingly intolerable.

As he was the reincarnation of the previous head lama, Kusho Tulku was invited to Jasa Hermitage in Shorong to give teachings. While in Jasa, Kusho Tulku was approached by Sangye Tenpa of the Lama Serwa clan, an extremely wealthy and powerful personage who wanted to build a celibate monastery at Chiwang, who asked him to take charge of the new monastery. The Shorong Sherpas also wanted to take part in the changing trend toward monasticism and were very keen to have monks who could perform the rituals well. And, whether the Shorong Sherpas were interested or not, the wishes of Sangye Lama were not to be challenged by the common people.

Sangye Lama did not need to exert much persuasion in order to convince him, and in 1923 Kusho Tulku took with him the Mani Rimdu masks, costumes, and ritual instruments and, together with his brother and the best monks of Thangme Gompa, left for Shorong. The married lamas and monks who chose to remain at Thangme elected Lama Dondrub[196] as their new leader and breathed a sigh of relief.

Lama Dondrub immediately undertook some important reforms. The old temple was too small for the growing number of resident lamas, so he decided to build a new one. With donations from the villagers, he was able to build a large two-storied temple a few meters below the old building, with a large courtyard ample enough for the performance of the Mani Rimdu dances. Although at that time there were not enough monks and no costumes or masks for the dances, the empowerment and rituals of the Mani Rimdu continued every year without interruption.

Meanwhile, the construction of Chiwang Gompa, situated on a beautiful spot above a steep mountain slope, began in the year of the ox, 1925, under the supervision of Kusho Tulku and his brother.[197] It was consecrated in the fire snake year, 1929. The Lama Serwa family was very generous and pledged support for fifty monks in perpetuity.[198] Many young Sherpas from Shorong and Khumbu were attracted by the prospect of a good monastic education and by the absence of worries concerning livelihood, and the monastery quickly filled up with monks. Kusho Tulku gave empowerments and teachings, while his brother taught the use of ritual musical instruments. Just as at Tengboche, the Chiwang monks began to perform the Mani Rimdu each year during the tenth month.

Some Sherpa women, including Kunzang Yeshe's daughter Karzang, had taken monastic vows from the Rongphu Sangye, and in 1925, a group of nuns approached Lama Gulo and asked permission to build a nunnery. Lama Gulo agreed and gave them a piece of land at Deboche, not far from Tengboche, where the first Sherpa nunnery was consecrated in 1928.

In the Thangme Valley, the mountainside between Gyachog Stream in the east and U Labtsa in the northwest became a haven for those wishing to engage in solitary contemplation. At Lawudo, Kunzang Yeshe continued his meditations without ever leaving his cave. At Charog, Gelong Ngawang Samten,[199] a monk from Thangme Gompa, settled in a large cave below the Tashi Nyi-öd Khyilba hermitage and soon became a famous meditation teacher. At Genupa, Au Palden from Namche and others built small houses and engaged in long retreats. Lama Wangchug of the Shangkhug clan built a large house above the caves of Chatang Chöying Rangdrol and organized the interior of a small cave behind it as his meditation place. To the north of Genupa, in a large cave known as the Sanyer, or Saogpa, Cave, lived Ani Ngawang Drolma,[200] an accomplished

17. U Labtsa chörten

disciple of the Rongphu Sangye renowned for the healing pills she prepared with clay and sacred substances.

Under the slopes of the sacred Khumbilha, the Akar Hermitage was filled with practitioners, while Lama Ralchagpa had settled at the Khangsarba Cave on the Gongdog Hill above Khumde.[201] At Tengboche,

Drag-ri Gompa, Deboche, Pangboche, Namkha Dzong, Chagmiteng, and so forth, many practitioners went into retreat for life and passed away amid wonderful signs. Externally they looked like unassuming, ordinary men and women, but their minds were free from self-grasping, and they were able to attain high realizations through the practice of the dzogchen path. Thus, during those years Khumbu was overflowing with many ordained and lay practitioners, both men and women.

# 11. Lessons in Impermanence

AFTER SOME FRUITFUL YEARS at Chiwang Gompa, the Kusho Tulku felt that his days as a monk were over, so he took a daughter of Sangye Tenpa as his consort. A quarrel then broke out between the Lama Serwa family and the Kusho Tulku, and in 1931 the lama left Chiwang with his brother and his consort Ganden Zangmo. Most of the Khumbu monks followed him as well. Thus, Chiwang Gompa suffered a great spiritual loss.

The Kusho Tulku was invited to teach near Patale at Tolu, or Toloka, a hermitage in the Okhaldhunga district where there is a cave with the imprint of Guru Rinpoche's body. The following year, after traveling to Tibet to meet the Rongphu Sangye, the Kusho Tulku and his family undertook a lengthy pilgrimage to Rolwaling and Yolmo. Eventually, they reached the Kathmandu Valley and spent some weeks visiting the holy places there.

Around that time, on the thirtieth of the tenth month of the water bird year (December 17, 1933), the Holder of the White Lotus, His Holiness the Thirteenth Dalai Lama, left his precious body. Messages were sent to all the monasteries in Tibet, even in the remotest corners of the country, so that rituals and prayers could be performed for the speedy return of the Precious Protector and for the welfare of Tibet.

When his pilgrimage to the holy places of the Kathmandu Valley was complete, the Kusho Tulku and his retinue took residence near the great Bouddhanath stupa.[202] The Kusho Tulku had many followers and sponsors among the Newar and Tamang communities and was offered hospitality in many homes, but he refused all the offers. Instead, he decided to set up a large Tibetan tent in the garden of one of his benefactors and stayed there most of the time. While in Kathmandu, the Kusho Tulku developed a good relationship with the prime minister, Juddha Shumser Rana, and was granted a certificate, or *sheel,* acknowledging him as the teacher of the Rana family and pledging him support.

It was now January 1934 and the pilgrimage season was at its peak. The bird year, which has a special significance for the Bouddhanath stupa, was coming to a close. Sherpas, Tibetans, Bhutanese, Dolpopas, Tamangs, and other Buddhist pilgrims could be seen circling the sacred stupa from early morning. Some devotees performed full-length prostrations on wooden boards at the eastern side, while others performed circumambulations by prostrating themselves along the path.

On January 15, the thirtieth of the eleventh Tibetan month, the Kusho Tulku was invited to visit the king and prime minister of Nepal, but he declined the invitation. Early that morning he told his relatives and followers to remain in the garden and not go to Kathmandu that day, not even to the marketplace. From among them, one Sherpa couple had made plans to visit Kathmandu that day; the wife was determined to go, even though her husband tried to convince her to listen to the lama.

Among the pious pilgrims in Bouddhanath—also known as Bouddha— was a dzogchen practitioner who was performing prostrations at the chörten. He was renowned for his clairvoyance, and people used to interrupt his practice with endless requests for divination about different matters. The dzogchenpa always complied, and his *mos,* or divinations, were reputed to be very accurate. That day, he suddenly started to feel very strange, and his whole body began to shake uncontrollably. "I need a drink," he thought, and went to the tent of Kusho Tulku to chat with him and drink some chang. The sponsor in whose garden Kusho Tulku was staying invited them to come into his house, but the lama refused and asked that the chang and *rakshi,* or arak, be served outside. The dzogchenpa gulped down three full glasses of liquor in a row. "Ah," he said, "I feel much better now. And you, Kusho-la, are a real emanation of Padmasambhava. You know the past, present, and future, and that is why you don't want to go inside the house."

Right at that moment, at exactly 2:13 in the afternoon, the ground shook fiercely for what seemed an eternity. Houses fell like paper cards, the top of the sacred chörten collapsed, and large cracks appeared in most of the temples and houses that did not fall down altogether. Everywhere one could see clouds of dust from the fallen buildings and hear the screams of people, the howling of dogs, and the noise of collapsing roofs and walls. It is recorded that 8,519 people died in the Kathmandu Valley alone. Some survivors went on a rampage, looting whatever they could lay their hands on and drinking whatever liquor they could find among the ruins. Massive landslides altered the course of rivers, and the whole eastern region of Nepal suffered terrible damage and loss of life.[203]

The Kusho Tulku consecrated water in a ritual vase and sent his brother to the streets to bless and comfort the people with the holy water. People were trying to rescue survivors from underneath the rubble, while long lines of corpse-bearers were forming at Pashupatinath[204] and other cremation grounds. The Sherpa woman who had disregarded the advice of the Kusho Tulku was among those who died.

Up in Khumbu, Lama Gulo and the Tengboche monks had been very busy. The son of the prime minister of Nepal was due to visit the gompa that day, bringing with him a large donation from his father in foodstuffs and cash for the Tengboche Monastery. That morning, however, something strange happened. When the temple keeper tried to open the door of the assembly hall for the morning service, he was unable to do so. No matter how hard he tried, the large iron lock would not open. When Lama Gulo was informed, he came to the temple, grabbed the lock with both hands, and broke it in two. Under the astonished eyes of his monks, the lama went inside and proceeded to make arrangements for the reception of the Kathmandu visitors.

It was around two in the afternoon when the Rana delegation passed through the gateway that marked the gompa's grounds. Lama Gulo was already sitting on his throne inside the temple, where the visitors were to proceed to offer him their respects. All the Tengboche monks and Deboche nuns were outside in the meadow, lined up in a procession to escort the illustrious visitors, when the earth started to shake wildly. The rear part of the roof of the temple collapsed, as did many of the monks' houses. Although the ceiling immediately above Lama Gulo did not fall down, he was hit on the back by a stone. That same evening Ngawang Norbu Zangpo, the beloved Lama Gulo, passed away, not so much of broken bones but of a broken heart at the destruction of his monastery.

The Thangme Gompa and the Lawudo, Genupa, and Charog hermitages escaped with very little harm, but the Kyabrog Gompa[205] suffered serious damage. Kunzang Yeshe sent Wangyal to find out whether anyone had been hurt, and he returned with the sad news of the death of Lama Gulo and others, and the destruction of Tengboche Gompa. Lama Kunzang Yeshe felt extremely distressed at the news, as Lama Gulo had been his teacher, friend, and companion on many journeys. Together they had received teachings and empowerments from many lamas, and the bond between them was stronger than any ordinary friendship or family ties. Besides, Tengboche Gompa was the main symbol of the spiritual development of the Khumbu Sherpas. Kunzang Yeshe plunged himself into deep meditation, unifying his mind with the deceased and transferring their consciousnesses to Amitabha's pure realm.

The Sherpas in general and the monastic communities of Tengboche and Deboche in particular were overwhelmed with grief at the sudden calamity. A man was dispatched immediately to Rongphu to convey the sad news. The Rongphu Sangye was dismayed at the news of this second misfortune and composed a sorrowful song about impermanence and the lack of true self-existence of the world.[206]

At Tengboche, the monks gathered under the guidance of Au Yeshe and Umdze Gyaltsen to perform the elaborate forty-nine-day rituals of the *Peaceful and Wrathful Deities* for their deceased lama. When the ceremonies at Tengboche were over, a large group of monks went to Tibet to request advice from the Rongphu Sangye. The lama was very optimistic. "Do not worry," he told them. "Tengboche Gompa will be rebuilt and will become even more magnificent than before. Now, you must commission a chörten to enshrine the relics of Lama Gulo and bring it to me for consecration. Then, after two years you should begin the search for his reincarnation." The Rongphu Sangye gave them a donation for the reconstruction of the monastery and sent them back to Khumbu. Umdze Gyaltsen and Au Yeshe assumed responsibility for the reconstruction and for leading the community, the Sherpas donated generously, and soon a new, larger temple presided over the Tengboche meadow.

At Lawudo, Peni gave birth to another child. The baby died soon after birth, and the grief-stricken mother cried and lamented, refusing to be comforted either by her husband or by Lama Kunzang Yeshe. Around 1936, Lama Wangyal went to Tibet to receive instructions from the Rongphu Sangye, but on the way back he contracted a disease and passed away shortly after. Peni was never able to recover from the loss of her husband, and two years later she too passed away. The children stayed at Lawudo under the loving care of Kunzang Yeshe, Ama Tsamchi, and Ani Karzang.

Meanwhile, the Kusho Tulku had been requested to build a new monastery at Toloka, but he passed away in 1936 before he could start the construction. Ngawang Sherab Zangpo, now known as Kusho Mangde, accepted the villagers' request to continue the work of his brother and remained in Toloka for the next forty years.[207] In 1938, Kusho Mangde found the reincarnation of his brother, and the Rongphu Sangye gave him the name Ngawang Lozang Yeshe Gyatso. The boy was enthroned the following year at Charog and Thangme, and later at Chiwang and Toloka. The Lawudo Lama Yeshe attended the ceremony at Charog and offered a beautiful porcelain cup to the young tulku, praying that he might benefit many beings. After the enthronement, the boy was taken back to Toloka, where his education was supervised by Kusho Mangde.[208]

In 1938, the earth tiger year, the monks from Tengboche traveled to Rongphu Sangye, carrying with them the chörten containing the relics of Lama Gulo to be consecrated by the Rongphu Sangye. The following year, the lama recognized Pasang Tenzin, the son of a Khampa trader from Namche, as the reincarnation of Lama Gulo and gave him the name Ngawang Tenzin Zangpo.[209]

In 1940, sorrow struck again when the precious Dzatul Ngawang Tenzin Norbu left his body. The Rongphu Sangye was the pure source of all the teachings that the Khumbu Sherpas had received, and they regarded him as their tsawe lama, or root teacher. Extensive rituals and prayers were performed at Tengboche, Thangme, and all over Khumbu and Shorong for his speedy rebirth. The Do-ngag Zungjug Ling Monastery at Rongphu now came under the guidance of Trulzhig Rinpoche, the young tulku of Trulzhig Kunzang Thongdrol.[210]

## 12. The Last Years of the Lawudo Lama

A LREADY IN HIS LATE SEVENTIES, the Lawudo Lama Yeshe was widely respected. By now, his long pigtail had become white, and all his teeth were gone. He wore dark spectacles and the round, white conch-shell earrings of tantric practitioners. His habitual clothing was a *logpa,* a thick sheepskin coat, except during the warmer months when he would wear a dark red woolen cloak. Years before he had replaced his old, worn-out yellow hat with a white and red *pesha,* the "lotus hat" similar to the one worn by Guru Rinpoche that lamas of the Nyingma tradition are allowed to wear.

People from Khumbu, Pharag, Shorong, and Kulung flocked to the Lawudo Lama for teachings and divinations, and his long-life empowerments were eagerly sought after. Although his feet were already healed, Kunzang Yeshe did not like to visit the villages. But on a few occasions he was requested to preside over the Dumche ceremonies at Thangteng and to perform the *torgyab,* the throwing away of the ritual cake imbued with the negative energies of the whole valley. This ritual can only be performed successfully by someone who has enough power to control the local spirits, and the status of Kunzang Yeshe as a high lama was thus acknowledged.

Ama Tsamchi sat in the kitchen or outside in the sun, turning her prayer wheel and reciting mani (Chenrezig's mantra). Sometimes she circled the cave or the mani stone, but she was now unable to perform any of the heavy tasks required by daily Sherpa life. Ani Karzang directed the household with the help of Karma Tenzin and Pemba Dekyi, who were already grown-up young people. Lama Kunzang Yeshe had taken special interest in their education. Not only could they read the scriptures, but they had learned how to prepare the altar and the offerings for the different rituals.

Karma Tenzin was a very bright young man. After the untimely death of his father Lama Wangyal, he was to become the holder of Kunzang Yeshe's lineage and receive all the transmissions and empowerments that the lama had received from his own teachers. Karma Tenzin had a short temper, but he tried his best to keep it under control. One of the things he strongly disliked was his grandfather's fondness for chang. He used to beg Kunzang Yeshe not to drink so much, but the lama did not pay any attention to him. Alcoholic drinks did not affect his level of awareness and served only to enhance his perception of ultimate reality, but common people were unable to understand his profound realizations. Karma Tenzin would get very upset when Kunzang Yeshe refused to stop drinking, and to vent his anger he devised a simple and effective method: he would fill up his hat with earth and twist it very hard as if he were beating someone!

Pemba Dekyi's job was to bring water from the spring nearby. During the dry season, just before the monsoon rains set in, the spring was almost empty, and she had to fetch water from Genupa, crossing the large landslide and carrying uphill a full, heavy wooden water container that was almost bigger than she was. She also learned to take care of the cows. Every morning she would open the door of the cowshed and lead them out onto the mountain. In the afternoon she often had to scan the forest and look for a missing cow that had become engrossed in munching the juicy grass and forgotten that it was time to return home. Sometimes snow leopards or wolves could be heard howling on the forested slopes above Lawudo; Ani Karzang or Karma Tenzin would climb the steep path to the Dragkarma or to Kabsale and make sure that the Lawudo cows did not fall prey to the hungry visitors.

Pemba Dekyi also helped Ani Karzang to milk the cows. The first bowl of milk each day was offered to the buddhas at the shrine in the cave; the remaining milk was used for tea or to prepare butter and cheese. During the summer months, the cows were taken to the higher pastures to keep them from damaging the potato crop and to spare the grass near the villages, but one cow was always allowed to remain at Lawudo to supply the lama with milk.

Occasionally, Ani Karzang had to go south to Katitenga to get grains and butter. Later, when the children grew up, it became their turn to make the journey. They both enjoyed the freedom afforded by a few days of walking through the mountain paths and meeting other people their age. Those journeys, however, were not frequent. Potatoes, radishes, and green onions were grown at Lawudo itself, and the lama's fields at Mende, Thangme, and Tarnga yielded enough potatoes for the whole family. Besides, the Lawudo Lama had many disciples and sponsors who provided him and his family with most of their needs.

Around 1943, Ama Tsamchi passed away at Lawudo. Kunzang Yeshe cremated the body of his wife on a flat spot on the ridge above Lawudo, and her ashes were mixed with clay and molded into small Buddha images that were placed inside a small cave under a large boulder east of Lawudo.

The Lawudo Hermitage was always full of people. The villagers from Mende never failed to stop by when they were on their way to the top of the mountain to check their cattle or to collect yak dung or wood. "Ya peb!" ("Come in!") Kunzang Yeshe would say, while sticking out his tongue and stretching his hand in a welcoming gesture. He would chat with them and give them good advice about whatever they needed, while Ani Karzang or Pemba Dekyi brought food and drink for the visitors.

Among the regular Lawudo visitors was Nyima Yangchen, a girl from Mende who belonged to the Shangkhug clan. Sometimes she helped the lama's family with their potato and grass fields in Mende and brought them salt and other commodities from Tibet. Kunzang Yeshe was very fond of her, and Nyima Yangchen enjoyed sitting at his feet and chatting with him. Sometimes the lama handed her his own cup and bowl filled with chang or tsampa and said, "Here, drink this." Nyima Yangchen was embarrassed to drink and eat from the lama's own utensils, but Kunzang Yeshe always insisted, and she had to comply. Then, when she tried to wash the cup or bowl, the lama would stop her. "There is no need to wash it; we are both human beings," he would say.

The Lawudo Lama enjoyed the company of young people. Nyima Yangchen's brother Pasang and Ang Dekyi, a girl from Mende of the same age as Pemba Dekyi, also came often. Kunzang Yeshe would then mix some tsampa with butter, powdered cheese, sugar, and black tea inside a small leather bag, knead it well into lumps of *pak* (dough), and give it to the girls. Ang Dekyi was fascinated by the statues of the two ladies attending Guru Rinpoche. Kunzang Yeshe told them the stories of Mandarava and Yeshe Tsogyal, and the girls developed a strong devotion toward them, particularly toward Yeshe Tsogyal, the Tibetan consort of Guru Rinpoche, who had been instrumental in concealing termas in Tibet and the Himalayan regions. In a country where women had very few opportunities to study and practice the Dharma, the example of Yeshe Tsogyal seemed very inspiring to those young Sherpa girls.

Then, a little boy called Ang Chötar came to study at Lawudo. The boy could remember his previous life when he had been a first cousin of the Charog Lama Kunzang Dechen Gyalpo, and he would talk about how he had drowned in the Yamdrog Lake in Tibet. Ang Chötar stayed at

Genupa with his maternal grandmother Ani Kalden, the sister of Lama Dondrub and Kusho Mangde, and the Lawudo Lama offered to take care of his education. The boy learned to read and began to memorize some prayers with the help of Kunzang Yeshe and Karma Tenzin.

### The Lawudo Lama Meets Ngawang Chöphel

Lama Yeshe Dorje, or Au Yeshe, was the eldest monk of Tengboche Monastery. After the disastrous 1934 earthquake, he had worked very hard to collect donations and rebuild the monastery. Later, however, there were some disagreements with the new management of the gompa, and Au Yeshe decided to leave. He settled in a cave at the Menchelo Hermitage above Pangboche, near Lama Sangwa Dorje's cave.

In the first month of the water horse year (1942), Au Yeshe began to give teachings on the preliminary practices and the actual meditations of the *Unobstructed Primordial Mind* to a few young men, such as Pemba Gyaltsen from Dunde, Ang Pasang from Kyongma, Lama Dorje from Domphug (Jorsale), and Ngawang Chöphel Gyatso from Kulung. After three months, however, the porch outside the cave broke down under the heavy rains. Au Yeshe thought that it was an inauspicious occurrence and decided to move to the Akar Hermitage above Khumjung, where he began to give teachings on the *Peaceful and Wrathful Deities* and *The Union of the Three Precious Ones*.

One day, Au Yeshe became very sick. His students were extremely worried and did not know what to do, but Au Yeshe told them, "My best Dharma friend is the Lawudo Lama Kunzang Yeshe. We often traveled together, and together we received teachings from the Rongphu Sangye and from Trulzhig Kunzang Thongdrol at Rongphu. I have no faith in anyone else. You should go to Lawudo and ask him to come." Pemba Gyaltsen and Ngawang Chöphel then took some scarves and a jar of chang and left for Lawudo.

It was now the tenth month of the year of the sheep (November or December 1943), and a sudden snow blizzard had covered the mountains with a thick layer of snow. All the birch, fir, juniper, and rhododendron trees were white, and only the precipitous rocky cliffs of the sacred Khumbilha Mountain stood free of snow. The young men took a shortcut to Phurte and were able to reach Lawudo in about two hours. When they arrived at the hermitage, they found the kitchen locked and no one in sight. Pemba Gyaltsen and Ngawang Chöphel had never been to Lawudo before, so they went around the building looking for the cave and the lama. They found the cave and an old man wearing a worn sheepskin coat sitting outside.

"Au, where is the Lawudo Lama?" asked Pemba Gyaltsen. "We have an important message for him."

The old man went inside the cave and motioned them to follow. The two men took off their boots and entered the cave. The old man was now sitting in his meditation box and said, "I am the Lawudo Lama." Pemba Gyaltsen felt his face flushing red out of embarrassment for not having recognized the lama and did not dare to lift his eyes from the floor. Kunzang Yeshe laughed and laughed until tears streamed from his eyes, while the two young men prostrated themselves and offered the khatags and chang to the lama.

"Where do you come from?" Kunzang Yeshe asked.

"We are coming from the Akar Cave Hermitage, Rinpoche-la. We have been receiving teachings from Au Yeshe, but he fell sick and is now on the brink of death. He has sent us to request that you come to Khumjung to perform *kurim* (rituals to avert illness and obstacles) for him. He insists that there is a strong Dharma connection between the two of you and that you are the only lama he can trust. Please, come to Khumjung with us immediately."

"Well," Kunzang Yeshe replied, "I never go anywhere to do kurim, but because Au Yeshe is my Dharma friend, I will make an exception." Kunzang Yeshe then took a text and his ritual implements, and the three of them left for Khumjung. Pemba Gyaltsen was thinking, "The lama is old and the path is covered with snow. I wonder whether we will have to carry him on our backs." But Kunzang Yeshe, who was nearing his eightieth birthday, walked faster than either Pemba Gyaltsen or Ngawang Chöphel, who were in their early twenties.

While they were walking down the hill toward Mende, Kunzang Yeshe told them, "This is the first time in twelve years that I have left this mountain. Only once in all those years I went to Mende to do kurim, and a few times I visited Charog, Genupa, and Thangteng. I spend my time meditating and do not like to waste my life in meaningless activities."

The three of them took the shortcut to Kyisa and followed a very steep path up to Khumde and then to the Akar Hermitage. Au Yeshe was very relieved to see his friend, although he knew that he did not have much time to live. Kunzang Yeshe stayed nine days at the hermitage performing elaborate rituals, and Au Yeshe recovered his health. The Lawudo Lama then returned to Lawudo escorted by Pemba Gyaltsen and Ngawang Chöphel.[211]

Au Yeshe was able to complete the teachings, but he passed away a few months later. After cremating his body, Pemba Gyaltsen, Ang Pasang, and Lama Dorje returned to their villages in Pharag, but Ngawang Chöphel felt a great respect and devotion for the Lawudo Lama and offered his services to him in return for meditation instructions.

Ngawang Chöphel Gyatso was born in Chereme, not far from the southern door to the secret Khenpalung Valley. When he went to stay at Lawudo, he had already received many teachings and engaged in many retreats.[212] At Lawudo, he moved into Wangyal's house next to the cave, from where he could easily hear the lama's call. Lama Kunzang Yeshe became very fond of him. The youth was a bright and dedicated practitioner and spent the day and a good part of the night meditating and reading scriptures. He was always ready to serve the lama, and Kunzang Yeshe found in him the helpful attendant he had missed since the death of his own son. Ngawang Chöphel received many teachings and instructions from the Lawudo Lama, such as the *Unobstructed Primordial Mind,* the *Self-Created and Self-Luminous Primordial Purity,* the *Goddess Chandali, The Union of the Three Precious Ones,* and many others.

During his last years, Kunzang Yeshe exerted himself wholeheartedly in the practice of thögal, the dzogchen meditations that lead directly to the highest level of realization. For that purpose, he dug a hole on the mountain slope east of the cave. There, sheltered from the continuous wind, he sat day and night under the sun and the moon, his mind firmly established upon the nature of reality. By practicing in accordance with the most secret instructions of the *Unobstructed Primordial Mind* and *The Heart Drop of the Great Expanse,* Kunzang Yeshe attained the realization of the manifestation of the absolute nature, the first of the four visions related to thögal. During the last years of his life he acknowledged having actually completed the four visions.

Ngawang Chöphel also practiced the meditations related to thögal, and at night he contemplated the intrinsic purity of the mind. He dug another shelter in the mountainside below the one used by Lama Kunzang Yeshe, and both lama and disciple spent their days and nights practicing in the open.

## 13. How the Lawudo Lama Kunzang Yeshe Dissolved the Illusory Appearance of His Form Body into the Expanse of Reality

ONE DAY, while his disciple was reading scriptures in the sun near the cave, Lama Kunzang Yeshe called, "Ngawang Chöphel, come here!" Ngawang Chöphel wrapped the text he was reading, put the wooden cover on top of it to prevent its loose pages from being blown away by the wind, and went inside the cave. "Sit down," said the lama. Kunzang Yeshe looked straight into his disciple's eyes and in a sorrowful mood recited the four Buddhist seals:

All compounded phenomena are impermanent;
All contaminated things are suffering;
All phenomena are empty and devoid of a self;
Nirvana is the complete pacification of all mental elaborations.
That is the Doctrine of the Buddha.

Ngawang Chöphel was perplexed and wondered what was going on in the mind of the precious lama. Then the expression in the eyes of Kunzang Yeshe changed.

"I just want to test your level of understanding and your spiritual development," Kunzang Yeshe said, laughing. "Now tell me, what is the meaning of the inseparability of appearance and emptiness, sound and emptiness, clarity and emptiness, awareness and emptiness, and bliss and emptiness, the reality free from the five poisons?"[213]

"Those are just objects of the dualistic mind. For the great wisdom mind free from intellectual concepts, the duality of object and subject has never been established," Ngawang Chöphel replied.

Lama Kunzang Yeshe continued, "My lama, the hermit Yonten Gyatso Rinpoche, does not have any attachment to the pleasures of the five senses."

"There is no such thing as forms or objects of desire," Ngawang Chöphel said.

These words brought a broad smile to the face of the lama, and he continued, "At this present time both of us, father and son, have the opportunity to enjoy the precious teachings of secret tantra. This is the result of the powerful prayers we made during many past eons. Accordingly, you should not waste your life performing rituals in the villages. Instead, you should meditate continuously with great energy. When you meditate, sometimes your mind will appear as angry, sometimes as peaceful, and at other times as sad. No matter what aspect your mind presents, you should continuously abide in a mental state that is unperturbed and beyond appearances, without letting your mind wander. As for myself, although in this life I was able to take the essence of this precious human body and live a meaningful life, I have not been able to benefit others in an extensive way. However, I make many prayers to be able to do vast work for others in the future."

Truly, after every practice he performed, the Lawudo Lama always recited a great number of dedication prayers, such as the *Prayer of Good Deeds*,[214] the dedication chapter from the *Bodhisattvas' Way of Life*,[215] and so forth. He would then conclude by remaining for a while with his hands folded at the heart, praying to be able to serve the Dharma and to benefit beings.

It was now the first month of the fire dog year (1946) according to the Khumbu tradition of celebrating the New Year one month ahead of the Tibetans, or the twelfth month of the wood bird year according to the Tibetan calendar. The New Year celebrations were taking place in every Sherpa home when on the sixth day, Lama Tenzin, the eldest son of Thangme Lama Dondrub, passed away. The Lawudo Lama was invited to attend the cremation and ritual ceremonies and went to Thangme Gompa with Ngawang Chöphel. A week later, on the twelfth of the month, he returned to Lawudo with his attendant. Kunzang Yeshe was having difficulty walking, and somewhere along the way he had to stop for a while and fell asleep. When he woke up, his eyes had a sad expression, and Ngawang Chöphel inquired, "Rinpoche, is your body in good health?"

"How could the body of a true practitioner possess any cause of sickness? Nevertheless, it seems that I have caught a cold."

Karma Tenzin, Ani Karzang, and Ngawang Chöphel were worried about the lama's health and thought that he might have eaten some dirty food while in Thangme, but Kunzang Yeshe told them to stop worrying about him. He sent Karma Tenzin to Charog to call Kusho Mangde and told Ngawang Chöphel to continue with his retreat.

Kusho Mangde had recently arrived from Toloka and was on his way to Rongphu with the young tulku of his brother. He had always shown deep affection for the Lawudo Lama and did not waste a moment in coming to visit him. Kunzang Yeshe then confided an important matter to him. "It seems that my life is over," he told Kusho Mangde. "On my way back from Thangme, I fell asleep and had a very clear, visionary dream. I saw a little boy, two or three months old, in a house at Thangme. His father's name was Puthar and his mother is Nyima Yangchen. That little boy is my *yangsi,* my reincarnation. He is the one who will continue my work for sentient beings. But for now you should keep my words secret and not talk about this until the right time comes."[216]

The next day, Kunzang Yeshe sent Karma Tenzin to Thangme with some errand that was going to keep him busy there for a few days. Pemba Dekyi had gone to Katitenga with some other young people to get corn and rice, and only Ani Karzang and Ngawang Chöphel were at Lawudo. On that day, there was a small landslide right behind the cave. Later, when Karzang went to fetch water, she found that the spring had almost dried up. Ngawang Chöphel also noticed that the tree growing at the side of the cave that is the residence of the local protecting god seemed withered and lifeless. Then, at midnight Ngawang Chöphel heard the sound of many female voices crying and lamenting in front of the cave. Thinking that the lama might be scolding his daughter, he went out quickly, but there was no one outside the cave. Everything was quiet and no one was there. Ngawang Chöphel later realized that the local virtuous or "white" deities were showing their sorrow at the imminent passing away of the Lawudo Lama.

The next day (the fourteenth of the month) in the afternoon, a young cousin of Kunzang Yeshe named Dargye brought a bag of rice as an offering to the lama. It was already late in the day, and Karzang invited Dargye to sleep at Lawudo that night. In the evening, Ani Karzang suddenly asked Ngawang Chöphel to come into the cave. When he came before the lama, he noticed that Kunzang Yeshe looked tired and was having difficulty breathing. The lama laid his hands for a while upon the head of his disciple as a blessing and told him to sit down. Then Ani Karzang brought a bowl of shagpa soup with dry meat in it.

"When I ask the lama to drink a bowl of soup, he does not accept. Please request him yourself and maybe he will eat," she said sadly. Ngawang Chöphel took the bowl in his hands and offered it to the lama.

"Please, Rinpoche, have some shagpa."

"I do not need any food, but I will accept it as an auspicious circumstance, so that you may have sufficient means of sustenance for the rest of your life." And with these words, Lama Kunzang Yeshe drained the bowl of shagpa without leaving a drop.

After Ani Karzang had left the cave, Kunzang Yeshe asked his disciple, "What day of the month is today?"

"Today is the fourteenth day, Rinpoche."

"That is good. Jetsun Milarepa went to the pure land of the dakinis on the fourteenth day of the first month. Now, go outside and look at the sky. How does it look?"

"The sky is clear, without center or boundaries as it is said, Rinpoche."

"And the moon, how does it look?"

"There is a rainbow around the moon, Rinpoche."

"Can you hear a sound 'uhr uhr,' as if there were an earthquake?"

Ngawang Chöphel listened attentively and replied, "Yes, Rinpoche, I can hear such a sound."

"Very good. Now, light a butter lamp on the altar and close the door of the cave. No matter what happens, do not let anyone inside, not even Karzang."

Ngawang Chöphel bolted the door and lit a butter lamp. Unexpectedly, Lama Kunzang Yeshe got up from his meditation seat and adopted successively the postures of the three bodies of the Buddha.[217] Afterward, he sat with his hands folded at his heart and recited many prayers with great fervor. At the conclusion of his recitation, Kunzang Yeshe said, "Our Teacher Shakyamuni passed away in this supreme posture," and he lay down on his right side with his right palm under his cheek, in the lion posture.

Then he sat upright and said, "Now the time has come for both of us, father and son, to stop our conversation for a while." Ngawang Chöphel thought that the lama intended to enter into meditation as usual, and replied, "*Lagso.* Very well, Rinpoche."

At that moment, Lama Kunzang Yeshe recited *Ah, Ah, Ah,* and with a slight movement, left his body. Thus, at midnight of the full-moon day of the first month of the fire dog year (Friday, February 15, 1946), the precious and compassionate Lawudo Lama Kunzang Yeshe passed away into the expanse of bliss.

Kyema kyehu! Knowledge-holder, Dharma lord,
You have gone to the primordial ground, the expanse of the
    Primordial Buddha's mind.
Deprived now of your compassion, a time of sorrow and weariness
    has arrived for your disciples and close ones!

For a while, Ngawang Chöphel cried and lamented and did not know
what to do. Finally, around three o'clock in the morning, he locked the
door of the cave and walked quietly around the outside of the kitchen,
where he met Dargye who had just come out to empty his bladder. "Keep
quiet," Ngawang Chöphel told him. "The precious lama has gone beyond
sorrow."

Without informing Ani Karzang, they both walked under the full moon
and went to the Dechen Chökhor Gompa. They woke up Lama Dondrub and told him of Lama Kunzang Yeshe's death. Then the three of
them returned to Lawudo. The first light of dawn was making its appearance behind the Tamserku and Gangtega peaks as they passed the chörten
at U Labtsa, and soon they were at Lawudo.

Ani Karzang heard them coming and had to be told about the death of
her father, but in accordance with the lama's instructions, Ngawang
Chöphel did not let her enter the cave. The body of the Lawudo Lama was
upright and his face was radiant, as if he had merely been asleep. Lama
Dondrub and Ngawang Chöphel locked themselves inside the cave and
performed the ritual for the deceased related to the *Unobstructed Primordial Mind* composed by Jamgon Kongtul Lodro Thaye.[218] While they were
performing the ritual, a large amount of holy water began to drip from the
ceiling of the cave.

The sad news spread quickly throughout Khumbu, and the next day
many people gathered at Lawudo. Everyone wanted to have a final glimpse
of the Lawudo Lama, but following the wishes of Kunzang Yeshe,
Ngawang Chöphel stood at the door of the cave and kept everyone out
with great zeal, using a big stick whenever they tried to force their way
inside. Messages were sent to the Khumbu lamas inviting them to attend
the cremation and related ceremonies, and many soon arrived.

After four days had elapsed, in the first watch of the morning, Kunzang
Yeshe arose from his absorption into the spacelike concentration. Having
purified even the subtlest defilement of his mind and energies, he attained
the exhaustion of phenomena into the ultimate nature, the fourth and last
stage of the thögal training. The ultimate reality of his intrinsic awareness

based upon the physical body became unified with the natural, absolute expanse of reality, just as the space inside a vase merges with the surrounding space when the vase breaks.[219] Kunzang Yeshe's mind entered into the spacelike primordial ground, indivisible from the mind of the Primordial Buddha Kuntu Zangpo. As a sign of his enlightenment, the sound of emptiness was heard.[220] The radiant face of the lama underwent a change, and drops of the white and red substances (sperm and blood) came out from his nostrils. That was the unmistakable sign of Lama Kunzang Yeshe's consciousness leaving his old body. It was then time to cremate the corpse.

In the early morning of the fifth day after the death of the lama, a cremation chamber was built on a large boulder east of Lawudo, close to Khumbilha Mountain. The precious body of the lama, sitting in meditation posture, was wrapped in his white and red shawl. His face was covered with a scarf, and the five-pointed crown of the five buddhas placed on his head. Ngawang Chöphel, Karma Tenzin, and other lamas carried the body, preceded by a procession of monks and lamas playing cymbals, gya-lings, drums, and conch shells. Sherpa men followed behind holding scarves, flowers, and incense in their hands. Ani Karzang placed a scarf on her father's body and sat in the kitchen wiping her tears, while other women busied themselves preparing food and tea.

The precious body was placed inside the cremation chamber and covered with scarves and flowers, the last offerings of his devoted disciples and friends. Walls were built around the body, leaving a large opening at the top and a smaller one at the side. Carpets and cushions were spread on a flat patch of ground nearby, and from sunrise till noon the lamas performed the ritual of *The Great Compassionate One Liberating All Migrators*. When the ritual was over, a simple-minded man from Pangboche, the only one present that had never received religious instruction or empowerment from Lama Kunzang Yeshe, lit the funeral pyre.

At that moment, although the sky was completely clear and the sun was shining brightly, a canopy of clouds and a circle of rainbows formed around the sun, and a few snowflakes in the shape of flowers fell from the sky. Arising from behind the Kongde peaks, a little white cloud drifted by, while rainbow clouds shaped like various auspicious offerings began to gather above.

Pemba Dekyi, Nyima Rithar, and other Sherpa boys and girls were returning from Katitenga when they noticed the rainbow formations above Lawudo. When they came into full view of the mountain, they saw a swirl of smoke and a large crowd. Pemba Dekyi's heart sank. "*Kyab su chi!* It looks as if someone has died!" and she rushed up the mountain.

Various musical sounds and melodious voices resonated through the valleys and across the mountain slopes. Everyone in the surrounding villages could see and hear these portents, and a great faith and devotion for the Lawudo Lama arose in their hearts. With tears in their eyes, they prostrated again and again toward Lawudo.

Although Lama Kunzang Yeshe was a respected lama and many people had received empowerments and instructions from him, he did not show external signs of being an accomplished dzogchen practitioner. Thus, for the ordinary, simple Sherpa folk unable to understand his level of realization, he was just an ordinary lama. But when they saw the rainbows with their own eyes and heard the music with their own ears, a strong devotion was born in their hearts. Those simple villagers did not understand much about the Buddha's doctrine and were mostly illiterate, but they all knew that dzogchen practitioners who have attained realizations are able to display wondrous signs at the time of their passing away.

For the next seven days, the lamas performed the ritual of the *Peaceful and Wrathful Deities* inside the cave. During that time the cremation chamber could be seen surrounded by rainbow clouds. On the eighth day they opened the cremation house and found that most of the bones had been consumed by the extremely hot fire. Among the ashes, however, they could see a large blackish lump and a few pieces of bone. Kusho Tsultrim Gyaltsen (who was known as Log Khyenpa, "proficient in reading"), a Khampa lama who was staying at Genupa, collected everything and brought it to Lawudo. The lamas performed a purification ritual and opened the large lump. Inside they found the skull with the brain, tongue, and heart, as symbols of the lama's body, speech, and mind, all of which had taken the shape of a wonderful jewel. The knee bones had also been spared by the flames and were marked with three wheels.

Kusho Log Khyenpa then took the remaining ashes and bones down to Kyisa and together with Riku Dorje of Tramoteng and Pasang from Mende, washed everything in the Gyachog River, searching carefully for relics. They found another bone marked with the syllable *Hum* and a great quantity of small, very hard balls of different colors[221] endowed with the power to bring liberation from cyclic existence merely by seeing, touching, hearing about, or remembering them. Kusho Log Khyenpa also found a small white piece of bone the size of a thumbnail, with a syllable *Ah* clearly marked in black upon its surface, and kept it as his own object of veneration.

The relics were distributed among the relatives and disciples of the Lawudo Lama. The skull with the jewel-like brain, tongue, and heart was given to Karma Tenzin, while Ngawang Chöphel received five relics the size of a pea.

Some days later, Tragtho Ang Dawa of Thangteng, Migmar Gyaltsen of Kyisa, Dargye, and others brought a few bags of very fine white clay from a particular spot below Mende. The remaining bones and ashes from Kunzang Yeshe's body were ground into powder, mixed with the clay, and molded into small Buddha statues. A square purkhang was built at the spot where the cremation had taken place, and the statues were deposited inside. The remaining clay was used to make a statue of Lama Kunzang Yeshe holding a *vajra* in his right hand and a bell in the left. Ani Karzang commissioned a copper and silver chörten to enshrine the relics of the lama, and the villagers offered many precious jewels to adorn it. The skull and the jewel-like relic were deposited inside and kept in the cave as objects of devotion for Lama Kunzang Yeshe's followers.

18. Purkhang of the Lawudo Lama Kunzang Yeshe

*Kyema kyehu!*
*Magnificent, compassionate protector, to you I pray:*
*From the peaceful expanse of great manifest enlightenment,*
*With the wisdom body that is the illusory display of great love,*
*Appear to your vajra disciples, give predictions, and*
*Bestow the blessings of your holy mind.*
*Until the ocean of existence is emptied,*
*Remember your aspiration to lead all living beings to enlightenment, and*
*Emanate different bodies according to your disciples' needs.*

—Ngawang Chöphel

# PART TWO

*The Reincarnation of the Lawudo Lama,*
*Thubten Zopa Rinpoche*

19. Lama Zopa in Beding, 1952 (T. Weir)

# 14. Continuity

*If there are no disciples to be trained, the trainer vanishes into*
    *the expanse of reality;*
*The self-manifested body of emanation dissolves into the body of*
    *reality.*
*If there are disciples, the…teacher gradually manifests as before.*
*This is the spontaneously accomplished fruit of Dharma practice.*
                                —Longchen Rabjampa[222]

AFTER THE LAWUDO LAMA PASSED AWAY, Karma Tenzin became the successor of his grandfather's lineage and moved into the cave, while Ani Karzang and Pemba Dekyi stayed in the kitchen. For a few years, on the anniversary of Kunzang Yeshe's death, his students gathered in the cave to offer tsog and perform rituals.

Ani Karzang passed away in 1958 at the age of seventy-two. Three years later, Karma Tenzin left for Shorong with Diu Rinpoche, a Tibetan lama who had been a friend of Kunzang Yeshe. Pemba Dekyi stayed for a while at Lawudo, but after her marriage to Pasang Namgyal she also left, taking with her the chörten with the lama's relics. All valuable statues and texts were stored in boxes and kept in Kunzang Yeshe's old house at Thangme Gompa. Various Tibetan meditators stayed for shorter or longer periods at Lawudo, but no one really took care of the place. The buildings began to deteriorate, and the cave and the large clay statues became black from the smoke of fires that were lit inside.[223]

Meanwhile, in accordance with his bodhisattva vow to help suffering beings, the Lawudo Lama Kunzang Yeshe did not waste time relaxing in some blissful buddha-land. Even before his old body had been consumed by the flames, his compassionate mind had already emanated another physical manifestation.

Nyima Yangchen was the eldest daughter of Shangkhug Nulu from Thangme and Tragtho Nyima Chökyi, whose father had been very religious and had performed many retreats at the Sanyer Cave near Charog. She was born in the fire sheep year 1907 and was followed by two girls, Lhamo and Dawa Butri, and three boys—Pasang Dorje, Ngawang Trinle, and Ngawang Yonten. When their father passed away in 1926, Nyima Yangchen engaged in trade in order to help her mother take care of the family. They lived in Mende, right below Lawudo, and would often visit the Lawudo Lama Kunzang Yeshe and his family.

Nyima Yangchen married Khampa Pasang Puthar of the Tsogo Drongsar ("new household of Tsogo") family, who was a couple of years younger than she was. Pasang Puthar's father Ang Dawa, or Da Pache, was a Tibetan from Nechung, a small town situated between Kyatrag and Shartö in the Dingri area.[224] Ang Dawa came to Khumbu in search of work and was hired as a servant by a Thangme family. Later he married his employers' daughter and built a house in the village under the Nasa Tsering, the northern ridge that separates Thangme from Thangteng, next to the path to Thangme Gompa.

Ang Dawa had six sons. The eldest, Ngawang Gendun, became a monk at Thangme Gompa. He went to Chiwang with Kusho Tulku but left a few years later and finally settled in Rolwaling as the resident lama and teacher. The second son was Ayulha, who became a soldier in the Indian army. He married a Tibetan lady, became a trader, and settled in Phag-ri in southern Tibet. Pasang Puthar, the third son, was born around 1909, and the fourth son, Rithar or Ngawang Legshe, became a monk at Thangme Gompa. The fifth son was Ang Tenzin, who had a problem in one leg and could not work or walk properly. One day he left for Darjeeling and was never heard from again. The youngest son was Ngawang Jigme, who also became a monk at Thangme Gompa and spent long periods of time at Rolwaling.

In accordance with Sherpa tradition, when Ang Dawa passed away, his youngest son Ngawang Jigme inherited the family houses. Being a monk, Ngawang Jigme renounced his property rights in favor of Pasang Puthar, who was the only married son living in Khumbu. Pasang Puthar and Nyima Yangchen were reasonably wealthy and happy, but shortly after the birth of their fifth child—a boy whom they named Dawa Chötar— Pasang Puthar became sick and died. Nyima Yangchen was left with three small children and another one in her womb—her sixth pregnancy—and a precarious economic situation.

When she was told that her son Dawa Chötar had been recognized by three high Tibetan lamas as the tulku of the Lawudo Lama Kunzang

Yeshe, Nyima Yangchen was not surprised. She had always wondered why the old Lawudo Lama had often insisted on sharing his cup with her. The boy studied in Thangme Gompa and then in Rolwaling with his uncle Ngawang Gendun. In 1957, Dawa Chötar—now Gyaltsen Zangpo—traveled to Tibet with his uncles and refused to return to Khumbu. In 1959 he fled the Chinese occupation and was able to continue his studies in the Buxa Refugee Camp, where he met Lama Thubten Yeshe, a deeply compassionate and learned monk from Central Tibet.

In 1968, when Lama Yeshe and Gyaltsen Zangpo (now known as Thubten Zopa) came to Nepal with a Russian lady named Zina Rachevsky, Lama Thubten Zopa Rinpoche was reunited with his family after an absence of twelve years. Karma Tenzin, the grandson of the Lawudo Lama Kunzang Yeshe, offered the Lawudo Cave and the possessions of the previous Lawudo Lama to him with the request to build a monastery at Lawudo where young Sherpas could receive proper education.

In 1971 Lama Thubten Zopa taught his first meditation course for Westerners at a place called Kopan in the Kathmandu Valley. Soon Lama Yeshe and Lama Zopa began traveling around the world and opened Dharma centers in different countries. When Lama Yeshe passed away in 1984, Lama Zopa had to assume the enormous responsibility of caring for the spiritual needs of thousands of students and directing the organization known as the Foundation for the Preservation of the Mahayana Tradition. His life became extremely busy, and he had very little time for his Lawudo Gompa and the Sherpa people.

Meanwhile, some significant changes were taking place in Khumbu. The number of climbing expeditions and trekkers increased dramatically, and the social structure and economy of the Khumbu people underwent a profound transformation. The great practitioners of the previous generation took birth again in their country, but many of the Sherpa tulkus, monks, and nuns left Khumbu and went to study at the large monasteries in Shorong, the Kathmandu Valley, and India.

In accordance with the aspirations he made in his previous life, Lama Thubten Zopa Rinpoche is now a world-famous Buddhist teacher. His life is fully devoted to serving the Dharma and sentient beings, and his beneficial activities continue in spite of age and health constraints. But the full account of the latter part of his life and his deeds will be recorded in a future volume. Now, let us hear what the second Lawudo Lama has to tell about his childhood, his youth, and life in his native Khumbu.

## 15. My Family and Early Childhood

I WAS BORN IN THE HIMALAYAN MOUNTAINS of Nepal, two or three days' walk from Everest Base Camp. That region is called Khumbu and is divided into two parts, Upper Khumbu and Lower Khumbu. Lower Khumbu, or Pharag, is a little bit warmer, but Upper Khumbu is extremely cold, with many high snow mountains and some forests, and a small, very primitive village called Thangme. That's where I was born.

I do not remember my father at all. I am sure that he helped to form my body, but I have no idea what he looked like. I have been told that when I came out of my mother's womb he was still alive, but I have no mental picture of him. People say that he was tall, with long hair and a small beard. It seems that he was a religious man who did many practices and was very good at reading scriptures and performing rituals for the villagers. He could sing very well but did not like to talk too much and was known as a very placid person with a "big stomach" who could "swallow" anything. That does not mean that he never got angry, but that he practiced patience and always tried to be calm. In any case, even though I do not remember him, I know he was very kind to me. If he had not created the karma to give me this body, by now I would not have this precious human body qualified with eight freedoms and ten endowments, which is the foundation for obtaining both temporal and ultimate happiness.[225]

My mother Nyima Yangchen was an extremely kind and generous woman, always concerned about others and ready to help at any time. In the morning she would make plenty of food and tea to be offered to whomever came to the house. Like most Sherpa women, she was completely illiterate and unable to recognize even *ka,* the first letter of the Tibetan alphabet, but although she could not read or study any text, her heart was a hundred times better than mine, one who has learned so many Dharma words. She could not read the scriptures describing the different sufferings of sentient beings, but she had innate compassion toward everyone, not just her family and friends.

The main residence of my parents was at Thangme, where all our possessions were stored in large wooden boxes. During part of the winter and early spring, my parents would move to Zamte on the opposite bank of the Nangpe Tsangpo. When the potato crop was planted at Zamte, they would move to Thangme and plant potatoes there and in Tengbo. After the Mani Rimdu and Dumche festivals, they would send the cattle to

20. Lama Zopa's family home in Thangme

Tengbo and go there sometimes to check on the animals and the potato fields. Then, when the potato crop was ready, they would spend several days or weeks digging potatoes, first at Zamte, then at Thangme, and finally at Tengbo.

My parents were regarded as being a little bit better off than other families and had a large number of possessions, although according to Western standards they might have been considered as "rich in garbage"! They possessed many domestic animals but only a few fields. As Sherpas do not like to sell their ancestral land, my paternal grandfather, who was a new arrival from Tibet, could buy only a small amount of land. But when my maternal grandfather died, my mother inherited some grass fields and potato fields.

My father took care of the yaks, naks, zobgyos, cows, and sheep, and went on trading journeys to Tibet. My youngest maternal uncle *(ashang)*

Ngawang Yonten used to take our animals to the high pastures together with his own cattle, while my mother worked in the potato fields and took care of the house and the children and sometimes accompanied my father on trading journeys to Tibet. When one of the yaks that carried their goods fell down a cliff and died, my parents dried the meat and went to Dza Rongphu to offer part of it to the Rongphu Sangye Ngawang Tenzin Norbu. They offered the rest of the meat, one cup of rice, and some dried potatoes to each of the meditators who were in retreat for life.

My mother had great devotion toward the lamas and the Three Jewels, and although she could not comprehend what was going on, she attended the teachings of the Rongphu Sangye in order to receive his blessings. She was unable to understand the actual teaching, but she paid attention to the simple bits of advice that the lama gave. On one occasion, the Rongphu Sangye told them that in front of a lama one should not wave the hands around but should keep them folded together in a calm and subdued manner. That was something she always remembered. Another piece of advice she never forgot was that while reciting the mani mantra, one should count one bead for each mantra, not two, and that the mind should not wander around. When the Rongphu Sangye gave the empowerment of the *Great Compassionate One Liberating All Migrators,* my father helped her to memorize a beautiful, short prayer for invoking Phagpa Chenrezig. For the rest of her life, my mother recited this prayer three times a day in the morning, afternoon, and evening, and she continuously recited Chenrezig's mantra, *Om mani padme hum hrih.*

Many children were born to my parents, but some of them did not survive childhood. The eldest was a boy who died when he was just six months old. He was followed by another boy who used to talk continuously about a place in Jang, north of Dingri, and had a kind of "double head" or pinnacle like the Buddha. When he was six years old, his body became completely swollen and he passed away. The Thangme Lama Dondrub told my parents that the body had to be carried to the cremation place by a fully ordained monk, and so they asked Gelong Ngawang Samten from Thangme Gompa to carry it. It was cremated at a spot high in the mountains from where one could see Tibet.

The third child was a girl, born on the third day of the third month of the water horse year 1942. In accordance with the Sherpa custom of naming children according to the day of their birth, she was named Phurbu Butri, which means something like Thursday Bringer of Sons. Sherpas like to give that name to their first baby girl in order to create auspicious circumstances for having male sons after her. When they have too many children, they give the name Tsamchi, which actually means making a demarcation or fence.

For a few days after she had come out of the womb, my elder sister did not cry or drink milk. My parents were worried and decided to call her Kami, which is the Nepali name for blacksmith. Since Sherpas did not have much knowledge about hygiene or medicine, they would attribute every sickness to evil spirits. They thought that by giving the child a lowly name such as Kami, the evil spirits would not want to come near and the danger of sickness would thus be averted. I do not know exactly how it works, but I guess it is a question of interdependence. If a name with a high, lofty meaning is given to a person who does not have enough merit to receive it, the person may get sick or even die, but if a "low" name is given, somehow the person may be able to recover. This is one of the methods that Sherpas and Tibetans employ to ensure the survival of their children. Whatever the case, after she got her new name, my elder sister recovered from her illness.

Another girl was born after Kami. She had a tiny tail on the back, like a thick needle; I saw it with my own eyes. That girl, Ang Chökyi, was very intelligent, and some high lamas said that she was a dakini or *khandroma,* a special being. She was very sensitive, and whenever she ate in the homes of other people or had unclean food, she would vomit it. I remember that she was very affectionate and used to take care of me with great love.

When my mother was five months' pregnant with me, she had an auspicious dream. In it she saw two caves on the mountainside near the Genupa Hermitage. One of the caves was small with a short staircase, while the other was much larger and had a long flight of steps. Although my mother wanted to go into the small cave, she entered the larger one instead. The staircase was lined on both sides with stone statues of the female deity Vajrayogini. On her way up, my mother paid homage by touching her forehead to the feet of the statues on the right side, and on her way down, to those on the left. When she woke up, she thought that the dream could mean that the child in her womb was someone special, but she did not tell anyone.

I was born at sunrise on a Monday, the last day of the tenth lunar month (or the eleventh month by Sherpa counting) of the wood bird year (December 3, 1945), in our Thangme house. Just as I was coming out of my mother's womb, a large black raven alighted on the roof of the house and began to caw. That is regarded as something very auspicious because black birds are considered to be manifestations of the Dharma protector Mahakala, the Great Black One. I did not move or cry, and my mother thought that I was dead. Nevertheless, she gave me a little bit of butter to eat and placed me inside a rectangular basket. She had much work to do and could not afford to take even one day of rest after giving birth, so she left me in the basket and went out to work. After a few days, my parents held a "birthday beer" party, or *kyechang*,[226] and gave me the name Dawa Chötar, Monday Dharma Expansion.

## My Father's Death

Just as happened in the case of Jetsun Milarepa, right after my birth things started to go wrong in the family. My father used to go to Tibet to buy salt and other items and then to Lukla and Katitenga to exchange them for grains and other things. Once, when he was returning home, he spent the night at Gomila below Rimejung Gompa. The next day when he reached Thangme he was feeling very sick with acute stomach pains. It seems that he had been poisoned by the lady of the house where he had spent the night.

In Khumbu and Tibet there are many cases of poisoning. Poison can be extracted from animals such as scorpions and causes very heavy and dangerous diseases. Some women become servants of evil spirits, and the spirits order them to poison some person who is good, powerful, or prosperous. The higher the status of the person who is poisoned, the happier the spirit becomes. Also, the good fortune of that person is transferred to the woman. But if she does not give the poison, the spirit gets very angry, and she then has to take it herself or pass it to another woman. I heard that in such cases the woman has to go to the center of the village and shout loudly for everyone to hear that she is passing the "lineage" to so and so. Usually, however, nobody knows whether a woman has poison or not, not even her family members. For that reason, Sherpas are always very careful not to accept food and drink from strangers. They also try to get bowls from Tibet made from a special wood that undergoes a change when poisonous food or drink is poured into them.

My father took special pills made by some lamas to counteract poison and was able to recover a little, but he never regained his health completely and was unable to go on trading journeys as before. As a consequence, our family's economic situation began to deteriorate.

About two years after my birth, Amala (the Tibetan term for "mother") became pregnant again. My father spent most of his time at home reciting prayers and mantras while Amala had to do all the work. One day, when she came home during a break, our father was sitting in his usual seat next to the fireplace. She called out, "Phala (Father), do you need anything?" There was no answer. As in all Sherpa houses, the room was very dark and Amala could not see his face; she thought he was meditating because he was sitting very straight. Finally, she realized that Phala was dead, and she began to cry and wail. My elder sister also started to cry; we small children did not understand what was the matter, but we joined in the crying anyway.

Amala did not know what to do, but after a while she collected herself and called the other amalas, neighbors, and friends. They all came into our house and discussed what had to be done. They were all very simple-minded villagers and did not even think about asking a lama for advice, so they decided that the only thing to do was to take the body away and cremate it.

In accordance with Sherpa custom, Amala stayed at home while some men took my father's corpse to a remote place to be cremated. They noticed that his face looked very fresh, not like the face of a dead man, and they were very surprised. Neither those villagers nor my mother knew that when someone is engaged in meditation on the clear light of death, the complexion of the body does not fade and there is no bad smell. In fact, when some meditators die, they look more magnificent than when they were alive, and their body emits a fragrant scent. These are the signs of having practiced pure morality and having developed bodhichitta, the altruistic mind of enlightenment. Because no one checked with lamas familiar with tantric practices who knew how to deal with such cases, I suspect that my father was not actually dead when they took him to the cremation place. Probably his subtle mind was still in the body, but the cremation took place before he had time to complete his meditation.

A few months before his death, my father had told Amala: "When I die, you don't need to perform rituals for me. The best way of accumulating virtue on my behalf will be not to sell our cattle to other people who may kill them but to keep them until they die." After my father's death, however, Amala felt that it was not right to not have any ritual performed, and she arranged everything in accordance with Sherpa custom, even though she had to borrow money to pay for the expenses.

About one month after Phala's death, Amala went to Tengbo to check the potato fields. There, in the early morning of the fourth day of the fourth Tibetan month of the year of the mouse (1948), my youngest brother was born inside a cave. Because he had been born after only seven months of pregnancy, Amala expected the child to be dead. The baby did not move, and she was just going to wrap it in a cloth and leave it there, when suddenly it began to cry and Amala took it home.

My brother was named Pemba Chötar, Saturday Dharma Expansion. Later, the Thangme Lama Dondrub changed his name to Sangye Chötar, and many years later Trulzhig Rinpoche changed it again to Ngawang Sangye. But Amala used to say that I was the one who had first started to call him Sangye. My brother grew up as a very kind and sensible boy who used to ponder such deep matters as the purpose of life and the deeds that cause beings to be reborn in heaven or hell.

## Hardships

After my father's death, life became very difficult for us. Most of our animals died of some strange disease, and only four or five cows were left, most of them old and with broken horns. In order to feed us, Amala had to work for other people carrying heavy loads and working in their fields, which Sherpas consider to be the lowest type of work. She engaged in trading, just as my father had done, and she also spun wool, had it woven into long strips of cloth, and sold it to people. We had become a very poor family, but we still had three good houses to live in and enough tsampa, potatoes, and radishes to fill our stomachs. We did not have to suffer like the poor people in the West who have to sleep on the streets and live on a sandwich or an apple a day.

My elder sister Ang Kami (*ang*, or *anga,* means child), or Kami Drolma, was soon able to do a little bit of work, such as taking the animals to graze on the mountain slopes above our house. The rest of us, the very small children, were completely useless. All we could do was break things and cause trouble for our mother.

Amala would get up very early in the morning, light the fire, and make butter tea by churning the tea brew with salt and butter in a *dongmo,* a wooden churn. Our breakfast consisted of tea and tsampa, or the leftovers from the previous evening's soup. Amala would breastfeed my younger brother Sangye and sometimes me also. Sherpa children are given mother's milk until they are three or even four years old, which creates a very strong affectionate bond between Sherpa mothers and their children.

After breakfast, Amala had to fetch water from the spring and carry it into the house in a very heavy wooden container; in those days lighter plastic drums and buckets were unknown in Khumbu. Then she would go to work in the fields or collect firewood, yak dung, or grass. Ang Kami led the animals to the pasture grounds, and the rest of us ran outside to play.

Back wall: On the shelves are large brass water containers, wooden utensils for carrying water, and wooden chang pots; a donmo for churning tea on the right; the stairs from the basement are just behind the wooden wall.

Shrine, folded yak wool blankets, wooden chests

Clay and brass cooking utensils, flat stone for mashing potatoes

Front wall: Hearth with pots for making arak, sitting and sleeping benches

21. Interior of Sherpa house

After a few hours, Amala would come back and prepare food and tea. She used to call us from the window, and we would scramble and crawl our way up the very steep and narrow staircase to the kitchen. We would then sit on the floor and enjoy boiled potatoes or potato pancakes. Sherpa houses used to have two stories, but now some Sherpas build their houses with three or even four stories. The animals are kept on the ground floor, which is filled with leaves for them to be warm and comfortable, and the people live upstairs in the kitchen.

After lunch, Amala would go out again and we would continue our games. Late in the evening, when it was getting dark, she would come back home and make sure that all the cows were in the cowshed downstairs, where my elder sister gave them grass and potato peels to eat. Sometimes one of the cows would not return, and Amala would have to go out and search for it.

While dinner was being prepared, we used to sit on the floor near the fireplace in order to keep warm. In those days there was no electricity, kerosene, or even candles. The only thing we had to light the house was a torch made with a few dry bamboo branches. Often we would fall asleep while the food was being cooked, and Amala would wake us up when dinner was ready. Our evening meal was usually shagpa, a kind of stew prepared with sliced potatoes, radishes, flour, *tsilug* (animal fat), and whatever ingredients were available. Rich people put meat in their shagpa, but since we were quite poor, we usually ate a very simple shagpa with no meat and scarcely any tsilug.

Because of the kindness and compassion of the Khumbu lamas and particularly because of the teachings of the Rongphu Sangye, the Sherpa people had made a rule forbidding the killing of animals. If someone was caught killing birds or wild animals in the forest, the Nepali policemen would keep them in jail for a few days, and they would be given some punishment. Nevertheless, some people hunted wild goats and wild chicken, and even killed yaks and cows very secretly. But in general, fresh meat was available only when an animal died naturally. In autumn and winter there used to be plenty of meat because wolves would sometimes kill sheep or cows. The very tasty dried mutton from Tibet was also often available.

After finishing our food, we carefully licked our bowls clean and went to bed. We all slept together, crowded under a very warm and large white sheepskin coat, a logpa. That, we were told, was "Father's logpa." It was our only covering; we had no other blanket or sleeping bag. In the mornings we small children did not get up early but lay in bed chatting and laughing under Father's logpa. So, although I cannot remember my father at all, at least I remember his coat very well!

Amala had to go through many hardships and sufferings for our sake. Sometimes she had to borrow money but was then unable to repay her debts. I don't know whether she also had to pay taxes for the house and fields, but I remember that on a few occasions people came to our home asking for money and threatened to confiscate the house and possessions if she did not pay.

From time to time, Amala made arak (potato wine), a very strong alcoholic drink. In our country people do not eat the very small potatoes; these are given to the animals or used for making arak, which is a long and complicated process. After the potatoes have been cooked and allowed to ferment for some weeks, the mixture is placed on the fire in a large pot covered by a clay pot with holes in the bottom for the steam to come up, and a small container inside to collect the arak. The upper part of the clay pot is then sealed with a small conical vessel filled with cold water. When the steam from the potatoes goes up, it condenses on the surface of the conical vessel, and the drops fall slowly into the small container inside the clay pot. To me, the whole structure actually looks like a stupa!

Amala served chang and arak in nice porcelain cups and talked politely with those people who came to ask for money. I used to be playing around in the room, and I remember Amala saying things like, "Yes, tomorrow," or "Next time," or "I don't have it." I was too young to catch the whole conversation, but I do remember very clearly that as soon as they went downstairs and left our house, Amala would pick up the dust from between the wooden planks of the floor and throw it in their direction. This is something that Sherpas consider very inauspicious. Then she would make some strong prayers by saying things like, "May he die soon," and other bad things. Actually, she was very kind and did not really mean to harm anyone, but I guess they were giving her a very hard time.

When she had to go into the forest to collect firewood, Amala would leave early in the morning, come back at midday with a huge load of wood on her back, and then go back to the forest in the afternoon. She used to return very late in the evening, and we had to wait for her outside because the house was very cold and dark inside. I remember one specific occasion when we were sitting outside waiting for Amala. The moon had already risen in the sky, but still she had not come back. We were all crying and screaming because we were cold, hungry, and afraid. Finally, after what seemed to us a very long time, Amala appeared carrying an enormous load of firewood. She took it into the house, closed the downstairs door, and went upstairs followed by a band of sobbing children. We had stopped crying and were expecting to get a nice, warm fire and food, but our mother collapsed onto the bed and began to cry and weep, calling for her own mother, "Ama, Ama!" Our grandmother lived nearby in Thangme, but there was no way she could hear. We children just sat there staring at Amala, unable to do anything. I was feeling very sad and sat close to her, but there was nothing I could do to help. Many years later, I learned that when one is experiencing difficulties, the most beneficial thing that can be done is to invoke the help of one's lama or spiritual friend. But ordinary people instinctively call for their mother because they consider the kindness of the mother to be the greatest of all.

In short, during the early years of my life, my mother underwent great hardships for our sake and suffered very much. Her only comfort and hope was to pray continuously to Phagpa Chenrezig, and in this way our difficulties helped her to develop greater and greater compassion.

## 16. I Am the Lawudo Lama

I SPENT MY EARLY YEARS EATING, sleeping, and playing with other children of my age. We did not have sophisticated toys, so we just played with earth, stones, pieces of wood, and anything we could find lying around.

Next to our Thangme house there is a large rock carved with mantras. Many years before there had been a landslide; a very large boulder had fallen down the mountain and had come to a halt next to the house without causing any harm. My grandfather, Ang Dawa, had felt that the protection of the buddhas had spared his house, so he had the boulder carved with the mantras *Om mani padme hum hrih, Ah a sha sa ma ha,* and *Om ah hum vajra guru padma siddhi hum.*

My favorite game was to sit next to that boulder, arrange a few stones as *tormas* (ritual offering cakes), and pretend that I was giving empowerment to the other boys. My best friend was Wangyal, who was the mentally retarded son of my mother's cousin. He always sat very quietly while I pretended to give teachings. (Actually, I still feel nowadays that I may be playing at giving teachings, since I do not really know anything.)

I also used to play with Ang Migmar (now he is called Ngawang Ingnye) and Ngawang Nyandrag, who was just a few months older than I. We used to fill a box with sand, stick a few feathers on it, and put it on our heads as if it were the black hat of the Mani Rimdu dancers. Then we would jump around pretending we were dancing. (Later, both Ngawang Ingnye and Ngawang Nyandrag became monks at Thangme Gompa, where Ngawang Nyandrag is one of the best dancers and gyaling players.) Sometimes we played at performing rituals. Of course, we did not know any prayers, and so we would just make some noises like "wa, wa, wa," mimicking the chanting of the lamas and banging metal tins as if they were cymbals. Some of the boys were the "sponsors" and served "soup and vegetables" (earth mixed with water) to the "lamas" on small flat stones.

On quite a few occasions I told Amala and Ang Kami, "Tomorrow such and such a person from Lukla (or from Monzo, Yulnying, Namche, or other places) will be coming to receive my empowerment." It seems that

I used to mention names of disciples and benefactors of the Lawudo Lama Kunzang Yeshe, who had passed away a couple of months after my birth. Every now and then I would mention that "my daughter" Karzang or "my grandson" Karma Tenzin were coming to visit. I had never met any of them, and my mother was very surprised at my words.

When we were staying in Zamte and Amala had to spend the whole day working in the potato fields, Ang Kami took care of us small children. Although I was still very small and could just barely walk, I always tried to half-crawl, half-walk toward Lawudo. Ang Kami had to watch over the other children and the cows, so Amala would have to leave her tasks and come running after me. She would scold and beat me and drag me home, lamenting about the extra difficulties I was causing her. But I also would get upset and tell her, "I want to go to Lawudo; Lawudo is my home!"

Whenever she had to go on a journey or to check the Tengbo fields, Amala left us at Zamte with the family of Lozang Dorje, a married lama who had been the Thangme headman and, like the previous Lawudo Lama, was a Sakya Khampa. Lama Lozang was very kind to me, and I used to have a great time playing with his son Ngawang Gyatso. Because I was always playing at giving empowerments and trying to go to Lawudo, the villagers began to tease me and called me Lama *Daju,* or Elder-Brother Lama in Nepali. On the other hand, I also gained a bad reputation as a very naughty and mischievous boy: when my playmates did not comply with my wishes, I would grab them by the hair and twist it around, or else I would throw stones at them!

I told my mother many times, "I do not want to stay here; I want to go with Ngawang Chöphel." I did not know anyone with that name, but Amala, who had been a disciple of the Lawudo Lama Kunzang Yeshe, remembered the young man from Kulung called Ngawang Chöphel who had been the lama's attendant. Therefore, because of all these signs, both Amala and the local people began to think that I could be the reincarnation of the Lawudo Lama.

### Recognition

After the death of the Lawudo Lama Kunzang Yeshe in February 1946, Ngawang Chöphel went to Rongphu to study with Trulzhig Rinpoche and performed many retreats. Around 1949, when I was three or four years old, Ngawang Chöphel came to Thangme. He heard that my mother had been telling people, "This boy of mine is always crying and saying that he wants to go with Ngawang Chöphel," so he came to our house to check. As soon as I saw him I said, "Oh, now Ngawang Chöphel has come, so I won't have to stay here!" Ngawang Chöphel was deeply moved and became firmly convinced that he had found the *yangsi,* the reincarnation of the Lawudo Lama. That night he slept in our house, and I insisted on sleeping with him. The next morning, when I saw him going away, I began to cry and said, "I am going with you!" Amala also started to cry. Ngawang Chöphel told me, "I am going to Lawudo to get Karma Tenzin and Ani Karzang and will be back very soon," so I stopped crying, and he left.

Ani Karzang, the daughter of the Lawudo Lama Kunzang Yeshe, was living at Lawudo with the grandchildren of the lama, Lama Karma Tenzin and Pemba Dekyi. Ngawang Chöphel told them, "I think I have found the reincarnation of precious Lama Kunzang Yeshe. The son of Ama Nyima Yangchen has clearly recognized me and cries all the time saying that he wants to come to Lawudo."

Ani Karzang offered him chang and potatoes but kept quiet. Ngawang Chöphel insisted that I was the tulku and that some kind of examination should be done in order to have clear proof. Reluctantly, Ani Karzang agreed to come with Ngawang Chöphel to our house. They brought many objects such as drums, rosaries, nice cups, and so forth, that did not belong to the Lawudo Lama. When they displayed those objects on a large *chara* blanket in front of me, I did not show the slightest interest. "These are not mine," I told them. So, a few days later, Ngawang Chöphel came back with Ani Karzang and Lama Karma, bringing with them the rosary, cup, hat, drum, water bowls, and texts of the Lawudo Lama, together with some other things. When they showed them to me, I immediately exclaimed, "This is my rosary, this is my hat, this is my cup," and so forth, and grabbed them. Thus, everyone was convinced that I was the tulku of Lama Kunzang Yeshe.

Ngawang Chöphel said that I should be enthroned at Lawudo and offered to help with whatever was needed, but Ani Karzang and Karma Tenzin said that first it was necessary to seek confirmation from some high lamas. So, a few days later Ngawang Chöphel offered me a new set of clothes and said, "Rinpoche, I am going to Tibet to request divination from some lamas. I will be back very soon, and then we will go to Lawudo together." Then he departed.

First, Ngawang Chöphel went to the Drakar Taso Hermitage in Kyirong to meet Kagyu Rinpoche.[227] The mo, or divination, was favorable to me, but the lama advised him to check also with the Tripön Lama Pema

Chögyal at Tsibri.[228] That mo was favorable as well, but the Tripön Lama told him to check once again with Trulzhig Rinpoche at Rongphu. Trulzhig Rinpoche confirmed what the other two lamas had said and stated that I was the true reincarnation of the Lawudo Lama Kunzang Yeshe. Ngawang Chöphel then crossed the Nangpa La back into Khumbu and went straight to Lawudo to report the outcome of the div-

22. Kagyu Rinpoche and Drakar Taso Tulku Tenzin Norbu (courtesy of Kunzang Rinchen Lama)

23. Tripön Pema Chögyal (courtesy of Abo Rinpoche's gompa, Manali)

inations. He insisted that I should be enthroned at the cave, but Ani Karzang and Karma Tenzin said, "Yes, the boy should be enthroned, but there is no need to hurry." They did not promise anything or make any commitment.

Ngawang Chöphel was very disappointed, but he understood that there were other matters to be taken into account. Traditionally, the lineage of married lamas is transmitted to their blood descendants, and their reincarnations are seldom recognized. The family of the Lawudo Lama enjoyed a comfortable economic situation and high social status; an enthronement would imply that all the possessions of the Lawudo Lama, including the cave, houses, and fields, would have to be handed over to me as his tulku. Besides, Ani Karzang was ashamed to acknowledge that her father had been reborn into a poor and insignificant family. And on top of everything else, I had been born two months before the death of the Lawudo Lama. Although my case was not unique, some people still had difficulty accepting it.

On certain auspicious days, such as the anniversary of Lama Kunzang Yeshe's death, the full moon of Saka Dawa, and so forth, the close disciples of the lama used to gather at Lawudo to perform rituals. On one of those days, Ngawang Chöphel took me to Lawudo. I had been trying to get there for a long time, but this was actually my first visit. I remember that there were many tall trees around the cave and a hollow tree trunk that was used to channel water from the spring. I was taken into the cave and the kitchen, which I remember as very dark. Some lamas were drinking tea and chang, and Ani Karzang gave me boiled potatoes. She was very nice and kind to me. I was still quite small, and while the lamas were doing rituals, I fell asleep. Sometime later someone took me out to relieve myself, and I could see the extremely green potato fields at Mende, just below Lawudo.

Around that time, the Thangme Lama Dondrub was giving a long series of empowerments, and Ngawang Chöphel took me with him to the gompa. Lama Dondrub had long white hair and a beard and looked like the Long-Life Man, the *mi tsering* actor of the Mani Rimdu. He was a ngagpa, a married tantric lama. He was not a great scholar but had done many retreats and was extremely kind to everyone. One day, when I was in Lama Dondrub's room with Ngawang Chöphel, the lama asked me to choose a set from among a large stack of cymbals. I chose a particular set. They mixed all the cymbals and asked me to choose again; again I took the same set and said, "These are mine." Lama Dondrub then explained that those cymbals had been offered to him by Karma Tenzin after the death of the Lawudo Lama.

During the empowerments I sat on the lap of Ngawang Chöphel in one of the front seats, but I was asleep most of the time. When I was awake, I could hear the words of the lama, but I did not understand what was going on, and only many years later I learned that the Thangme Lama had given a series of empowerments from the Northern Treasure.[229] But I still can remember being banged on the head with ritual vases, tormas, pictures of deities, and so forth, and being given holy water and sweet tsampa pills. I liked the music of the drums, gyalings, and dungchens very much and was fascinated by the chant master clashing the cymbals. I thought that the sound was coming from the red paint in the inner part of the cymbals!

I also enjoyed looking at the lama because he emitted such a peaceful and warm feeling. He used to talk for a while and then fix his eyes somewhere on a pillar in front of him. Then I would turn around and look in the same direction, but I could not figure out what held the lama's attention. Sometimes another elder lama gave the oral transmission of the texts, and the Thangme Lama just relaxed in his throne and took the aspect of being asleep. In front of him was a beautiful, foreign-looking glass jar full of chang, which the lama sipped slowly through a glass pipe. I was quite impressed by that jar. One day the lama noticed my interest, burst out laughing, and passed the jar to me. That was the first time I ever tasted an alcoholic drink.

Later, I was taken to the Dumche celebrations presided over by Lama Dondrub and his younger brother Kusho Mangde. Someone asked me, "Do you know that lama?" "He is Kusho Mangde," I replied, although I had never seen him before. It seems that around that time Kusho Mangde disclosed to some of his intimate friends the last words of the Lawudo Lama concerning my being his reincarnation.

I continued to run toward Lawudo whenever I could and to give more signs of being the Lawudo Lama. Once, when Amala was working in the fields at Thangme, a man from Kyisa called Migmar Gyaltsen came by on his way to the gompa. Amala invited him for a drink and they talked for a while. I was playing nearby and Amala asked me, "Do you know this man?" "He is my cousin," I replied. They both were startled by my answer, because Migmar Gyaltsen was indeed the cousin of the Lawudo Lama Kunzang Yeshe. Amala then related this incident to my paternal uncle *(aku)* Ngawang Legshe and to some other people.

In short, I was generally accepted as the reincarnation of the Lawudo Lama, but it took many years until Kunzang Yeshe's relatives acknowledged it in public. People in the remote mountainous areas love to gossip and make up all kinds of stories about everyone. Some Sherpas were saying that Ani Karzang wanted to keep all the possessions of the Lawudo Lama for herself and that she had a tin full of coins hidden under the wooden floor of the kitchen. I do not know whether those stories were just fabricated by idle villagers, but I do remember that even though she came a few times to our house, she never gave me any money or gifts.

From my own side, I know that I am not a high lama. Some highly realized incarnate lamas can remember past lives as clearly as what they had done the previous day, but I am not like them. My own proof of being a reincarnate lama is based upon some meditation experiences that I had, which seem to confirm that I have practiced meditation in my previous lives.

Ngawang Chöphel discussed with my mother and uncles the possibility of taking me to Kulung and performing the enthronement ceremony there, but somehow it never happened.

## Education at Thangme Gompa

The fact that I am now able to read the scriptures and have the possibility to understand their meaning is mainly due to the kindness of my mother. If she had not sent me to study, by now I would be unable to read a single sentence, and I would not be able to explain the meaning of the scriptures to others. Therefore, I always remember the great kindness of my mother, and I try to repay her with my Dharma practice.

Beginning at birth, I would often become sick, and my mother worried about me. When I was about four years old, she asked Lama Dondrub to perform the *trashe* ceremony in order to improve my health. The trashe ritual involves cutting a small tuft of one's hair, which symbolizes renouncing worldly life, giving one a new name, and making prayers for one's long life and success in Dharma practice. But Lama Dondrub said that I should be taken to the Tengboche Rinpoche because in our previous lives we had been very close Dharma friends.

Shortly afterward, the Tengboche Rinpoche Ngawang Tenzin Zangpo, who was fifteen years old at that time, came to Thangme with his tutor Umdze Gyaltsen. Rinpoche was going to Tibet to study at various monasteries and spent a few days in the house of his maternal grandfather, Shangkhug Jiwa. On that occasion a few villagers requested him to perform the hair-cutting ceremony for their children.

My mother was quite poor and had nothing to offer to the lama, but Urgyen, the husband of my Aunt Dawa Butri, who was a nephew of Lama Dondrub and a ngagpa at Thangme Gompa, came to my mother's rescue. He gave her a very good old *chara* blanket as an offering to the Tengboche Lama and a white and red shawl to wrap around me during the ceremony. The shawl was huge and I was tiny, but they somehow managed to make me look smart. Then somebody took me on his shoulders while my mother walked alongside. On the way it began to rain, and my mother jokingly told me to blow away the clouds and stop the rain. She was quite surprised when I actually did it and the rain turned to mere drizzle.[230]

The Tengboche Lama recited some prayers and cut a tuft from my hair. He made many mos by throwing the dice again and again and finally gave me the name Gyaltsen Zangpo, Good Banner of Victory. From then onward I became known as Ang Zangpo.

After the hair-cutting ceremony, it was decided that I should stay at Thangme Gompa with my Aku Ngawang Legshe, who was a very learned fully ordained monk, or *gelong*. He also had a great sense of humor; he used to play the part of the *mi tsering* during the Mani Rimdu, and people laughed very much at his jokes.

My uncle was also very good at carving mantras and images on stones and was always busy carving large boulders or the large flat stones that we call *emba,* which are also used for roofing. The sponsors gave him food and

24. Tengboche Rinpoche Ngawang Tenzin Zangpo and his mother, 1950 (Dr. Charles Houston)

money, and when the carving was complete, they would bring many wooden containers filled with chang and arak, balls of cooked rice, tsampa, dried meat, and kabse pastries, and perform a tsog offering ceremony near the carved stones. Afterward they would drink a lot, dance, sing auspicious songs, laugh, and joke. The sponsors gave khatags to my uncle and to everyone who had helped. They also offered khatags to the stones because now they were no longer ordinary stones but representations of the Buddha's holy speech. Later they would make a path for people to walk clockwise around the carved stones.

Buddhists think that walking clockwise around a holy person or a holy object helps to purify negative actions, particularly those committed with the body, and this creates a great amount of merit. Sponsors accumulate more merit than those who merely walk around the holy objects, but the person who does the carving accumulates an unbelievable amount of merit, provided he does his work with the pure motivation to benefit others and not just for money. There was a Sherpa man in the Pharag area between Phagding and Yulnying who spent most of his life carving mantras on stones. When he died and his body was being cremated, his skull suddenly burst, and everyone could see the six-syllable mantra *Om mani padme hum* clearly formed on the skull's surface.

The Thangme Gompa is about fifteen minutes' walk from our house. Although it had traditionally been a gompa for married lamas only, at that time there were about twenty monks and ten ngagpas. The married lamas had larger houses and lived with their families in the area below the temple, while the monks had built small huts on the upper part of the mountain. A few old nuns also lived at the gompa. The monks had to attend some of the ceremonies at the temple and do some of the rotating jobs such as *umdze* (chant master), *konyer* (caretaker of the temple), and *nyerpa* (manager).[231] Apart from those specific duties, both the monks and the lay lamas were free to live their lives as they wished.

Aku Ngawang Legshe lived in a small stone house with a courtyard surrounded by a wall. He used to give lessons outside in the sunshine instead of inside the cold, dark house. Two other boys, Ngawang Nyandrag and Lama Kami, were studying with me. Ani Ngawang Samten, a nun who lived in the uppermost house next to the Takugug, used to help my uncle with the cooking. She also took care of me by taking me out to pee at night and helping me to get dressed and undressed.

To begin with, Aku Ngawang Legshe taught me the *ka kha ga nga,* the Tibetan "alphabet." I did not find it difficult and managed to learn everything in a couple of days, except for the very complicated syllables made out of two or three letters stacked together. My uncle was very pleased with me and reported to my mother that I was learning very fast. Soon I also learned all the complicated syllables, except one. That particular syllable was giving me a lot of trouble. I struggled with it for a while, and then I had a brilliant idea. When teaching how to read, teachers use a long, sharp stick to point at each syllable. So, when my uncle was not around, I took his stick and made a hole in the paper right through that trouble-some syllable! At that time I did not know that any letters used to explain the teachings of the Buddha are regarded as his holy speech and should be respected as the real Dharma. In that way, I created the heavy negative action of destroying the speech of the Buddha, which brings the result of decreasing wisdom and increasing ignorance.

25. Thangme Lama Ngawang Tsering Dondub (center), Gelong Pasang Wangchug (left), and Genupa Lama Ngawang (right) (courtesy of Thangme Rinpoche)

After two or three days with my uncle, I became bored because I did not have enough friends to play with. One day, when my uncle went inside to prepare lunch, I ran away to my mother's house. The path from the gompa to the village runs along a mani wall and is surrounded by many large boul-ders and bushes. I was still very small and was afraid of the dark and shady spots because I had heard Amala telling stories about ghosts and spirits who live in those dark places and who could grab a small child at any moment. In any case, mountain children do not know how to walk slowly, so I ran very fast, like water falling from a cliff, and did not stop for even a minute until I reached home. Amala scolded me, and the next day she sent me back to the gompa with somebody. A few days later, I again ran back home, and again Amala scolded me and sent me back to the gompa. That went on for quite a while.

One of those flights took place during winter, when the whole country was covered with snow. I was wearing a very simple dress made by my mother consisting of a thick woolen shirt and trousers sewn together. I did not know how to put it on or take it off, or how to open it when going to the toilet; there was always some grown-up person to help me. So, that time I did everything inside my trousers and ran all the way from the gompa to my house with the "toilet" inside. When I reached home, I found Amala sitting outside with some people. As soon as I arrived, she could smell something foul, so she took off my clothes, cleaned everything, and again scolded me harshly. After two or three days she sent me back to my uncle.

My neighbor Ang Chötar, who was seven or eight years older than me, was the reincarnation of his paternal grandfather, who had been the father of Urgyen, the husband of my Aunt Dawa Butri, and had died in Tibet under mysterious circumstances. Ang Chötar had learned to read with the previous Lawudo Lama. In the summer I would run to meet him, and we would go into the forest to collect mushrooms or a medicinal plant called *churtsa* (rhubarb) that has large, bitter leaves used for dyeing clothes. Needless to say, my uncle and my mother used to get very upset with both of us.

People began to gossip about me, saying that since I was such a disobedient and obstinate boy, probably I was not the tulku of the Lawudo Lama after all. My mother wanted to boost my (and her) reputation and used to tell many lies about me. She just wanted to hear people say some empty words, such as "Oh, her child is a very good boy!" When people came to visit, she would make up all kinds of stories and tell them that I was a very special child. She exaggerated the few good things that I did and tried to conceal my faults as much as she could. In this way, out of concern for empty reputation, she committed various negative actions of speech and accumulated much negative karma.

At the gompa I memorized prayers such as the *Prayer of Good Deeds* and the *Prayer for the Spontaneous Accomplishment of All Wishes*. I became very fond of Lama Dondrub, who was extremely good-hearted and loved children. Every morning around eight o'clock, he would do some rituals with a drum and bell. As soon as I heard the drum, I would run to his house, lift the curtain of the door, and wait quietly until the ritual was over. Then Lama Dondrub would call me in and give me a small present, such as popcorn or kabse.

Whenever Lama Dondrub gave teachings, my uncle would take me to the gompa with him, but I slept most of the time, and even when I was awake, I did not understand a single word. Many years later, when I met the great bodhisattva Kunnu Lama Tenzin Gyaltsen[232] in the Kathmandu Valley, I asked him whether I should regard Lama Dondrub as my spiritual friend. I had been visualizing him as one of my teachers, but I did not know what he taught. Kunnu Lama replied, "If you found his teachings beneficial for your mind, then you should regard him as your spiritual friend; otherwise, there is no need." I do not remember a single word of Lama Dondrub's teachings, but just seeing him was beneficial for my mind and made me always feel happy and peaceful, so I do consider Lama Dondrub as one of my spiritual friends.

The very first thing Aku Ngawang Legshe told me was, "The only reason that we do not achieve realizations is due to our lack of effort and determination." It was very good advice, but I was too young to grasp the meaning of his words, and I continued to run home and to waste my time playing with friends instead of studying.

## 17. Rolwaling

*Our eyes were drawn to a little boy who sat wearing a cardinal's cap and looking down on all this. He could not have been more than four years old, but there was something almost majestic about him. There was dignity and refinement in his features, yet he never stopped smiling. His was the face of a saint. By his side sat a good-looking lama who was his guardian. The little boy was the reincarnation of a very holy lama, we were told, which meant that his was a very special place on earth. It was as if he knew he had a high mission in life to perform and was already ordained for it. We felt that the astrologers who had selected him knew their job. We were to see him round our camp often enough. The other little boys were mischievous, and like boys the world over were anxious to be noticed and larked with. But not the little lama. He took a keen interest in all that went on, smiling happily to himself with secret pleasure, but he made no attempt to talk or attract attention to himself.*

—EAST OF KATHMANDU by Tom Weir[233]

AFTER ONE YEAR AT THANGME GOMPA, during which I would run home every few days, my mother became very concerned about my future. She wanted me to receive a good education and decided to send me somewhere else where I could concentrate better on my studies. Aku Ngawang Legshe suggested that I should be sent to Rolwaling with his elder brother Ngawang Gendun, but my mother could not afford to give money for my food, and my uncle was not wealthy either. Finally, the problem was solved when Au Summi, a man of the Sakya Khampa clan from Rolwa-ling offered to sponsor my studies for three years. My mother borrowed a little bit of money for my expenses, and I was taken to Rolwaling on the back of Wangyal, a friend of my father. I was about six years old at that time.

### The Tashi Labtsa

The way to Rolwaling from Khumbu goes through the Tashi Labtsa, a very high and extremely dangerous pass always covered with snow and ice. During the autumn and spring, if there is good weather and if one starts very early from Thangme, a strong person can reach Rolwaling on the same day. Usually, however, it takes two days to get there, and one has to spend the night in a cave that is also used as shelter by the yaks that are in the high pastures.

26. The Tashi Labtsa (T. Weir)

The journey through the Tashi Labtsa is not easy. First, one has to climb a very steep mountain covered with snow and strewn with large boulders, from where one can see to the north the five lakes of different colors related to the Five Sisters of Long Life, the Tsering Che-nga. Sometimes there are avalanches in that area. All of a sudden the snow begins to move, and in one second, the people walking on it completely disappear. Once, when we were returning to Khumbu from Rolwaling, a small avalanche hit those walking ahead of us. Everyone was knocked down and all the loads were scattered, but luckily the avalanche was just a small one, and the people were able to stop their fall near some boulders just above the lakes. Then they got up and climbed back to collect their belongings. They seemed neither shocked nor afraid, and they kept on walking, singing, and smiling.

That area is also dangerous because of the crevasses in the snow. I could see large cracks as if I was looking down from the top of a many-storied house, with very blue and deep water at the bottom. When people or animals would fall down, it was difficult to get them out. The Sherpas who climbed mountains with Westerners had learned to cross such dangerous places by binding themselves together with a rope tied around their waists. In that way, if one person fell into a crevasse, the person behind could pull him out with the rope. The person walking in front was always somebody who knew the route well. He would carry a pointed stick that he

27. Porters on the Tashi Labtsa (T. Weir)

thrust into the snow in front of him. If there was a hole, he would turn back and tell the others to retrace their steps.

After the snow mountain there is another dangerous area with many waterfalls, where huge rocks and small stones are constantly falling down. There is a continuous noise at that place, the large boulders falling with a deafening crash and the small ones dropping with a "ting, ting" clatter, a different sound each time. Before crossing that spot, everybody would stop to drink *arak,* the strong potato wine. Drinking alcohol seems to be the main source of inspiration for the Sherpas, whether for walking, working, or any other occupation. With the exception of a few who keep their monastic vows pure, Sherpa monks follow the local custom and habitually drink chang and arak. So, before that crossing, everyone would drink arak, including the monks, and rub their hands together to generate heat. I always wondered how that heat would help them cross the dangerous places, but that is what they do.

Then they take up their huge loads weighing thirty-five or forty kilos, or more. They carry things to sell, as well as food, blankets, firewood, and grass. The Sherpas often bring their yaks along, and the animals would have to be pushed through those dangerous places where sometimes they would fall and get killed. The people carry grass to feed the animals and to spread as a mattress on the ground in caves. The finest dry grass was used as "socks." Sherpas used to wear very primitive boots made with felt and leather and they never wore socks. Instead, they would just put a little bit of grass inside the boots to keep their feet warm. The grass would get wet in the snow, so they would carry some extra grass to replace it.

When the drinking was over, everyone would begin to cross that dangerous slope toward the ridge, hoping that everything would be all right. Everyone was afraid of death, so they would stop speaking and pray very hard. That was probably the only time during their lives when they really took refuge in the Three Jewels. They would concentrate one-pointedly on reciting the refuge prayer and whatever mantras they knew, such as *Om mani padme hum* or *Om ah hum vajra guru padma siddhi hum.* Then, as soon as safety was reached, all the mantras and prayers stopped and everyone relaxed. They thought that the danger was now over and there was no need to practice Dharma. Actually, if we are continuously able to keep in mind the fact that everything is impermanent and that death can happen at any moment, we would practice the Dharma not just when a particular danger threatens us, but for days, weeks, months, and years. The duration of our life would be equal to the duration of our Dharma practice. But those simple Sherpa people had no Dharma education at all.

I made my first journey to Rolwaling in a basket on top of the grass, food, and blanket. Altogether I went back and forth through those dangerous places four times, I never walked; I was always carried by someone. I have heard that many Sherpas and a few Westerners have died on that mountain, so I find it quite amazing that I was not killed or hurt by the falling stones. Another thing I found strange was that whenever we stopped for food and tea or just to take a rest, no stones would fall. But as soon as we passed the dangerous area and reached the top of the mountain, the stones would again begin to fall, making a loud and frightening noise. I used to think, "Oh, now whoever comes behind us might get killed or injured!" but the boulders began falling only after all the people had reached the safe edge of the mountain. This may have been due to the power of prayers; I don't really know the cause, but I found that fact quite amazing. Only once did a little stone hit a finger of one of my uncles. And another time, when I was being carried by Aku Ngawang Gendun and he was passing me some food, he was hit by a rock. He fell down a few steps and I fell with him, screaming with fear.

## *The Rolwaling Valley*

Rolwaling is one of the valleys hidden by Padmasambhava, a beyul. It is surrounded by high snow mountains and presided over by Tseringma, or the Deep-Blue Queen Mountain. People say that Guru Rinpoche created the Rolwaling Valley with a plough given to him by Tseringma. She then created two streams, and the valley was covered with trees and flowers. The Rolwaling Sherpas believe that if they cut the trees, the goddess will get upset and send floods and avalanches to punish them.

The largest lake in Rolwaling is the Tso Rolpa, which can be seen when coming from the Tashi Labtsa. People say it is the largest lake in the Himalayas.[234] On the upper part of the valley is the Ome Tso, or Dudh Pokhari, the Milk Lake. Its waters are very clear and transparent, and sometimes a large, white yak can be seen inside. When that happens, it is possible to ask questions about one's future. If one sees blood, that means that one will die soon. To see yaks, nomads' tents, and so forth, means long life and prosperity. I heard that a monk from Tashi Lhunpo Monastery saw himself riding an elephant and the next year was appointed manager of the monastery by the Thirteenth Dalai Lama. On the full-moon day of the sixth and ninth months, the local Sherpas and the people from the lower valleys perform rituals at Ome Tso. After washing themselves very well, they offer a bamboo container filled with milk mixed with the three sweets (sugar, molasses, and honey) and a piece of white cloth. They burn juniper branches, perform circumambulations, and take great care not to make the lake dirty.

During the summer Rolwaling becomes very green and beautiful. On the mountain slopes grows a type of grass called "summer grass winter insect" *(yartsa gunbu)* because it grows from the mouth of a brownish insect that looks like a shrimp. The Sherpas eat the dead, dry body of that insect because they say that it gives strength, in the same way that we take vitamins, but I never tasted it myself. It seems that people make a good profit by selling it.

The Rolwaling Valley is very narrow, and it is forbidden to build houses in land that can be used for cultivation. The main village is Beding, which means something like "the innermost plain of the hidden valley." Three hours up the valley is Na, which used to be the main settlement and has the oldest gompa, and halfway between Beding and Na is a huge boulder completely covered with carved mantras known as Urgyen Shugtri, Padmasambhava's Throne. People say that when Guru Rinpoche flew to Rolwaling, Tseringma offered the boulder to him as his seat. Nearby is another, smaller boulder also carved with mantras and known as Khandro Yeshe Tsogyal's Throne. On the mountain above Urgyen Shugtri is the Phurbi Drubkhang, a cave where Padmasambhava did the Phurba practice and left his footprint. Seen from outside, the cave looks exactly like Padmasambhava's hat, roundish and pointed in the middle. During Saka Dawa, all the villagers go to the Phurbi Drubkhang to perform ceremonies and make offerings. Once, my uncle took me with him. After we cleaned the cave really well, performed the *Ribo Sangcho* by burning juniper branches, and recited some prayers, nectar began to drip very strongly from certain spots on the rock ceiling, which were marked by a waxlike substance.

Across the river is a huge rocky cliff that the Sherpas say is the entrance to the inner hidden valley. There are many wonderful and blessed caves in Rolwaling, with water springs inside, where wandering yogis and ascetic practitioners spend long periods of time in meditation.

I heard that in that area can be found a special kind of grass called *tsa kunzang* ("excellent grass") that grows only during a short time in the summer and is very much prized for its medicinal properties. It has a very strong scent during the day and at night it shines like a lamp. That grass can only grow in places blessed by Padmasambhava, and one needs to perform purification rituals and pray strongly to him to be able to find it.

My uncle lived in Beding in a house above the gompa[235] and was the caretaker of the temple. Every morning he would offer water bowls on the altar by reciting the seven-limb offering from the *Prayer of Good Deeds,* and in the evenings he emptied the bowls and lit butter lamps. He was known locally as Gelong Che, the Eldest Gelong, and was very learned and extremely good at storytelling. There were two other teachers in Rolwaling, Gelong Pasang from Yulhajung in Khumbu and Lama Tsampa Ngawang Puntsog, who was known as Gelong Chung, the Younger

Gelong. The head lama of Beding Gompa was Umdze Pemba, also known as Gomchen-la, the Great Meditator. He lived in a house below Aku Ngawang Gendun and had a big goiter, as did many Sherpas.

## Reading and Memorizing

My education continued in accordance with traditional Tibetan and Sherpa methods. First, I had to start again with the *ka kha ga nga* and learn how to spell correctly, which is extremely important in the Tibetan language. After that, I memorized prayers and practiced reading. The gompas in Khumbu follow the tradition of the Rongphu Monastery, which in turn follows the tradition of Mindroling Monastery, so I memorized mainly the prayers and rituals of the Mindroling tradition. I had to read and memorize from early morning till sunset, with a few breaks for meals and tea. The only opportunity to rest was to go out to relieve myself and then wander around for a while instead of returning quickly.

We were about twenty young monks in Rolwaling, either of my age or a little bit older. My best friends were Ngawang Tharpa, who lived next door with his *gaga ani* (the sister of his grandfather), and Ngawang Özer.[236] The other boys had to go to the winter or summer settlements with their families, but these two boys stayed always in Beding, and the three of us would eat together.

Many Sherpas take empowerments into the secret mantra vehicle, but most of them are illiterate and cannot even recognize the Tibetan syllables. When bestowing empowerments on those who can read and understand the texts, the lamas give commitments to recite ritual texts and perform retreats. To others, the lamas usually give the heavy commitment to recite millions and millions of mantras. Although that is something they are able to do by themselves, most of the people go to lamas and monks, bringing a basket of potatoes as offering, and say to them, "I have received the commitment to recite so many millions of mantras from such-and-such lama. Please, recite a certain number on my behalf." So, instead of practicing the Dharma themselves, they ask others to practice for them.

Although ordinary Sherpas have a firm belief in the law of cause and effect, their understanding is not completely right. They believe that sickness, death, unsuccessful business, bad crops, and other problems are brought about by the local gods and spirits and are the result of bad actions committed in the past. To avert those problems, they sponsor the recitation of mantras, reading of scriptures, carving of mantras and Buddha

images in stones, making paintings or statues of a particular deity, building, repairing, or whitewashing stupas, building prayer wheels, offering
tea and food to religious practitioners, and so forth. It never occurs to
them that the most effective way to stop problems is to tame their minds
and not be controlled by hatred, greed, ignorance, jealousy, or pride.

To find out what needs to be done, a person requests a lama renowned
for his clairvoyant powers to perform a divination, or *mo*. After throwing
the dice or checking with the beads of his rosary (some people can see past
and future events in a small mirror or even on their thumbnail, like images
in a TV screen), the lama consults the outcome of the mo in a particular

28. Aku Ngawang Gedun (T. Weir)

text and gives advice about the rituals or virtuous activities to be performed. One of the easiest methods is to request some lamas to read the
Perfection of Wisdom texts, the *Diamond-Cutter Sutra,* or *Dorje Chöpa,*[237]
or the *Condensed Scriptures (Sungdu)* on their behalf. These activities,

known as kurim or *zhabten,* are one of the main sources of income for monks and lamas.

Many people would request Aku Ngawang Gendun to read scriptures for them. He used to spend the whole day reading, and we had to do the same. Even when nobody had requested it, my uncle made me read the *Dorje Chöpa* over and over again as an exercise in reading fast. I read it for months and months. At that time I did not know the benefits of reading the scriptures, but now I understand the great kindness of my uncle. Realizing emptiness is a process that can take many years or many lifetimes. Moreover, to have even a little understanding of the meaning of dependent arising and emptiness depends on purifying the mind and leaving positive imprints. These imprints might come from previous lives, but also from childhood. Since my teachers gave me the opportunity to read again and again the teachings of the Buddha on emptiness when I was a child, now I have developed unshakable faith in Tsongkhapa's explanation of interdependence, which is like a great protection from the wrong view of emptiness.[238] Even after meeting the Dharma, it is possible to waste one's life meditating on something that is actually not emptiness; this is a very subtle and delicate point. Not everyone has the merits and good fortune to hear the correct explanation of emptiness, let alone to reflect and meditate on it. There are many wrong explanations, so it is difficult to find the correct view.

On the tenth day of each month, the villagers took turns sponsoring the tsog offering ceremony. All the lamas and monks gathered in the gompa to perform the ritual of *The Union of the Three Precious Ones* and have lots of food, tea, and chang. The elders drank liquor the whole day, sipping it through a bamboo straw from wooden containers. At least once a year, the village as a whole would sponsor the reading of the Kangyur and the Tengyur to ensure a good potato crop and to protect people and cattle from natural calamities and from leopards, wolves, and yetis. The reading took a very long time, and the sponsors gave us food, drink, and money.

One of the rituals that we performed very often and that I had to memorize was the *Shitro,* the ritual of the *Peaceful and Wrathful Deities* that is performed when someone dies. I was so familiar with it that even many years later, when I was alone I could hear the chanting and remember the words as if I were actually performing the ritual.

## A Naughty Lama

It was obvious that I could not run home from Rolwaling, but I continued to misbehave. I terrorized the younger boys and was always playing
tricks and throwing stones at people. During the winter, when the villagers came from Chumig Golchag to collect the grass they had stored for
feeding the animals, I used to wait for the people coming down from the
mountain with huge loads of grass on their backs and throw stones at
them. The Rolwaling people still remember that.

29. From left: Ngawang Özer, Ang Gyaltsen (Lama Zopa Rinpoche),
and Ngawang Tharpa (T. Weir)

On one occasion, I was sitting in the courtyard of my uncle's house
with a thick volume on the low table in front of me. Tibetan texts consist
of loose pages, which are held together by wrapping them in a cloth and
keeping them between two wooden boards tied with a leather string. I was
reciting the text very loudly because that is the way we read. At some point,
my uncle left the courtyard and went out somewhere. When I was sure
that he was gone, I quickly turned over quite a large number of pages and
started to amuse myself by braiding the threads of the cloth and so forth.
Although I did not know it, my uncle had not gone very far, and he

noticed that my voice could no longer be heard. When he came back, he looked at the number of pages I had pretended to have read, took a thick bamboo stick, and hit the ground very hard in front of the table. All the pages flew away and got mixed up, so I had to put them back in order and start the reading all over again from the beginning. Although I was quite upset, I had to admit that my uncle was right.

Reading and memorizing the whole day can become quite boring for a small child, so I always tried to make things more lively and interesting. One of my amusements was to make drawings with charcoal on the edge of the text, and another was to kill flies. In summertime there were many tiny flies that bothered me very much by flying around my face. When my uncle was not nearby, I would clap my hands and find that two or three flies had gone beyond this life. Then I would feed them to the spiders. The house of my uncle consisted of the main meditation room and a kitchen. Outside there was a courtyard and a small room where I slept and where my uncle sometimes performed rituals. The walls of that room had many holes, and the spiders put their "tents" or webs in them while they stayed inside the hole waiting for food. When I threw the dead flies into the web and it moved, the spider would notice and come out of hiding to check. But the spiders were not interested in the flies that were already dead, eating only those that fell into their web while still alive. Maybe dead flies are not very tasty. I also learned how they eat flies, starting from the bottom and leaving the head until the end.

Another of my pastimes was to kill lice eggs. Since the weather in Rolwaling and Khumbu is extremely cold, we used to wear thick woolen pants. We never washed either the pants or our bodies, and the woolen cloth was always full of lice. They bit continuously to feed on our blood, and they left many tiny white eggs on the cloth, mixed with the hairs of the wool. I hated those lice and their eggs and did my best to get rid of them by crushing them between my nails. Years later I realized that lice also have consciousness and the right to enjoy life, just as we humans do. Now I try to amend the wrong I did, and whenever I find lice or lice eggs in my clothes, I keep them in a warm woolen piece of cloth or in my woolen socks and feed them butter.

Now and then my uncle punished me by pushing me back into a cluster of nettles, or else he would push my face down into the pools of water that formed in the courtyard in such a way that my face just touched the water without getting wet. He beat me very often. My youngest paternal uncle (*aku*) Ngawang Jigme, who was also a gelong at Thangme Gompa, used to come often to Rolwaling to do retreat. When he happened to be there, he would hold me in his arms and protect me from Aku Ngawang Gendun's beatings. As far as I remember, neither my mother nor Aku Ngawang Legshe ever beat me very much. Most of the beatings I received in my life came from my holy uncle Ngawang Gendun. But being such a naughty child, I guess I deserved those beatings.

Now I have observed that most young tulkus are very naughty, and I have seen many of them beaten by their tutors when they misbehave. It seems that they are full of energy that needs to be put to use. Then, as they grow up, they learn to control that energy and to use their intelligence to benefit others instead of causing trouble.

At some point, Aku Ngawang Gendun went to Rongshar to receive teachings from a lama called Chuzang Rinpoche and sent me to study with Gelong Pasang,[239] who was the most learned teacher in Rolwaling and the only one in the whole of Khumbu and Rolwaling who did not drink chang. He was staying above Beding in a very nice hermitage high up in the mountain. The place is very warm because it receives lots of sunshine. It also has a water spring inside the main cave next to the fireplace, so one just has to take the water with a ladle. I stayed there for a few months and had a very good time. Gelong Pasang was very kind to me, and from him I learned a little bit of *ume,* the "headless" Tibetan writing. His two nephews from Khumbu, Sonam Puntsog and Ngawang Sherab, who were much older than I, were also staying at the hermitage, and sometimes we would go together to collect wild garlic in the forest. I used to tell them, "When I become as big as you, I will do very important, outstanding deeds." Many years later both of them moved to Pharping in the Kathmandu Valley, where Sonam Puntsog spent fifteen years taking care of Guru Rinpoche's cave at Yanglesho until the local Hindus took over as caretakers of the place.

As could be expected, I was not always happy in Rolwaling. At the beginning I missed my mother very much, so I decided to send a letter telling her that I wanted to come back home. Since I did not have a pen, I used a piece of charcoal to write on a piece of paper, "You *must* write to Aku Ngawang Gendun saying that I should come back to Thangme." Without my teacher's knowledge, I tried to find a way of getting the letter to my mother. At last I found a man going to Thangme, and I asked him to deliver the precious letter to my mother. The man agreed to do so and, in order to keep it safe, put it inside his boots. When he reached Thangme, however, he could not find the letter—or maybe he forgot about it. On his way back to Rolwaling, after crossing the snow-covered pass, he stopped to change the wet grass inside his boots, and when he shook them very hard, the letter came out. At that point, there was nothing to do but bring the precious, important letter back to me.

## Meeting Westerners

In those days very few Westerners visited Khumbu and Rolwaling, but I had heard about the *mig karpo,* the people with "white" eyes and yellow hair. For us they were something similar to the yeti: we had heard about them, but most of us had never seen them. Then one day, in October or November of 1952, a group of mig karpo arrived in Rolwaling. Below the gompa there was a large chörten and right across the river, a pleasant green meadow where they camped.[240]

The Rolwaling people were astonished at their appearance and said that those strange people were probably bad because they were not Buddhists and were coming from a strange, faraway country, and that they most likely brought some evil spirits with them. They were afraid that the local gods and nagas would be angered at their intrusion into our country and would cause floods, landslides, earthquakes, avalanches, and bad crops. Therefore, at first the villagers did not want the Westerners to come into their houses, and least of all into the gompa. Taking photographs was also considered very bad because the blessings of holy objects or the life force of persons and animals would be taken away with the photo. Such was the general feeling toward Westerners among the Rolwaling Sherpas.

The mig karpo came accompanied by porters, some of them Sherpas who had been in contact with many Westerners in Kathmandu and Darjeeling. They told the Rolwaling people that their ideas about Westerners were wrong. These people were human beings just like us, and besides, they were generally very kind and generous. Sherpas are friendly by nature, so they relaxed a bit, and my uncle invited the Westerners into the gompa and allowed them to take pictures of whatever they wanted.

The first time I saw Westerners camping across the river I had the wish to bring them something, since they were our guests. Sherpas always give food and drink to whoever comes to their village. Accordingly, I asked my uncle whether I could bring some boiled potatoes to the mig karpo. Aku Ngawang Gendun was not very happy with the idea, but I insisted so much that finally he filled a brass container with potatoes and let me go.

I ran down the hill toward the river and went over the small bridge made of two tree trunks tied together, carefully clutching the potatoes and quite excited at the prospect of seeing the mig karpo at close range. When I reached the middle of the bridge, somehow the tree trunks began to move and shake, and it seemed as if the bridge was upside down. The potatoes fell into the water and I fell after them, right in the middle of the river. The stream was neither wide nor deep, but the current was very swift and strong, and my little body was carried off toward a dangerous area with very deep waters. Sometimes my head came out closer to one shore and sometimes closer to the other. One time when my head came out, I saw my uncle running down from his house, which is actually quite far from the river. He had taken off his *chuba* and was wearing some simple pants, which he held up as he ran in the hope of catching me before I reached the dangerous area.

At that time I had no understanding about the meaning of emptiness or about the fact that everything, including ourselves, is merely labeled by name and concept. But at that moment the thought came into my mind, "Now this thing that people call the Lawudo Lama is going to die, is going to end." There was no fear at all in my mind. It will probably be much more difficult now to accept death, but at that time my mind felt quite comfortable.

Finally, my uncle managed to grab me and take me out of the water. He took off my wet clothes, wrapped me in a blanket, lit a big fire, and made me sit near the flames until I got warm again. Someone came with hot butter tea, so after a while I felt at ease again. Later I heard that one of the Western tourists had come running with a camera and had taken pictures of me while I was being carried away by the water!

My uncle did not punish me, but he scolded me very strongly, saying, "I told you not to go! Now you can see what happens when you disobey your teacher!" That episode was a good lesson about the advantages of following correctly the advice of spiritual friends.

The next day, the Westerners came to the gompa to attend a ritual ceremony sponsored by one of their Sherpa porters. They sat for a while drinking tea and chang and looking out of place. They took pictures of the beautiful paintings on the gompa walls, of Aku Ngawang Gendun beating the drum and clashing the cymbals, and of many other people as well.

The Westerners had blue eyes and yellow hair indeed, and talked very strangely, making funny sounds like "wee, wee." I had learned from the scriptures that in addition to the Southern continent called Dzambuling on which we live, there are three other large worlds, or continents, in the east, west, and north.[241] I thought that the Westerners probably came from one of those other worlds because they looked so strange. As a matter of fact, they were extremely kind. To the children they gave something brown and sweet that they called "choclet." I did not like it at all and found the taste very boring because it was not spicy like our food. Many years had to pass before I managed to swallow some chocolate; in the late seventies, when we were driving from Sydney to Melbourne in Australia, I was so hungry that for the first time in my life I ate a whole bar.

They also gave us two tablets each, probably vitamins, and taught us how to swallow them. One of the Westerners was a doctor who managed to cure a very sick Sherpa man, and from that moment on many Sherpas came to him asking for medicines. Afterward, the Westerners left to climb some high mountains with their Sherpa porters and guides. We thought that too was very peculiar. Sherpas go up on the mountains to graze the yaks, to cut grass or *masur* bushes for incense, or on pilgrimage to the holy lakes and caves. No one ever thinks about climbing dangerous mountains and going through ice and boulders just for the pleasure of doing it. When the Sherpas went to the mountains with the Westerners, it was only because they were well paid, as they needed the money. Life in Khumbu and Rolwaling was, and still is, very hard, and people were very happy to earn a large amount of money just by carrying loads up the mountain for the Westerners.

My sister Ang Kami came a few times from Thangme to bring me food and clothes and to collect rice as payment for clothes that Amala had made for some Rolwaling people. She also took a few tins of butter back home because Rolwaling butter was very good and cheap.

During those years I went only once to Thangme to attend the empowerments given by Lama Dondrub. Although I was already accustomed to life in Rolwaling and did not miss my mother so much, I was still very glad to spend a few days with my family. One day, my mother served a glass of arak to both my uncle and myself. I probably did not drink the whole glass, but when it was time to leave, I discovered that I was unable to move my arms or legs. I felt like a spider with long, unmanageable limbs. My uncle had to grab me and drag me all the way to Thangme Gompa. That was the second time I drank alcohol.

After a few years I began to understand the great kindness of my two alphabet teachers. The reason why I can now read as many texts as I wish and can try to understand their meaning is because of the kindness of my teachers. If they had not introduced me to the Tibetan syllables, how could

I have become able to understand them by myself? Without the help of my teachers, I could never have learned how to read, and I would not be able to explain the Dharma to others. Therefore, the teachers who have given us such opportunities have been extremely kind to us, and we should always remember them with deep gratitude.

In Rolwaling I read the life and songs of the great yogi Milarepa three or four times. Although I did not know much grammar and was just reciting the words without understanding them well, what I read had a very strong impact on me. I was quite young and my mind was clear and sharp, so I was able to remember all the details of Milarepa's life. It filled me with a great desire to find a teacher like Marpa, Milarepa's teacher, and to become a strong practitioner like Milarepa himself. That is how the Sangha Jewel guides us.

## 18. Tibet

While I was in Rolwaling, my Aunt Dawa Butri went to Kyatrag in Tibet to get salt and died there from food poisoning after eating some bad meat. Her husband Urgyen had passed away the previous year, so my mother assumed the responsibility of helping their four children (Bu Dargye, Nyima Lhakyi, Pemba Butri, and Pema) even though it meant an additional economic burden for her.

In the year of the monkey 1956–57, Beding Gompa was torn down and rebuilt.[242] Just around the time the work was completed, Thangme Lama Dondrub passed away. It was the night after the Mani Rimdu dances, and it seems that he had drunk a lot of chang during the day. He stayed three or four days in meditation, and then his body was cremated in the courtyard of the gompa, with the twenty-two-year-old Tengboche Lama presiding over the ceremonies. When they checked the remains, they found the syllable *Om* clearly visible on his skull.

Around that time, my uncle received a letter from his brother Ayulha, who lived in Phag-ri in southern Tibet, inviting him and Aku Ngawang Legshe to come to his house and join him on a pilgrimage to Lhasa and the holy places of Central Tibet. My uncles were very keen to accept the invitation, but they did not think it a good idea to leave me behind and decided to take me with them. Shortly after the consecration of the new Beding Gompa, we left for Thangme and Tibet.

My mother was not happy about my going away and shed many tears, but my uncles convinced her that it was the best arrangement for me. Since I needed provisions for the journey, Amala again had to borrow money and contracted more debts. It was arranged that my younger maternal uncle Ashang Ngawang Yonten, who had been sick for quite a long time with stomach pain, would carry our luggage on his five yaks up to Dingri Gangar, where he would see a doctor and buy salt to bring back to Khumbu.

Ashang Ngawang Yonten, who was thirty-one at that time, was extremely kind. He took care of the animals and used to spend the summer at Tengbo, where he had many encounters with yetis. Tengbo is a summer settlement and the houses have a ground floor only; the animals spend the night outside in the courtyard. One evening, when it was almost dark and the yaks and naks were already back in the enclosure next to the house, Ashang Ngawang Yonten suddenly heard the cry of a yeti. Ashang is quite short and frail, so he ran toward the house of his friend Lozang, who was tall and strong. In order to alert the other Sherpas, Lozang started to bang a metal plate with a stick while shouting, "Yeti is coming! Yeti is coming!" The village dogs—those very vicious mastiffs that fear nothing—began to howl and hid in corners inside the houses.

The yeti became angered by the noise and came toward Lozang's house. Two large red eyes appeared above the stone wall, and the two young men became petrified with fear. Somehow, Ashang Ngawang Yonten managed to get inside the house. Lozang came inside after him and slammed the door closed with all his strength. But Sherpa doors are kept in place without any sophisticated means such as hinges or screws, and the door collapsed onto the floor. The two of them spent the night hidden under a bundle of grass in a corner of the house, hungry and thirsty and shaking with fear, while the yeti kept on screaming outside the wall all throughout the night. In the early morning, the yeti went away and the boys came out. The animals were all there, so they concluded that the visitor of the previous night had been a *miti,* the type of yeti that eats dogs and humans rather than cattle....

### The Journey

Our party included my two teachers Ngawang Legshe and Ngawang Gendun, Ashang Ngawang Yonten, Ani Ngawang Samten from Thangme Gompa, a Sherpa layman, and myself. The first night we slept at Marulung, and the next day we crossed the Nangpa La and reached Kyatrag. That village was unbelievably dirty. The fields were covered with human excrement, and the inside of the houses were also very dirty and even darker than our Sherpa homes. All the Tibetan women in that region wore a head decoration that looked like an upside-down bow, and they looked very strange sitting around the fire with those bows on their heads. Beyond Kyatrag, the country became more clean and beautiful. In fact, some valleys were extremely beautiful, with willow trees and flowers, and the monasteries especially were very clean and nice.

On the way to Dingri we stopped at Shartö, where some relatives of my father lived, and the next day we reached Dingri Gangar, a trading town on the eastern slope of Ding Mountain. All the rich traders from Namche had houses in Gangar, from where they conducted their business. People from Shigatse, Lhasa, and even Kham would come there to trade, so the town was busy with many people, yaks, and horses. There was also much drinking and gambling.

Ashang Ngawang Yonten visited a famous Tibetan doctor in Gangar, but he did not benefit from the treatment. Later, he went to Tsakor to see another doctor. The new medicines did not help either, so he finally decided to go to Dza Rongphu to see Trulzhig Rinpoche. Rinpoche told him that his sickness was due to karmic obscurations and could not be cured by medicines but only through purification practices. My uncle requested to be ordained as a monk, and Trulzhig Rinpoche advised him to do the preliminary practices first. My uncle stayed six months at Rongphu receiving teachings. Then he returned to Khumbu with his five yaks loaded with salt and decided to sell the animals and devote himself fully to Dharma practice.

We continued our journey without Ashang Ngawang Yonten or the yaks. My two uncles carried their luggage—clothes, a blanket, books, and food—tied onto a bamboo frame on their backs. Since we could not get porters, Ani Ngawang Samten agreed to come with us to Phag-ri; she carried her things and most of mine in a basket. She was also carrying a few bags of *shagpa,* the dried, sliced potatoes used in the Sherpa stew, some of which was being sent to a Sherpa monk in Tashi Lhunpo Monastery. I carried just a very small load.

At Tsakor, a Tibetan who had been to Khumbu many times invited us to stay in his house. Tibetan houses are very different from those in Khumbu. They are built with blocks of dry mud and have flat roofs surrounded by stacks of dry wood and yak dung on the edges. In that area of Tsang Latö the people grow barley and wheat on the flat land beside the rivers; the rest is just wasteland, very arid mountains where nothing grows except for a few flowers and bushes. But the sky is a fantastic deep blue color, and as a whole, I found the Tibetan landscape very beautiful and magnificent.

After Tsakor we went to Shelkar Chöde, a Gelug monastery situated on top of a high rocky mountain that is considered to be the goddess Drolma; the monastery had been built on the lap of the goddess.[243] I was wondering how one could reach the monastery, but the path was very cleverly made. They had made holes in the rocks and fitted some logs in between, which were then covered with earth and grass. The monastery itself was very clean, and everything looked shiny and neat. There were about 350 monks, many of them young boys.

After visiting Shelkar, we went to Lhatse. On top of the very high Lakpa Pass between Shelkar and Lhatse, I found many stones with conch shell marks, fossils from about 300 million years ago when Tibet was a large ocean.

We walked along the road and stopped occasionally to make a fire and cook Sherpa food, such as *sen,* and tea. Since we were pilgrims, we carried only a small amount of food with us, and we would beg for tsampa in the villages. I had a very nice wooden bowl, and people would fill it with chang and tsampa. In the evenings we would ask for shelter in the houses and would offer some dried potatoes as payment for the fuel we used to cook our meals.

The Chinese had already made a motorable road in that area, and once in a while a car would pass by. We had been walking for many days on that hard road, so every time I saw a car, I used to think, "How wonderful it would be to go in a car!" I must have created a lot of craving karma at that time. One day we met two Tibetans riding on horses and leading a donkey that was not carrying anything. I was so tired that my uncle asked the men if I could ride the donkey. The Tibetans accepted and I rode with them for about three hours, leaving my uncles behind until they disappeared in the distance. That evening we spent the night in the house of the Tibetans, and they gave us delicious Tibetan soup, or *thugpa,* for dinner, with lots of meat in it.

## Tashi Lhunpo Monastery

When we reached Shigatse, we went to stay at Tashi Lhunpo, a very large Gelug monastery whose abbot was the Panchen Lama. Although Sherpas generally follow the Nyingma tradition, some Sherpa monks would go to study at Tashi Lhunpo because it had a reputation for learned teachers. Others went to Rongphu or Mindroling, but Tashi Lhunpo had the advantage of being on the main trading route to Lhasa and close to Khumbu. Many Sherpa traders went to Shigatse, and it was easy to bring food and messages from their relatives at home. At the time of our visit, there were about fifteen Sherpa monks at the Dzongka *khamtsen,* or hostel, which they shared with the monks from Kyirong.[244]

We stayed in the house of Drongpa Sangye (or Gyaltsen, I cannot remember his name exactly), a monk from Thangme. He looked like a *dob-dob,* a kind of anarchic or unruly monk who did not like to study and who wore dirty and torn clothes. His *shamtab,* or monastic skirt, was black from dirt and grease, and from his belt hung a large iron key that made a loud noise as he walked. He did not study or attend the ceremonies at the monastery, but went to the market many times every day. He used to do business with yaks and zobgyos, and it was rumored that he had even killed some animals himself.

One of his businesses was to sell butter. In Tibet everybody drinks butter tea, and the tea served in large and prosperous monasteries, such as Tashi Lhunpo, is prepared with large amounts of butter. Before drinking, the monks blow away the butter, which then sticks to the edge of the wooden bowls. After drinking the tea, they remove the butter from the bowl and keep it in a container. When they have collected enough, they press it into large lumps, wash it, and sell it. Drongpa Sangye used to buy that butter from the monks and then resell it to the people who dealt in animal hides. The butter was utilized to soften the leather used in making the soles of boots, coracles, bags to keep butter and grain, and so forth. Since there was a great demand for leather and for the butter to soften it, Drongpa Sangye made quite a large profit from his butter business.

The evening of our arrival, the Chinese were showing a movie in the monastery. It was the first time we had ever seen a movie. I sat on the lap of a monk from Thangme called Ang Dorje and followed the film with great interest, but now I cannot remember what it was about.

Although we had planned to stay a couple of days only in Shigatse, my uncles heard that the Panchen Lama was going to give a public audience, so they decided to stay a little longer. In all, we stayed for about ten days. On the day of the audience we went to the palace of the Panchen Lama. We stood in line for a long time with many other people, and then some very tall monks with large shoulder pads pushed us along. The Panchen Lama was sitting on a high throne and gave blessings by touching everyone's head with the silk hangings of a long stick. Everything finished very quickly and I hardly saw the Panchen Lama.

The monk Sangye (or Gyaltsen) became very fond of me and would take me to the temple with him. We did not go to the ceremonies but arrived just at the end and lined up with the rest of the monks to receive the money offered by the benefactors. He wanted me to stay at Tashi Lhunpo and become his student, but I did not like the idea at all. On the last day that we spent at his house, Sangye insisted very much and finally my uncles decided that I would stay there instead of going to Phag-ri.

That night I did not get any sleep and spent the whole time considering all the possibilities for escaping that situation. I went through a lot of suffering that night. Then, the next morning something happened, and at the last moment my uncles agreed to take me with them.

The highlight of our journey was supposed to be a visit to Mindroling Monastery, the most important Nyingma monastery in Central Tibet. Our way of making tormas, playing musical instruments, and performing religious dancing was done according to the Mindroling tradition, so I wanted very much to study there; I was not interested in the other temples and gompas that we visited on the way. Actually, just before leaving Khumbu I had a dream in which Jetsun Drolma appeared to me and predicted that I was to stay in Tibet, so I thought the dream meant that I would stay at Mindroling. But we did not go there and went straight to Phag-ri instead.

## Phag-ri

Phag-ri, Pig Mountain, is named after a nearby mountain shaped like a pig. It is situated near Jomolhari Mountain on a very high and cold plateau where the wind blows fiercely all the year round. Because of the cold, even barley never ripens, and the stalks are sold as fodder to the traders. The water and grass are good for the cattle, however, and there are many nomads in that area. During the spring and summer the plain becomes completely covered with flowers and is very beautiful. The local people have a song that says, "In summertime, we buy Phag-ri. In wintertime, we sell Phag-ri!"[245]

The houses in Phag-ri are built half underground because that helps to keep them warm, and the doors are low as in Khumbu because that keeps out the *rolang*, the animated corpses. Some Westerners have written that Phag-ri is "the filthiest town in the world,"[246] but I did not find it any dirtier than other Tibetan towns; in fact, it was much cleaner than Kyatrag. The town is on the main trading route between Tibet and Sikkim, and with the many caravans that passed through, it was always very lively. You could get everything there. It was not exactly like San Francisco or Paris, but it was one of the biggest marketplaces in Tibet. The two richest Tibetan families, the Pomdatsang and Tsangdutsang, who were known as "the sun and moon," had houses in Phag-ri. Many other important and rich families lived there, and there were many good schools,[247] so the people of Phag-ri were well educated, polite, and cheerful.

We stayed in the house of Aku Ayulha and his wife Drolma Tsering. Aku Ayulha had left Khumbu many years before and had gone to Darjeeling in search of a job. Eventually he had enrolled in the Indian army and was posted in the Dromo Valley, north of Sikkim. He married a lady from Phag-ri and when the British left India, he stayed in Tibet and became a trader. He used to travel a lot between Shigatse, Lhasa, Dingri, and even Amdo. Ayulha and Aja Drolma were famous for their good-quality delicious chang and arak. They used to make chang from different grains, such as rice, barley, and millet, and arak from fruit that they brought from Bhutan.

Winter was approaching and the weather became extremely cold. My three uncles and Ani Ngawang Samten decided to go to Lhasa, but they thought I was too young to undertake the difficult journey. They left me with Aja Drolma and my cousin Lozang, who was the same age as me and was a monk at the Nyachung Lhakhang, a Gelug monastery in Phag-ri. Although I wanted very much to go to Mindroling, I was happy to be left alone for a while without my strict Aku Ngawang Gendun. My teachers told me to continue memorizing and reading while they were away, and I saw them off with a large caravan of traders bound for Lhasa.

## 19. I Become a Gelug Monk

THE BUDDHA HAS SAID that the most difficult and profound point of his teaching is not the realization of emptiness but the understanding of the workings of the law of causality, or karma. Every single action we perform with our body, speech, and mind is the cause of a result that will be experienced sooner or later, in this life or in future lives. As we are completely ignorant of the actions we have performed in the past and the imprints that have been left in our mindstream, we therefore do not know what results we are going to experience. We just cannot foresee what direction our life is going to take. Thus, during my stay at Phag-ri some previous imprints bore fruit, and my life took a very different course.

I used to sit outside the house of my uncle reading a text and watching what was going on in town. Since there was no one to keep an eye on me, I spent most of my time wandering around and playing instead of memorizing. On one occasion, the thought of throwing a stone at a bird came into my mind, so I just threw a stone at a small bird that was perched on top of the firewood pile. I went to see what had happened, and I found the small bird lying on the grass, not yet dead but moving its wings and seemingly in great pain. I felt extremely sad, and since that day I never again threw stones at birds or people. It seems that children like to harm others without any particular reason. Maybe when the thought comes they just follow it, or maybe they think there is some enjoyment in it. In any case, those bad imprints are now in my mindstream, making preparation for my journey to the lower realms of suffering.

One day, while I was memorizing some prayers next to the dogs' kennel, a tall monk with a scar across his forehead came to me and asked, "Do you want to be my student?" I had never seen him before, but I immediately answered, "Yes!" The monk went inside the house and talked to Aja Drolma. Actually, it seems that both of them had already been discussing me. His name was Lozang Gyatso, and he was the manager of the Nyachung Lhakhang, where my cousin Lozang was a monk. Aja Drolma agreed that I could go and study with that monk, and the next day she filled a thermos with good butter tea, put one of her very nice breads into a round Bhutanese basket, and took me to the monastery, which was very near the house.

That morning, *Gen* ("elder" or "teacher") Lozang Gyatso took me to the house of a man called Pema Tsewang, where the monks were performing

*kurim,* or *zhabten.* The monks sat in the shrine room, but since I did not know the rituals of the Gelug tradition, Gen Lozang Gyatso told me to sit outside and gave me the Yamantaka sadhana[248] to memorize. I was wearing a red woolen chuba and a red hat and looked like a poor, insignificant boy. I sat on an old animal skin on the floor of the courtyard and spent the day memorizing, while the family who was sponsoring the zhabten gave me food and tea. Lozang Gyatso then realized that I could read very well, and the next day I was invited to come inside the shrine room with the rest of the monks.

30. Gen Lozang Gyatso
(courtesy of Gen Pasang, Ghoom)

A few days later, I moved to the monastery with Gen Lozang Gyatso. The Nyachung Lhakhang was a branch of Dungkar Gompa, a large Gelug monastery in the Dromo Valley, one day's walk south of Phag-ri. Dungkar Gompa had been founded by Dromo Geshe Rinpoche[249] and had branches in Phag-ri, Darjeeling, and some other places. Monks from the main monastery were sent to the branch monasteries for a few years to perform rituals for the local people as a kind of public service. Tibetan monks do not usually run hospitals, schools, or charitable institutions as Christians do, but they help people by performing rituals on their behalf whenever needed. Gen Lozang Gyatso had been sent from Dungkar to help with the management of Nyachung Lhakhang. The abbot was Khenpo Puntsog Dorje, and there were about a hundred monks in the monastery.

In the early mornings we memorized prayers and texts, and then went to perform zhabten in different houses. At first nobody knew that I was an incarnate lama, but after a while Gen Lozang Gyatso heard some rumors and checked with his teacher, an ex-monk with a large nose who was the oracle of Dungkar Gompa.[250] The oracle said that I was certainly a tulku and that I should be kept very clean. He also emphasized that I should abstain from "black" foods, such as garlic, radish, and raw onions, and from "red" foods, which means meat. Chicken and fish were especially forbidden because these animals feed on worms and other small animals, whereas goats, yaks, and so forth are vegetarians. It was difficult for me to be strictly vegetarian because we had to eat in the house of the benefactors and everyone ate meat, but I tried to abstain from it on the auspicious days, such as the full moon and the last day of the month. Later, when I was in India I became a vegetarian for a long period of time.

## I Am Not Going Back

Meanwhile, my uncles had been in Lhasa for a few months, where they had an audience with His Holiness the Dalai Lama and attended a Chenrezig empowerment at the summer palace, the Norbulingka. They visited the three main Gelug monasteries (Sera, Drepung, and Ganden), and when one monk they knew passed away, they went to the Phabongkha charnel ground to witness the ceremony of offering the corpse to the vultures.

My uncles had walked to Lhasa, but they returned to Phag-ri by truck. They had been away for about five or six months, which seemed to me a very, very long time, and now they wanted to return to Khumbu and expected me to go back with them. But during those months at Nyachung Lhakhang I had seen that the Gelug monks were better educated than the Nyingma monks in my country and, what was even more important to me, they did not drink chang and they kept their vows purely. Besides, Gen Lozang Gyatso was very kind and never beat me like Aku Ngawang Gendun did. Therefore, I had no wish to go back to Khumbu or Rolwaling.

One evening, when we were sitting by the fireplace in the house of my uncle, they told me that we were to leave soon. Then I said I would not go with them. Aku Ngawang Gendun, who was extremely kind to me even though I did not realize it at the time, stood up and spanked me very strongly. They asked me again whether I would go with them, but I kept quiet and did not reply. Aku Ngawang Gendun gave me a piece of paper and told me to write down that I was going with them, but instead I wrote, "I am not going back." Then my uncle got furious with me, grabbed me by the ear and twisted it until it bled, then spanked me again. My other uncles and Aja Drolma stopped him, and then Aku Ayulha tried to convince me by different means. He took out a new set of beautiful monastic

robes made of brocade and the very fine wool called *nambu,* and a carpet
and decorations for a horse. They had bought all those things in Lhasa
because they wanted me to return to Khumbu as a high lama and bring to
an end the controversy about my being the tulku of the Lawudo Lama.
Ayulha showed the clothes to me and said, "If you go back to Khumbu,
you will get all these beautiful things." But I was not interested in those
clothes, and again I said I would not go.

Gen Lozang Gyatso was very worried about me and went to ask advice
from Trungyig Dawa-la, the secretary of the Pomdatsang family, who was
one of the benefactors of Dromo Geshe and a very powerful person in that
area. Trungyig Dawa-la suggested that I should go back to my country,
but I insisted that I did not want to go. Then Gen Lozang Gyatso went to
consult the *dzongpon,* the local magistrate. The dzongpon called my uncles,
and while the discussions were taking place, they locked me in the shrine
room in my uncle's house. The room was very cold, and I was shivering the
whole day. The benefactors who knew me were worried because they heard
that I had been locked in the cowshed without any clothes, and some ladies
came to check on me. Tsering-la, the daughter of Trungyig Dawa-la who
was like a mother to me, gave me candies through a hole in the door.

After many hours, I was taken into the room where the dzongpon, my
uncles, and Gen Lozang Gyatso had been discussing my case. The dzongpon then told me that I was old enough and had the right to decide myself.
Therefore, my uncles had to accept my decision and return to Khumbu
without me.

The next day I moved back to the Nyachung Lhakhang and went to
perform rituals in the houses of benefactors as before. Aku Ngawang Gendun had been my teacher and tutor for about six years and was obviously
worried about leaving me in Phag-ri, so he came to check what I was
doing. On that particular day we were in the house of a lady called Aja
Pendog. I was sitting in the shrine room next to Tashi Dondrub, a monk
who had come from Tashi Lhunpo. He was playing the cymbals and the
drum, and I was playing the bell and *damaru,* the small drum. Although
I was sitting with my back to the window, I kept on turning around to
look at what was going on. I could see the main street where the traders
were passing dressed in colorful clothes, carrying long knives and riding
horses or mules; I could also see Aku Ngawang Gendun across the street,
looking intently at me. Afterward, he told people that I was just looking
through the window instead of doing the ritual properly. He was extremely
unhappy about my staying there.

Finally, my two uncles and Ani Ngawang Samten left for Sikkim and Darjeeling, from where they walked back to Khumbu. Many years later I heard that when my uncles returned to Thangme without me and explained to my mother everything that had happened, she did not believe them. She cried and cried, thinking that I was dead and they were just trying to conceal it from her. She sent many letters to my uncle Ayulha in Phag-ri asking him to send me back, but by the time her letters arrived in Phag-ri I had probably left for India already.

Around the time we went to Tibet, my sister Ang Chökyi got a very bad throat infection. There were no doctors in Khumbu, and Amala could only give her blessed pills and recite mani. One day, Ang Chökyi died in my mother's arms. At that time my elder sister Ang Kami and our cousins had gone somewhere, and only my brother Sangye was there. My mother and brother cried for a long time, and then Amala asked someone to check the Tibetan calendar for an auspicious day and place to burn the body, because that could have great importance for her future rebirth. Finally, she was cremated near the river at Thangme. So, when my uncles had returned without me, my mother became extremely depressed because she thought she had lost another child. In this way, I caused her a great deal of suffering.

Meanwhile, my admiration for the Gelug monks was increasing day by day, as was my determination to build many gompas and teach many monks when I grew up. Gen Lozang Gyatso had a very good heart and took care of me with great kindness. The only thing he ever taught me were the *Twenty-One Praises to Tara,* but he gave me food and clothing and provided for all my needs. I felt great respect and affection for him.

In Rolwaling I had read the life of Milarepa many times, and deep in my heart I had a strong wish to find a teacher who would take care of me in the same way that Marpa the Translator had taken care of Milarepa. So, one day I asked him, "Can you be my teacher, just like Marpa?" I am not sure that Gen Lozang Gyatso understood what I was talking about, but he answered, "Yes, sure," and I was thrilled to have found such a teacher at last. Since that time I have been very fortunate to meet many virtuous friends with qualities equal to those of Marpa. My problem is not that I did not find a qualified teacher. From the side of the teachers, most of them have qualities equal to those of the great masters of the past, such as Tilopa, Naropa, Marpa, Milarepa, Tsongkhapa, and so forth. The problem is that from my own side I do not practice the Dharma. Since I am unable to practice Dharma, no positive changes have taken place in my mind, and it has remained in the same state as before, without any improvement.

As members of the Nyachung Lhakhang, our duty was to go to a different house every day to perform rituals. Early in the morning we did prayers in the temple and spent some time memorizing texts. Then, we would smear Vaseline on our faces as protection against the cold, put our dorjes, bells, and damarus in a bag, and go to a benefactor's house. At five in the afternoon we would return to the monastery, still filled with the delicious food and with the pollution attached to offerings,[251] drink black tea, and again memorize for a few hours. After a while I got bored with doing rituals as if it were a job and started to wonder when that would finish.

Soon I became well known among the benefactors. They heard that I was a tulku but did not know whose tulku I was, and began to call me Dromo Rinpoche Chungwa, the Small Rinpoche from Dromo. Even many years later, people from Phag-ri used to come to our monastery in Nepal asking for Dromo Rinpoche, meaning myself.

Aku Ayulha and Aja Drolma continued to take care of me, but my main sponsor was Aja Dekyi Pendog. She was extremely kind to me, and I used to call her "Amala." She always gave me small presents; once she gave me a small watch, which I tried to take apart. In the house of Aja Pendog there were only women, and even the domestic animals were only females. The eldest daughter wore a short chuba, boots, and a long earring like a man, carried a long knife on her belt, and had a very deep, low voice. She did business and would go back and forth to Lhasa in trucks with the merchandise.

After a while, Gen Lozang Gyatso consulted Mili Khentul, the lama of Richung Pote Gompa in Phag-ri,[252] regarding the monastery where I should continue my education. According to the divination of that lama, Sera Je Monastery was best for me. Gen Lozang Gyatso then wrote to their *khamtsen,* or hostel, in Sera and began to make preparations for me to go there.[253]

## Dungkar Monastery

At Nyachung Lhakhang I memorized the *chöjöd,* the two volumes of prayers and rituals performed at the monasteries of Dromo Geshe. After I had memorized the first volume, I went to Dungkar Monastery to have an examination in front of all the monks. I had to sit on the monk's mat *(dingwa)* on the floor in front of the abbot; he asked me to repeat something from the text, and I recited one or two pages. The examination went quite well, and afterward the abbot gave me a scarf and praised me by saying that I had done a good job. I was feeling very proud and happy, but some of my friends became jealous because the abbot did not praise them!

After the examination, I took the *getsul,* or novice, vows from the abbot Thubten Jinpa, a very kind monk, and was given the name Thubten Zopa. "Thubten" means the doctrine of the Buddha, and "Zopa" means patience or forbearance. In Tibet it is customary, when ordaining monks and nuns, to give the first name of the abbot. Like many elder lamas of his generation, Gen Thubten Jinpa had received the vows from His Holiness the Thirteenth Dalai Lama, whose name was Thubten Gyatso, and because of that I was also called Thubten. Zopa was probably chosen because I was so naughty that the abbot hoped the name would help to subdue my mind.

Gen Lozang Gyatso, whom I used to call *Changdzo-la,* "manager," arranged everything for me and made offerings of tea, food, and money to the abbot and monks on my behalf. At that time I had not been recognized officially as a tulku, and I had to sit at the end of the line, with just one boy after me. But Gen Lozang Gyatso made some special offerings to the monastery on my behalf and I became a *chomdze,*[254] which meant that I did not have to do any work in the monastery like the rest of the boys.

Before taking me to Sera Monastery, Changdzo-la consulted the oracle of Tashi Öbar, the protector of Dungkar Gompa,[255] and the answer was that I should not go to Sera but should do a retreat instead. I was a little bit confused by the prediction, but one or two months later we heard about the revolt in Lhasa and the flight of His Holiness the Dalai Lama to India. Then everything made sense.

Even after the Chinese had taken full control over Tibet, we continued to go from family to family doing zhabten. Since we were close to the Indian and Bhutanese borders, the atmosphere was a little bit more relaxed than in Lhasa. In the evenings, while we were taking dinner, we were able to listen to the radio and learn what was happening outside Tibet (the Chinese later confiscated all the radios.) Thus, we heard that those monks who had escaped to India and wanted to continue their studies had been taken to a place called Buxa and were receiving food from the refugee relief committee of the United Nations.

After six months in Dungkar Gompa we went to Pema Chöling, a hermitage halfway between Phag-ri and Dungkar, where Gen Lozang Gyatso had been appointed *lopön,* or master of ceremonies. It was a small monastery, very quiet and isolated, situated on top of a hill overlooking a very green valley with a small river. Across the river was the main road between Phag-ri and Dromo, and behind the mountain lived many nomads who used to bring us milk, cheese, and clay pots filled with curd.

It seems that some time before, a Mongolian known as Namkha Barzin had done a retreat at Pema Chöling. He died on top of a pass very near the monastery in an angry state of mind and had been reborn as a spirit.[256] The previous Dromo Geshe had been able to control him, and he used to give advice through an oracle. I could see that pass from my window, and whenever I looked, I could see a kind of palace at that place as clearly as if I were watching a video. It seems that it was the palace of Namkha Barzin. I observed that everyone going on that road, even the Chinese, would dismount from their horse or stop their car and make offerings to Namkha Barzin's shrine. I heard that many people had died on that road because they did not pay respect to the spirit.

I did my retreat in a small room next to the Tsenzang Lhakhang, where traditionally many golden statues of Lama Tsongkhapa, the founder of the Gelug tradition, were kept. But when I was there, the room was filled with dried meat and large piles of butter stored in Bhutanese baskets. Probably the monks had hidden the statues for fear of having them stolen or destroyed by the Chinese.

I was supposed to do the *guru yoga* of Lama Tsongkhapa and recite 100,000 times the prayer that we call the *Migtsema*.[257] Gen Lozang Gyatso did not explain how to meditate or how to visualize, but he gave me a small text of a commentary on the *Jorchö*[258] practice, which contains the preliminary practices and the gradual path to enlightenment. Since it was my first retreat and I did not know how to meditate, I just sat on my bed and recited the prayer again and again. I enjoyed the good, delicious food they were giving me, and sometimes I read a few pages of the *Jorchö* text. I think that retreat was just like a joke, like playing a game. I am sure there was some benefit, but my recitation was like a tape recorder playing, with no mind. In any case, I was able to complete the prescribed number of recitations.

When the retreat was over, Gen Lozang Gyatso offered some butter lamps on the shrine, and we performed a tsog offering. I remember that there was an open text on a small table in the center of the shrine room and a cup filled with tea as an offering to Namkha Barzin, the local protector.

## Escape

That same evening, a group of monks that included Gen Pasang and Geku-la came from Phag-ri riding on horses. They told us that the Chinese were giving a very hard time to the monks, the wealthy people, and those who were important or were leaders in their communities. The Chinese had organized torture sessions during which the "enemies of the people" were beaten, tortured, and even killed in front of everybody. The torture team was just two days away from Pema Chöling, so the monks were very worried and were planning to escape to Bhutan and India. Gen Lozang Gyatso did not know what to do; there were many Chinese spies at the temple and among the nomads, so he had to be very careful. Late at night he performed a divination with dice in front of the statue of Namkha Barzin, and the outcome was that we should escape. The divination indicated that there would be some loss of material possessions, but apart from that, the journey would be safe.

Everyone expected that the situation would improve and that we would be able to come back after a few weeks, or maybe a few months, so they packed away some tsampa and dried meat to last for just a few days. The monks were afraid of being attacked on the road by the Chinese spies and took small knives to protect themselves. Although everyone was very worried and afraid, that night I was feeling extremely happy and peaceful and not afraid at all. I just could not see any reason to be frightened.

We left very secretly in the middle of the night, around two o'clock. It was the beginning of October. There was some snow on the path, and our steps made a kind of interesting, distinctive sound. We were worried that the nomads might hear us, but nobody came out. At the pass near Pema Chöling there were some prayer flags and stones. We added some stones as an offering to Namkha Barzin and continued on our way toward the Tremo La, the pass between Tibet and Bhutan. Normally that pass was not being used to cross into Bhutan, and some of the first Tibetans who escaped had been beaten by the Bhutanese. Afterward, however, it seemed that many people went that way and that the Bhutanese had accepted them.

The road was very muddy and we fell down many times, but we were able to see the path by the moonlight. Then, when the moon went behind the mountains, we lost our way. At dawn we heard some dogs barking and reached a nomad camp. The nomads, who lived in a bamboo hut, offered us milk soup and pointed up the road. A short while later we reached the actual border and met a Bhutanese border guard carrying a very primitive, long gun of the type we used to call an *inji* (English) gun. That man took us to Drukgyal Dzong, the first Bhutanese town, and the next day we continued to Kyerchu Lhakhang.[259]

When people discovered that I was a tulku, they came out of their homes to receive my blessings. Gen Lozang Gyatso bought some cheap red cloth that we cut into strips. Then I made a knot and blew over each strip to bless it, and I distributed them to people as protection cords. That was my first experience of performing "tulku activities."

At Kyerchu Lhakhang we met a benefactor from our monastery in Phag-ri. We stayed in his house for seven days, and then he took us by horse to Paro, where we stayed for another week before traveling to the Indian border. Bhutan is a very beautiful and inspiring country, with many monasteries and temples. The police officer who accompanied us told us very proudly that even one year would not be enough time to visit all the monasteries and temples of Bhutan.

One day we were invited by a Bhutanese government official to recite the *Twenty-One Praises to Tara* at his house. He gave fifty *paisa* to the monks and one rupee to me, and told me, "When you reach the Indian border, you will have to sign a paper, so I will teach you how to write your signature in English." That was my first English lesson. Actually, at the border I was requested to put my fingerprints on the registration paper instead of my signature.

On the way to the Indian border we met more monks and laypeople from Phag-ri until we were a party of thirty-seven. Some of us were riding horses and the rest walked. The road was very muddy and ran through forests full of leeches. Whenever we stopped and sat down to rest, a few leeches would jump on us and suck our blood. There were many people working on the road, and they offered us puffed rice and chilies. Bhutanese people like very hot food and eat tsampa with small fried chilies. They don't eat as much tsampa as Tibetans, but they love to eat puffed rice instead. Just as people in the West love to eat chocolate and cookies, the Bhutanese cannot stop eating puffed rice, either alone or with their tea.

After seven days, we reached the border and entered India at a place called Tala on October 27, 1959. I was almost fourteen years old.

# 20. Life in India

THE INDIAN POLICE OFFICERS at the border took our names and photographs. Before being allowed to proceed we had to report to the superintendent of police, a Tibetan or Sikkimese called Tashi Babu who was in charge of Tibetan refugees. As they came through the border, the majority of Tibetan laypeople were being sent to Missamari in Assam, a very hot and unhealthy place, and only those who had money or relatives well established in India were allowed to go to Kalimpong or Darjeeling. The monks and nuns were sent to Buxa Duar, unless they belonged to a monastery in India. In my case, although I told the police that I was born in Shar Khumbu in Nepal, I was registered as a Tibetan.

Dungkar Monastery had two branch monasteries in Ghoom near Darjeeling—Yiga Chözin and Samten Chöling. We were planning to stay in one of those monasteries, but Tashi Babu would not allow me to go. He sent all the other monks to Darjeeling, but said that I had to stay in Buxa with one monk to take care of me. I never found out whether he had been asked by the monks of Sera Je to keep me there or if there were some other reason. I don't think he got any *bakshish* for doing that. In any case, due to the kindness of the policeman Tashi Babu, I went to Buxa and had the opportunity to meet many high lamas, study the teachings on philosophical tenets, and then debate on those subjects. If I had gone to Darjeeling, my life might have been very different. Maybe I would have given up monastic life and become a coolie at the train station, then gotten married and had many children and grandchildren!

## The Buxa Duar Lama Ashram

When it became obvious that the Tibetan refugees were not going back to Tibet in the near future, the Indian government provided an old fort at Buxa Duar,[260] not far from the Bhutanese border, where the Tibetan monks could continue their studies.

During the British rule, Mahatma Gandhi and Jawaharlal Nehru were imprisoned at Buxa. When the Tibetans arrived, the building where Gandhi had been became a nunnery under the direction of the Kagyu lama Khenpo Tsultrim Gyatso, while Nehru's prison became the residence of about 1,500 monks from all the four traditions of Tibetan Buddhism, as well as Bonpos. It was a very long building with strong doors reinforced with iron bars, and windows covered with barbed wire with small holes for guns in between. There was a barbed wire fence around the perimeter, and large forts could be seen on the surrounding hills. The whole place looked like a military or concentration camp. It seems that much fighting and killing had taken place there.

The building was set in a low area surrounded by hills where there was no wind, and the weather was extremely hot and humid. The area was full of poisonous snakes, while in the surrounding forests lived tigers and elephants. During the rainy season there were many leeches, and every time we went to the toilet we got a few of them on our body. The Bhutanese, Indians, and Nepalis made them fall out with a lump of rock salt, then they would place them on a stone and crush them or chop them into small pieces, like they do with chilies. I heard from some monks that the pieces of dead leech would dry out, but that when the rain came again, somehow the consciousness would re-enter the dry pieces and each one would become a new leech!

When we arrived in Buxa, all the monks were sleeping together in a large hall. There was always a strange noise, like "ru, ru, ru." At first I thought that it was the sound of the monks singing prayers, but it was just the resonating sound of so many people talking inside that large room. After a while, the different groups of monks wanted to do their own practices, so they cut bamboo in the forest and built some sort of wall or room dividers.

Gradually, as more and more monks arrived in Buxa, the place became very crowded. Some monks built rooms on the verandah and in the yard next to the main building, until there were small bamboo huts everywhere. Instead of glass, they put simple pieces of cloth in the windows. The beds were also made of bamboo, and everything, walls and beds, was full of bed bugs. We had mosquito nets, but they were quite useless and unable to keep the insects out.

Poisonous snakes used to make their nests between the ceiling and the beams, and sometimes they would drop down on top of our beds. The monks learned to catch the snakes with their bare hands, but I never heard of any monk being bitten. I guess that must have been due to the power of taking refuge in the Three Jewels. Instead, the Indian policemen who killed snakes would often get bitten. Once, when the monks were making their half hour of prayers before a debate session, a very large snake suddenly appeared. It was quite thick and long and frightening. One of the monks caught it, and as he was holding it, the snake became shorter and fatter; the monk then threw it out. When the policemen saw the snake, they threw kerosene on it and set it on fire. The snake managed to crawl away, but I guess it soon died.

Behind the place where I was staying was a long row of toilets. The weather was always extremely hot, and the Tibetans had no experience in cleaning toilets, so during lunch there used to be a strong odor coming from that place. Although in Tibet and Khumbu we never washed our bodies, in Buxa it was so unbelievably hot that we went everyday to the river to bathe, and at night we would wash under a water tap.

Because of the heat, we never wore our robes except during special ceremonies. All the monks walked around in their underskirts or underpants except for the disciplinarian and a few lamas. I remember that Gen Jampa Wangdu, who later became a highly realized meditator, always wore his robes in a very proper way in accordance with the Vinaya rules. I used to wear pants most of the time.

The monks were divided into eating groups called *tobsang;* the monks in each group would eat and do rituals together. Due to the kindness of the Indian government and many voluntary organizations, we were able to have food, clothes, and medicines, but the food was very poor (rice and *dhal* only), and it was quite different from Tibetan food. Because of the unbearable heat, bad food, and sadness, many monks became sick and died. Some of them even committed suicide because they could not cope with the situation. Every week we saw the corpses of a few monks being taken to the cremation place by the river.

We performed rituals and debated together in the large hall. Each monastery did their own daily practice separately, and once a week all the monks performed a long ritual together. In Sera Je College they have the custom of chanting the *Heart Sutra* extremely slowly; the chanting can take many hours. In Tibet, the monks would say that in the time they were chanting the *Heart Sutra,* one could go to Lhasa and back. Of course, chanting slowly is effective for the mind because one can meditate at the same time, but in Buxa the prayer hall was hot and crowded, and the monks found it difficult to sit for so long. It was so crowded that it was almost impossible to get out, and at least a couple of times I had to relieve myself on the bed where I was sitting. When I stood up, I was completely wet!

At night, when we debated outside, we often saw orange-colored lights or flames moving about. One night, when we were walking through the forest, we saw a light shining through the trees. We thought that it was a fire, but when we went toward the light, it moved away. It seems that those lights were flames coming from the mouths of *pretas,* or hungry spirits.[261] Some monks could see the pretas at mealtimes sitting with the monks. When the food was offered, the spirits would also put out their bowls, but since most people could not see them, they were never given food. There are different types of pretas, but generally the scriptures mention that their bellies are as large as mountains and their necks as thin as needles. We may find this difficult to believe because we cannot see them (there is no preta country where we can go as tourists to take pictures or videos), but if we look at the different shapes of human bodies, we can understand that the body of a preta is something that could definitely exist.

When the rains did not arrive on time, the Indian villagers would request the monks to do prayers to bring rain. We would go down to the river, burn some incense, and make prayers to the *nagas,* the beings who have control over water. Most of the time our prayers worked and the rain came just as we were getting back into the house. The local people developed great faith in the Tibetan monks.

In spite of the hardships and difficulties, we were happy to have the opportunity to study and continue our Dharma practice. We heard reports from Tibet about monks being killed and monasteries destroyed, so we realized how lucky we were to have the freedom to study and practice. Above all, we were extremely grateful to His Holiness the Dalai Lama. It was thanks to his efforts that the Indian government had allowed Tibetans to stay in India instead of turning them back into the hands of the Chinese. Due to the immense compassion of His Holiness, Tibetan monks and nuns had a place to stay, and the precious Buddhadharma could continue to exist and develop.

## Studies

When we arrived in Buxa, I was taken to the abbot of Sera Je to request admission to the monastery. Gen Lozang Gyatso offered tea, bread, and money to the Sera Je community on my behalf, and I became an official member of the monastery.

The main concern of Gen Lozang Gyatso was that I should have a good education, and he began to inquire about the different teachers. We had been given a place to sleep together with a monk from Drepung, who suggested that I could study with Geleg Rinpoche[262] and so took me to him. The monks of the four traditions were studying and debating together, and they had decided to start teaching from the very beginning, so I began my studies in the first class and had to memorize the text for debate called *Collected Topics*.[263] But after only three days, Geleg Rinpoche told me, "I cannot be your teacher; you should take teachings from Geshe Rabten, who is a very good master." In that way, thanks to the kindness of Geleg Rinpoche I was able to meet Geshe Tamdin Rabten, one of the greatest teachers of Sera Monastery.[264]

Geshe Rabten, or Gen Rinpoche as he was called by his students, was staying in a small room on the verandah of the main building. I went to see him with Gen Lozang Gyatso, bringing some tea offering, and he accepted the request to become my teacher. Afterward, I came almost every day to receive teachings from him. Geshe Rabten used to sit on a high bamboo bed, and because of my being a tulku, I was also supposed to sit on the bed. I was already fourteen years old, but my body was still quite small. (Sherpa and Tibetan children are very small until they are sixteen or seventeen years old, and then quite suddenly they develop into young adults; I think Western children grow up in a different way). I remember wearing a long shamtab that had to be folded almost double over the belt to fit my body.

One of Gen Rinpoche's students called Thubten Yeshe used to lift me up and deposit me on the bed next to the teacher, while the rest of the students sat on the floor. Thubten Yeshe would sit facing Geshe Rabten with a large pile of scriptures on the table in front of him and would look at Geshe-la with great devotion. I experienced some special feeling toward that monk because he seemed to be very learned and devoted.

Geshe Rabten spoke often about the advantages of meditating on emptiness and practicing *shamatha*, or calm abiding meditation. Since he was very busy teaching the monks, he took advantage of the rituals to remain single-pointedly concentrated on his meditational deity. I decided to give it a try, and one night, after Gen Lozang Gyatso had put the mosquito net on my bed, I sat down and tried to concentrate one-pointedly on the silver lid of my teacup. Then—I don't know what happened—I fell down. My body just collapsed onto the bed. That happened several times, so after a while I gave up. Nevertheless, I think that my interest in meditation is due to the imprints of my past life, together with the kind explanations of Geshe Rabten. Some time later I did my first Yamantaka retreat, and I began to understand how meditation truly benefits the mind.

After just two or three months in Buxa, I became sick. First, I discovered that I had worms, and a doctor gave me medicine to get rid of them. In those days there arose some controversy among the monks regarding worm medicine because it kills the worms. Most of the lamas thought that since the Buddha did not allow killing any sentient being and as worms are also sentient beings, it was not permitted to take worm medicine. Other lamas were of the opinion that it might be permitted to take worm medicine according to the circumstances. As for me, I never took worm medicine again. My experience is that after some time, when your karma to have worms is exhausted, they just leave by themselves, even without medicine.

I probably also got hepatitis, because I could not eat anything and just the smell of food made me sick. I could only swallow food if I ate it with many green chilies. Then, in 1961, the doctors discovered that I had contracted tuberculosis, like many of the monks, and Gen Lozang Gyatso took me to Darjeeling for a few months to regain my health in the cooler climate.

## Darjeeling

We stayed in Ghoom at Samten Chöling, the new monastery of Dromo Geshe. Shortly after we arrived, I met my uncle from Phag-ri, who had escaped through Bhutan in December 1959 with his whole family. Aku Ayulha and Aja Drolma were very concerned about my health and insisted that I should stay for a while in their house, which was located somewhere between Sonada and Ghoom. Aja Drolma was a particularly good cook, and she would give me all kinds of delicious dishes, such as fried rice and eggs. Aku Ayulha knew that exercise was good for my health, and in the early morning he would take me for long walks on the mountain. He also made a ball with some rags and we played together. Although he was not young, he would spend two or three hours every day helping me to get some exercise. My cousin Lozang was no longer a monk and had been sent to the Tibetan Children's Village in Dharamsala.

Once I had returned to Buxa, Aja Drolma used to send me food there from time to time. Aku Ayulha died in 1965 in Tibet. It seems that he was planning to return to Khumbu and had decided to first of all take his valuable goods to Thangme, including the jewelry of his wife. Along with another Sherpa from Namche—who ironically was known as Tsering

*Kang-gyog* ("Swiftfoot") because he had some problem with his legs—they loaded about twenty yaks with goods and started toward Khumbu through Tibet. But when they reached Tsakor, near Dingri, Aku Ayulha died of food poisoning. Ang Tsering took the yaks through the Nangpa La into Khumbu and gave Ayulha's goods in custody to the police in Kathmandu. Then the Nepali police sent a telegram to the family in Darjeeling, telling them that Ayulha was dead and they should come to Nepal to collect the goods.

31. Lama Zopa Rinpoche in Darjeeling, early sixties (unknown)

Since the time I had left Khumbu in 1957, I had never sent any letters to my mother and had had no news from my family. I knew that my Aunt Lhamo, my mother's sister, lived in Darjeeling. There were many Sherpas there (many of them worked on mountaineering expeditions), so I went to the Tongsum Bhasti area where most of the Sherpas were staying and asked around until I found her. She was married and had a son called Dawa Tsering, and she was working in the Planters' Hospital. To verify my identity, she asked for the names of my father, my mother, and my uncles and aunts. Finally, when she was convinced that I was her nephew, she felt very happy and invited me many times to her house. My aunt gave me money and clothes and sent a letter to my mother in Khumbu telling her that I was alive and well. At her house I also met my childhood friend Ang Chötar from Thangme, who was working at the Himalayan Mountaineering Institute, which had been founded by Tenzin Norgyay Sherpa after he had climbed Mount Everest with Sir Edmund Hillary in 1953.

I had a very pleasant time in Darjeeling and discovered many new and interesting things there, such as horse races and lotteries. Gen Lozang Gyatso bought lottery tickets once, but we did not win anything. We heard that a poor woman had won a large amount of money in the lottery. She wrapped the money in her sari and went home, but she had no chance to use or enjoy her wealth because the next day she was found dead, probably killed, and her money had been stolen.

A couple of months later, Kyabje Ling Rinpoche, the senior tutor of His Holiness the Dalai Lama,[265] came to Darjeeling for medical treatment and stayed for about two months in Samten Chöling. Rinpoche had arthritis and every morning went for a walk on a path parallel to the Siliguri-Darjeeling railway track. He always called me to accompany him, and we would walk up and down that road and sit for a while on the ground. Sometimes a monk of my age called Dorje came with us and tried to play with me by pulling my shamtab and doing all kinds of tricks behind Ling Rinpoche's back, but I was not interested and always tried to behave respectfully in the presence of Rinpoche.

Almost every day Rinpoche asked me to join him for lunch and dinner. In the evening, everyone would listen to the Tibetan news bulletin and Tibetan music on All India Radio. I liked that music very much, so Rinpoche would play the radio for me. Sometimes I played ping-pong with Kyabje Ling Rinpoche and Dorje. Rinpoche would throw the ball to Dorje, Dorje to me, and I would throw it back to Rinpoche. A few times the ball hit Ling Rinpoche's shiny, bald head, making a "ting" kind of sound! Ling Rinpoche had a great sense of humor and enjoyed telling funny stories about tantric monks who had made mistakes. They were similar to Aku Tonpa stories, which are very popular in Tibet. Very often his benefactors would organize picnics, and whenever it was an informal occasion, I was invited to join them. I also had the opportunity to meet Trijang Rinpoche, the junior tutor of His Holiness the Dalai Lama,[266] who was staying in Sonada and came a few times to visit Ling Rinpoche.

I did not receive many teachings from Kyabje Ling Rinpoche at that time, but I remember very clearly one of his instructions: "Do not wet with saliva the pages of the Dharma texts to turn them or you will be reborn in the vajra hell. The scriptures represent the holy speech of the Buddha and the Dharma Jewel; therefore, one should show respect and not make the pages dirty. One should use water instead of saliva." Sometimes Kyabje Ling Rinpoche would hold my hand and walk with me around the large Buddha Maitreya statue in the temple while he recited prayers and mantras or gave me teachings. Rinpoche asked me a few times which teachings I wanted to receive from him, and I always replied that I wanted teachings on the *Ritual Offering to the Teacher,* or *Lama Chöpa.*[267] At that time, Rinpoche gave me only a very brief explanation, but twelve years later, in January 1973 in Bodh Gaya, I was able to receive from him the detailed commentary of that profound teaching.

32. Picnic in the Darjeeling Botanical Gardens, 1961. Front row from left: Geshe Ngawang Jinpa, Lama Zopa Rinpoche, Mingyur-la. Behind: Kyabje Ling Rinpoche and his manager Lozang Kunrig (Thubten Tsering)

After six months in Darjeeling we returned to Buxa. Geshe Rabten had moved to a house on top of the hill and was extremely busy teaching different classes, so he had no time to teach me. He sent me to Gen Yeshe, a very learned Khampa lama from Trehor. From him I received the very precious teachings of the *Lama Tsongkhapa Guru Yoga,* and the development of the altruistic mind of enlightenment by reflecting upon the fact that all sentient beings have been our mothers in our previous lives and have been extremely kind to us.[268]

Gen Yeshe gave the teaching without using a text, and I wrote every-thing down. At that time I did not know how to write the very quick Tibetan script properly. I just wrote according to my own idea, without following any rules. As a result, my writing has always been quite illegible. Later, I was able to receive writing lessons from Trungyig Chenmo Angu-la, a very humble monk from Sera Je. Actually, in Tibet he was a very important person. He was one of the four Trungyig Chenmo, or Great Secretaries, two monks and two laymen, who worked in the Tibetan gov-ernment. Trungyig Chenmo Angu-la was later given the job of obtaining land to rebuild the three monasteries of Sera, Ganden, and Drepung in South India.

# 21. The Young Lamas Home School

*...The behaviour of these [children] was strangely adult. They sat smiling and talking quietly in Tibetan, accepting everything that was done for them with perfect courtesy and no trace of anxiety or fuss.*
—THE PRESENCE OF TIBET, by L. Lang-Simons

ONE DAY, a tall English lady with blue eyes, dressed in a yellow sari, came to Buxa. Her name was Frida Bedi. She was a friend of Pandit Nehru's family, and when the Tibetans came to India, she had been asked by the Central Social Welfare Board to work for them.[269]

Mrs. Bedi realized that the Dharma would soon spread in the West and that the young Tibetan tulkus needed a proper education. One possibility was to send them to good Christian schools in Darjeeling or Kalimpong, but in that case they would have had no chance to study Buddhist philosophy. In the end, she decided to open a school herself for the young tulkus of all the Tibetan traditions where they could learn English, Hindi, and some other basic subjects without having to give up their daily prayers and Buddhist studies. The school ran for a six-month term, at the end of which they would return to their monasteries.

Mrs. Bedi explained the advantages of the school to each young tulku and invited them to attend. Since I carry the title of tulku, she also persuaded me to go to the school. Therefore, it was due to the kindness and foresight of Frida Bedi that I learned a little bit of English and am now able to give meditation courses and talk about the Dharma with a few words of broken English.

The Young Lamas Home School started in Delhi in 1961 in the house of Frida Bedi, with Chögyam Trungpa, Akhong Rinpoche, Tulku Pema Tenzin, and Geleg Rinpoche as the first students. After a while, Mrs. Bedi rented a beautiful new house at L-7, Green Park, in the Hauz Khas area of New Delhi. When I joined the school in 1962 there were twelve tulkus attending. Every morning we did some prayers, or *puja,* and then we were taught English, Tibetan writing and grammar, and Hindi. After the classes we would go back to our rooms to play, and in the evenings we did our homework, filling our notebooks with big letters so that we could get new notebooks quickly!

I attended the school in Delhi for about four months. I did not learn much, but I did put a little bit of effort into learning English, even though the classes were not very useful. The teachers were volunteers who happened to come by and agreed to teach us for a few weeks or months. They did not speak Tibetan, and nobody ever asked us whether we understood or not. They would explain grammar, but we could not understand what they were talking about. It was a complete waste of time. For months and months I could not understand a single thing. Later I found a Tibetan book with English grammar, and that helped a little bit. The good side of it was that Mrs. Bedi chose only British teachers so that we could learn a good accent right from the very beginning.

Most of our time in Delhi was spent in sightseeing. Mrs. Bedi had many Western friends and sponsors for our school, and often some of them would come and take a group of tulkus for a tour of the city. On Saturdays and Sundays we were invited by the staff of the different Western embassies. We played with the Western children and were taken to the zoo or watched cultural movies. They took us around in nice cars and gave us delicious food, so we had a very good time.

Once somebody gave us a ball and we enjoyed playing football in the school compound, until the day when Mr. Shakabpa, the representative of His Holiness the Dalai Lama, happened to come to the school when we were playing. Mr. Shakabpa belonged to an aristocratic family and had been educated in India and other foreign countries, but his ideas were very traditional. He was shocked to see the young Tibetan tulkus playing football and told Mrs. Bedi that it was not correct. From that day onward, we were not allowed to play football anymore.

After I had attended the school for a while, I got smallpox and was taken to a hospital very far away. I had to stay fifteen days in that place. Then I got TB again and was sent to another hospital together with Yeshe Losel, the brother of Akhong Rinpoche, who was a little bit older than me. When they told me that I had to stay there for a few weeks, I was extremely upset. The Indian doctor was very kind and gave me bananas and sweets, but I cried continuously for three days. Actually, I was crying because I wanted very much to learn English, and in the hospital there was no opportunity to do so.

They put me in a room with three Indian boys and gave me the hospital shirt and pants to wear. One of the boys took away my pants and books, shot ink inside my mouth with a pen, and tried to beat me with his sandal. Yeshe Losel, who could speak a few words of Hindi, tried to explain the situation to the nurse. When she finally understood, the Indian boy was sent away to another place.

Yeshe Losel did not stay long in the hospital and I was left alone, crying and feeling very sad. I used to sit near the fence where I could see the cars passing on the street, with an English book on my knees. It was a book with very simple conversation, such as how to go shopping and so on, that had been given to me by Thubten Tsering, the secretary of Ling Rinpoche. But I found it impossible to learn English on my own and I kept on crying. The Indian boys used to come around and tell me, "Lama, do not cry, do not be upset!" But I was really sad and did not want to talk with them. Then, after a few days I met a kind old man who agreed to teach me English, so I stopped crying. Everyday I would go to the old men's section and learn some English words from him.

The hospital staff treated the Tibetans very well. We were given meat because they knew we needed it, as without it we would become even more sick.

After a few weeks I got better and was sent back to the school. At the end of the six-month term we had to pass the English examination, and then we had an audience with the Indian Prime Minister Jawaharlal Nehru. We waited in a small room and were then taken to a courtyard. Nehru was quite old and his skin looked bluish. He was sitting in a reclining chair and spoke a few words to us, but I cannot remember what he said. We were given cold drinks and one lady, probably his daughter Indira Gandhi, gave us each a pen.

I returned to Buxa and continued my studies on Buddhist philosophy. Although I practiced a little bit of debate, it seems that I did not have the karma to study the whole set of philosophical texts. However, I did receive many teachings from very learned lamas and at least some imprints have been left in my mindstream.

At that time I was more interested in studying English, but I did it in a useless sort of way. I was trying to memorize English words just like we memorize the Tibetan texts; in fact, I was planning to memorize the whole dictionary! I did not realize that one needs to learn the grammar and practice speaking in order to learn correct pronunciation, so I just memorized words from different books. That was definitely not the correct way to learn English, and I wasted a lot of time. Finally, I decided to look for someone to help me. Every day I wrote down the words I did not understand, and after lunch, when we had free time, I would go to the storekeeper, who knew some English and ask him, "Babuji, please, what does this mean?" Some other times I went with my book to talk with the Indian officials. They wanted to sleep for a couple of hours in the afternoon, but I took up most of their resting time with my questions. After a while, a Tibetan from Phag-ri called Abu began to teach English to the monks at Buxa, and I was able to make some progress.

## Dalhousie

I was not very enthusiastic about the school for young tulkus, but the next year Frida Bedi came back to Buxa and strongly insisted that I should return. The school had moved to Dalhousie, a former British hill station in Himachal Pradesh in northern India, where Mrs. Bedi had rented a large house named Kailash. So, in April 1963 I went to Dalhousie with Gen Lozang Gyatso.

We were now forty or fifty tulkus from all the traditions;[270] each tradition had its own room, teacher, and abbot. The principal of the school was Drubthob Tulku, a Sakya lama who also acted as translator for Frida Bedi, and the main disciplinarian was Geshe Tenpa Tenzin, a Gelug lama from the Lower Tantric College. Every morning and evening we met in the shrine room to do a short ritual from each tradition and to recite some common Buddhist prayers. On the tenth day of the month we did our own separate rituals. Gen Lozang Gyatso took care of the shrine room, arranged the offerings, and so forth. The school term lasted from April to October, and we were taught many different subjects, such as English, Hindi, Urdu, mathematics, geography, writing, Tibetan grammar, and *thangka* painting. This time I found the school more beneficial.

On Sundays we had a holiday and most of the tulkus spent their time playing, but I liked to sit on my bed, cover my head with my *zen* (the monastic shawl), and recite texts. Someone would always run into the room and tell me, "Come to play with us, today is a holiday!" But I enjoyed reading texts and would reply, "You go play if you like, that is your holiday; staying here reading is my holiday!" Khorchag Tulku was full of admiration for me and used to tell me that I was going to become a great geshe (I never became a learned geshe, but he became a very skillful thangka painter). In any case, during those months at Dalhousie I was able to memorize the 400 pages of the root text of the *Compendium of Valid Cognition*.[271]

His Holiness the Dalai Lama had offered to help those monks and nuns who had completed their studies and wanted to meditate. Many of them, including Gen Jampa Wangdu, had moved to Dalhousie to practice meditation under the guidance of Trehor Kyorpon Rinpoche, a very high lama from Drepung Monastery.[272] On Sundays, when I went for a walk on the mountain, I used to meet Gen Jampa Wangdu collecting firewood. He was staying in an old ruined house, a tiny place with just a roof and broken stone walls. It seems that during the British occupation many people had been killed in that house and it was full of spirits. At night, while Gen Jampa Wangdu was meditating, the spirits used to walk around and make a great deal of noise, but he was not afraid. Sometimes he even gave them teachings on bodhichitta. Gen Jampa Wangdu achieved calm abiding at that place.

At Kailash House we also had many strange experiences. Every morning, around 4:30, one of us had to ring the bell. One morning, Gala Rinpoche saw an Indian man without legs next to the bell. He got very scared and ran back to his room. Other boys also saw that man. Even Mommyla, as we used to call Mrs. Bedi, had a very strange experience. One night she heard a baby crying near her bed. She switched on the light and saw a small baby, but as she tried to hold it in her arms, the baby just vanished. Some other times we heard footsteps and the noise of plates in the kitchen when there was nobody there. But our visitors were not only spirits. One morning, when one of the tulkus opened the door of the toilet, a leopard unexpectedly jumped out!

At Dalhousie I learned a little bit of drawing and painting, first from Palden Sherab, who later went to Samyeling in Scotland, and later from Sangye Yeshe, who became the main teacher in the art school at Dharamsala. From them I learned how to draw the face of the Buddha and the body of the female deity Drolma (Tara). I enjoyed painting very much and began to make paintings to send to the benefactors.

Besides getting sponsorship for the school, Mommy-la found sponsors for each one of us. One of my benefactors and pen friends was Mrs. Rachel Levy, a Jewish schoolteacher from England. I think she also wrote books. I never met her, but I know she had a very good heart and was very kind to me. She wanted very much to learn the Dharma, but at that time I was not able to communicate properly in English, and there were no Tibetans at Buxa who could write English well enough. The only alternative was to ask the Indians, but then they would write something other than what you wanted to say; I had that problem many times. Later she met a few Tibetan lamas in England and was very impressed by Trungpa Rinpoche.

33. Guru Rinpoche painted by Lama Zopa for Sister Vajra

Once, Mrs. Levy sent money to make me a new set of robes. Sister Vajra, a Scottish nun who was also my pen friend, had them made and sent to me. In return, I painted a Guru Padmasambhava for her. Sister Vajra's Western name was Miss Robinson. First she had followed the Theravada tradition, worn yellow robes, and lived in Sarnath in a small hut; then she became a follower of His Holiness the Gyalwa Karmapa. I first met her in Sarnath and later in Darjeeling, at her house in Tongsum Bhasti. She continuously recited Chenrezig's mantra, just like my mother did. She was trying to find sponsors for the Tibetan monks among the rich Tibetans of Darjeeling and Kalimpong, but she did not succeed. The extremely wealthy Tibetan families were not willing to give anything, and some of them even tried to get help for their own children from the charitable organizations. But Sister Vajra, although she was not a Tibetan and was not rich, dedicated her life to the Tibetans.

Sometime later I heard that she had died. One day there was a landslide in her neighborhood and everyone had run out of their houses. Unfortunately, she had decided to go back inside to get an umbrella and the money for the Tibetans. At that moment there was another landslide, which caused the house to collapse on her. She was in her late seventies.

At one point Mrs. Levy did not write for about two months. I was wondering what had happened to her when I received a letter saying that she had had an operation and had been in hospital. Her handwriting had deteriorated very much, and it looked as if someone else was helping her to write. That was her last letter. After some days, I dreamed that someone was bringing a letter written on very white paper, and the next morning I received a letter like the one in my dream that had been written by her friend, who was the pen friend of another young tulku, explaining that she had died. She was about eighty-seven years old. Her body was cremated electrically and her ashes strewn on her garden. We performed an extensive ritual on her behalf and requested the high lamas to pray for her good rebirth.

Afterward, her cousin, Mrs. Audrey Cohen, became my main sponsor. She took complete care of me as if I were her child, and I used to call her Mother. For seven years she paid for all my expenses and all the medicines and milk I needed because of the tuberculosis, and she also sent me paints. Every week I would receive a letter from her; my room was full of them, but I would answer only occasionally. I wrote in my broken English and asked her to correct my letters and send them back, so that I could learn proper English. But then, probably to make me happy, she replied that I should not worry too much because even in London nobody spoke English correctly![273]

After six months at Dalhousie, I returned to Buxa in November 1963 and never went back to the school for young tulkus. In 1965, Mommy-la, who had been ordained again as a nun and had become Sister Khechog Palmo, closed the school and moved to the monastery of His Holiness Karmapa in Sikkim. Some tulkus who had nowhere to go decided to stay, and Kailash House became a nonsectarian monastery. Then, a new abbot, a monk from Tashi Lhunpo with crooked feet, arrived. The evening after his arrival a violent storm took place and the roof was badly damaged. The lamas interpreted this as a bad sign, and many of them left immediately. The ones who stayed discovered that the abbot would give all the food and milk powder sent as donations for the lamas to the Tibetan Government minister who had appointed him. The tulkus were quite upset, and I heard that on one occasion they decided to play a trick on him as a kind of "punishment." They threw many chickpeas on the stairs, and when the abbot with the crooked feet came by in the evening, he fell all the way down the stairs. Very naughty tulkus!

# 22. Lama Thubten Yeshe

I WAS APPROACHING my eighteenth birthday and had been studying with Gen Yeshe for two years, when he decided to leave Buxa and go to Bhutan to meditate in a remote area. Some of his friends advised him to join the meditators in Dalhousie, but Gen Yeshe replied, "I have read the texts explaining the gradual path many times, and I have enough material to meditate on. I do not need to be guided by anyone." He stayed in the mountains for a few years living with the local people and then wandered around India, staying at any place suitable for meditation. I never saw him again. I heard that after some years he gave back his monastic vows and settled in Bir in Himachal Pradesh, where he passed away.

When Gen Yeshe left, I was again without a teacher. Gen Lozang Gyatso used to spend long periods of time in Darjeeling, leaving me with Geshe Rabten, but Geshe-la was extremely busy and suggested that I could take teachings either from Geshe Thubten or Lama Thubten Yeshe.[274] He did not say specifically that I should go to one or the other; he just made the suggestion.

The monks from each class had to study the same texts, but they could have different teachers. Chöphel (pronounced "Chumbi"), who was the leader of my class, lived in the room next to me and we became very close friends. He was studying with Lama Thubten Yeshe and suggested that I too should take teachings from him, but somehow I was reluctant to go. One day he insisted that I should go with him to meet Lama Yeshe, who had moved to a house on top of the hill, about a half hour's walk from our place. We went out for a stroll and he pushed me in that direction, but I refused to go. I tried to turn back, but Chumbi insisted, "You must go!" We went outside the fence of the monastery and reached a large mango tree where people used to take a rest. I wanted to go back, but again Chumbi pushed me a little farther. Again I refused to go, and again Chumbi pushed me. Finally, we reached the house of Lama Yeshe and again I said, "I do not want to go inside." There was nothing wrong with Lama Thubten Yeshe, and there was no particular reason why I was refusing to take teachings from him, but somehow I did not want to meet him. Anyhow, Chumbi pushed me inside the house.

It is said in the scriptures that when one makes first contact with a spiritual teacher, it is extremely important to perform offerings correctly. The circumstances surrounding that first meeting will determine how many teachings you will be able to receive from your teacher in the future and how much your practice will progress. For instance, when Milarepa met his teacher Marpa he had no material possessions, but he offered his body, speech, and mind to the lama. Afterward, he went begging and was able to offer an empty pot with four handles. To create auspicious conditions, Marpa filled the pot with butter and lit a wick, then shook the handles making a loud sound. In this way, Marpa created the conditions for Milarepa to become enlightened in one lifetime and benefit many beings.

When I went to meet Lama Yeshe I had no offerings with me, and that is probably the reason why I received very few teachings from him. Chumbi had brought a little bit of rice, which he put on a bowl together with one rupee and an old khatag, and offered those things to Lama Yeshe on my behalf. Lama Yeshe asked, "Did he receive permission from Geshe Rabten?" and Chumbi replied, "Yes!" So I was asked to go inside the room, and Lama Yeshe made me sit on the bed next to him because of my having the title of "reincarnated lama." The room was very small, and I noticed that on the window behind Lama Yeshe there was a nest of ants; they were crawling everywhere.

During that first hour that I sat on the bed with Lama Yeshe, I did not understand a single word of what he was teaching. I only remember that it had something to do with cause and effect. All I could think about was, "Why is Lama Yeshe speaking so fast? Why can't he teach slowly?" Since I came with the wrong attitude, that day I did not understand anything, and I had a difficult time. The second day, however, it became easier for me to understand Lama Yeshe's teachings.

It seems to me that the above episode shows that in many lifetimes I have been guided by Lama Thubten Yeshe. Even though I did not have the wish to study with him, there was a strong karmic link between us. He had helped me in many previous lives and continued to do so in this present one, taking care of me better than a mother and father. The help we receive from parents is limited to this present life, but the help of spiritual teachers extends to future lives also, and their great kindness is difficult to repay.

After a while, when he saw that I was being well taken care of by Lama Yeshe, Gen Lozang Gyatso decided to leave Buxa for good and go into retreat. He offered some money to Lama Yeshe on my behalf and requested him to take full responsibility for my life and my studies. Lama agreed and Gen Lozang Gyatso left for Bhutan, giving me a big watch as a farewell present.

I then moved to the house of Lama Yeshe on top of the hill and shared his room. Two monks, Lhundrub Rigsel and Lozang Nyima, were also staying there and helped with different tasks. Lama Yeshe had asked the office of the monastery to give them separate rations of rice, dhal (lentils), cooking oil, and so forth, and they did their own cooking. Sometimes Lama himself would prepare the food, but most of the time it was done either by Lhundrub or Lozang Nyima. Lozang Nyima also took care of me, washing my clothes and accompanying me everywhere.

After becoming my official tutor, the first thing that Lama Yeshe did was to take away all my possessions, including the watch that Gen Lozang Gyatso had just given me. I was very sad to lose my nice new watch, and I cried all day long. Lama Yeshe did not know why I was crying and thought I was sad because Gen Lozang Gyatso had left. I did not say anything and just kept on crying, but after a while I forgot about the watch. Many years later I told the story to Lama Yeshe and he said, "So, you were attached to your watch?" Then he opened a box, took out the old watch, and gave it back to me, so I started wearing it again.

In the afternoons, when it became too hot, Lama Yeshe used to lie down and pretend to sleep, although he was in fact meditating. He would tell me, "Kusho, lay down and take a rest!" but I did not want to sleep and just sat on the bed reading or painting. At night, when it was quiet and cool and we could hear people snoring, Lama Yeshe used to read the scriptures. I also spent the night reading and meditating on the teachings, and I found that I needed very little sleep. I often reflected on the great usefulness of having a perfect human body and on suffering of being born as an animal, such as a dog or a mosquito. By reflecting on these sufferings, I reached a point when it was harder for me to sleep than not to sleep. I wanted to spend all my time creating merit to make sure that I would never be reborn as an animal again.

Over the next few years, Lama Yeshe gave me teachings on philosophical tenets, logic, parts of the Madhyamaka and Prajnaparamita commentaries by Jetsun Chökyi Gyaltsen,[275] and parts of the *Five Treatises* of Maitreya.

During those years at Buxa I suffered greatly from TB. I used to cough a lot and became very thin. One day, Gen Lozang Gyatso sent a letter inviting both Lama Yeshe and myself to visit him in Darjeeling. Lama Yeshe was also not feeling well, and he thought that the cold climate would be helpful to restore our health. We went to Darjeeling at the beginning of 1967, sometime around Tibetan New Year, and stayed at Samten Chöling with Gen Lozang Gyatso.

While in Darjeeling, I kept trying to improve my English by reading *Time* magazine. The words I did not know I would ask Mingyur-la, the benefactor of Kyabje Ling Rinpoche, who lived nearby. Whenever I asked him about the meaning of scientific words, he would say that those were new words and that he had studied English a long time before. Mingyur-la used to wake up around nine in the morning, wash, and then go into the shrine room. A monk from Dromo Geshe's monastery was staying in his house and took care of the shrine room, so when Mingyur-la came in, the monk would hand him a few sticks of lit incense. Mingyur-la would then light a butter lamp in the beautifully carved shrine and recite a few mantras while turning his prayer wheel. Then he would take his jeep and go into Darjeeling town to gamble until nine P.M. That was his daily schedule. He was a very jolly man with a great sense of humor, and very kind also; whenever a monk was sick he would take him for treatment to Darjeeling and cover all the expenses.

## Zina Rachevsky

The sixties were the "hippy era." Young people were opening their minds to spiritual matters and reading books on Eastern religions, and many of them came to India and Nepal in search of spiritual guidance (and to enjoy the cheap, plentiful *hashish* and *ganja* of those countries!). Some of them were taking LSD and had out-of-body experiences, and by reading the *Tibetan Book of the Dead* became inspired to follow the Buddhist path.

Others were attracted to the spiritual path by reading the life of Milarepa. Some years later in Nepal, our first Italian student brought his three Italian friends to take teachings from Lama Yeshe. One of them had been taking heavy drugs, but when he read Milarepa's life story he developed a great sense of renunciation. He then gave away all his possessions and came to India and Nepal. When I met him, he was wearing only a yellow *lungi* (loincloth) and had no money. Actually, he did not understand the true meaning of renunciation. True renunciation does not necessarily mean giving away material possessions. It means giving up selfishness and the wrong concept of a self-existent I.

In those days there were very few books on Tibetan Buddhism in English. The most popular were those of Alexandra David-Neel, W. Y. Evans-Wentz, and Lama Govinda. In particular, Lama Govinda's *The Way of the White Clouds* became a classic. (I wonder which one happened first—LSD or this book!) Lama Govinda's teacher was the previous Dromo Geshe Rinpoche Ngawang Kalzang, who had been a very highly realized meditator.

One of the Darjeeling truth-seekers was the Russian "princess" Zina Rachevsky, whose family had escaped the Communist revolution and had settled in France. Zina went to the United States, married a wealthy moviemaker, and had a son and a daughter. Her life had been very interesting. I think she did everything one can possibly do in the West (Hollywood star, fashion model, can-can dancer in Paris, and so forth), except becoming a president or a prime minister.

Zina believed herself to be an incarnation of H. P. Blavatsky and came to the Himalayas looking for a Tibetan lama. She arrived in Darjeeling from Sri Lanka in April 1967 with her small daughter Rhea and took a room in the Windermere Hotel. The manager of the hotel, Rai Bahadur Dondrub-la (people knew him as Tenduf-la), was also the director of the management committee of Dromo Geshe Rinpoche's monasteries in Ghoom; he knew me from Dungkar Gompa. Soon Zina made friends with Gene Smith, an American who was studying Buddhism in Darjeeling, and he gave her a list of the most important lamas in the Darjeeling and Kalimpong areas. She then started to visit each of the lamas, accompanied by either Gene or Jampa Gyaltsen Mutugtsang, a nephew of the Gyalwang Karmapa who had been in Frida Bedi's school with me in Delhi.

Zina was not satisfied with the lamas she met and was looking for someone else who could answer her questions. It seems that she had read *The Way of the White Clouds* and had some strong desire to meet Dromo Geshe Rinpoche. One day, Tenduf-la suggested that she should meet the "Dromo Rinpoche" and his teacher, who were staying at Ghoom and could speak some English (at that time everybody knew me as the Small Dromo Rinpoche). Jampa Gyaltsen also knew me, and one Sunday morning he and Gene brought her to Samten Chöling to meet the "Dromo Rinpoche."

Lama Yeshe was reading a text and I was painting when a monk called Drugta (Sound of the Dragon) opened the door and said, "Someone is looking for you." Zina came into the room with Jampa Gyaltsen, who introduced me saying, "This is Dromo Rinpoche." She sat on a chair and Gen Lozang Gyatso offered her a huge mug of Tibetan tea. I thought that she seemed surprised. Maybe she was expecting to find a venerable lama in a luxurious apartment instead of a couple of ordinary monks in a small room. In any case, that did not matter to her. As soon as she saw the big smile of Lama Yeshe, she immediately realized that he was the teacher she had been looking for.

The next morning she came back with Jampa Gyaltsen and asked Lama many questions. She kept coming every day to Ghoom by car and spent a few hours asking us all kinds of questions about East and West. Lama Yeshe answered all her questions very kindly, and Jampa Gyaltsen translated. After a few days, I gained confidence in my knowledge of English and started to translate for her. She used to praise us saying that we were polite and answered all her questions. I guess the other lamas were too busy and gave her only minimal answers.

Ghoom is a few kilometers outside Darjeeling, and it was difficult for her to come every day, so after a while she asked whether we would like to move to her house. We agreed, and after two months in Samten Chöling, we went to live with Zina at the Villa Altomont. Her house was near the house of Gyalo Thondup, the brother of His Holiness the Dalai Lama. The upper floor was rented to an Indian who was in charge of the Darjeeling zoo, and Zina was living in the ground floor with her daughter, a Nepali servant, a small dog, and many friends. She asked whether we wanted to be in the main house with her and her friends, but we preferred to stay in a glass teahouse at the back of her garden. It was a very small room with space for only two beds and a little table in between; so small that Lama Yeshe's feet would stick out the door when he stretched out on the bed. We stayed almost nine months in that house.

Zina knew most of the important, famous people in town and throughout the world, and also many ordinary people, and her house was always full of visitors. Among her friends were Allen Ginsberg, Bhagawan Dass, and Ivan Surita, an Armenian who was the Commissioner North for the Siliguri area and was very fond of me. That is probably the reason that Zina was allowed to have two Tibetan refugee lamas staying in her house. In those days, the Indian Intelligence Service was very suspicious, and both Tibetans and Westerners were kept under close watch.

Zina used to get up around seven and go to the bathroom. We had to use the same toilet, and on the way had to pass her, sitting in her underpants in front of the mirror. She would spend about two hours every morning putting creams and make-up on her face. When she first got up from bed, she looked like a sixty-year-old lady, but after all that work, she would become extremely beautiful and young, like a sixteen-year-old girl. We found that fact quite amazing.

After Zina's toilette was finished, we would join her for breakfast. Then she would come to receive teachings from Lama Yeshe and I would translate. She usually brought a book with her to leaf through, sat with her legs up or stretched out because she did not know that this is considered disrespectful, and would nibble on biscuits, chocolate, or *pakoras* (an Indian snack). Most of the time it was not a formal teaching, and we would just talk about cause and effect and the things she had done in her life.

At midday we would have a big lunch, and in the afternoons Zina would dress up and go to the movies. Once or twice she took us with her. In the evenings we were given a thin soup made with the leftovers from lunch and two slices of bread, but we were used to eating thugpa in the evenings and were always quite hungry. Sometimes Tibetan visitors brought us bread, for which we felt very grateful, and many times, when she had gone to the movies, we would sneak out and go to eat *momos* (meat dumplings) at the local Tibetan restaurants. We really practiced a lot of patience during those nine months, but seen in retrospect, it was worthwhile. If we had not stayed with her, we would probably have continued our studies like the other monks and would not have had the opportunity to teach the Dharma and benefit so many Westerners.

While we were in Darjeeling, the Tibetan School for Higher Studies (now known as the Central Institute of Higher Tibetan Studies) was being started at Sarnath, and the Tibetan Administration was selecting the monks that could attend. Lozang Nyima sent us many letters from Buxa with the notification that Lama Yeshe, Lozang Nyima, and myself had been selected, but Lama Yeshe decided not to accept. Lozang Nyima also declined and later joined us as our attendant.

Around that time, His Holiness the Dalai Lama had been offered large tracts of government land in South India to relocate Sera, Drepung, and Ganden monasteries. The job of obtaining the land had been given to Trungyig Chenmo Angu-la, who was teaching Tibetan writing at Buxa. Trungyig-la spent many months in Delhi visiting the Indian official who was supposed to give the land, but without success. He then became very depressed and went back to Dharamsala to report to His Holiness, but His Holiness did not want to listen to the story and sent him back to Delhi right away. Trungyig-la left the same evening, and the next morning went again to see the official. Usually, that official did not pay any attention to the Tibetan, but that day he called him and said, "My son wants a small Tibetan puppy, can you find one for him?" Trungyig-la said he could and went out. Nearby he met an Indian *swami* walking along with a beautiful, long-haired Lhasa Apso. Trungyig-la asked the swami, "Could you please sell me that dog?" The swami readily agreed, and Trungyig-la went back to bring the puppy to the official. As he entered the house, the dog ran to the son of the official waving its tail and licking his feet, so everyone was delighted. The official then gave the land right away. Actually, Tibetans believe that the swami was an emanation of His Holiness the Dalai Lama.

Around Christmas 1967, Zina began to have trouble with her Indian visa and thought about going to Sri Lanka to start a Mahayana monastery there with Lama and I as teachers. We agreed to go with her, and she wrote to the Office of His Holiness the Dalai Lama asking permission for us to be sent to Sri Lanka to teach Dharma. Zina then left for Sri Lanka and returned to Calcutta a few weeks later.

Lama Yeshe and I went back to Buxa to collect our belongings and then on to Calcutta to meet Zina. We traveled to Dharamsala with her and stayed in the large house of Trijang Rinpoche in the mountains. (A couple of years later, Lama Yeshe bought that house and it became Tushita Retreat Center.) The teachings of Lama Yeshe had definitely brought a change in Zina's mind; she had decided to become a nun and spend the rest of her life purifying her negative karma. We had an audience with His Holiness, and she offered all her jewels to him and requested permission to be ordained. Then, on July 31, 1968, she received the novice vows from Trijang Rinpoche.

His Holiness gave us much advice regarding our new teaching job, and we were given official permission to go to Sri Lanka as Zina's teachers. We obtained our visas without any trouble, but Zina experienced many obstacles in obtaining hers. Perhaps because she was a Russian princess, or because she was with us, the Indian Intelligence Service always had some spies checking on her. We used to see a tall, fat man with a moustache walking back and forth in the train stations and everywhere. Even as she was receiving her vows in Trijang Rinpoche's house, that man could be seen pacing back and forth on the road below.

Since we could not go to Sri Lanka for the time being, Lama Yeshe suggested that we go to Nepal instead. I would thus have the opportunity to see my mother and relatives, whom I had not seen for almost twelve years. Thus, in October 1968, when I was nearing my twenty-third birthday, I returned to Nepal.

## 23. Return to Nepal

As soon as we arrived in Nepal, I wrote a letter to my mother telling her, "If you want to see me, you should come now to Kathmandu. Afterward, we may be going to the West, and it could be a long time until I can come to Nepal again." At that time Zina was talking about bringing us to New York to Allen Ginsberg's house.

Lama Yeshe and I went to stay at Samtenling Monastery[276] in Bouddha. We were given a room in a little house at the back of the gompa without any furniture, so we slept on grass mats on the floor. Zina and her friend Jacqueline Fagan from New Zealand took a room at the Double Dorje house, which belonged to the son of the Chini Lama, the caretaker of the stupa.[277]

### Serkong Dorje Chang

Shortly after arriving in Nepal we went with Zina to meet Serkong Dorje Chang, a very high lama from Ganden Monastery. In Buxa I had heard that his behavior was similar to that of ancient yogis such as Tilopa and Naropa. He used to suddenly disappear and reappear somewhere else, causing much trouble to his attendants, who had to run around looking for him. The lama himself told one of his monks that he was in actuality Marpa the Translator, the teacher of Milarepa. His previous incarnation had been a great scholar, learned not only in words but also in experience of the Buddhist path. His Holiness the Thirteenth Dalai Lama recognized him as having enough realizations of the tantric path to practice with a consort.[278]

Serkong Dorje Chang was staying in the house of one of his benefactors near the Swayambhu stupa. When we arrived at the door and called out, a simple-looking monk came down, and we asked him, "Where is Serkong Dorje Chang?" He told us to wait and went back into the house through a different door. Then somebody else came and took us upstairs, and we found out that the simple monk was actually Serkong Dorje Chang himself!

We made prostrations and offerings and sat down on the floor. There was a large pile of texts next to Rinpoche's bed, and Zina suddenly said, "Please read something from those texts for us." Normally one does not ask a lama in such a way. In fact, whenever we took her to see high lamas, we had to prepare the questions beforehand so that she would not shock them with her Western manners. Anyway, that is what she asked on that occasion, and I had to translate it. Serkong Dorje Chang replied, "No, no, I know nothing, I know nothing!" But then she asked about guru devotion and Rinpoche gave an unbelievable, profound teaching. I cannot remember all the words, but the essence of his advice to Zina was, "If your lama is sitting there on the floor, you must think that Shakyamuni Buddha is sitting there."

During the commemoration of the Buddha's descent from heaven (Lhabab Duchen), which falls on the twenty-second of the ninth Tibetan month, the monks of Samtenling Monastery would do nyungne, the fasting retreat of Avalokiteshvara. In those days, all Gelug practitioners would do nyungne together at Samtenling because there was no other Gelug monastery in the valley. That year the retreat was sponsored by a disciple and benefactor of Drubthob Rinpoche, a lama from Drepung Monastery.[279] The benefactor wanted Drubthob Rinpoche to give the eight Mahayana precepts in the early morning and to lead the nyungne, but the monks wanted Serkong Dorje Chang. The reason was that Drubthob Rinpoche practices the Most Secret Hayagriva, which is the main deity of Sera Je Monastery and is, in fact, a Nyingma practice; for some reason those Gelug monks did not want to have anything to do with the Nyingmapas, even indirectly. There was a slight conflict with the benefactor, but finally the monks had it their way, and Serkong Dorje Chang was invited to give the precepts and lead the retreat.

On the first morning of the nyungne, Rinpoche came into the gompa with the text, opened it, and said, "If the lama tells you to lick fresh, warm excrement, you should get down on the ground and lick it immediately like this," and he made some licking sounds with his tongue. "That is the way to practice Dharma," he concluded. Then he closed the text and left, so the monks had to take the eight precepts from the Buddha image on the altar. The words of Rinpoche were an extremely powerful teaching, like an atomic bomb. It really affected my mind, and on the basis of that instruction, I consider Serkong Dorje Chang as one of my teachers, even though I never received any empowerments or complete oral transmissions from him. My mind is often filled with doubts and wrong ideas, but whenever

I went to visit Serkong Dorje Chang, I had no doubt that I was in the presence of Yamantaka, the wrathful aspect of Mañjushri, the bodhisattva of wisdom. I had not a single doubt that Rinpoche was an enlightened being.

## Max Mathews

Although she had taken the vows of a novice nun, Zina did not know exactly how Buddhist nuns should behave and kept going to parties with her friends and so forth. On the occasion of an American holiday called Thanksgiving, Zina went to a party at the house of Maryjane (Max) Mathews, a black American woman from New York whom she had met in Greece a few years before. Zina was wearing her monastic robes and told many stories about "her Tibetan lamas." A few days later Max came with Zina to meet us. She was so impressed by Lama Yeshe that when he looked at her and smiled, she began to cry and could not even speak.

Max had spent some years traveling and teaching at American schools all over the world. In those days she was teaching at the Kathmandu Lincoln School and had an art gallery, Max's Gallery, where she sold all kinds of beautiful statues and objects from Tibet and Nepal. She had rented two floors in a very nice house in Indrachowk, right in the middle of Kathmandu, with a roof garden and many interesting objects from all over the world. She also had some Tibetan ritual objects, but she did not know their meaning and used them for different purposes. I remember a set of silver water-offering bowls being used as wine cups and butter lamps that served as ashtrays. Her house was always full of people—embassy people, Nepalis, Tibetans, hippies, travelers, movie stars, writers, princes, and so forth. She had five servants working for her and gave parties very often.

Shortly after our first meeting, Max began to invite us to her house for the weekends and to pay Zina's bills for our expenses. Lama Yeshe would give teachings to her and her friends, and I would translate for them. On Sunday afternoons she would drive us back to Bouddha in her convertible car, an old 1928 Hudson. It was the second car that had been carried by coolies into the Kathmandu Valley for the king of Nepal. Sometimes we all went for picnics in that car.

We enjoyed sitting on her roof terrace, from where we could see the whole valley, and talking with Westerners. An American couple, Chip Cobalt and Judy Weitzner, who were also teaching at Lincoln School, were often at her house. Judy began to teach English to Lama Yeshe, and soon he was able to say a few simple sentences, such as, "Be happy, dear."

34. Picnic in the Arniko Highway. From left: Lama Zopa, Lama Yeshe, Chip Cobalt, and Max Mathews (Judy Weitzner)

Around that time, Max bought a very old and expensive Tibetan statue. We realized that it was extremely blessed and might contain very special relics, so Lama decided to open it and check its contents, then again perform the consecration. We did the ceremony in Max's bedroom while some Westerners were upstairs on the terrace listening to the Beatles. The statue contained the relics of one of the previous buddhas and was extremely valuable. Afterward, as we sat there drinking tea, Zina began to talk about getting a place where Lama could teach and people could come from all over the world to learn meditation. We thought that it was a very interesting idea and assured her that things would work out perfectly. Everyone became enthusiastic about that project and offered to help.

Soon Zina began to look for a suitable house. From the window of our room in Samtenling, we could see in the distance a small hill with two large trees on top. Lama Yeshe felt some kind of attraction for that hill, and one day we all went there for a picnic and to have a look. The area was called Kopan, and on the hill there was a very nice old house that had been built by one of the previous Nepali kings for his astrologer. On the very top of the hill a smaller brick house had been built—perhaps for watching the stars or for recreation—but it had fallen down during the big earthquake in 1934 and many bricks were still lying around.[280] Lama Yeshe liked the place very much, and Zina began to make inquiries about the possibility of renting the house.

## Meeting My Brother

News travels extremely fast among Sherpas and Tibetans, and it wasn't long before my brother Sangye heard about our arrival and came to meet me.

Sangye had always been interested in the Dharma but had no inclination for monastic life. The Thangme monks and our grandmother used to tell him that if one does bad things one goes to hell and there is much suffering, but if one does good, one goes to heaven and life is very pleasant there. Sangye never forgot those words, and he often reflected about the meaning of life and death. Amala used to tell him that one can die at any moment and that he should pray as much as possible, because prayer always helps to solve any problem. During the winter, when most of the villagers had left Thangme for Zamte or Mende and when the wind was blowing fiercely, Amala and Sangye spent the nights reciting the mani and Vajra Guru mantras and the prayer of taking refuge in the Three Jewels.

Every summer Aku Ngawang Legshe and Aku Ngawang Jigme would put up a tent in the forest across the river near Thangme, where they would practice chöd at night. During the day they taught my brother how to read. Later, Sangye spent six months at Genupa with Ashang Ngawang Yonten.

In 1959, thousands of Tibetan refugees had come into Khumbu, bringing with them whatever material possessions they could carry and a large number of yaks and sheep. Many of them settled in tents on the large plain at Thangteng, but there weren't enough grazing grounds for so many animals, and many of them had to be slaughtered. One day, when Sangye was on the Nasa Tsering ridge above Thangme with the cows, he saw a Tibetan man tying the legs of a yak with a rope and cutting its belly with a knife. The yak managed to break the rope and run away dripping with blood, but the Tibetan caught it again and cut off its head. Sangye was horrified and began to cry and to pray for the yak to be reborn in Dewachen, the pure land of Buddha Amitabha.

When he was about twelve years old, Sangye decided to run away from home because he wanted to become rich and help Amala. One night, when everyone was asleep, Sangye and a group of boys left Thangme and began to walk to Darjeeling. The next morning, quite a few people from Thangme were running around the village asking everywhere, "Where is my boy? Where is my boy?" Later, some people reported that the boys had been spotted walking down the road in Pharag, but it was too late to bring them back.

Sangye and his friends went first to Punakha in Bhutan and spent six months doing different jobs. Afterward, they worked in Darjeeling chopping bamboo to be used as scaffolding on construction sites. Sangye then returned to Khumbu and stayed for a while at Thangme, but when he was fifteen he left again, this time as a kitchen boy on a trekking expedition to western Nepal. He spent the next few years working on expeditions as a cook and later as *sardar,* or headman. In this way he was able to earn a good amount of money, most of which he sent home. Thanks to Sangye, the economic situation of my mother and sister improved substantially. Now Amala no longer had to work for other people except when she did so in return for help she received from other villagers.

My brother was staying in Chetrapati, an area of Kathmandu where most Sherpas used to live. Shortly after we met, Sangye went to Khumbu to bring my mother and sister down to Kathmandu.

## Meeting My Mother, Sister, and Uncles

It was now February 1969, the beginning of the earth bird year. The Tamang, Newar, and Tibetan communities were performing very elaborate ceremonies at the stupa, and many pilgrims arrived. It seems that the construction of Bouddhanath Stupa had been completed in a bird year, so on those years there are special celebrations.[281] That particular year people were also coming to attend the oral transmission of the Kangyur from Dilgo Khyentse Rinpoche,[282] an eminent Nyingma lama.

My maternal uncles Ashang Trinle and Ashang Ngawang Yonten were planning to come down to Kathmandu to receive the transmission of the Kangyur, and after receiving my letter and talking to my brother, my mother and sister decided to join them. There was already an airstrip at Lukla in the Pharag region,[283] but there were no regular flights and the Sherpas always walked to Kathmandu. Although Sangye had enough money to cover the expenses of the journey, my mother and sister took with them needles from Darjeeling, yak wool blankets, and salt to sell along the way. Those items were in great demand in the lower hills, and they were able to make a good profit.

My relatives rented a house near the stupa and came to Samtenling Monastery to meet me. When they walked into the room, I said, "Amala, how are you?" My mother looked at me, then looked at Lama Yeshe, and could not figure out which one was her son. Then somebody pointed at me and said, "This is Lama Zopa." When I had left Khumbu twelve years before, I was a rather plump little boy with a round face, but now I had become an extremely thin grown-up man, with protruding cheeks and dark skin. My relatives were completely startled, and all they could do was cry. They sat down and cried and cried for a long time, without being able to speak. When the emotions calmed down and we were able to talk, I told them about my life, and I learned everything that had happened to them during those years.

My mother and sister had had a difficult life. They were forced to sell the house and fields at Zamte for the ridiculous amount of 400 rupees, and had to work very hard in other people's fields and carrying loads. In 1959, when she was seventeen years old, my sister had become very sick, and half of her body became paralyzed. Soon after, Trulzhig Rinpoche came to stay in Thangme Gompa, where he gave many teachings and empowerments. My sister attended some of the empowerments and somehow recovered from her sickness. A few years later she fell sick again, and Trulzhig Rinpoche, who was then staying in Phugmoche in Shorong, told her that she had many life obstacles and that the only solution was to become a nun. In 1967 she took novice vows from Trulzhig Rinpoche in Phugmoche, together with many other Tibetan and Sherpa women, and was given the name Ngawang Samten, Powerful Speech Meditation. Back in Thangme, she learned the *ka kha ga nga* from Ashang Ngawang Yonten, so she was able to read some texts and devote a little bit of time to spiritual practice.

Ashang Trinle was still a monk at Chiwang Gompa and came often to Thangme to help my mother cultivate the fields. Most family members were monks or lived far away, but Ashang Trinle was the only one that they all trusted when they needed some practical help. Even though he was always busy, he never failed to do a one-month retreat every year, and every night, no matter how much he had worked or how much he had walked up and down the mountains, before falling asleep he always recited the confession prayer to the thirty-five buddhas.

Ashang Ngawang Yonten, who had accompanied us to Dingri Gangar when I left for Tibet, had taken monastic vows with Trulzhig Rinpoche and devoted his whole life to Dharma practice. In accordance with Sherpa family rules, as the youngest son he took care of his mother, who was old and blind and could not be left alone. For a while he stayed with her at

Genupa; then he obtained permission from Charog Lama Kusho Mangde to build a small hut under the cliff at Charog. The hut was very small, so my uncle would spend the night in a small square meditation box while his mother slept on a wooden bench next to the fireplace. He did prostrations on a wooden board outside the hut. In addition to his own Dharma practice, he did all the cooking, collected firewood, and fetched water, because his mother could do nothing except recite mani.

My uncle spent eleven years in that hermitage, performing preliminary practices and taking care of his mother. He was able to complete four *bum* (pronounced "boom," means 100,000) of prostrations, six bum of Vajrasattva mantra recitations, four bum of mandala offerings, and four bum of guru yoga. Over the years his health improved so much that he never got sick anymore. Later, he moved to Thangme Gompa, where he bought a small house from a nun. My grandmother had recently passed away.

The main teacher of Ashang Ngawang Yonten was Gelong Ngawang Samten, a very pure practitioner who lived in a cave at Charog, at a short distance from my uncle's hut. I had met him a few times when I was a child, and I always remember the good feeling that I got from him, which was somehow different from the rest of the monks. He loved children and used to play with me a lot.

At that time I also met my first two teachers again. Aku Ngawang Legshe was still a monk at Thangme Gompa, but Aku Ngawang Gendun was now married and had a daughter. Aku Ngawang Jigme was staying in Rolwaling. Gelong Pasang built a school in Beding and had come to Bouddha with his students.

## Meeting Ngawang Chöphel, Karma Tenzin, and Other Sherpas

Many Sherpas who had been disciples and benefactors of the previous Lawudo Lama came to see me. Ngawang Chöphel, the disciple of the Lawudo Lama Kunzang Yeshe, was extremely pleased to learn that I had been able to receive a good education. He himself had received many teachings from different lamas and done many retreats. He was a great practitioner who had been able to complete a whole set of the five preliminary practices in forty days, and had spent one week in a cave offering his body in charity to the insects. I was quite impressed by him. Later he had to marry and take care of a family, but he continued practicing Dharma and was able to help very much in his country.[284] It was probably on that occasion that Lama Yeshe requested Ngawang Chöphel to write down everything he could remember about the previous Lawudo Lama.

One day, Karma Tenzin, the grandson of the Lawudo Lama Kunzang Yeshe, came to visit me with Au Palden from Namche. Ani Karzang had passed away in 1958, and after her death Karma Tenzin spent most of his time at Thangme Gompa. His sister Pemba Dekyi also left Lawudo and moved to Thangme and later to Mende with her husband Pasang Namgyal and their children. Then, in 1959 a Tibetan lama called Dephug (Sherpas pronounce it "Diu") Rinpoche,[285] who had been a friend of the Lawudo Lama, came to Khumbu. At Karma Tenzin's invitation, Diu Rinpoche stayed two years at Lawudo with some of his students. Karma Tenzin became his devoted disciple, and when the lama was offered land to build a gompa in Shorong, he packed the books and possessions of the Lawudo Lama in large wooden boxes, stored them in his house at Thangme Gompa, and left for Shorong with Diu Rinpoche. Pemba Dekyi took the copper and silver chörten containing the lama's relics to her house in Mende for safekeeping because the two winglike silver ornaments at the sides had disappeared, and she was worried that the chörten itself would be stolen.

Karma Tenzin settled in Chubarma, where Diu Rinpoche built the small Lhundrub Chöling Gompa. Diu Rinpoche was an expert in medicine, grammar, astrology, and rituals, and Karma Tenzin learned a great deal from him. He helped the lama by collecting medicinal herbs and making pills for him, carrying his luggage, and so forth.

When I was a child, the family of the Lawudo Lama had not wanted to acknowledge me as the true reincarnation of Lama Kunzang Yeshe, but now Karma Tenzin and Au Palden requested me to go back to Lawudo and take possession of the cave and belongings of my predecessor. They brought some offerings and told me, "Now Lawudo is empty, please come back." Karma Tenzin seemed very sincere and devoted, and I accepted. We then agreed that on the full-moon day of Saka Dawa, which is a very auspicious day, the cave and the property of the previous Lawudo Lama Kunzang Yeshe would be officially handed down to me.

After a while, we received the visit of another Sherpa from Namche who had been a disciple of the Lawudo Lama. His name was Ang Nyima, and he was famous in the Kathmandu Valley. After being a monk at Tashi Lhunpo Monastery for some years, he gave back his vows and had become very rich by selling thangkas and statues to tourists. He also sold small mani wheels that moved with the wind and could be fixed on the top of a car. Once, Ang Nyima had invited His Holiness Karmapa to his house; he drove the Karmapa from the Kagyu gompa at the top of Swayambhu Hill to his home, with a big pot of incense on top of the car and clouds of smoke filling the streets.

Ang Nyima brought a few old Tibetan texts printed in Tibet as presents for Lama Yeshe and me. To Lama he offered the ritual practice of Chakrasamvara, and to me he gave the *Great Thought Transformation,* written by Kachen Yeshe Gyaltsen.[286] I used to carry that book with me all the time, and for many years it became like my pillow or my blanket. To mark the chapters, I filled the edges with the postal stamps that Zina received in letters from her friends in Sri Lanka. Later, that text inspired me when I was teaching the first meditation course to Westerners and gave me the best opportunity to practice the *lamrim* meditations.

Ang Nyima and his family were probably the only vegetarian Sherpas. Once he invited us to his house to do incense offering and put up some prayer flags, but for some reason we were late and he did everything himself. When we reached his house, he was not there. We did the *Lama Chöpa* ritual, and when we asked his wife for a little bit of meat to be offered in the tsog, she said that they did not have any because they never ate meat. We were really surprised.

A few years later I heard that Ang Nyima had died in jail. Together with his brother Urgyen and another Sherpa man, he had gone to an ancient Vajrayogini temple above Sanku, east of Kathmandu, and tried to steal the main statue.[287] It seems that they had made a deal with someone, and if they were able to bring the statue to the airport, they would get a very large sum of money. One night, Urgyen and the other man went quietly into the temple while Ang Nyima waited in the car. They managed to get the statue, but then the caretaker woke up and rang a bell that alerted everybody. The villagers ran after the Sherpas and beat them until the police came and took them to jail. I do not know what happened to Urgyen, but I heard that the other Sherpa was released and went to Darjeeling. As for Ang Nyima, he became famous even in prison. He taught handicrafts to the prison inmates, and they made some business: for one plate of food, they would give an incense pot. Then his family gave 100,000 rupees to get him out of jail, but he died the day before he was to be freed.

One day we went with Zina to visit Trulzhig Rinpoche, who was attending the transmission of the Kangyur and was staying in the house of Lama

Babu, the grandson of Sangye Lama, who had built Chiwang Gompa. Trulzhig Rinpoche is extremely learned and lives in pure moral conduct, and at the same time he is a noble bodhisattva with an unbelievably good heart. Although he belongs to the Nyingma tradition, he has received teachings and empowerments from all the schools of Tibetan Buddhism and is one of the teachers of His Holiness the Dalai Lama.

When we arrived at the house, Rinpoche had just returned from the teachings. He was taking off his zen and his meal was being brought, so he told us to come back later. But Zina insisted in asking her question: Why is it necessary to practice the three principal points of the sutra path (renunciation, bodhichitta, and emptiness) before taking tantric empowerments? It was an uncomfortable situation because Rinpoche was in a hurry, but anyway he answered, "Before the crops can grow, you have to fertilize the fields." That was exactly the same explanation that Lama Tsongkhapa gives. Some years later, Lama Yeshe and I received the oral transmission of *The Great Compassionate Lord* from Trulzhig Rinpoche, and Lama invited him to Kopan to give the transmission of the *Spontaneous Fulfillment of One's Wishes* prayer to the monks.

The oral transmission of the Kangyur lasted for quite a while. My mother, sister, and uncles stayed in Bouddha until its conclusion, but Lama Yeshe and I went to Dharamsala instead to receive teachings from His Holiness the Dalai Lama. We came back after a few weeks and began to plan the journey to Khumbu.

# 24. Back in Khumbu

ONE EVENING, Max invited us for dinner at the American Club. The restaurant was full of Americans, all of them looking very clean and wealthy, and everyone was staring at us because we were an unusual group—Tibetan monks, a Western woman in robes with a shaved head, Max in amazing clothes, and a few hippies.

After eating some strange food, we went out. We then noticed many lights on Swayambhu Hill and decided to go and have a look. When we reached there, we found that a group of French people were making a film about a statue being stolen and that Zina knew all of them very well. She introduced us to the moviemakers, Georges Luneau and Cecile Roulet, and told them everything about the trip to Lawudo that we were planning. They became very interested in my story and decided to come along with us to the mountains to record the "historic event" of my return to Lawudo.

## The Trek

The trip was planned for early April 1969, the second month according to the Tibetan calendar, which coincided with the two-week Easter holiday of the Lincoln School where Max, Chip, and Judy were teaching. The party would also include my brother Sangye, Zina and her friend Jacqueline, and a German photographer friend of Max called Prinze Lorenz, who was planning to go to Khumbu with his assistant to take pictures for a book.

With much difficulty, Judy managed to charter a plane for all of us. Most of the aircrafts flying to Lukla were six-seat Pilatus Porter, but the only one available at that time was a sixteen-seat Twin Otter that belonged to the king and was a little too big for the Lukla airstrip. (Now the airstrip has been considerably lengthened and Twin Otters can land without any problem.) In those days, many of the planes going to Lukla were flown by Western pilots. There was a particularly well-known Swiss pilot (Captain

Emile Wick) who enjoyed playing and whirling around in the air with the aircraft and drinking chang and having fun with the Sherpas on the ground. The Sherpas loved him, but I am not sure about the passengers.

When we arrived at the airport, we were informed that the pilot was sick and that they were sending a replacement. Finally, a Nepali pilot arrived and told us that he had never flown that plane to Lukla before. We became a little nervous, but we went anyway.

35. The trek to Namche: Lama Yeshe and Chip in the foreground, Zina and Max behind, Lama Zopa and Sherpas at the back. Lama Zopa's brother Sangye wearing a white shirt is standing in front of the house (Prinze Lorenz?, courtesy of Kopan Gompa)

It was our first time on such a small plane. The Westerners were looking at the snow peaks and taking pictures, while Lama Yeshe and I sat at the back reciting mantras and prayers, just in case—we were flying very close to huge mountains and being tossed about by gusts of strong wind. Then, when we saw the tiny Lukla airstrip at the bottom of the valley between huge mountains, we were all terrified. The pilot suddenly had to turn the plane around and make some kind of whirling movements before he could manage to come down and land on the airstrip. Prinze's assistant fainted. Finally, we landed amid a large cloud of dust and came out of the plane alive. Later we heard that the same pilot flew back to Lukla that day and crashed when he again tried to land. He was not injured, but the plane was damaged and had to be left at Lukla. I think it is still there.

My sister Ngawang Samten and Ashang Ngawang Yonten were waiting for us in Lukla, and a Sherpa called Ang Dorje invited us to his house. There were no hotels, so everybody came to stay in Ang Dorje's and in another house nearby. We were offered butter tea, tsampa, and delicious Sherpa food, maybe sen or potato pancakes. I had not eaten Sherpa food for many years and I enjoyed it very much, but the Westerners had a hard time swallowing the thick, dark brown lumps of sen accompanied by a soup of strong-smelling rotten cheese and chili.

The next day, Ang Dorje and my relatives arranged coolies to carry everyone's luggage, and we began the trek through the Pharag region. The path follows the valley of the Dudh Kosi, and we had to cross its turbulent waters quite a few times on swinging and shaking bridges. The Westerners were having a great time. At a spot where the stream coming from Kusum Mountain forms very nice, large pools, all the Westerners jumped into the water to take a bath. Soon they all caught a cold, and Prinze actually got pneumonia. Later, when he banged his head on the door of a Sherpa house, he told us that he had only one lung and that, due to brain surgery, he had no skull in some spots but only skin. We were becoming worried about him and suggested that he should go to the Hillary Hospital in Khumde.[288]

All along the trail, people were coming out of their houses to greet me and to receive blessings, showing great respect. Some of the Westerners were surprised because they thought that I was just a young, unimportant monk. Only then did they realize that the title "reincarnate lama" gave me priority over Lama Yeshe in the eyes of the Sherpas.

We spent the second night at Pemkar, where there is a cave and hermitage on top of the hill, and the next day we reached the foot of the mountain where Namche is situated. The trail went straight up above the river, and it was a difficult and tiring climb. We were all feeling exhausted and thirsty when we saw Au Palden and Ashang Trinle coming down with thermos flasks full of tea and with carpets to sit on. We stopped at a spot where there are the ruins of an old Tibetan fort and from where one can see Mount Everest and had a nice tea party. We then continued on toward Namche, but then Max fainted and had to be carried the rest of the way by a Sherpa.

At Namche, Lama Yeshe and I stayed in the house of Au Palden, very close to the Kangyur Lhakhang. Zina and Jacqueline came with us, while the rest of the Westerners found accommodation somewhere else. Au Palden had been a disciple and benefactor of the Lawudo Lama, and the father of his wife was a brother of the wife of Wangyal, the son of the previous Lawudo Lama. After being a monk at Chiwang for five years, Au Palden had married and had thirteen children. He did the preliminary practices at Genupa near Lawudo and had recited the *Diamond Cutter Sutra* more than 10,000 times. He was very skillful at building large prayer wheels.[289]

In the evening we went to check on the other westerners of our party and sat with them in the sun for a while. They were feeling cold and thirsty, and Judy suddenly said, "Oh God, I'd give anything for a Coca Cola!"

Lama Yeshe asked, "What is Coca Cola?"

"It is a drink that we have in America," she replied.

Lama said, "No worry, dear, here is Coca Cola for you," and he poured tea in their cups. The tea seemed to have some sort of bubbles. Judy and Max drank the tea, looked at each other quite amazed, and said that it tasted like Coca Cola! That is just one small example of how Lama Yeshe could work for the happiness of sentient beings.

Without our knowledge, Zina had told Max that she did not want "her group" (meaning Max, Chip and Judy, and Prinze and his assistant) to come with us to Thangme and Lawudo. Max was our main sponsor and obviously she got very upset. We had no problem about everyone coming with us, but Westerners sometimes become very possessive about "their" teachers and create all kinds of unnecessary trouble for themselves and others. In any case, in order to visit the Thangme Valley, everyone, even Lama and myself, needed a special permit because it is on the way to the Tibetan border. Westerners were only allowed to visit Tengboche Monastery and the Imja Khola Valley. Chip wanted very much to see the Lawudo Cave, so he went with Lama to the police station above Namche and somehow obtained a permit.

36. The chörten at Phurte

After two nights in Namche we left for Thangme, while Max and her friends accompanied Prinze to the Khumde Hospital and then went to Tengboche Monastery. The trail to Thangme, the "Namche-Thangme

highway," is almost flat by Khumbu standards. It runs through forests of
fir and rhododendron trees, with a magnificent view of the the Kongde
peaks. Shortly after Phurte, at a turning of the path, we saw Lawudo right
in front of us. We could see the large boulder of the cave, a couple of
ruined houses, and a small white purkhang to the left, in the middle of an
impressive mountain slope.

We continued down the road past Samshing and crossed the Gyachog
River at Tesho, right below Lawudo. We passed Tramo, where we were
told that a new Gelug monastery had recently been built, passed through
Tomde, crossed the Nangpe Tsangpo below Zamte, and climbed the steep
trail to Thangme.

## Thangme Again

My mother and cousins and many Thangme villagers were waiting for us
with khatags and incense. All of us stayed in my mother's house, which
actually is quite small. Lama Yeshe and I were given the largest beds;
Sangye, Zina, and her friend slept on wooden benches, and my mother,
sister, and cousins slept on the floor. The French film crew was already in
Thangme, taking pictures and filming.

Over the next few days many people came to see me, bringing offerings
and requesting blessings and empowerments. Usually they brought a bowl
of corn or rice with a few rupees on top and a khatag, or else a tin of potatoes. Most of them brought a thermos of tea from their homes, so we continuously had to sip butter tea, then sweet tea, then again butter tea, and
so forth.

The villagers who had young sons and had been disciples or benefactors
of the previous Lawudo Lama[290] requested me to build a small gompa at
Lawudo, where eight or ten boys could receive a good education in accordance with Sherpa tradition. In 1961 Sir Edmund Hillary had built a school
in Khumjung, followed by other schools in Thangme, Pangboche, Namche, Chaurikharka, and Junbesi, but the traditional religious education
was gradually disappearing. I accepted their request, and Lama Yeshe and
I began to make plans for fixing the cave and the old houses and for building a small gompa at Lawudo.

During the twelve years that I had spent in Tibet and India, life in
Khumbu had undergone many changes. A large number of Tibetan
refugees had settled in the area and had small shops and lodges in Namche, but the most important change was that Sherpas were not allowed to

trade in Tibet anymore.²⁹¹ For a while they had experienced economic difficulties, but now they were able to make quite a lot of money by working with climbing expeditions. But although there had been many changes and improvements in my homeland, something remained unchanged: the Sherpas still loved to laugh and joke, and to drink lots of chang and arak!

My mother and sister noticed that I spent the nights reading texts and meditating and did not lie down to sleep, and they were very worried about my health. Previously, when we were in Darjeeling and I was feeling quite sick, Lama Yeshe had checked with an oracle, and the answer had been that my health would improve if the possessions of my predecessor were returned to me. As soon as Lama Yeshe related this incident to my relatives, Ashang Ngawang Yonten gave me a set of water bowls that had belonged to the Lawudo Lama. Gradually my health began to improve, and when the cave, books, and so forth were also returned to me, I became quite healthy again.

During my stay in Thangme, I gave teachings and the empowerment of Vajrapani and visited the Thangme Gompa. Zina did a one-week retreat in a house at Thangme Gompa, and Sangye cooked for her.

### Lawudo

One evening, Chip appeared in my mother's house. He told us that as he had watched us disappear behind the ridge above Namche, he had made up his mind: he had come all the way to Khumbu to visit the famous Lawudo Cave and did not want to miss it. When they returned from Tengboche, he left Max and Judy with the luggage and porters at Namche and began to walk in the same direction that we had, without knowing exactly where he was going, until he arrived at Thangme and somehow found his way to our house.

We had had dinner and gone to bed when suddenly we heard some shouting outside and two soldiers came into the kitchen. They pointed a flashlight into Chip's face and took out their *khukuris,* the large Nepali knives. They had found out that a Westerner had passed on the road unchecked and were very upset. It seems that somewhere along the way, Chip saw a checkpost with two soldiers inside playing cards and laughing, so he just walked past them. We talked to the soldiers and calmed them down, while Chip looked around for his passport and permit. The soldiers had a look at his papers and seemed satisfied, so they left without causing any problem.

The next morning all of us—my relatives, Zina, Jacqueline, and Chip—

walked to Lawudo while the French movie crew filmed everything. At Genupa we were greeted by a lama called Ngawang Zopa, his wife, and two nuns who were relatives of the Tengboche Lama. We crossed a very large landslide and soon reached Lawudo. We had been told that a Tibetan monk called Jamyang was doing 100 nyungnes in the cave, but on that day he had gone elsewhere, and the door of the cave was blocked with two large stones. Chip and I removed the stones, he pushed the door with his foot, and we both went inside.

The cave looked to me then just as it had years before, when I had been taken there as a child. The meditation box of the Lawudo Lama Kunzang Yeshe was still there, as well as the statues of Guru Rinpoche, his two consorts, and the Lawudo Lama. There were also some thangkas and a few other small things, but the meditators who had used the cave had built fires inside, and everything had become completely black with soot. The adjacent kitchen was still in good condition. It was a long structure with a small room in one corner for storing wood, where the first two sons of Pemba Dekyi had been born. The other house was in ruins, and the potato fields were overrun with weeds.

We rested for a while and ate boiled potatoes outside the cave. The French took a few shots of the whole group, and we started to walk back to Thangme, while Chip went to Namche to rejoin Max and Judy. The three of them had to go back to Kathmandu to teach at the school, but we decided to stay a little longer and do a retreat.

## The Khari Lama and Tramo Gompa

One day we were invited to visit the Khari Lama Lozang Tsultrim, the Tibetan lama who had built a new gompa at Tramo, below Lawudo. The lama looked very old and was wearing an old hat and old clothes that were not colorful or nice; extremely simple clothes that seemed to have been picked out of the garbage. At that time he was quite sick. Sometimes he would vomit large amounts of blood, but whenever he heard good Dharma news, he would get better. Then, when people thought he was cured, he would get sick again.

The Khari Lama was an unbelievable ascetic practitioner. In his youth he had joined Shelkar Chöde Monastery and had eventually been appointed manager. His job was to collect grain from the villages that belonged to the monastery, sell it, and make a profit for the monastery. He worked very hard, but he failed to make a success of it, and a great sense of renunciation arose in his mind. Realizing that life is impermanent and that there is nothing definite in cyclic existence, he gave up everything and went to receive teachings from a learned lama called Lingka Kangyur Rinpoche. After receiving from him all the essential teachings on sutra and tantra of the Gelug tradition, Lozang Tsultrim went into retreat in the

37. Khari Gompa, Tramo (Thubten Yeshe)

mountains in order to actualize the teachings. He performed many *bum* of the preliminary practices and spent many years practicing calm abiding, and in this way he actualized renunciation, bodhichitta, and an understanding of emptiness, and also developed clairvoyant powers. As his realizations increased, people began to flock to his cave to receive advice and guidance. Soon he became famous in that area, and the villagers of his hometown in Phadrug offered him the old Khari Monastery that had been abandoned many years before.[292]

In 1959, the Khari Lama escaped to Nepal with his monks and nuns.[293] They lived in tents at Kyabrog and Thangteng, where they were asked to perform rituals for the villagers. In this way, they never went without food.

After three years, the Khari Lama and his followers planned to settle at Dzarog, a small hamlet above Namche, but then a Sherpa woman offered them a large plot of land in Tramo. The lama foresaw that a monastery would be beneficial only if they were able to build it in three days, otherwise there would be many obstacles. So, in the tenth month of the water hare year (1963), they began to build the gompa. Although he was very old, the lama himself carried stones and helped in the construction process. They used the stones just as they were found, without breaking them, and in this way they managed to build the walls of the prayer hall and the lama's quarters in three days. The roof was built in the Tibetan-style with flat stones covered with earth and gravel. The building looked a little bit rough, but there was a very good and relaxed feeling there. After the gompa was completed, they built houses for the monks and nuns. Gelong Tsultrim Yeshe directed the work, and they managed to build one small, simple hut every day.

The Tramo monks and nuns were offered two fields in Tarnga and had to plant and collect the potatoes. After the potato harvest, they went to beg in the villages. They had to cut firewood in the forest and work for other people as coolies. Each person took care of his or her own food, and the community ate together only during ceremonies. The lama was very generous and shared all the offerings he received with his disciples, without keeping anything for himself. During those early years, they recited the *Twenty-One Praises to Tara* ten million times and read the Kangyur and Tengyur on many occasions. Although they did not study much, they did many practices, particularly the meditations of Vajrayogini. The tradition of the Khari Lama was to start rituals at three o'clock in the morning so that by sunrise the long Vajrayogini sadhana, the self-empowerment, and even the tsog offering had already been completed. While in Tibet, the lama, monks, and nuns used to do three sets of eight nyungnes every year and performed the chöd practice according to the lineage of Zagalung Rinpoche. Many of them engaged in a three-year retreat of Vajrayogini. The lama made the rule that every year at least half of the community should not eat meat.

The Khari Lama was very pleased to hear that we were planning to build a monastery and teach Dharma. He told me, "You should not have narrow mind and build a small monastery because of the expenses involved. You should have a very wide, strong mind and build it as large as possible. It will be very beneficial for the Dharma." At that time I did not think that I would be able to build a large monastery. Karma Tenzin and the villagers had suggested that I build a small gompa for about eight monks, and that had been my intention. But Lama Yeshe and I decided to follow the advice of the Khari Lama.

The lama also gave me some books, the *Lamrim Chenmo*[294] and some tantric scriptures, and asked me to take them to America. He said, "Either yourself or someone else should take those books to America. It doesn't matter where, as long as the books are in the country." I asked him to pray for the success of building the monastery and for other things, and he replied by quoting Lama Tsongkhapa, "If the mind is noble [pure, endowed with bodhichitta, opposite to evil] everything becomes noble and successful—the place, the path, everything. If the mind is evil, everything, all your enjoyments, become evil." He then mentioned, "I have only one year to live," and that proved to be true. He also predicted that both Zina and her friend from New Zealand would be able to realize emptiness in this life, but whether that became true, I cannot say.

When I met the Khari Lama, I was fully satisfied. I thought, "Now I can stay at Lawudo, and there is an incredible lama here from whom I can receive teachings and advice." I had great expectations, but in fact, I was not able to spend much time up there. I had to go to Kathmandu to raise funds and arrange things for building the gompa, and we were still living with Zina. Thus, I was not able to receive teachings from the Khari Lama because the next year he passed away. I was very disappointed.

After one month in Thangme, we decided to go back to Kathmandu to get some money and then fly back to Khumbu before the full-moon day of Saka Dawa, when the Lawudo Cave and the possessions of my predecessor were to be officially handed over to me. When we reached Lukla, the weather was very bad and the plane could not fly from Kathmandu, so Lama Yeshe decided to go back to Thangme. I was to fly to Kathmandu alone and return in a couple of weeks with building materials and enough money to fix the cave and rebuild the old kitchen.

## Saka Dawa

In Kathmandu, I told Max about our project of a monastery school at Lawudo. She was very enthusiastic and promised to take care of the children and provide funds for the building. She has always been extremely generous and kind to us. Zina had no money, but she offered enough to build a small structure for burning incense in front of the cave.

Ten days later I flew back to Lukla alone. We attended the Mani Rimdu and met the tulku of Lama Dondrub,[295] who was studying with Trulzhig Rinpoche and came to Thangme only for the Mani Rimdu and the Dumche. After the death of Lama Dondrub, his son Lama Ngodrub had taken over as the head of the Thangme Gompa, but it seems that the monks were not happy, and many of them had gone to Chiwang or Tengboche. Others gave back their vows and became businessmen or went trekking with the climbing expeditions.

After the Mani Rimdu, we moved to Lawudo. Lama and I stayed in the cave, and about ten of my relatives stayed in the old kitchen and in makeshift tents. Then, on the full-moon day of the Tibetan fourth month (Saturday, May 31, 1969), Karma Tenzin, Pemba Dekyi and her husband Pasang Namgyal, Au Palden, about twenty-five people from the Thangme area, and four or five Tengboche monks gathered at Lawudo. Karma Tenzin, Pemba Dekyi, her husband Pasang Namgyal—who was the son of the Thangme *gembu* (the headman)—and some of the elder villagers signed a document written in Nepali giving me the Lawudo Cave and houses, as well as the fields, books, and belongings of the previous Lawudo Lama. Karma Tenzin kept only the old house at Thangme Gompa and a few fields. Ashang Ngawang Yonten offered me his own potato fields and the wood from his old house in Mende.

The Sherpas had the custom of placing the surrounding land under the care and protection of the gompas and hermitages. In that way, they said, the trees and wild animals were protected because the lamas and hermits do not use much wood and do not kill animals. Thus, the Lawudo Hermitage was permitted to make use of the land from the cliffs in the east to the water spring in the west. We could collect dry firewood and build houses in that area, but had to prevent other people from doing so.

Following the tradition of my predecessor, I gave a long-life empowerment and teachings on *The Thirty-Seven Bodhisattva Practices,* using the commentary written by the Rongphu Sangye Ngawang Tenzin Norbu.[296] When giving empowerment it is customary to wear a hat, so I had borrowed the very blessed yellow hat of Serkong Dorje Chang. Then, when we offered tsog, Pasang Namgyal stood up, made three prostrations, touched his head to the altar, and requested me to perform the nyungne ritual at Lawudo in the following year. He pledged to sponsor the dinner of the first night. Other people stood up as well and offered to sponsor the meals and teas. I accepted

38. The Thangme Lama Ngawang Tsedub Tenpe Gyaltsen (left) and Lama Zopa Rinpoche at the Mani Rimdu, 1969 (courtesy of Pemba Butri, Lukla)

the request and gave them some tsog offerings in return. So, that is how we started to perform yearly nyungnes at Lawudo during Saka Dawa. (Later, thanks to the kindness of Lama Yeshe, the nyungne practice spread to our centers all over the world.) Then, at the conclusion of the ceremony, the villagers danced and sang auspicious songs in front of the cave.

One of the first things that was returned to me was a brass "pee pee" pot that the Lawudo Lama used to keep in the cave, and his sheepskin trousers. The pot was a nice, large container with a handle, and very useful. When I was building the monastery, I used it at night and even sometimes during the day because I was too lazy to go out. Lozang Nyima had to take it out and empty it.

Karma Tenzin gave me a small Tara statue that the Lawudo Lama had always carried with him. Her face and hands were worn and her left ring finger was broken. He told me that it was a very old Tibetan statue and that the finger had been broken by Langdarma, the ninth-century Tibetan king who had an ox horn on his head and had destroyed the Buddhist monasteries and objects of worship. I cannot say for sure whether that story is true, but the statue is certainly very blessed, and I always carry it with me. In 1979, while I was teaching in France and doing intensive Tara practice, I found that the spot on the table where the image was sitting was completely wet, even though there were no external conditions for that to happen.[297]

39. Lama Zopa and Lama Yeshe near Namche (courtesy of Lawudo Gompa)

## Rebuilding and Looking for Benefactors

Right after the full-moon day we started to rebuild the old kitchen, adding a second floor to it. Pasang Namgyal was in charge of the construction, helped by my two uncles Ngawang Trinle and Ngawang Yonten, my sister, the Tramo nuns, and the two Sherpa nuns from Genupa (Ani Phurbi and Ani Pema). Lama Yeshe used to carry stones on his back and went around collecting cow dung to spread in the potato fields as fertilizer. He seemed to enjoy himself very much. I was not strong and could not do physical work, but I helped to prepare the food: Amala would boil the potatoes and Lama and I would peel them to be used for making *rildog* (a kind of thick mashed potatoes).

During that time we did many rituals to pacify the local spirits by offering incense and *serkyem* or "golden drink" to the buddhas and Dharma protectors. Then, we began to make plans for the construction of a large gompa and decided to go to Namche to look for benefactors. On the way we went again to see the Khari Lama, and I requested the initiation of the Most Secret Hayagriva, the special deity of Sera Je College. I did not mention that we were going to Namche to raise funds for the gompa, but the lama told me, "You should not ask many people, but rely only on one person."

Lama and I spent one week in the house of Au Palden. Au Palden filled many wooden pots with chang to be offered to the people who would come to give us money (in Khumbu, chang is the most important thing; it is what makes Sherpas joke and laugh, the whole essence of life!), but not many people came. Finally, one rich man called Tenzin Tashi, who had been a monk in Tengboche, offered to sponsor the roof for the gompa (corrugated iron sheets that had to be brought from Kathmandu) and tea offerings for the monks for one year. He sent a box of tea bricks and one old Tibetan Buddha statue to Lawudo, but somehow he never gave the money for the roof. It seems that at the beginning, the Namche people were very interested in our project and had decided to send one boy from each family to become a monk at Lawudo, but when they heard that the gompa was to be Gelug instead of Nyingma, they changed their minds and were reluctant to sponsor it.

We went a few times to Namche. Wealthy Sherpa families have large shrine rooms with many statues, paintings, and texts. Even if they themselves cannot read, they like to have at least the twelve volumes of the *Perfection of Wisdom in One Hundred Thousand Verses* in the shrine room. Every morning they offer water bowls in front of these holy texts, and in the evening they offer butter lamps. They are extremely fortunate, because making offerings to the Perfection of Wisdom brings unbelievable merits.[298]

At Namche I gave long-life empowerments and teachings about karma, death and impermanence, and the suffering of the lower realms. Lama Yeshe and I used to come back to Lawudo carrying on our backs whatever offerings had been given to us—rice, potatoes, dried meat, tea bricks, and so forth.

Sometime in July we walked down to Kathmandu with Sangye, and my sister Ngawang Samten moved to Lawudo to take care of the place. During the next winter, Ashang Ngawang Yonten, helped by my mother and sister, rebuilt and enlarged the old house near the cave to provide accommodation for the monks. I had given specific instructions concerning the building. I wanted large windows with glass panels so that the sunlight could come inside, but my relatives had never seen a house like that and were unwilling to follow my advice. In the end they did as I had instructed, and the new house was very nice. Unfortunately, because the foundations had been laid in the winter when the ground was frozen, after some years the walls cracked and the house had to be rebuilt.

# 25. Building Lawudo Gompa

IT WAS NOW CLEAR that we were not going to Sri Lanka, and we began to look for a place to settle down. Lozang Nyima brought our belongings from India, and the three of us stayed for a while in Bouddha. Zina rented the house on Kopan Hill, and after a few months in Bouddha, we moved to Kopan. The house was full of Zina's friends—hippies taking drugs and playing music with guitars and so forth. We were given the smallest room, with enough space for only two beds and a very small table in between. Lozang Nyima had to sleep on the floor.

Actually, during the years that we were with Zina we really had to practice thought training. One evening she got very upset about something and threw the bamboo tray with bowls of thugpa all over us. We just laughed and cleaned everything up, and the next day she apologized. On another occasion I did not practice well. Zina had a dog called Ross that she had found in Bouddha. Zina would eat and read at the same time, while the dog licked her plate. One evening she sent us some bread and a little bit of peanut butter for dinner in a small rusted can, similar to the ones we used to relieve ourselves in at night. Ross came into our room at the same time, and I took the peanut butter and smeared it on the dog's face. Ross ran back into the kitchen and Zina got into a rage!

With the help of Max and other Westerners, we began to expand on the idea of the school at Lawudo. We decided to call it Mount Everest Center for Buddhist Studies and organize it like a monastic school where the boys could learn Buddhist philosophy and at the same time study English, Nepali, art, and other subjects. I made a brochure to raise money for the project. A Dutchman called Matti de Wijs, who used to take us in his Land Rover for picnics and visits to the holy places of the Kathmandu Valley, became very interested in the Lawudo project and helped to raise money for the school.

## *My Walk from Rumjatar to Lawudo*

In the spring of 1970, Lozang Nyima flew to Jiri with building materials and organized porters to bring everything to Lawudo, and a couple of months later I went up to Lawudo on my own. At that time we were staying in a nice house that Max had rented in Tinchuli, north of Bouddha, with a geshe from Sera called Geshe Tashi. Max gave me 10,000 rupees to take to Lawudo, which in those days was a substantial amount of money, and Geshe Tashi's attendant, Nyima Dondrub, made a money belt for me out of very cheap green cloth. I was to wear it tied around my chest and pretend it was something I had to wear to keep my body in good health.

The monsoon rains had already arrived and planes could not land at Lukla, so I flew to Rumjatar in the Okhaldhunga district of eastern Nepal. When we landed at the tiny airfield surrounded by very high cliffs, I went to look for a teahouse and a porter. Actually, I was a little scared because I was carrying a large amount of money with me and the people of that area are quite rough. The weather was extremely hot and I started to sweat, and soon the green dye from the money purse spread all over my body and clothes. It was heavy, too, so after a while I took it out and carried it in my hand. Later I put it on the porter's load.

While I was walking alone on the road, I kept on checking my motivation and praying that every single atom of the stones used to build the Lawudo Gompa would benefit sentient beings.

The first night we slept in the house of an old woman, and during the night people kept coming in to drink chang. I was afraid that someone would steal the money, so I put the purse inside a nice box made of banana leaves that Max had given me, and used it for pillow. Then I tied a thread to the box and wrapped it around my finger. I also kept a flashlight nearby, but nothing untoward happened.

The next day we arrived at Jasa. I knew that my eldest *ashang* Pasang Dorje was working in the carpet factory at the Tibetan refugee settlement in nearby Salleri, but I did not find him. I had breakfast in a Tibetan restaurant, and one woman called Aja Metog, who knew me from Buxa, invited me to her house and found a Tibetan coolie for me, a man called Dorje. Dorje and I went on our way and stopped for lunch near a huge boulder. I was quite hungry, but I only had some cheese, so I gave a piece of my cheese to Dorje, and he gave me a piece of bread he had brought from his home. Normally I would not have accepted his food because his body and clothes were extremely dirty; around his neck he wore a piece of rock salt and a chili completely black with dirt.

The next day we met a Sherpa family who asked me to make a divination for them and offered me some corn in return. That evening we came to a place where there were only two houses. The family had gone to attend a funeral, and there was only a young girl in the house. We asked her to give us rice, but she refused. We asked for potatoes, and she again refused, so Dorje took out the corn that I had been offered, washed and roasted it, and went to the mill to grind it. By then it was already dark. Then he made a small bread with the corn flour, put a little bit of butter on top, and gave it to me.

When we finally arrived at Lawudo, we found that everyone had gone to Thangme. I had to spend the night in Mende at the house of Au Summi, a man from Thangteng, who treated me very kindly. I had no blanket or sleeping bag and it was quite cold, so I had to cover myself with his chuba. Summi was very kind to me. He gave me tea, butter, and cheese and tried to make me feel as comfortable as possible until my relatives came back.

## Building Activities

My sister and uncle had fixed the cave during the winter, and now it had a nice new door and a large window. Lozang Nyima and I slept in the cave, my relatives in the kitchen, and the workers in the new house next to the cave. My sister did the cooking, and Wangyal, my dumb childhood friend, carried water from the spring. My mother stayed in Thangme taking care of the fields and the house and sometimes came to Lawudo to help with whatever was needed.

Since Sherpas need to drink chang and arak all the time, my mother and sister began to make it at Lawudo. I did not want alcoholic drinks at Lawudo, but there was nothing I could do about it; the workers would not come unless they got plenty of chang and arak.

We began to fell trees and flatten the land for building the gompa. My uncles and Lozang Nyima organized the building activities while Pasang Namgyal broke stones. Pemba Dekyi and the nuns carried the stones and dug the earth. Karma Tenzin also came a few times to Lawudo and brought his eldest son Sangye Yeshe to become a monk. He helped and worked like an ordinary coolie, and sometimes we performed rituals together in the cave. Every morning I offered serkyem to the buddhas and local protectors because we had to cut many trees and bushes and dig the earth, and many small creatures were killed in the process. Besides, such activities disturb the local protectors, nagas, and spirits that live in the area, and before undertaking any construction work it is necessary to ask permission and give them some offerings so that they do not cause trouble.

My job was to check whether the workers were cutting stones and working or just wasting time chatting. Instead, I spent most of the time inside the cave reading texts. Compared to what I do now, at that time I was able to do a lot of things, but what I could not do was to read texts and watch the workers at the same time. Only when I went out to the toilet could I see what they were doing. Most of the time they were just sitting there, laughing and joking instead of working, but I found it difficult to tell them anything. Probably Lama Yeshe would have been able to reprimand them, but to me that seemed a strange thing to do. In the evenings before sunset I went out to pay the wages, even though I knew that some people did not actually do a full day's work. I also felt uncomfortable doing that because I was used to receiving money from others as an offering rather than giving it myself.

During that summer I had to do everything myself—I was the secretary, treasurer, bookkeeper, everything! I kept the money in a small plastic suitcase, and as I paid the workers each day, the pile of money would go down, down, down. Then, when the pile was almost gone, somebody would appear with offerings, and the pile would start to go up again. I never learned mathematics at school, so I had to learn at Lawudo while paying the wages. We were paying three rupees to the common workers if we gave them food, and six rupees if they ate their own. The stone cutters got twelve rupees and the carpenters seven. Slowly, I learned to calculate how much money we had to spend and how much was left. I would then divide that amount according to the new things that had to be bought.

In addition to the building, I also had to organize the school. I sent Lozang Nyima with two Sherpas to the main villages—Thangme, Tramo, Khumde, Khumjung, and Namche—to explain what we were planning to do and take the names of boys who wanted to join the school. The children were to be given room, food, clothing, medicine, and school materials. The parents were expected to pay fifty rupees a month or the equivalent in foodstuffs, and provide the child with his first set of monastic robes.

During that summer I checked all the texts of the previous Lawudo Lama. Apart from a set of the *Rinchen Terdzö* and a few other volumes, most of the texts were written by hand. In the past it was difficult to obtain printed copies, and it seems that the Lawudo Lama had put great effort into copying scriptures. There were practices of different deities, commentaries, and teachings from the Nyingma and Kagyu schools, but I found a text that contains the fundamental practice for all four schools of Tibetan Buddhism. It is called *Opening the Door of Dharma, Training the Mind at the Very Beginning*,[299] and is a collection of instructions from Kadampa geshes on how to practice Dharma, written from their own experience. The text combines their life stories and their advice about how to differentiate what is holy Dharma and what is worldly Dharma, what we should practice and what we should abandon.

I read this text from beginning to end, and it was only after reading it that I came to understand what Dharma really means. Before, even though I memorized and recited scriptures and performed rituals, I did not really know the meaning of Dharma. But at that time, when I looked back at my life, I could not find anything that had been Dharma practice. I clearly saw that since the mind does not exist independently but depends upon causes and conditions, it can become either good or bad. Thus, if one practices, one can attain realizations. Even if one has just a small experience of one's mind having changed into good, that itself is logical proof that enlightenment is possible. In short, I understood that it is possible to attain realizations, and that having realizations had not been my experience.

As I was reading that text, I became afraid of accepting offerings. Many Sherpas and Tibetans would come to Lawudo and offer me tins of potatoes or brass containers filled with corn, rice, or barley, with a few rupees and an old khatag on top. They had great faith in me, but I knew that I had no realizations and I could not really benefit them, and also that by accepting their offerings I was receiving some kind of pollution. Geshe Rabten had once explained that anything offered with devotion carries mental pollution because of the responsibility on the part of the recipient to benefit the donor. Mental pollution is like poison and is a great obstacle for developing the mind and receiving realizations.

Another text I found was the *Mani Kabum*, which was composed by the Tibetan king Songtsen Gampo. In that text I found a short explanation about the lineage and the benefits of constructing and turning prayer wheels. It seems that the practice, which is related to Chenrezig, originated with Nagarjuna. Later, Guru Rinpoche brought the teaching to Tibet. In Khumbu and Tibet all the elderly people have prayer wheels; when they sit at home or walk around, they hold a rosary in their left hand

and turn a small prayer wheel with their right hand while reciting mantras. Many houses have small prayer wheels next to the beds or at the entrance, so that when people go in or out, they can turn them and accumulate merit. Next to the temples it is customary to build at least one large prayer wheel containing many millions of mantras. Large prayer wheels have a metal stick attached at the top. Every time the wheel turns, the stick strikes a small bell that hangs from the ceiling, making a very nice sound, the "sound of emptiness."

Since real Dharma practice means training the mind, I used to wonder how turning a prayer wheel becomes Dharma practice. I did not have much faith in it, but after reading the *Mani Kabum,* I realized that this practice has valid references and is very meaningful. Just touching and turning a prayer wheel purifies negative karmas and brings unbelievable merit. I wanted to build a large prayer wheel at Lawudo, but it was only many years later in 2000 that it could be constructed.[300]

Just as he had foretold the previous year, the Khari Lama passed away during the winter. Although he was quite sick, just before his death he seemed to be feeling better. One day, when they were about to perform a long ceremony, the lama ordered that everyone should attend. Then, that night, he called his closest disciples and gave them instructions on how to run the monastery. They had been able to collect some money offered by the villagers and were using it for the special rituals on the tenth and twenty-fifth of the Tibetan month, but the lama told them, "Do not keep that money. Use it right away; otherwise, it will become the cause of fighting and problems." He spent many hours talking to them and giving them advice, and then he asked his two attendants to fill his bowl with good tea and to leave him alone. He passed away at around five o'clock in the morning, sitting in meditation. He stayed seven days in thugdam, the meditation on the clear light of death. The cremation took place next to the gompa, and when the disciples opened the purkhang a week later, they found two small footprints and the mantra of Vajrayogini drawn with red powder. The bones and ashes were also red colored. This happened because the Khari Lama had done extensive practice of Vajrayogini, who is visualized as red in color. Afterward, 100,000 clay images of Vajrayogini were made with the lama's ashes and enshrined in a chörten. Those that did not fit inside were thrown into the river to benefit beings living in the water.

After the Khari Lama's death, Gen Lama Tenzin Tsultrim, a very learned Sakya lama from Kham, became the abbot of Tramo Gompa.

After the Chinese takeover of Tibet, he had escaped to Drakar Taso and pretended to be a simple man so that the Chinese would not bother him. But after a while people began to ask his advice, and the Chinese became suspicious. He had to hide in a very secret cave that only one person knew. The cave was very damp, and the lama's legs eventually became extremely painful. After eight months, the Chinese suspected his presence in the area, and again he was forced to escape. His benefactor had to carry him on his back because he could not even walk, but they managed to reach Khumbu safely, and Gen Lama settled in Tramo. Although he had studied in monasteries of the Sakya school, he also practiced the Gelug and Nyingma traditions and was highly respected.[301]

After two months or so I went down to Kathmandu, leaving Lozang Nyima at Lawudo to supervise the work. In October I flew back with David, an American Peace Corps volunteer who knew about building and was going to check the foundations of the gompa. David made some calculations, put a stick on the ground, and said that it was very important not to move the stick, but I never understood why. He also checked the mountain for underground water but could not find any.

At the end of November we came back down to Kathmandu with Lozang Nyima. Soon after, Max was ordained as a nun by Geshe Rabten in Dharamsala together with her Canadian friend Ann McNeil, Sylvia White, and an American called James.

## 26. I Become a Teacher

*The Kopan Meditation Courses*

AT THE BEGINNING OF JANUARY 1971, we went to Bodh Gaya with Zina to receive the Yamantaka empowerment and commentary from Kyabje Ling Rinpoche. On that occasion, I received the vows of a fully ordained monk from Ling Rinpoche.

The famous Indian master Goenka was giving a *vipassana* meditation course in Bodh Gaya at the Burmese Vihar, and a zen master called Zengo was leading another course. Lama Yeshe and I went with Zina to attend one session with the zen master. He was guiding the meditation, but I could not understand what he meant. I could not see any difference between that type of meditation and dark, unconscious sleep without any awareness of the objects of mind.

Zina was very enthusiastic about the courses and wanted Lama Yeshe to teach a meditation course at Kopan, but Lama flatly refused. His point was that the monks in Sera Monastery, even though they spend their whole time thinking about the path and studying, all of which is actually meditation, do not normally call that "meditation." It is only after taking tantric empowerments that they do retreats and formal meditations. Zina insisted very much, but Lama refused. I had a very strong wish to teach, but Zina did not even consider asking me. Finally, when she was convinced that Lama Yeshe would not teach a course, she turned to me and asked whether I would like to do it. I asked Lama Yeshe for advice, and he replied, "Well, if you think that you can do it and that it would be beneficial, then you do." So, I happily accepted to teach.

The First Kopan Meditation Course took place in March 1971 and lasted for about ten days, with fifteen people attending. There was no room in Kopan for everyone to stay, and some Westerners had to stay in the two houses of Ram, a Nepali man who lived nearby. The two new nuns, Ann and Sylvia, helped with the course. We prepared about two or three written pages so that the students would have something to study.

Together with Sylvia I translated a few lines about the main topics of the lamrim, such as the perfect human rebirth, suffering, karma, and so forth. The explanation about the sufferings of the lower realms—animals, pretas, and hell beings—was the longest part. I stopped after describing the suffering of humans and also included a short "equilibrium meditation" to develop equanimity.[302]

40. Lama Zopa Rinpoche in Kopan (Ursula Bernis)

When I taught about bodhichitta, I used the text of Kachen Yeshe Gyaltsen that Ang Nyima had given me a couple of years before. That text was my main source of inspiration. Probably due to the blessings of that great lama, everyone, including Zina, liked the teachings very much. But deep in my heart I believe that whatever I taught that benefited others was, in fact, coming from Lama Yeshe.

## Lawudo Gompa

Right after the course, I flew alone to Lukla. Ann was to spend the summer at Lawudo and help me with bookkeeping, but she trekked all the way up with Lozang Nyima, who organized the coolies to carry glass for the windows, other building materials, and food supplies. We had discovered that the food in Khumbu was at least three times more expensive than in the Kathmandu Valley. Since 1965 there had been Saturday market at Namche, where the Limbus and Rais from the lower valleys, about three or four days' walk from Namche, brought rice, sugar, barley, wheat, corn, millet, milk powder, eggs, chilies, and other goods. The Sherpas from Solu and Pharag sold butter, erma, beans, and bamboo mats. Now the Khumbu people did not have to walk to distant towns to buy food, but it was expensive.

41. Lama Zopa Rinpoche at Lawudo. The old man with white beard holding a rosary is Ang Phurba, who died at age 103. At the right is Gelong Tsultrim Yeshe of Tramo Gompa (Ueli Minder)

I attended the Mani Rimdu at Thangme Gompa and stayed at Ashang Ngawang Yonten's house. Ann and Joseph, a hairdresser from New York, stayed one night at my mother's house in Thangme and enjoyed a long, sleepless night thanks to the fleas, which in Khumbu are very large and lively, particularly during the summer months.

During Saka Dawa we did three nyungnes at Lawudo, one in the kitchen upstairs and two in the new house. The Tramo nuns, who are real experts in nyungne, led the ritual. Some Thangme monks wanted to attend, but the nyungne coincided with the Mani Rimdu at Thangme Gompa and they had no time. Some old disciples of the previous Lawudo Lama came to do the nyungne. One of them, Ang Phurba from Kyabrog, had recited the *Diamond Cutter Sutra* every day of his adult life. He died a few years later at the age of 103.

The day after the last nyungne I gave a long-life empowerment and explained the purpose of the school. We had typed a couple of pages in English explaining the conditions of the school, and the parents had to sign or put their thumbprint on it; that was the registration. During that summer we already had about ten boys at Lawudo, the oldest being Ngawang Namgyal (the eighteen-year-old brother of my friend Ngawang Nyandrag) and Ngawang Khenzin. One of the boys was the nephew of Wangyal, the water carrier. When his father Kami Tenpa began to talk about "offering" him to me, the boy became very upset and told his father, "What are you talking about offering me to the Lawudo Lama? I am not a bag of potatoes!"

42. Lama Zopa and Nepali government officials at Lawudo Gompa
(courtesy of Lawudo Gompa)

Some of the children were quite small, and my sister was like a mother to them, consoling them when they cried and cleaning up when they wet their beds. She had a lot of work and used to complain to Ann, using the few words of English she had learned from the Westerners: "Me much tired! Lawudo, difficult!" Ngawang Samten was very good at cooking and shopping in the market on Saturdays, and she also organized the making of tsampa with the help of the Tramo and Genupa nuns. First, the barley had to be bought in the market and cleaned and dried in the sun. It was then roasted on hot sand, sifted to get the sand out, and then taken to Tesho at the foot of the mountain, where the Tibetan family in charge of the water mill would do the grinding. Finally, a few days later the tsampa would be carried up to Lawudo. (Now, most Thangme villagers buy tsampa from the Dingri Tibetans who come through the Nangpa La to sell all kinds of goods in Khumbu).

The very first thing I taught the little monks was how to make prostrations while reciting the prayer known as *Common Confession (Thunshag)*, or the *Sutra of the Three Heaps*, which contains the names of the thirty-five buddhas. I gave teachings on emptiness to the Westerners who were at Lawudo, but my English was not good enough, and they probably did not understand much of what I said. I also tried to inspire them to make prostrations, but they did not really like the practice. Only Ann was very enthusiastic and tried to make prostrations as quickly as me. In any case, the Westerners seemed to enjoy Lawudo very much.

Every couple of days, my mother would come from Thangme to bring me curd because she knew that it was good for my health. She would stay for just a short time in Lawudo and then walk back to Thangme. The Westerners were amazed that she would walk three hours up and down the mountain just to bring me food.

The monks memorized prayers and helped with small tasks. They used to sit in the mountainside below the cave and recite prayers at the top of their voices, so that even the people working in the fields at Mende could hear them. Merely by hearing the Lawudo monks reciting while she was digging potatoes, the daughter of Au Palden learned by heart the prayer that says,

| | |
|---|---|
| *Pal den tsa wai lama rin po che* | (Precious, magnificent root guru, |
| *Dag gi chi wor peme den shug la* | Please sit on the lotus at the crown of my head. |
| *Ka drin chen po go ne je zung te* | Take care of me with your great kindness and |
| *Ku sung tug ki ngo drub tsel du sol* | Bestow on me the attainments of your holy body, speech, and mind.) |

During that spring I had an inauspicious dream about a particular place where some kind of spirit or life-threatening energy abided. In order to counteract it, I did the Yamantaka sadhana and *Drugchuma*[303] every evening and invited Ann to join in, even though she could not read Tibetan.

Ann helped me to keep track of the expenses. Lozang Nyima and Ashang Trinle would tell her how many hours each person had worked and how much their wages were, and then Ann would write everything down and then help me to count out the correct amount.

Now that the foundation and walls of the gompa had been built, the most important thing was to get wood for the pillars and beams and for making the doors, windows, and so forth. In order to apply for permission from the Nepali government to cut trees, Lozang Nyima and Ashang Trinle went to Salleri, the district office in Solu, about four or five days' walk from Lawudo. The larger trees that could not be found in Khumbu had to be brought from Pharag. Lozang Nyima supervised the felling and sawing of the trees by Nepali woodcutters and found porters to bring them up to Lawudo. After paying for the wood, our funds were finished, and I had to send Lozang Nyima down to Kathmandu to get more money from Max. He worked really hard and had a difficult time walking up and down the slippery, leech-infested mountain trails.

After obtaining the wood, we needed carpenters, but good carpenters were in great demand and were asking high wages. Lozang Nyima and Ashang Trinle went to Pharag to request Kunzang Legshe, a well-known carpenter from Pemkar, to please come to Lawudo. Kunzang Legshe used to come up to Lawudo, work for five or six days, and then go back to his home, promising to return the next day. After a few days, Lozang Nyima had to walk again to Pemkar and very sweetly and nicely request Kunzang Legshe to please come back to Lawudo to finish the job. When he would finally agree, he walked up looking like a very important person, with Lozang Nyima behind carrying the carpenter's wooden box with his tools.

Two more carpenters were hired, Sonam Tobgyal and a man from Kyabrog. Sonam Tobgyal had worked on at least seven Tibetan monasteries and was considered to be the best carpenter in Khumbu. I asked him to make a throne and a table with some elaborate carvings for His Holiness the Dalai Lama. We were not expecting His Holiness to ever come to Lawudo, but that is the custom in Tibetan monasteries; it creates a good connection between the monastery and His Holiness.

The carpenters had to be continuously served tea and chang, and they ate four meals a day. In the morning they had either tsampa or *kyu*—a kind of porridge with millet, tsampa, and dried cheese. Around twelve, they had a big lunch of rice and potatoes, or sen, or potato pancakes. At three or four in the afternoon, they were served boiled potatoes or sen, and in the evening they had shagpa. I think the carpenters were one of the greatest expenses we ever had.

In the kitchen, Lozang Nyima built a very nice hearth with stones and mud instead of the open, Sherpa-style fireplace, and he would joke about how primitive the Sherpas were. But he could not manage to build a chimney, and the smoke still had to go out through a small hole in the wall, Sherpa style. Ann was sleeping above the kitchen, and as soon as the fire was lit at six o'clock in the morning, she had to come down to avoid getting "smoked out."

I gave Ann a warm red woolen chuba and a hat, and she looked like a Sherpa nun. She made herself useful by helping my mother and sister in the kitchen, volunteering to wash the cooking pots, and she became quite proficient at scrubbing the soot off with juniper branches. Whenever she went to wash clothes at the spring in Genupa, she offered to wash my mother's and sister's shirts. Their clothes were full of lice, and Ann was not sure how to save the lives of the tiny creatures and to wash the clothes clean at the same time. I guess she would pick off as many as she could and then recite mani to benefit those who went to their next rebirth.

Ann tried hard to learn the local customs. She was always very careful to respect the sitting arrangements in the kitchen and tried to keep the texts in a high place. One day, however, she placed a Tibetan text on the wooden stairs thinking that it was a safe place to keep it from being trampled on, but everyone in the kitchen became upset because texts should not be put on places where one walks or sits.

Because of the construction, Lawudo was always full of people. The kitchen had a door right next to the cave, and I could hear people talking and all the noise they were making. Sometimes I would go to meditate alone on the mountain, but then I would forget about the time. When I did not come back before dark, my sister would become very worried and had to search for me all over the mountain, calling loudly, "Rinpoche, where are you?" until she found me.

Ann also wanted to find a spot or a cave where she could sit to read and meditate during the day. Once we went together to the mountain above Charog to check a water spring and the possibility of piping the water to Lawudo, since we always had a water shortage. On the way back we passed a large boulder standing alone in the middle of the mountain slope, not too far from Lawudo. That night Ann dreamed that there was a cave beneath that boulder. The next day she went up to have a look, and she found that there was indeed a very nice, large cave inside. She was extremely happy, and from that day onward she would spend many hours there. Acording to my mother, when Padmasambhava was staying in that cave, a female demon began to throw rocks at him. Padmasambhava made a hole on the upper part of the cave and flew out from there toward the top of the mountain.

Actually, there are many interesting stories about Lawudo and the surrounding area. Below Lawudo there is a small boulder with a triangular mark on it, which, according to my mother, was made by Padmasambhava with his phurba, or ritual dagger. Above Lawudo is a large cliff known as the Dragkarma, or the White Cliff, which some people say is the entrance to the secret Beyul Khumbu. It seems that a few years back, Sonam Puntsog, the nephew of Gelong Pasang from Rolwaling, went up there with two Tibetan refugees from Gaba in Kham. When they reached the Dragkarma, one of the men went into a trance. Speaking through him, the local goddess said that Guru Rinpoche had hidden many termas in the Dragkarma and the Lawudo Cave.[304] Later, Sonam Puntsog carved the three syllables *Om Ah Hum* on the Dragkarma.

Another special place in that mountain is a large boulder, quite a long way up the mountain above Charog, known as Shongmi Do or Mandalphung, because it looks like Mount Meru in the center of the mandala or the universe. Some locals say that it also contains termas.

Karma Tenzin came a few times and helped with the construction for a while. Although there had been some initial reluctance on his part to give me the possessions of the Lawudo Lama, Karma Tenzin was devoted to me and requested Diu Rinpoche, who was at that time in Kyabrog Gompa giving the empowerments of the *Unobstructed Primordial Mind,* to write a prayer for my long life. He offered me the prayer and taught the monks how to chant it with a very melodious tune. His son Sangye Yeshe spent a few months at Lawudo, but Karma Tenzin wanted him to study the Nyingma tradition and took him to Mindroling Monastery in India.

Sometime in August I decided to organize a picnic, taking advantage of a few days of good weather. A Japanese company was building a large hotel in the forest near Khumjung on a spot where there is a very good view of Mount Everest. It was called Everest View Hotel, and it was to become a luxury hotel for rich tourists. The Sherpas were not happy about it because the water for the hotel had to be brought from Khumjung, where the water supply was not sufficient even for the village. A few days earlier we had received a message from Max saying that she was sending 6,000 rupees

# VISUAL JOURNEY

57. Khenpalung: view from the Tsechu Cave
(Gary McCue)

58. Maratika Cave
(courtesy of Lopon Karma Wangchug)

59. Rolwaling: the Phurbi Drubkhang (T. Jinpa Sherpa)

60. Rongphu: Do-ngag Zungjug Ling Monastery; Jomo Langma (Everest) in the background (Gary McCue)

62. Pangboche Gompa

61. Lama Sangwa Dorje
(painting by Nyima Dorje Sherpa)

63. Thangme Gompa

64. Rimejung Gompa

65. Lukla Gompa

66. Chörten at Namche

67. Guru Rinpoche, Guru Dragpo, and Sengdongma; stone carved by the Charog Lama Ngawang Trinle Lhundrub at Zamte

68. Shrine of the local protector and prayer flags above Lama Dorje's house at Yulnying

70. Way to Thangme Gompa

69. Shrine of the Khumbilha above Namche

71. Statue of Chatang Chöying Rangdrol at Genupa

73. Genupa: Lama Zangpo in Ngodrub Chöling Palgyi Drubkhang

72. Charog: Tashi Nyi-öd Kyilba Hermitage

75. Tengboche Monastery (F. Klatzel)

74. Shrine room of the Tragtho family in Namche

76. Namche: the Kangyur Lhakhang

77. Mende

78. Gangtega (left) and Tamserku peaks

79. The Lawudo Cave

80. Statues of Guru Rinpoche, Mandarava, and Yeshe Tsogyal in the Lawudo Cave (F. Howland)

81. View from the top of the Lawudo cave

82. Karma Tenzin (courtesy of his son Sangye Yeshe)

83. Pemba Dekyi

84. Dargye and his wife

85. Manuscript illustrated by the Lawudo Lama Kunzang Yeshe

87. The postures of the Three Bodies. Manuscript of the *Ati Zabdon Nyingpo* from the Lawudo Lama collection

86. Ngawang Nyandrag holding the old lotus hat of the Lawudo Lama

88. Tamserku and Gangtega at dawn

89. Copper and silver chörten containing the relics of the Lawudo Lama

90. Purkhang of the Lawudo Lama

91. Ruins of Lama Kunzang Yeshe's house at Thangme Gompa

93. Trulzhig Rinpoche Ngawang Chökyi Lodro (courtesy of *Mandala* magazine)

92. View of Thangme from the Sumdur Mountain; Zamte down the valley

94. Carved stone near Thangme Gompa

95. Beding village and chörten; Tseringma in the background (T. Weir)

96. Urgyen
Shugtri;
Umdze
Pemba in
the fore-
ground
(T. Weir)

97. Gelong
Pasang
(Janice
Sacherer)

99. Ani Ngawang Samten of
Thangme Gompa

98. Ang
Gyaltsen
(Lama Zopa
Rinpoche)
with Aku
Ngawang
Legshe
(T. Weir)

100. Thubten
Zopa Rinpoche
and the Gyuto
monk Kalzang
Tsering in
Phag-ri (cour-
tesy of *Mandala*
magazine)

101. Geshe Rabten and Lama Thubten Yeshe
(courtesy of Kopan Gompa)

102. Lama Yeshe, Chip, and Lama Zopa on the terrace of Max's house in Kathmandu (courtesy of Chip Cobalt)

104. The Khari Lama Lozang Tsultrim (courtesy of Venerable Thubten Sherab)

103. The first visit to Lawudo. First row from left: Lama Yeshe, Chip, Lama Zopa, Zina, Ashang Tinle. Second row: a lady and a nun from Genupa, Lama Ngawang Zopa of Genupa, and Jacqueline Fagan (courtesy of Chip Cobalt)

105. Diu Rinpoche Dela Longchen Yeshe Dorje (courtesy of Kusho Yonten-la)

106. Rehearsal of the Mani Rimdu dances

107. Au Palden

108. Gomchen Gampa-la (Thubten Yeshe)

109. Lama Zopa and Ann McNeil, 1971
(Ani Thubten Pemo)

110. Trulzhig Rinpoche and Zina in Thubten Chöling
(courtesy of *Mandala* magazine)

111. Gen Tashi, Ron Brooks,
and Lama Zopa with two
young monks above
Lawudo, 1972 (Massimo
Corona)

112. Lawudo monks debating in Namche, Dalai Lama's birthday (M. Corona)

113. Ashang Ngawang Yonten in front of the Lawudo kitchen

114. Statue of Jetsun Milarepa in Pelgyeling Gompa

116. Ordination in Bodh Gaya, 1974: Amala (Thubten Zangmo) in the foreground. Second row: Thubten Thardo and Thubten Pemo. Third row: Thubten Pende, Thubten Wangmo, and Thubten Donyo. Behind: Thubten Palgye, Lama Zopa, Thubten Chökyi, Jampa Konchog "Yogi," Thubten Chösang, and Thubten Chödron (courtesy of Nick Ribush)

115. Group photo, second Kopan course. Sitting in the center is Gen Tashi, with Ann sitting at the left. Standing from left are P. Kedge, M. Corona, J. Zangpo, Gen Wangyal, Age del Banco, Ron Brooks, Lozang Nyima, Lolly Smith, Liselotte Kolb, Chris Kolb, and Lama Zopa's cousin Pema (Carol Corona)

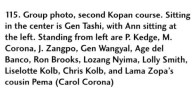

117. Preparing for fire offering ceremony at Lawudo, 1976
(Cuban Camilla)

118. Kusho Mangde (courtesy of Lama Ngawang Tsultrim)

119. The Lawudo Gompa

120. Lama Zopa in the Lawudo Gompa
(courtesy of Kopan Gompa)

121. Sherpas at Lawudo (Roger Kunsang)

122. Amala and Ngawang Samten

123. Lama Zopa, Kusho Mangde, and Lama Yeshe at Lawudo, 1981 (Trisha Donnelly)

125. Chörten at Samshing in memory of Amala

124. From left: Sangye, his friends Mrs. and Mr. Hammond (England), Tsultrim Norbu, Amala, and Jean Marie Tampi, 1990 (courtesy of Sangye Sherpa)

127. Ngawang Samten and Ngawang Jigme (courtesy of Ani Ngawang Samten)

126. Lawudo nyungne, 1992; Gen Lama Tenzin Tsultrim sitting under the ceremonial umbrella

128. Chörten in memory of Ngawang Jigme

129. Dzatul Ngawang Rigzin Kunzang Chökyi Gyaltsen (courtesy of Kulnarsingh Shakya, Subash Printing Press, Patan)

130. Khumtul Ngawang Tenzin Jigdral Wangchug Chökyi Gyaltsen (courtesy of Khumtul Rinpoche)

131. Kusho Tulku Ngawang Lozang Yonten Gyatso (courtesy of Kusho Tulku)

132. Tenzin Ösel Rinpoche, the tulku of Lama Thubten Yeshe

133. Ngawang Jangchub Rigzin, the tulku of Diu Rinpoche (courtesy of Kusho Yonten-la)

134. Ngawang Rigzin Tenpa, the tulku of Gomchen Gampa-la

135. Tenzin Chögyal, the tulku of Ngawang Chöphel Gyatso (courtesy of Lopon Karma Wangchug)

136. Lama Zopa Rinpoche with Charog Lama Ngawang Rigzin Tenzin Gyatso, the tulku of Kusho Mangde (Roger Kunsang)

with someone to the Japanese hotel, so I took everyone there and chose a nearby spot for the picnic. Suddenly, I recognized the place as the one I had seen in my previous, inauspicious dream. Anyway, we had lunch there, and the boys played around and enjoyed themselves. Ann and I went to the hotel to ask the manager about the money, and he was extremely surprised to see us because the money had arrived less than an hour before.

A day or so later, I fell sick. I was sure I was going to die, but at the beginning no one would take me seriously. Ann would come in the morning to the cave and jokingly say, "So, you are still alive!" But I could feel that the energies in my body were completely out of balance and changing, and I really thought I was going through the death process. After a few days, when everyone saw that I was getting worse, they became very worried about me, and my two uncles went to get medicine from Gomchen Gampa-la,[305] a Tibetan lama who was staying in the Akar Hermitage above Khumjung. Gomchen-la was well known for his medicines and healing powers. When people took his medicine against poison, they would excrete snakes, frogs, and scorpions. After Gomchen-la passed away, nobody in Khumbu could help those who had been poisoned. Once they sent a person who had been poisoned to Khumde Hospital, but the Western doctors could not do anything and the man died. When they performed the autopsy, a large, live frog jumped out of his stomach. They cut the frog open and it was empty inside.

I told Ann to go to Namche and send a message to Lama Yeshe and Max with my last wishes, and with the request that they send a helicopter immediately. Ann ran down the mountain really worried and praying all the time to White Tara, a long-life deity. It was Saturday, and Namche was full of people. Finally, she found the police station and asked that an urgent message be sent by radio to Kathmandu. The policemen were sympathetic, but they told her that the radio was broken and that she would have to go either to Lukla or to Everest Base Camp to send the message. Ann was desperate, but then she decided to try to get help at Khumde Hospital. So, she went all the way to Khumde and told the whole story to the New Zealand doctors in charge. The next day the doctor came to Lawudo and said that I had the mumps, which can be dangerous for adults. The little monks had contracted the mumps a few weeks before but had recovered very quickly. The doctor gave me some medicine, and after a few days I got better.

Ann left at the beginning of September, and I waited for Lama Yeshe to come and close the school at the end of the month. Most of the monks returned to their homes for the winter because there was nobody to teach them. The walls of the gompa were complete, but there was still a lot of work to be done. During the winter and spring, my relatives, Pasang Namgyal, Wangyal, and two young monks—Thubten Ngodrub and Thubten Monlam—continued with the building.

43. Serkong Tsenshab Rinpoche (left) and Serkong Dorje Chang
(courtesy of Lama Yeshe Wisdom Archives)

Zina went for a few months to Thubten Chöling, the monastery of Trulzhig Rinpoche, to build a small retreat house and to make preparations for a long retreat. Ann then moved to Kopan to take care of us. By this time we had been able to buy a large part of the hill and were planning to build a monastery there. Our idea was to bring the Lawudo monks to Kopan for the winter, so that they could continue their studies all year round. In January or February of 1972, a group of monks from the Upper Tantric College came to Nepal to take part in the re-consecration of the Bouddha Stupa,[306] and Lama Yeshe invited them to Kopan to bless the land.

## Serkong Tsenshab Rinpoche

Serkong Rinpoche, the *tsenshab,* or debate master, of His Holiness the Dalai Lama, used to come often to Nepal. Serkong Rinpoche had been recognized as the reincarnation of Dharma Dode, the son of Milarepa's teacher Marpa. In this life he was the son of the previous Serkong Dorje Chang, Ngawang Tsultrim Donden, the embodiment of Marpa.[307] When

Serkong Rinpoche and the tulku of his father were trying to escape from Tibet, the Chinese were coming from every direction. They were in Lhodrag, where there is a nine-storied tower that was built by Milarepa. Serkong Rinpoche, who always carried with him Marpa's damaru and the rosary of Marpa's wife Dagmema, went to the upper floor of the tower and offered the damaru to the statue of Marpa and the rosary to the statue of Dagmema, and told them, "Whatever happens to my life, my father and mother, please take care of me." Then they left, and everyone in his party was able to reach India safely.

I wanted very much to receive a Milarepa empowerment from Serkong Rinpoche. One day, as I was on my way to Pelgyeling Gompa in Swayambhu to visit him, I met Rinpoche on the bridge of the Vishnumati River, just below the Bijeshwari Vajrayogini temple. Rinpoche said that it was a very auspicious place to meet and accepted my request for the empowerment. He thought that it would benefit the Sherpas in Khumbu.

The monks of Pelgyeling Gompa were originally from a monastery next to the Stomach Cave of Milarepa, near Nyanam in Tibet.[308] They had brought with them a very precious statue of Milarepa, made by his disciple Rechungpa, that contains very blessed relics. It is said that when Rechungpa was giving a Vajravarahi empowerment in front of that statue, at the moment of invoking the wisdom being, the mandala absorbed into the heart of the statue. The caretaker told us that the heart of the statue is always warm and that the statue's hair is growing. The face had been repainted with gold, and Serkong Rinpoche himself had painted the eyes.

In front of that blessed statue, Rinpoche gave the Milarepa empowerment to an American called Steve Malasky, a French girl, and myself, using a text written by the first Dodrubchen Jigme Trinle Özer.[309] Afterward, Steve did the retreat in the basement of his tower. He had wanted to build a house in Kopan and had the unfortunate idea of asking me how he should build it, so I told him to build a three-storied tower in the shape of a mandala. The ground floor was round, made with stones and with very small windows—that was the meditation room. The first floor was square with windows in the four directions, and the top room was made of wood and had very large windows. To get to the main room, they had to build a small wooden bridge across a deep ditch, and Sonam Tobgyal carved the railing with dragons. I think that the cost of building Steve's tower was almost as much as the cost of building the entire Kopan Gompa.

The last piece of carving that Sonam Tobgyal undertook was a walking stick for Lama Yeshe with a handle in the shape of a sleeping cow. Sonam

Tobgyal's liver was damaged because he used to drink a lot of alcohol, and he stayed for one month in Bir Hospital in Kathmandu. When I went to see him, he was lying on his back and his face looked completely black. Although he could not move, he managed to put his hands together in the prostration mudra and tried to give me a piece of fruit that was on his table. He could not speak but he could hear, so I told him that he should not have attachment to his relatives and possessions. As death will definitely occur, there is no meaning in being attached to these things. The only thing to long for, always, continuously and consistently, is the Western Pure Realm of the Buddha Amitabha. He died either that night or the next morning.

# 27. Mount Everest Center for Buddhist Studies

ZINA REQUESTED ME to teach another course in March 1972. I worked with some students, particularly Massimo Corona, and we put together about thirty pages of teachings. But just a few days after the course began, we heard that Kyabje Trijang Rinpoche was giving some very special teachings in Dharamsala, so Lama Yeshe and I left immediately. Ann taught the rest of the course with the help of Jampa Zangpo, a Canadian monk who had recently been ordained in Dharamsala and had just arrived in Kopan.

After we returned from Dharamsala, Zina went to Thubten Chöling for a long retreat and Max moved to Kopan. Lama Yeshe was then given the best room, and Max took another large room next to him (years later her room became what we used to call the Chenrezig Gompa). I was given a nice room at the top of the stairs, next to the kitchen. Every morning at seven, Max would go down in her jeep to teach at the Lincoln School and then came back in the evenings. She was very generous and offered most of her money to Lama. She also sponsored the monks of Samtenling Monastery to do a one-month Vajrayogini retreat.

I went back to Lawudo in May with Geshe Thubten Tashi and Gen Wangyal, two lamas from Sera who had agreed to teach the Lawudo monks. The gompa was almost complete except for the roof, but then a French student of Lama, Philippe Camus, offered to pay for the 130 sheets of corrugated iron that were needed for the roof and chartered a plane to Lukla to bring them up. The carpenter came to Lawudo two weeks after the sheets and managed to finish the roof in time for the nyungne.

After attending the Mani Rimdu at Thangme, we did nyungne on the upper story of the gompa, while the carpenters were busy laying the wooden floor downstairs. Lama Yeshe arrived in time for the official opening of Mount Everest Center, which by now had about thirty monks. Geshe Thubten Tashi gave monastic vows to the boys, and we offered khatags to them. The parents seemed very happy and gave offerings for the

**44.** Logo of the Mount Everest Center for Buddhist Studies (drawing by Lama Zopa Rinpoche)

gompa, and some of them decided to build small houses around Lawudo for their sons.

We also had a Western boy at the school, Michael Lozang Yeshe, whose father was Greek and mother was American. Two years before, Michael and his mother Olivia (a niece of Aldous Huxley) came to Nepal with Matti de Wijs. Michael was about six at that time and stayed for a while with us at Max's house in Bouddha. Later, his mother took him to India, but Michael insisted that he wanted to come back to Nepal and stay with us. Lozang Yeshe was very enthusiastic about being a monk and from the very beginning felt completely at ease among the Sherpa and Tibetan boys. Years later other Western children became monks at Kopan, but none of them felt really comfortable with the monastic environment and had to leave sooner or later. Instead, Lozang Yeshe went to Sera Monastery and spent many years studying there.

Sometimes Lozang Yeshe slept inside my large meditation box. He would fall asleep while I was doing my prayers, and when he woke up in the morning, he found me again sitting up meditating. He seemed surprised, but did not dare to ask me why I did not lie down to sleep. One day I explained to him that if we could experience even for a short instant the suffering of being born as an animal, such as a dog, we would never sleep again. We would spend all our time creating merit in order to make sure that we would not take such a rebirth. I taught him some prayers and Ngawang Samten took care of him. Sometimes he would get into the storeroom where my sister kept the chang and would eat the sweet, delicious leftover fermented rice. I always found out because his breath smelled of chang, and I would scold him very harshly, telling him that monks are not allowed to taste alcoholic drinks.

Many Westerners spent that summer in Lawudo. At Genupa, Åge del Banco translated Milarepa's life story into Danish, while Chris Kolb meditated in the small hermitage of Ngawang Trinle Lhundrub above Charog, eating only tsampa, potatoes, and nettles, like a true Sherpa hermit. Ron, a very tall American, made a large offering of money to Lama Yeshe and some of it was used for the Lawudo Gompa. When he arrived at Lawudo, Ron had some problem with Nepali rupees and could not pay for food, so

he would eat the tormas that I took out every evening, which he mixed
with flowers and herbs. One day he asked my permission to put his tent on
top of the cave. Dorje, our female watchdog, was kept below the cave in the
potato field. I guess that the dog took responsibility for the safety of the
houses and at night used to be very sensitive, so every time Ron moved
inside his sleeping bag and made a noise, the dog would bark furiously and
disturb everyone's sleep. Then Ron would wake up very upset, even though

45. The Lawudo monks washing clothes (courtesy of Lama Yeshe Wisdom Archives)

the barking of the dog was caused by the noise he himself was making; he
did not realize that he was disturbing the dog. At one point he became so
angry that he told me he wanted to kill the dog.

In those days nobody had electricity in Khumbu, but Ron had a small
solar panel that he used to recharge outside during the day, and at night
he had light in his tent. After a while he moved the tent to another place
on the mountain. During the summer there is quite a bit of datura[310] growing around Lawudo; the cows like it very much. One day, Ron cooked a
pot of datura and ate it. Then he began to hear a loud noise like the sound
of many people talking and could see the particles of dust on the ground
moving like living creatures and the mountains swirling around. I think
he had a very difficult time. Jampa Zangpo and Massimo took care of
him, and after a couple of days Ron came to tell me the experiences of his
hallucinating mind. Then I told him to stop eating such things and to eat
normal food again.

During that summer I began to expand the small booklet I had prepared for the second meditation course. Jampa Zangpo helped me to translate the section about the creation of the universe and the mandala offering. Afterward, he went into a strict three-month retreat in my uncle's house in Charog. I continued the work with Massimo, and by the end of the summer we had completed the book, which I called *The Wish-Fulfilling Golden Sun of the Mahayana Practice*. It was just a simple booklet of seventy pages with the basic lamrim teachings and meditations, combined with verses from the *Lama Chöpa*. After we came down from Lawudo,

46. Lama Zopa in his cave (courtesy of Kopan Gompa)

somebody typed stencils and made copies for the students (in those days there were no photocopy machines or computers in Nepal).

Massimo and Matti tried to teach English to the boys, while Geshe-la taught them the basic debating text and Gen Wangyal helped them to memorize it. Then, I decided to do a ten-day Vajrasattva retreat in the cave with Geshe Tashi and Massimo. I led the retreat on the basis of the Vajrayogini sadhana, and we did four sessions a day, stopping at the Vajrasattva meditation; in the evening session we would complete the sadhana. Geshe-la was sitting very straight and completely concentrated, not like my monkey mind, which was always jumping here and there. He did not even move his lips and remained unmoving for the entire session, probably doing mental recitation. He recited 100,000 mantras in ten days, but Massimo and I did not manage to complete the number.

A few days later I started a Vajrayogini retreat, during which I had some auspicious signs and visions. Probably due to the fact that I had been reading the text of Kachen Yeshe Gyaltsen and from it I had understood how to practice Dharma, even on the very first day of the retreat I felt unbelievably peaceful and joyful. Because of a slight weakening of the eight worldly concerns,[311] my mind was more tranquil and slightly purer. Like a road with fewer boulders blocking it, there were fewer obstacles in my mind. This is what makes a retreat successful. Thus, even though I had not read the commentary of this tantric practice, the blessings of the deity were received in my mind. It seems that I have a strong connection with that deity. At one point I had some doubts regarding the way to recite the mantra; while that doubt was in my mind, I saw a white light and heard a voice telling me the correct way of recitation. Although at the beginning of the retreat I had a cough and some other obstacles, I felt an unimaginable joy, and I wondered whether that experience would last for the rest of my life. Usually one is allowed to perform the self-empowerment only after completing the retreat, but I think that I did the self-empowerment even before the retreat!

By the end of the summer, the construction and the carpentry work were complete. The cave now had a large shrine, a bedlike meditation box, a wooden floor, and wood panels on the walls. The first floor of the gompa had a large room with a shrine and a bed for Lama Yeshe or any other visiting lama and four smaller rooms for the monks. On the top there was a large attic to be used for storage or as a dormitory if the need arose.

Lama Yeshe came at the beginning of September to check on the school and left on September 20 with Jampa Zangpo and Robby Solick. Two days later I went to Tramo to preside over the enthronement of Tenzin Özer, the son of an ex-monk and ex-nun that His Holiness had recognized as the tulku of the Khari Lama Lozang Tsultrim.[312]

## Kopan Gompa

The Lawudo monks were to come down to Kathmandu for the winter to continue their studies at Kopan in the new Ogmin Jangchub Chöling Gompa. On October 6, 1972, we closed the summer school and left for Lukla, while my mother and sister moved to Lawudo for the winter. Max had chartered two or three flights to bring us down, but the weather was very bad, and we had to wait quite a few days in Lukla. Geshe Tashi and I flew in the first flight and waited for the others in the restaurant at the airport, where we met some Western students from Kopan. After having lunch in Bouddha, we all walked to Kopan, and that same evening I performed a ceremony in the new prayer hall. I stayed in a small room in the new building, while the monks settled down in the old house.

47. Lama Zopa teaching the third meditation course in Kopan Gompa, October 1972 (unknown)

The Third Kopan Meditation Course started a few days later in the new Kopan Gompa, which still did not have a wooden floor or a proper shrine. Besides giving teachings twice a day, every morning and evening I would sit on the floor below the throne and lead meditations on death and impermanence, the suffering of the lower realms, and so forth. The students seemed to enjoy my teachings and meditations, and over the following years quite a few of them became monks and nuns, although by now some have given back their vows.

In those days I was trying to practice at least a tiny bit of Dharma and was very scared of acquiring a good reputation, so I used to teach for a long time about the eight worldly concerns. It was probably during that course that I spent more than two weeks talking about the eight worldly concerns, like ice cream with the cherry of the hells on top!

Geshe Thubten Tashi never came to Kopan to teach the monks. Instead, he went to Pharping, a holy place of Padmasambhava and Vajrayogini south of Kathmandu, and engaged in a twelve-year retreat on his main deity, Chakrasamvara. Gen Wangyal continued to teach the monks for a few months and returned to Sera Monastery. Lama Yeshe then wrote to his student Lhundrub Rigsel, who was in South India working on the construction of the new Sera Monastery, and asked him to come to Nepal to teach the monks. His teacher gave him permission to come to Nepal for a few months only, but thirty years later Lama Lhundrub is still at Kopan and is now the abbot.

48. Watching the buffalo at the back of the old Kopan Gompa

In January 1973 I went to Bodh Gaya with Lozang Nyima, Ann, and my sister Ngawang Samten to receive the *Lama Chöpa* teachings from Kyabje Ling Rinpoche. Besides giving those very profound teachings, Ling Rinpoche would go to the Bodhi Tree every evening to lead the *Lama Chöpa* ritual with the monks. His Holiness the Dalai Lama and many other high lamas were also in Bodh Gaya and it was a very special time. After the teachings, Ngawang Samten did a short retreat in Kopan and then returned to Khumbu.

The Fourth Kopan Meditation Course took place in March 1973, with about 100 students. I expanded *The Wish-Fulfilling Golden Sun* booklet with the help of Dr. Nick Ribush and Marie Obst, and I also expanded the title. Now it was called *The Wish-Fulfilling Golden Sun of the Mahayana Thought Training Directing in the Short-Cut Path to Enlightenment.*

At the end of May, the monks and about eight Westerners went to Lawudo for the summer. Lama Yeshe, Lama Lhundrub, and I arrived just in time for the nyungne. That year we enthroned a boy from Namche called Tenzin Norbu (Thubten Zopa) as the tulku of a lama from Shugtö Gompa near Ngamring in Tibet. Tenzin Dorje, a boy from Thangme recognized as the tulku of the Charog Gelong Ngawang Samten, and Geleg Gyatso, the tulku of Togden Ngawang Tsultrim, who had been involved in the founding of Tragshingto Gompa[313] in Shorong, also joined Mount Everest Center. Thus, we had three young tulkus in our monastery.

49. Participants at the third meditation course. Sitting in the first row: Massimo Corona, Nick Ribush, Henk, ?, Claudio Cipullo, Steve Malasky, Piero Cerri, Lolly Smith, David Borrie, Darlene Darata, ?, Åge del Banco, Paula de Wijs, Eric. Standing in the first row: Carol Corona, Ira, ?, Chris Vautier, ?, ?, ?, Ann McNeil, Gareth Sparham, Lama Zopa Rinpoche, Helly Pelaez, Shan Cooper, Luca Corona, Suzanne Lee, ?, Marcel Bertels, Dieter Gewissler, ?, Barbara Vautier, Peter Kedge, ?, ?, ?. At the back are Ron Brooks (Ngawang Khedup), the cook Lozang Phagpa, Marie Obst, Nicole Lajeunesse, and others (courtesy of Nick Ribush)

Lama Yeshe and I left very soon for Shangboche, hoping to catch the very first plane chartered by the Japanese Everest View Hotel to the new airstrip. We stayed in a small tent next to the only teashop in the area, and the two young monks, Thubten Ngodrub and Thubten Monlam, took care of us. It was already late June and the weather was very bad, with a thick fog and rain. After ten days we lost all hope of getting a flight, so we decided to try our luck at Lukla. After waiting for another week or so, we were finally able to fly to Kathmandu and went to Dharamsala for the summer.

The Westerners stayed in retreat at Lawudo for the whole summer. Some of them taught English to the monks and painted the gompa walls. Pasang, another Tibetan disciple of Lama Yeshe, arrived some time in July to join the staff of Mount Everest Center. He taught writing to the monks and helped in construction and carpentry works. He had a very short temper and used to beat the boys very hard. Everyone was afraid of him.

## Zina's Death

Zina wrote to us describing her meditation experiences and her plans to come after the monsoon to receive teachings from some high lamas and do a one-year retreat in Dharamsala.

Then, at the beginning of August, a messenger came to Kopan with the news of Zina's death. It seems that she had been sick for only three or four days, but we do not know the exact cause of her death. Some people suggested that she had been picking up wild garlic and had mistakenly eaten another very similar plant that is poisonous. Just before dying, she was able to sit in meditation posture and recite a few mantras. Her daughter was holding her hand, crying and saying, "Please mother, do not die!" A message was sent immediately to Trulzhig Rinpoche, who was in Tengboche Monastery giving a long series of empowerments. He did many prayers and transferred her consciousness to the pure realm of Vajrayogini, a deity with which she had a strong connection. Zina's body was cremated after three days, and although the weather had been rainy and foggy, on that day it cleared up and everyone could see a rainbow.

I had a dream in which Zina was telling me that she was leaving, so I had the feeling that she was dead even before we received the message. She was very fortunate to die as a nun in a simple room in a monastery, more peacefully than those people who die in an expensive apartment surrounded by crying relatives. She had completed more than three million Yamantaka mantras, and her mind had changed a great deal. She had always wanted to help others, particularly Westerners. Some time later I checked with an old high lama who lived in South India, and he told me that Zina had gone to a very good realm.[314]

Lama Yeshe and I were able to benefit so many Western people because we met Zina. She knew many important, wealthy people, and also poor people, and that is how we were able to meet other Westerners. I think that what Zina did is a good example of "women's liberation." She was able to benefit beings extensively by creating the conditions for them to meet the teachings of the Buddha, and she also trained her own mind. She chose true freedom and true liberation. That is the real challenge.

In October, Lama Yeshe went to Lawudo for a short time with Wim, a Dutch man who had offered to paint the throne and table of His Holiness in the gompa, and a new Spanish nun called Jampa Chökyi. Lama closed the school term, and Lama Lhundrub, Lama Pasang, and the monks came down to Kopan. My mother and sister moved back to Lawudo to take care of the place, and Jampa Chökyi stayed in retreat for the whole winter at Charog in Ashang Ngawang Yonten's hut.

My mother came down to Kathmandu in December, and we went together to Bodh Gaya to receive the Kalachakra empowerment from His Holiness the Dalai Lama. There, she took ordination as a novice nun from Ling Rinpoche with a group of our Western students[315] and received the new name Thubten Zangmo. I had been telling her for a long time that she should become a nun, so I was extremely happy. The next summer she went to Thubten Chöling for two months and received many teachings and empowerments from Trulzhig Rinpoche.

Around that time I received a visit from Gen Lozang Gyatso, the manager from Nyachung Lhakhang in Phag-ri who had been so kind to me. He was living in Bhutan and told me that he was able to heal many people by reciting the mantra of Black Mañjushri. The queen of Bhutan invited him to perform rituals, and he became quite famous in that country. When he came to Kopan, he was wearing Bhutanese clothes and looked very thin. Some time later, when I was in Dharamsala, I received a letter from him telling me that he had TB, and two weeks later I heard that he had passed away. Before his death he left a will giving his belongings to different people and his money to his teachers and to the old people's home in Mundgod in South India. He left me a pair of very good cymbals (which I never received) and a large silver reliquary, a *gau*. Inside it was a small Vajrayogini statue, precious pills from Dromo Geshe Rinpoche made with the milk of a snow lioness, a Tara statue made of pure gold, and some other precious relics. Gen Lozang Gyatso was a very kind person and very learned in ritual dances and music. I always remember him with great love and respect.

## The Life of the Monks

The monks of Mount Everest Center were making good progress in their studies, and Lama Yeshe was very happy. He supervised their work and their living conditions and made sure they had what they needed. Lama was quite strict with them, and when they misbehaved, he would beat them with his rosary and scold them very harshly. Or else, when the monks fell asleep during the evening rituals, Lama would take a bowl of water from the altar and pour its contents over their heads.

The food the monks ate was very simple, not like the delicious dishes that Westerners were served at Kopan. They had a plain, flat bread and Tibetan butter tea in the morning, rice and dhal for lunch, and thugpa in the evenings. Max (now she was known as Mommy Max) felt very sorry for the little monks and convinced Lama to give them peanut butter on their morning bread, but the monks would rather have had chilies or spicy potato curry with it.

Chumbi, the monk who brought me to Lama Yeshe in Buxa, was not a monk anymore. He came to Nepal and we asked him to be the cook at Kopan. After a while, he came to my room and said, "I am always busy and have no time to practice Dharma. I am only creating negative karma. Instead, you are always sitting on the bed, meditating and saying prayers.

50. Lawudo monks, 1973 (courtesy of Nick Ribush)

After this life, you are going to be born in a pure realm." He was making his own projections, so I told him, "The one who is actually practicing Dharma is you, not me. I just sit here the whole day doing nothing, but you are accumulating unbelievable merit by working in the monastery and serving the students of Lama Yeshe. It is said in the teachings that making offerings or serving the disciples of one's own lama creates more merit than making offerings to the buddhas of the three times. Just think about the merit that you accumulate every morning, lunchtime, teatime, and dinnertime when you offer tea and food to the monks. Thus, in one day you accumulate incredible merit. You have heard more teachings than I have, so you should think in this way and rejoice. Even if you have no time to make prostrations or mandala offerings, you accumulate merit by following the advice of Lama Yeshe and serving the monks."

51. Genupa Lama Ngawang teaching *gyaling* to the Kopan monks

Around five to five-thirty in the morning, Lama Lhundrub would go around banging on the monks' doors and sometimes pulling the blankets off their beds. After washing, they would do a ceremony in the gompa for an hour and a half, during which time they had breakfast. Afterward, they cleaned the grounds, memorized scriptures for one or two hours, and had different classes. The younger boys learned painting; others had grammar and poetry classes. For a few years, all the monks learned how to paint and were able to make some beautiful paintings that were later sold to raise money for the gompa. At lunchtime they had one hour free, and afterward they would have English and mathematics classes. In the evening, the monks would receive teachings and debate about what they had learned that day. Then they had to recite by heart the passages they had memorized in the morning, and around half past ten in the evening, they would go to bed. In other monasteries, such as Sera, the monks have to memorize 400 or even 700 pages. If they do not practice, they forget, so sometimes they have to spend the whole night reciting scriptures.

The older monks studied the *Abhisamayalamkara* of Maitreya, *lorig,* (understanding the mind), and *tarig* (training the mind in logic). After a while they began to study *dura,* which contains many different subjects and starts with the definition of forms, colors, and so forth, and learned to debate about simple philosophical topics. Debate is considered very important in the Gelug tradition because it increases intelligence and makes the mind sharp.

The monks of Mount Everest Center did not have any holidays or even a single free hour to play. Their schedule was completely full from morning till evening. After some years, we asked Lama Yeshe to give them holidays and free time, so they had Saturdays free (in Nepal the weekly holiday is Saturday, not Sunday). Lama was very concerned about the monks' behavior, and whenever he found out that some monks had been to the movies or to watch videos in town, he sent them to work in the kitchen or to clean toilets for one month as punishment. Unfortunately, after Lama passed away, the monks started to spend their holidays watching videos in Bouddha and even gambling, so at one point it was decided to show videos at the monastery itself, so that at least they would not be hanging around and creating a bad example. Nowadays, however, their behavior has greatly improved.

I used to tell the monks how very fortunate they were. Since the schedule of the monastery had been set up by Lama Yeshe, following the schedule was actually following the advice of the teacher; thus everything they did became a way to accumulate unbelievable merit. Even just using the broom to sweep became purification. I told them that their motivation should be either to benefit sentient beings or to fulfill the wishes of the teacher by following his advice. In this way, even if they got tired, they would always be happy and have energy to do their studies. Without the proper motivation, they could lose interest and become bored.

In the spring of 1974, the monks went back to Lawudo with Lama Lhundrub, Lama Pasang, and a few Westerners. In October, the monks returned to Kopan and never went back to the mountains. The conditions at Lawudo had always been difficult, and the boys had to carry water, cut firewood, take care of the cows, plant and dig potatoes, and so forth, which was distracting them from their studies. Besides, the number of monks had increased, and it was too expensive to fly so many monks up and down. Thus, from 1974 onward, Mount Everest Center was established permanently year-round at Kopan Monastery, and Lawudo returned to what it had been in previous times: a hermitage.

# 28. Lawudo Retreat Center

INTEREST IN BUDDHISM was growing among Westerners, and the Kopan meditation courses became very popular. I continued to give courses twice a year until 1975. Since that time, the one-month Kopan course has taken place only in November.

In January 1975, Gomchen Gampa-la, who used to spend the winter months in Tulku Urgyen Rinpoche's monastery in Bouddha, came to Kopan to request the oral transmission of the Lama Tsongkhapa Guru Yoga from me. In return, I asked him to give a talk to the Western students. Gomchen-la gave a very detailed explanation of the meaning of guru devotion and offered me a text called *How the Previous Kagyu Lamas Practiced Guru Devotion,* written by his root guru Dzatul Ngawang Tenzin Norbu.[316]

Around that time I had the great good fortune to meet Kunnu Lama Rinpoche in Bouddha. Kunnu Rinpoche advised me to subdue the mind of the students and teach them how to have a good heart. He did not tell me to make them learned or strict in morality but to persuade their minds to practice bodhichitta, which is the best way to benefit others.

In that year, Lama Yeshe and I went on a tour to Australia and New Zealand and I was unable to go to Lawudo, but in May 1976 I returned to Khumbu with Lama Pasang. After the nyungne I did a short Tara retreat in the cave, followed by an elaborate fire offering ceremony. The Khari monks and nuns did not know how to perform fire offerings and the Thangme monks follow a different tradition, so there was nobody to help, and I had to organize everything myself. It was my first experience at drawing mandalas for fire offerings. I had brought the text describing how to do it, and I managed with the help of Ngawang Nyandrag, Ashang Ngawang Yonten, and Jampa Chökyi, who had been in retreat in the Sanyer Cave for a few months and was skilled in drawing and painting. A kind of tent was set outside the cave, and I started the ceremony when it was already dark and under heavy rain.

The next day I left for Lukla, and on the way I paid a visit to Gomchen-la. Since leaving Tibet, Gomchen-la had been moving around Khumbu without any fixed home, just like a hippie. He used to carry a small tent, a large damaru, and a thighbone. He would put his tent in the forest or in caves and at night practiced *chöd,* or slaying the ego. Then he built a small meditation hut above Khumjung and stayed there for some years with an old nun, his aunt, taking care of him.

Gomchen-la's main practice was to maintain continuous awareness of the fact that we can die at any moment. At some point he was totally convinced that he was going to die very soon, and he thought, "This nun is very old and she cannot collect dry wood to burn my body nor carry kerosene up the mountain to ignite the fire. I better do the arrangements myself. In this way, all she will have to do is drag the body from the meditation box outside and put the wood on top, so she will not get tired or worried." So he bought quite a lot of firewood and some kerosene and made everything ready. But he did not die for another ten years!

A couple of years back, Gomchen-la had built a chörten in Khumjung that had caused a big uproar. It seems that Geshe Urgyen Dorje, a Tibetan lama who lives in Pangboche,[317] had predicted that if a chörten were built to the east of Khumjung, the village would be destroyed. Gomchen-la was not aware of that prophecy, but the villagers became very upset and built a wall so that no one could walk around that chörten. After a few attempts were made to poison him, Gomchen-la left the Akar Hermitage and settled above Pemkar in a nice cave.

I met him in Rimejung Gompa, where he was supervising the molding of clay statues of Guru Rinpoche. Gelong Tsultrim Yeshe and Gelong Wangchug of Khari Gompa made many hundreds of them, some of which Gomchen-la took to his hermitage in Pemkar. The following year he offered to send some of those statues to Lawudo, but the Pemkar villagers refused to let us take them. They said that the statues belonged to the hermitage and that the Lawudo people were welcome to stay there if they wished, but the statues were not to be taken to Lawudo. I guess they understood how beneficial it is to have holy objects in the vicinity of the village, and they did not want to be deprived of the benefits. Gomchen-la later sent us a set of texts and three old statues that had been found buried under the ruins of his gompa in Tibet.

## The Mani Recitation

Ordinary Sherpas are not interested in meditation or in doing any practice to train their minds, but they do have strong devotion to the lamas and

the Three Jewels, and particularly to Chenrezig, the Great Compassionate One. I thought that it would be very beneficial for them to do some
purification practice, so I decided to organize the recitation of 100 million
of the six-syllable mantra *Om mani padme hum*. Reciting the six-syllable
mantra is a very powerful method to purify the six afflictive emotions and
avoid rebirth in the six realms of cyclic existence, and it can also help to
control the problems caused by an imbalance of the four elements.

We still did not have any objects of devotion in the gompa, so before
leaving Lawudo that year, I asked Jampa Chökyi to make a large thangka
of the eleven-face Chenrezig and have it ready for the mani recitation of
the following year. During the winter I translated some parts of the
nyungne sadhana, so that Westerners could follow the practice. Until then,
those foreigners who attended the nyungnes at Lawudo did not really
understand what was going on. They made prostrations and recited mani,
but that was all. Of course, Sherpas do not understand the deep meaning
of the practice either, but they have devotion and faith in Chenrezig. By
contrast, Westerners always try very hard to concentrate and to understand things but they lack devotion, so for them it was important to have
the text translated.

In the spring of 1977, I went up to Lawudo with some Westerners.
Jampa Chökyi was able to complete the large Chenrezig silk appliqué
thangka the day before I was to give the Chenrezig empowerment, and I
sent her to Pemkar to have it blessed by Gomchen-la. I told her that she
should go and come back the same day, so she left at 3:30 in the morning,
walked five or six hours to Gomchen-la's cave above Pemkar, and was
back in Lawudo before dark. I thought she was becoming a real Sherpa
coolie!

Not many people came to recite mani. Besides the three monks and
eighteen nuns of the Khari Gompa in Tramo, Ashang Ngawang Yonten,
Ashang Trinle, and twelve Westerners, only a few elderly Sherpas joined
the recitation. We recited mani for six weeks, but we could not complete
the number of mantras. Although the retreat had started after the potato
planting season, it seemed that the Sherpas were not interested in reciting mani. Most of them were trekking and carrying loads for tourists, or
preparing chang and arak for the Mani Rimdu celebrations, when all
their relatives and friends from Kathmandu would come to Khumbu to
spend a few days drinking, singing, and dancing. I heard that the next
year Gomchen-la also tried to organize the recitation of mani at Rimejung. He had to promise ten rupees a day to everyone as a kind of wage

for reciting the mantras, even though it was done for their own benefit, and even then very few people made the effort. Of course, Sherpas have a lot of work to do and life is difficult for them, but I found it strange that they would consider reciting mantras to be work.

While the mani recitation was going on, I gave teachings to the Westerners and translated a beautiful prayer to Chenrezig written by Dzatul Ngawang Tenzin Norbu for his mother.[318] Jampa Chökyi cleaned the old statues of Guru Rinpoche and his two female disciples, and when the black soot had been removed, we offered gold to the face of Guru Rinpoche, and I painted his eyes and moustache. We also cleaned all the texts of the previous Lawudo Lama. They were kept in the cave, which is extremely damp, so we took them out in the sun to dry and prevent them from being destroyed by worms. These are old texts written on Nepali paper, and the worms reincarnate among the pages and make interesting holes in them!

At the end of the retreat we did two nyungnes, and the following day the Tramo nuns did the practice and tsog offering of the *Great Compassionate Lord,* a Nyingma practice that Trulzhig Rinpoche had taught them. Then I left for Shangboche with Lama Pasang and two Australian students and tried to get a flight, but the weather was extremely bad. Finally, I started to recite some wrathful mantras while walking up and down the runway. All of a sudden, the sky cleared a bit and a Pilatus Porter was able to land. We quickly got our luggage and managed to fly out before the clouds came back.

My mother and sister had a hard time taking care of the Westerners, and the Westerners had a hard time with the Sherpa food, the cold, the fleas, and the general lack of comfort. There was no electricity, no chocolate, and not even a nice fire to sit around in the evenings to keep warm; the Lawudo kitchen was too small for so many people. There were also communication problems, so I thought that in the future we would try to improve the material conditions at Lawudo and have a Western person familiar with Sherpa customs taking care of the Westerners.

### The First Chenrezig Group Retreat

The following winter, Lama Yeshe asked Jampa Chökyi to organize a Chenrezig group retreat for Westerners at Lawudo during the next Saka Dawa. We thought that the example of the Westerners practicing Dharma would also indirectly benefit the local people.

One day, a Sherpa came to Kopan and offered to sell us an old set of the

Tengyur printed in Lhasa that his father kept in Namche. Lama Yeshe thought we should buy it for Lawudo, and a few weeks later we sent the Sherpa monk Thubten Ngodrub and a Western monk, George Churinoff, to Namche to carefully check the texts. For some reason, the owner wanted to keep the deal secret, even though afterward everyone came to know about it, and so the eighteen people who were carrying the texts left at three o'clock in the morning to avoid being seen.

In May I flew to Shangboche, and two hours later I reached the foot of the Lawudo Mountain. In those days there were no phones in Khumbu, and there was no way to send a message telling my family the exact date when we were coming. Many old Sherpas can understand the language of ravens and know that when they make a particular sound, it means that someone is coming from far away. Whenever they heard the ravens, my mother and sister, who were always thinking about me, would keep watch on the Namche highway in the hope that I would appear. If they saw someone wearing dark red clothes and followed by a porter, they would become excited thinking that I was coming. Needless to say, they were always disappointed. But whenever I flew to Lukla or Shangboche, it would never take long for the news to reach Lawudo, and then my sister or uncle would come to meet me on the way with a thermos of tea and carpets to sit on for a rest.

About forty Westerners registered for the 1978 Chenrezig Group Retreat, which lasted ten days. I gave many teachings, and we did two nyungnes with the Khari monks and nuns. Jampa Chökyi had bought many things in Kathmandu—food, mattresses, candles, chocolate, and so forth—and sent them to Lukla in a chartered plane. At Lawudo she organized a small shop where the Westerners could buy all the "goodies." Actually, one could get anything at Namche, from Nepali "Nebico Glucose" biscuits, to Spanish olives and olive oil, French foie-gras, Italian spaghetti, English porridge, Swiss muesli and chocolate, Australian butter, New Zealand cheese, and so forth. The climbing expeditions used to leave behind all their leftover food and the Sherpas would sell it to the tourists for a very high price. But the retreat participants were not allowed to go to Namche during the retreat, and the "Lawudo Shop" (a metal trunk that was opened only after lunch) helped them to survive during those days.

My sister used to get help from Yangchen, the eldest daughter of Pasang Namgyal and Pemba Dekyi, a Tramo nun called Donma Pande, and Ngawang Nyandrag's sister Ang Kyimzom. Kyimzom's son Thubten Kunga became a monk at Kopan, and a few years later her daughter Pasang

Dekyi became a nun at our Khachö Gakyil Nunnery. Unfortunately, both of them died very young. One Saturday afternoon, Thubten Kunga went to play football with other monks in a field below Kopan, even though the local people had warned them not to play there because of some local spirits. He was hit on the head by the ball and returned home not feeling well. At dinnertime, his friends came to get him and found him dead. A few years later, Pasang Dekyi also died in the Kopan nunnery.

### Kusho Mangde

The Charog Hermitage had been empty for quite a while, but in 1978 the Charog Lama Kusho Mangde came back to his ancestral home with his wife Ngawang Lozang, his son Sonam Zangpo and his wife, his daughter Ani Pema Chöden, and a couple of disciples from Toloka. Kusho Mangde came to Lawudo during the nyungne, and over the following years he always sent offerings for the nyungne, even though he could not always attend.

Kusho Mangde was around seventy-three years old at that time and had a beautiful, long white beard. He used to wear an old brocade chuba and dark round glasses, and he spent his time sitting on a square, wooden meditation box in the kitchen next to the fireplace, holding a crystal rosary in his hand and glancing at some texts. When the weather was good, he practiced chöd in a small tent outside or in a wooden shelter on the roof. Twice a day he offered *sur* to the spirits by burning juniper branches, tsampa, and butter, and in the evenings did an elaborate Phurba practice according to the Northern Treasure. He was very skilled at making astrological calculations and divinations, and he gave long-life empowerments that were attended by Sherpas and Tibetans from all traditions. The Tengboche and the Thangme lamas came often to receive instructions from him.

Trulzhig Rinpoche respected Kusho Mangde very much and used to joke about his beard, saying that it reminded him of Mindroling Trichen Terdag Lingpa. Once, when visiting Charog, Trulzhig Rinpoche grabbed Kusho Mangde's beard and exclaimed, "A beard like this cannot be bought even with 1,000 rupees!" Kusho Mangde used to send consecrated long life pills to Trulzhig Rinpoche at least once a year, and when Rinpoche's mother passed away, Kusho Mangde was requested to perform the transference of consciousness for her.

The Charog Lamas follow the ritual musical tradition of Mindroling and Dorje Drag monasteries, which I like very much. I wanted the Kopan monks to learn the melodies from Kusho Mangde or his son, but the monks had no time to go to Khumbu. A couple of years later, however, Lama Ngawang from Genupa came to Kathmandu, and I invited him to Kopan to teach ritual music to the monks.

52. Ashang Ngawang Yonten, Amala, Ngawang Samten, and Aunt Lhamo, 1983
(Andrea Antonietti)

I left Lawudo after the retreat and tried to get a flight from Shangboche, but the weather was very bad, and after a few days I had to walk to Lukla. While I was waiting at Shangboche, I made a short visit to the Akar Cave, where there is a footprint of Padmasambhava and a self-created syllable *Ah*. I left after lunch with a few Western disciples, thinking that the cave was near Khumjung, but it was quite a long way up the mountain. We only had time to do a very short tsog offering because it was getting dark and the mountainside was very steep. I thought that maybe we would all have to roll down the mountain instead of walking! We reached the hotel in Shangboche around nine or ten in the evening.

Meanwhile, the wife of the man who had sold us the Tengyur had come to see me and had left a khatag and some large packets of biscuits as offerings. I was afraid that they had been bought with the money they had obtained from selling the texts, and I asked Jampa Chökyi to take those biscuits to some spot high up in the mountains where no one could ever eat them. The money obtained from selling texts and statues should not be used for buying food, and if one does, that food carries a very heavy pollution because it has been obtained by wrong livelihood.

There is a story to illustrate that point. Once, a Tibetan practitioner of Chenrezig was invited to read the scriptures in the house of a benefactor. The family used to have the twelve volumes of the *Prajnaparamita Sutra* in their shrine room, but they had sold them and with that money they offered food to the monks. While they were eating, that practitioner suddenly felt great pain in his body. He then went into meditation to discover the cause and saw a white syllable *Ah* moving inside his body. Wherever the syllable went, there was great pain. Then he prayed very hard and had a vision of Chenrezig telling him, "The reason why you are experiencing such unbearable pain is because you have eaten food obtained by wrong livelihood. And the reason why you are experiencing it now is because you have only thin mental obscurations and can experience the result right away. These three monks do not feel anything now, but after they die they will definitely be reborn in the hells."

### The Second Chenrezig Group Retreat

That winter we invited Diu Rinpoche to Kopan to give a three-day course on Tibetan medicine. Rinpoche, who was originally from the same village as Lama Lhundrub, came accompanied by his attendant Ani Pewang and the Lawudo Lama's grandson Karma Tenzin. Rinpoche lived in the Terphug Hermitage above Pangboche and used to spend the winters in Bouddha in Tulku Urgyen Rinpoche's gompa. He was very learned in the *Kalachakra Tantra* and skillful in astrology. It seems that with astrological calculations alone he could even discover how much money a person had in his pocket.

At that time, my sister spent a couple of months in Thubten Chöling receiving chöd teachings from Trulzhig Rinpoche. That particular tradition of chöd is very strict, and the commitment after receiving the teachings is to do the practice at night for one week, completely alone, in solitary and frightening spots. When they returned to Khumbu, Ngawang Samten and a group of Dharma friends went together to the mountain above Thangme to do the practice. During the day they cooked and ate together and did some other prayers, but just before dark they would each take their large drum, thighbone trumpet, and small tent, and go far away where they could not see or hear each other. After performing the chöd, they would sleep for a while, and at dawn they would meet again to have tea and breakfast together.

In May 1979 we had another group retreat at Lawudo, this time with fifty Westerners. From Serkong Rinpoche I had received the nyungne commentary written by Kachen Yeshe Gyaltsen,[319] which includes the life stories of Gelongma Palmo and the lineage lamas. I read some of the stories to the students to give them courage to bear the difficulties and explained how to do the practice. By then there was already a rough English translation of the whole nyungne sadhana.

The previous year we had begun the construction of a new, large kitchen next to the gompa. Now the new kitchen was finished, and Jampa Chökyi sponsored the roof. I wanted a large, spacious room with large windows and a balcony where the Western people could sit in the sun and enjoy the view, but the carpenter Kunzang Legshe could not understand my idea and did something completely different. And as soon as I left that year, my mother and sister built a stone wall instead of the balcony door and transformed the room into an ordinary Sherpa house.

My relatives were staying in the old kitchen next to the cave, but now a fireplace was built upstairs and the ground floor was used for storage. My sister had a door opened in the back wall of the upper floor, and built a small covered courtyard between the house and the upper part of the cave. She used that space for making chang and storing firewood. In those days my mother and sister continued to make chang and arak at Lawudo, even though there was no need. I tried many times to stop them, but to no avail. They always said, "Yes, yes, we won't make chang anymore," but they kept on making it. One day, it seems that they had just cooked a large pot of rice for making chang when they heard me coming upstairs to the kitchen. My mother and sister quickly took the pot out into the courtyard and closed the door, so that I would not see what they were doing. I sat in the kitchen for quite a while, drinking tea, talking, and joking with my mother. When I finally left, my sister opened the back door and went to get the rice. But she found one of the cows walking away, looking very satisfied with a full stomach, and the pot completely empty of rice! I guess they were quite upset, but they did not learn their lesson, and for many years my sister continued to make chang and arak at Lawudo against my wishes.

One of the main problems we had at Lawudo was the scarcity of water during the dry season, which is exactly when the retreats and nyungnes take place and when Lawudo becomes crowded. During one of the fasting days, Jampa Chökyi, who had been organizing the retreat and wanted a day off, went for a walk up the mountain. She reached as far as the upper Gyachog Valley, where the yaks are taken during the summer and yetis are said to roam. She did not see any yetis, but instead found some long pieces of large, black rubber pipes. She was very puzzled to find rubber pipes in such an isolated spot, and as soon as she returned to Lawudo, she came into the cave to tell me. We thought that pipes left in such a place did not have much benefit, but at Lawudo they could be very useful, and the next morning I sent Ashang Ngawang Yonten with some of the Khari monks and nuns to Gyachog Valley to bring the pipes down. That was not an easy thing to do. The path goes through very steep rocky cliffs and is quite dangerous, but somehow they managed.

Ashang Ngawang Yonten and the nuns installed the pipe from the spring at Genupa to a spot on our side of the landslide; they also installed a large metal drum as a water tank. That saved the water carriers a good fifteen-minute walk across the landslide, and we had a nice spot for washing clothes away from Lama Ngawang's family, who were not very keen about having lots of people around their place.

We were wondering about the origin of the pipes until Pasang Namgyal told us the whole story. It seems that the previous winter there had been an attempt to bring water from the Gyachog River to Khumde, Khumjung, and the Japanese hotel. The pipes had been dropped by helicopter in the valley, and a team of Sherpas and Western experts had gone there through the Khumbilha Mountain and had attempted to set up the pipes. On the way back to Khumde, one Westerner fell down the mountain and was killed. The Sherpas concluded that the local deity was angry and refused to have anything to do with that project. The pipes had been abandoned at that isolated spot, and some Sherpas had carried off large sections and then sold them secretly to the villagers. We did not know that story, but a few days later we received a visit from the headman of Khumjung. He said that the pipes were theirs and that he wanted us to bring them back to the Gyachog Valley. It took many months of long discussions between that headman and my uncle and sister, but we were finally allowed to keep the pipes.

I had a very strong wish to remain in retreat at Lawudo during that summer, but I was supposed to go on a teaching tour to the West with Lama Yeshe. The monsoon had already arrived and planes could not land, but there was still the possibility of going to Kathmandu by helicopter. I then started a strict retreat, although I was not sure how long I was going to stay.

One morning, as I was finishing breakfast, I heard the sound of a helicopter approaching. It landed in Mende, and a short while later Jacie Keeley, Lama Yeshe's secretary, walked into the cave. She told me that she had come merely to invite me and that it was up to me whether I wanted to go. Then I did a *mo* in front of the Tara statue that had belonged to the previous Lawudo Lama. I made up my mind that even though Jacie had spent so much money to bring the helicopter, if the outcome was that I should stay, I would not go. But the outcome was that I should go, so I had everything packed very quickly and left. Later, I realized that I had done the right thing; otherwise, Lama Yeshe would have been very upset, and I would have disturbed the mind of my teacher, which brings very negative consequences.

## Teaching the Sherpas

Whenever I came to Lawudo I tried to help the Sherpas in whatever way I could. People came to see me with all kinds of requests. Generally, when they have some disease or problem, Sherpas ask a lama to give them a short blessing to stop the obstacles, but they do not expect to do much from their own side. If the lama tells them to do a practice, they ask monks or lamas to do it for them. I thought that I should give some practice to the sick people who came to ask for blessings; otherwise they would never change their minds or purify their negative karma.

There was a Tibetan man at Tesho who had been a medium, or oracle, all his life. He and his family took care of the water mill, where people brought grain to make flour and tsampa. He had been sick for a long time, so when he came to see me, I told him to recite 200,000 Vajrasattva mantras. He said, "I will ask the monasteries to recite those mantras on my behalf," but I laughed and told him, "No, no, this time you have to recite them yourself." Since he had never been to school and was not able to read the scriptures, I decided to teach him the mantra by heart. I spent about two hours with him, but the Vajrasattva mantra is so long that we could not finish that night. The next day I recorded the mantra for him so that he could listen to the tape and memorize it. I think he tried for a little while, but again he told me that he would ask the monks to recite the mantras for him. Later I heard that he got even worse and that his mind had become a little bit crazy. He was very good at making Tibetan boots, and my mother had ordered a new pair from him. One day he came to Lawudo bringing just one boot and could not explain what had happened to the other one. Then, after some days, a woman from Tramo found one lonely, brand-new boot somewhere on the mountain and brought it to Lawudo.

Many Sherpa families have things stolen—money, potatoes, or other possessions. For example, Sherpas dig a hole in the ground to bury their potatoes and then cover the hole with earth to make it look as if there are no potatoes in there. Then they go to stay in another village for a few months. But some local people are able to find where the potatoes of their neighbors are buried, and they steal them at night. Sometimes the problem is that people lend things or money, and they are unable to get them back. Sherpas know that worrying does not help to get things back, so they go to see a lama and ask him to dedicate their possessions, believing that if their missing items are dedicated or offered, somehow they will be returned to them. Of course, that does not make sense because the dedication depends on the person being able to completely renounce the possessions and feel compassion for the thieves. Without that kind of attitude, there is nothing to dedicate. The villagers would come to me with that sort of request, and I would try to explain to them that the best dedication would be to think that the person who took the things is also in need of them and is also suffering. If a feeling of compassion were to arise in their minds, then there would be merit to dedicate, and that would be a really powerful dedication.

I find it very difficult to teach the older Sherpas and Tibetans because they cannot read or write. It is much easier to teach the young boys and girls who go to school, even though they do not learn the Tibetan or Sherpa language. They study Nepali and English, so at least one can give them mantras and short prayers such as the refuge, bodhichitta, and dedication prayers in a form that they can read.

When I am in Khumbu, people come from very far to meet me. Some of them walk four or five hours to get to Lawudo and have to return to their homes before it gets dark. I give them many teachings about karma and purification, but although I try my best, they usually have difficulty understanding me because I do not speak Sherpa well enough, and most of them do not understand Tibetan. I have to ask one of the monks to translate my teachings into Sherpa language. The old fathers and mothers are very devoted; they recite many mantras and make prostrations and circumambulations, but they are not educated and have a hard time grasping the meaning of the Dharma teachings. After talking to them for about two or three hours, the only things they may be able to understand are the very simple points, such as if one does this or this or this, it is negative karma, *digpa*.

Westerners are extremely fortunate because they have received a good education and if they pay attention, they can understand the Dharma. And even if they do not understand at the moment, they can write it down or tape it and study later. So, I find it much easier to teach Dharma to Westerners than to Sherpas. What the Sherpas have is very great devotion. They accumulate merit every day because of their devotion, not because of their intellectual understanding. But if they lose the devotion, then their lives become completely empty and meaningless.

## The Third and Fourth Chenrezig Group Retreats

In 1980 we had another Chenrezig group retreat attended by seventy Westerners, and the following winter I did a short retreat in Kopan, just before the Tibetan New Year. Usually I am too lazy to do retreat, but due to the kindness of Lama Yeshe, who wanted me to do the retreat, somehow I did it. I moved to a small hut that a German called Dieter Khading had built on the very top of the hill; that was less noisy than my room. Lama was very happy and made many preparations in the hut. He bought a new carpet and a very expensive cup that was always filled with the best quality Tibetan tea that his brother Rinchen had brought from Tibet. Dieter stayed in a tent just behind the hut and would come whenever I called him; he did a very good job. I attained no realizations, nothing, but I had a wonderful time in his hut. It was not really a retreat, because retreat means keeping away from the worldly concerns and the self-cherishing thought, and that is something I am unable to do. In any case, I felt very fortunate and enjoyed the retreat very much, mainly because Lama was so happy. I could not find any other reason.

In the spring we sent a Tibetan artist to Lawudo, and in a record time of two months he was able to make four very large statues: of Shakyamuni Buddha, Guru Rinpoche, Thousand-Arm Chenrezig, and Tara. Lama invited Dilgo Khyentse Rinpoche to give a talk in Kopan, and the next morning Lama and I flew to Shangboche and went to Lawudo by horse. Lama stayed in the house next to the cave, but a couple of days later he became very sick. Actually, Lama had a very serious heart problem and should not have come to Lawudo, but he loved the mountains and wanted to be there once again. I did some rituals for him, and he was able to recover and teach the Westerners. I gave a Milarepa empowerment and we did two nyungnes. The Charog Lama Kusho Mangde attended the ceremony on the last day and seemed to enjoy very much being with Lama Yeshe and the Westerners.

In January 1982, my mother and sister came to Bodh Gaya to attend what we called the First Dharma Celebration. I gave the first part of the *Precious Source* empowerments,[320] and after the Tibetan New Year, we went to Dharamsala to receive teachings from His Holiness the Dalai Lama and Zong Rinpoche.[321] The teachings were quite lengthy, therefore I was unable to go to Lawudo for the nyungne that spring. Since then, neither Lama nor I have been able to go back to Khumbu every year as before, but the nyungnes have continued with the Tramo monks and nuns.

Around that time, my Aunt Lhamo came back to Nepal. Her husband had died and her son was gambling away her money, so she decided to leave Darjeeling. I then suggested that she could stay at Lawudo with my mother and sister.

At Lawudo, my sister continued to cook delicious Sherpa food and take care of the cows, while my mother looked after the cave and the gompa and recited mani continuously. Thubten Drolkar, the little second daughter of my cousin Pemba Butri, was staying at Lawudo and helped with small jobs. During the following years, a new retreat house ("Lama Yeshe's house") was built above the gompa, and three retreat rooms below the new kitchen. Westerners did retreats at Lawudo for a few weeks or months. Jampa Chökyi went almost every year, painted the gompa and the altar in the cave, and took care of the old texts and the "Lawudo Library." Merry Colony and her husband Jean-Marie fixed the cave of Gelong Ngawang Samten at Charog and did some retreats there, while Harry Sutton, an American monk, meditated in a small cave nearby.

53. Chörten at Tesho

## 29. Times of Change

*Lama Yeshe's Death*

DURING THE SUMMER OF 1983, there were some problems regarding our center in England, Mañjushri Institute; because of that, Lama Yeshe's health deteriorated considerably. After some months on tour in the West, Lama went to rest in Dharamsala, but I requested him to teach the students of the Kopan November Meditation Course and he finally agreed to come.

On the last day of the course, Lama gave a fantastic talk on bodhichitta.[322] That evening after dinner, I was eating some delicious canned cherries from India, and I began to promote them to Lama, like the TV advertisements where people eat something and look as if they are enjoying it very much. Lama ate some cherries and immediately started to vomit. For a couple of days he had to stay in bed and take medicines, but he was getting worse every moment. Finally, we took him to Delhi for treatment. After spending one week in a hospital, we rented a quiet farmhouse in the outskirts of Delhi.

While we were in that house, every evening I did a very powerful ritual of Kalarupa, the protector who helps one to realize emptiness and conquer death. There are four actions one can perform with this ritual—pacifying, increasing, controlling, and wrathful. I was doing the very wrathful one, which includes hooking the evil spirits who harm holy beings. That ritual involves concentration, and Lama did not want to do that part because whenever he concentrated his mind, his heart would stop. His concentration was very deep and stable, not like ours, and it seems that in that state of deep concentration when the person is meditating on the extremely subtle clear light mind, the heart does not function.

During that time in Delhi, whenever somebody came to visit, the aspect of Lama would change completely. He would become bright and magnificent, almost as if he were not sick at all. Then, the next day again he would look sick and dark. After one month we took Lama to California for medical treatment, but on March 3, 1984, the first day of the Tibetan New Year, the incomparable Lama Yeshe passed away in a hospital in Los Angeles.

A few years before his death, Lama had given to Jampa Chökyi detailed instructions about what should be done with his body. I had never heard about that, and it seems that only she and Jacie Keeley knew Lama's last wishes. He wanted his body to be preserved for one year and all his students to come together and recite Vajrasattva mantra near his body. That would have been an extremely powerful purification, and also a great source of inspiration. But when I learned about Lama's wishes, I had already invited Zong Rinpoche to come all the way from Switzerland to California to perform the last rites, and when I informed him about Lama's wishes, he said that the body should be burned. I had to follow his advice, and Lama's body was cremated on a ridge at Vajrapani Institute in Boulder Creek, California.

Lama Yeshe was kinder to me than all the buddhas of the past, present, and future. He guided my spiritual life and took care of me better than a father and a mother—like a mother hen feeding her chicks from mouth to mouth. He took care of my affairs in this life and provided for my next lives by giving me Dharma instructions and the opportunity to receive teachings and empowerments from many highly realized beings. His kindness can never be repaid.

When they heard that Lama Yeshe had died, many people felt sad—not only his students, but also people who had had only brief conversations with him. Those who had never met him but had read his words or listened to him on a video or cassette were able to get a warm feeling in their hearts and understand the special quality of Lama Yeshe, his great lovingkindness and unbearable compassion. Even someone who had never met the teachings of the Buddha could feel that Lama was somehow higher or different than ordinary people. Lama had an especially strong will and great courage to plan and implement great projects to benefit others and to spread the Dharma.

One of Lama's main characteristics was his ability to give teachings that were perfectly suited to each individual. From the time that we met Zina, just as when the sun rises the earth's darkness is dispelled, in the same way the darkness of ignorance in the mind of so many beings, particularly Westerners, was dispelled by Lama's teachings. Also, Lama Yeshe had a very broad mind, open to all the different Buddhist traditions and to all religions. Thus, because of his special qualities and his activities to subdue others by revealing the teachings through various means, many Tibetan lamas from all the traditions sent me letters expressing their sorrow at Lama's death. When other learned lamas or geshes pass away, there may not be such a sense of loss, but even though Lama had no reputation for having been a very learned, top-quality geshe, many Tibetan lamas felt that his death was a great loss. He was not concerned with the external words differentiating sutra and tantra or the different traditions, but he concentrated on the essential meaning of the teachings and put it into practice.

The qualities of Lama Yeshe's body, speech, and mind were beyond our comprehension. Years before, the doctors who had checked his heart could not understand how he could still be alive and traveling around, but Lama had achieved control over his body because of his great compassion and desire to help his students. Regarding his speech, his way of teaching was such that he did not need to speak about a particular subject; he would talk about many different things, in the same way as one serves different dishes of food. When different dishes are served, everyone might find something enjoyable. After one hour of listening to Lama, everybody was blissful and happy and had received some answer to their problems, whether they were intelligent and highly educated or not educated at all.[323]

Shortly after the cremation, I went to Switzerland to meet Zong Rinpoche again. Then I went on to Dharamsala. Afterward, I did a short retreat on top of the Kopan hill, while some of the students recited Vajrasattva mantra in front of Lama's ashes in the gompa. I commissioned a chörten to enshrine Lama's relics and a life-size statue of Lama, and then returned to Dharamsala to do retreat.

After Lama Yeshe passed away, my life underwent a great change. Until then, Lama had taken care of the administration of our Dharma centers all over the world, while I just gave teachings and advice to the students and relaxed in my room. Now I had to assume responsibility for continuing the work of Lama, and my life became extremely busy. Consequently, I had very little time to go to Lawudo, even though my mother continued to send messages asking me to come.

In December 1985, after giving the second part of the *Precious Source* empowerments at Kopan as part of the Second Dharma Celebration, I went to Bodh Gaya with the students and my whole family to receive the Kalachakra empowerment from His Holiness the Dalai Lama. Many

Tibetans had come from Tibet to attend the Kalachakra that year, and there were around 100,000 people in Bodh Gaya. At peak hours it was practically impossible to walk on the streets or to get into the temple compound, and the police had to use big sticks to keep the crowd under control. I used to go to the stupa late at night with the students when the gates were already closed. We all jumped over the fence, even my mother, and did practices under the Bodhi Tree or walked around the temple. But even at night there were always some Tibetans doing prostrations; by three in the morning the stupa would begin to get crowded, and we would all go home to sleep.

After the Kalachakra empowerment, we received teachings from His Holiness Sakya Trizin[324] and from Kirti Tsenshab Rinpoche.[325] Afterward, I went to Dharamsala to receive teachings from Geshe Senge, a Mongolian lama who was the abbot of Sera Monastery in Tibet.

Around that time, His Holiness recognized Ösel, the son of the Spanish students of Lama Yeshe Paco Hita and Maria Torres, as the tulku of Lama Yeshe. Ösel was officially enthroned in Dharamsala the following year, and stayed in Kopan with his family for a while.[326]

## The Panchen Lama and Tibet

During the summer of 1986, I went for a couple of weeks to Tibet with a group of students to take more teachings from Geshe Senge on the Most Secret Hayagriva. I also went on a teaching tour to the West.

When I came back to Nepal in November to teach part of the annual Kopan Meditation Course, a conference of the World Fellowship of Buddhists was taking place in Kathmandu. The Panchen Lama had been invited to attend as the representative of Tibetan Buddhism, and I registered for the conference as an observer in order to see him. The opening ceremony in the Kathmandu stadium was a very colorful function. The Newar Buddhists displayed a large collection of images of Dipankara Buddha, the first Buddha of this present era, and there were Buddhist dances from the Newar, Tamang, and Tibetan traditions. Then the Panchen Lama stood up and spoke a few words in Tibetan and Chinese, saying something like, "May the teachings of Lord Buddha always spread and flourish in all directions." He seemed very straightforward and powerful, and totally dedicated to others. I thought that the Tibetans in Tibet were very fortunate to have such an unbelievable lama in their country.

The following day we went to a tea party at Tribhuvan University, attended by Their Majesties King Birendra and Queen Aiswarya. The Panchen Lama and other dignitaries had tea upstairs with the king and queen while the rest of us sat in the garden. At some point, we heard that the Panchen Lama was leaving, and we all rushed toward the stairs to get a blessing from him. The Panchen Lama was dressed in a magnificent, shining yellow brocade chuba, and he walked down slowly, giving hand blessings to anyone who managed to place his or her head within his reach. In this way, I had the chance to see him at close range and take blessings from him, but it was not possible to have an audience or to speak even a few moments with him.

During that tea party I again met Ngawang Chöphel Gyatso, the disciple of the Lawudo Lama Kunzang Yeshe. In 1980 Ngawang Chöphel had built a monastery next to the Maratika Cave and became known as the Maratika Lama. He invited me many times to go there, but I have never been able to. Many great lamas do retreat in that cave and their life hindrances are dispelled. At the cave there is some special water that purifies the negative karma that causes one to be reborn in the lower realms and that can extend the life span. From time to time, Ngawang Chöphel used to send me a small bottle of this holy water. He passed away at his monastery in Maratika in 1997 while Trulzhig Rinpoche was there. Some tantric lamas wear a silver box with a mantra or text inside. It is called *tagdrol,* "liberation by wearing." If it is put on the crown of a great practitioner at the time of death, that person is able to obtain liberation and manifest rainbows and other special signs. Trulzhig Rinpoche put the tagdrol on Ngawang Chöphel's crown, which means that he was a highly advanced practitioner who had attained some realizations.[327]

In December 1986, shortly after the visit of the Panchen Lama to Nepal, I received a message that my mother had fallen down near the cave, and I went up to Lawudo immediately. My mother was not feeling so bad after all, but she was very glad to see me. I did a few rituals for her and she completely recovered. Then one evening, as we were preparing to offer tsog, someone burst into the cave with the news that my Aunt Lhamo had just passed away. She had been a little sick for a few days, but we did not think it was serious. I performed the transference of consciousness for her, and the next day Kusho Mangde's son Sonam Zangpo came to perform the death rituals and cremate the body.

In 1987 I went on a pilgrimage to Tibet with some lamas from Kopan and a large group of Westerners. I went to many interesting places and was able to pay a brief visit to Mindroling, the monastery where I had intended to study when I went to Tibet with my uncles in 1957.[328]

On the way back to Nepal we stopped in Shigatse and had an audience with the Panchen Lama. He seemed very pleased to meet such a large group of Western Buddhists. He gave us the oral transmission of the *Prayer to Be Reborn in Shambhala*[329] and a short piece of very helpful advice: "The essential religious practice is to not create negative karma, to subdue one's mind, and to not harm others. That applies to any religion." I was extremely impressed and very glad to have made a Dharma connection with him. After the teaching, he called me back and explained that he was planning to build a very large Kalachakra mandala in Shigatse, a mandala where you could actually enter inside, and asked me whether I could help raising funds for it. Panchen Rinpoche gave me some pieces of the robes of the previous Panchen Lamas and a few small statues to put inside the large Maitreya statue that I am trying to build in India. Two years later, when I was in Australia, I dreamed that the Panchen Lama was holding my hand and we were walking together down the street. His body was very tall, and he was wearing monastic robes. Later, I found out that he had passed away just that day.

The return journey from Shigatse to Nepal was quite hard and eventful. We were planning to spend the night in Sakya, but the Panchen Lama's entourage had insisted on showing us a film and in having us filmed watching it, and it was already quite late when we left. The driver refused to go to Sakya and took us to Lhatse instead. It rained continuously for the whole night, and the following morning we found the pass covered with snow. The driver could not see anything except a blanket of snow, and when we reached the top, the bus fell into a ditch by the side of the road. It did not completely overturn, but we could not pull it back onto the road. It was snowing and extremely cold, and some people were getting altitude sickness, so I went around giving blessed pills to everyone. Two hours later, after paying a large amount of money to a truck driver who agreed to pull the bus out of the ditch, we were able to continue the journey. After a few more incidents, we arrived in Nyanam around midnight, having had no food or drink for the whole day. The next morning we reached Kasa, or Zangmu, on the Nepali border, and crossed into Nepal, but the road had been washed away by heavy rains, and we had to cross some dangerous landslides and waterfalls and walk almost all the way to Kathmandu.

When we finally arrived, I gave a talk at our city center, the Himalayan Yogic Institute, about the benefits of pilgrimages and the advantages of experiencing hardships. In 1977, Serkong Tsenshab Rinpoche had given the first section of the *Precious Source* in Kopan. At the completion of the teachings, we had gone to the Spring of Enlightenment, or Jangchub Chumig, one of Padmasambhava's holy places.[330] Rinpoche had been offered a car by the representative of His Holiness the Dalai Lama in Kathmandu, but that day there was heavy rain and the car broke down. Fortunately we had the jeep from Kopan to take Rinpoche. We offered tsog at that holy place, and Rinpoche gave the oral transmission of Padmasambhava's mantra and other teachings. It was already dark when we started to leave, and again the car carrying Rinpoche would not go. We pulled it with the jeep by tying it with Lama Pasang's monastic shawl, but after a while we had to leave the car and the driver because it was too far to pull it all the way. On that occasion, Serkong Rinpoche explained that it is very good to undergo hardships when on pilgrimage because that helps to purify negative deeds, and that is the whole purpose of a pilgrimage.

Although I wanted very much to attend the yearly nyungne at Lawudo, it was not until 1990 that I was able to go again. I arrived only on the morning of the full-moon day. Everyone was prostrating silently in the gompa when the sound of the approaching helicopter was heard, and my relatives and some Westerners raced down the mountain with a large thermos of tea and a carpet. We landed in Mende on top of Pasang Namgyal's potato fields; luckily, the plants were still very small and there was not much damage. The monks, nuns, and laypeople welcomed me on the way holding khatags and incense and playing gyalings. My mother waited for me outside the gompa because she was already very old and had difficulty walking.

The next day many people came, and I gave them a long-life empowerment and some teachings. As usual, I talked for a few hours before giving the actual empowerment. Most of the people did not understand anything of what I said, even though it was translated into Sherpa. Nevertheless, at least I helped them to practice patience! I also gave teachings on the transference of consciousness, which I thought could be useful for some of them who were approaching the end of their lives.

# 30. My Mother

*...Indeed, mother is a lama from whom we gain our first instruction to the wholesome quality known as compassion. Dharma-teaching lamas come later. The quality of foundation built by the earliest lama, the mother, will determine whether the future lama's teaching on compassion will make any impression on the child or not.*

—His Holiness the XIV Dalai Lama [331]

DUE TO THE KINDNESS OF MY MOTHER, I was able to learn how to read and could study the Dharma. Now I can read the texts and teach students, but regarding compassion, which is the most important and real Dharma practice, I have none compared to my mother. She had unbearable compassion for everyone, her relatives, her friends, and those walking on the road without shoes and carrying huge loads.

In 1980, my mother came to Dharamsala and attended the spring teachings of His Holiness. She stayed at Tushita Retreat Center with us, and every morning after breakfast she would go all the way down the mountain to do *khora* (circumambulation). The breakfast at Tushita used to be some kind of porridge and a pancake that my mother was unable to chew because she had lost all her teeth, so she used to take the pancake with her and give it to the beggars who sat on the road to the temple. Every day she would give them some coins and bread, and after a few days all the lepers and beggars had become her friends. As she walked pass the beggars, she recited mani and said, "*Nyingje!* (How pitiful!) They may be feeling cold."

Usually she went alone, but soon she made friends with the other Tibetan ama-las who also did khora every day. When looking at the prosperous Kangra Valley, so different from Khumbu, she would say, "*Lungpa legmonog!*" (What a wonderful valley!) After walking around His Holiness's palace and temple at least seven times each day, she would walk back to Tushita, all the way back up the mountain. She was seventy-four at that time.

Amala did a Chenrezig retreat at Kopan, and I taught her some prayers. After a few years, when I listened to her, I found that some syllables were missing; her recitation was like broken teeth. Then she told me, "I do not know whether it is correct or not, but anyway, that is the way I pray." One of the prayers she used to recite was,

> Do not accumulate any negative actions,
> Always practice perfect virtue,
> Fully subdue your own mind:
> These are the teachings of the Buddha.

I found this prayer very effective for remembering the true Dharma practice, which is to subdue one's mind. So, I told my mother, "When you are with me, you must recite this prayer several times, and you must do it very loudly so that I can hear." Actually, this stanza summarizes a very vast subject; it contains the whole explanation of the Four Noble Truths.

In Khumbu and Tibet, when people have bad dreams or fear of death or if they have been sick for a long time, they ask a lama to give them practices to avert untimely death. One method is to liberate animals that are going to be slaughtered. People buy goats, chickens, or whatever animals they can and keep them until they die. Those large animals are expensive, but one can also buy fish or other small creatures. In Bodh Gaya, during the pilgrimage season, the Indians sell small fish in plastic bags with water. The pilgrims buy the fish to create merit and then put them into the large water pond south of the main temple. Then the Indians go back to the river to catch more fish. In any case, that method definitely prevents untimely death. You are causing others to have longer lives, and that itself is a karmic cause to prolong your own life.

When she had cataracts and was becoming blind, my mother asked the Charog Lama about her life span and whether she should have an operation. Kusho Mangde told her that she had only one year to live, but she could extend her life by liberating some animals. Regarding the operation, Kusho Mangde did not see much point and said that since she could not read the scriptures, she could continue to recite mani even if she were blind. But my mother did not agree.

Since she moved to Lawudo many years before, her daily routine had included cleaning my cave and making water offerings on the shrine. Then she would bring coals from the kitchen and burn some sweetly scented powder incense inside and outside the cave, prostrate to the Three

Jewels, and touch her head to the shrine to take blessings from the holy objects. After that, she would go down to the gompa and repeat the same ritual. Then she would walk around the building many times, reciting mani and turning her prayer wheel. She used to recite about 50,000 mantras every day. When she got tired, she would sit in the kitchen or outside in the sunshine. After she became old and was unable to hold the prayer wheel in her hand, I had a large one made for her. It was installed on the window so that she could sit in her bed and turn it easily.

After lunch, she would empty the water bowls, dry them in the sun, and wipe them thoroughly with a towel. In the evenings she lit a butter lamp in the cave and burned branches of juniper and tsampa outside to benefit the spirits and bardo beings. When she became blind, she was unable to do these chores and felt completely useless. All she could do was walk around the gompa with the help of Thubten Drolkar or whomever happened to be there. Finally, she went to the Khumde Hospital to have an operation and came back to Lawudo able to see again and very happy.

During the winter of 1983–84, my mother came again to Kopan. She liberated a few animals and brought a goat to Kopan. We gave it to the Nepali man who came to milk the cows to keep at his home and take good care of, but maybe it soon became his food! Amala told me that according to the horoscope and predictions made by Kusho Mangde, she had only one more year to live. "I am in the process of departing to the next life, to other realms of existence," she said. Then I told her, "That is fine, you don't need to worry. What you have been doing until now is already very good. You are always reciting mantras, so that is beneficial. Now, you should remember three things every day: I am definitely going to die today, material things do not help at the time of death, and only the Dharma can help. Remember these points day and night, morning and evening. Also, you should not gossip and should not criticize others with bad thoughts." This is what I told her, but actually she has a much better heart than I do. Compared to hers, my heart is completely black. When there was nobody around to engage her in gossip, she would always be reciting mantra and her thoughts were full of loving-kindness. Of course, she sometimes got angry, but her kind nature was stronger than the anger. She always wanted to offer something to whomever came to see her, no matter what, and was always willing to help. Amala was always concerned about those who took care of her and considered herself very low. When the monks brought her food or tea, she would say, "I am not worthy to be served by others because I have nothing. My stomach is empty," an expression that means, "I have no realizations."

When Lama Yeshe took the aspect of being extremely sick, my mother was in Kopan. She would sit the whole day in my room reciting mani without closing her eyes and making a great effort not to let her mind wander, dedicating her mantras for Lama Yeshe.

## My Mother's Death

His Holiness the Dalai Lama was scheduled to give a Kalachakra empowerment in Sarnath in late December 1990 and early January 1991, and my mother insisted that she wanted to attend. By now her mind was not so clear, and she could not do water offerings. Still, every morning she went to sweep the cave and made prostrations while reciting prayers. My sister did not think that my mother would be able to walk even as far as Shangboche, but somehow she managed.

When they arrived in Varanasi, my family was taken to the same hotel where I was staying, but neither my mother nor my sister felt comfortable there. Every day they had to go by car to Sarnath for the teachings and they were getting car sickness, so they decided to move to a tent on the roof of a house in Sarnath where the Kopan monks and nuns were staying.

The night before the actual empowerment there was a terrible storm, and the tents were blown away by the wind. Everyone got wet and cold, and my mother became ill. The next morning they were having an audience with His Holiness the Dalai Lama, and my brother had to carry her because she could not walk. His Holiness talked to her for a while and gave her a khatag and some blessed pills. That same evening, on January 1, 1991, she passed away peacefully in her bed. She stayed three days in thugdam, and her face became very beautiful and peaceful. On the fourth day, her face changed and some blood came out of her nostrils.

I felt very satisfied that my mother had such a good death. We offered many rituals on her behalf and took the body to be cremated on the shores of the Ganga River. Afterward, I went to Bodh Gaya and made extensive offerings and prayers for her good rebirth. The rest of the family went to Lumbini and made light offerings for her. In Kathmandu and Khumbu, money was offered to the monasteries to do prayers and light offerings on her behalf.

## Her Reincarnation

I asked my sister Ngawang Samten to build a large chörten on the main road between Samshing and Tesho to accumulate merit on behalf of our mother. In 1993 I went to perform the consecration of the chörten and the kani that I had asked to be built at Lukla. Shortly after I left Khumbu, my sister went to Genupa to visit Lhagpa, the wife of Lama Zangpo (Lama Zangpo is the son of Lama Ngawang, who was the youngest son of the Thangme Lama Dondrub). Although they live quite close to each other, the family of Lama Ngawang and the people at Lawudo rarely saw each other, but Ngawang Samten heard that Lhagpa had broken her leg and went to pay a courtesy visit.

The youngest son of Lama Zangpo had been born a few weeks after my mother's death and was now two years old. His mother told Ngawang Samten that he was very bright and was always talking about Lawudo. The boy seemed to recognize my sister and asked to be taken to Lawudo. Ngawang Samten went to visit him a few times, and the boy always asked her to take him to Lawudo and to bring him milk from the Lawudo cows. He also asked when Lama Zopa and Sangye were coming to visit, although he had never met us or heard about us. Finally, Ngawang Samten took him to Lawudo; the boy was very excited describing where everything was even before arriving. He embraced the large prayer wheel I had made for my mother and said that he wanted to stay there. My sister showed him some new robes together with my mother's old ones and asked him to choose. The boy immediately picked up my mother's old robes and ignored the very nice ones.

On another occasion, my sister made a shirt for him using some plastic buttons that my mother used to keep. In older times, Sherpas used to consider plastic buttons as something very precious because they could not be bought in Khumbu. Buttons, spoons, needles, and other similar things had to be brought from Darjeeling or Kathmandu. Sometimes people wore the spoons around their necks or on their belts, together with their keys. My mother used to collect the plastic buttons from old shirts and kept them in a bottle. So, when the boy put on the shirt that Ngawang Samten had made, he exclaimed, "Oh, these are my buttons!"

My sister checked with Lama Pasang Wangchug, a monk from Thangme reputed to do very good divinations, and he said that the boy was the reincarnation of our mother. She also checked with Trulzhig Rinpoche, and the reply was that the boy was definitely the reincarnation of our mother. Rinpoche gave him the name Ngawang Jigme and said that there was a need for many rituals to be performed for him, otherwise his lifeŪwould be very short.

Ngawang Samten and my brother Sangye invited Ngawang Jigme's family and the monks, nuns, and local people to attend a ceremony at Lawudo as a kind of enthronement for the boy. At the conclusion of the ceremony, everyone present offered khatags to Ngawang Jigme, and he returned them as a blessing, except to the monk Tsultrim Norbu, someone that my mother had not liked!

In May 1994, Lama Zangpo and Lhagpa took Ngawang Jigme to Kopan, where I was able to meet him for the first time. We performed an enthronement ceremony, and I offered a set of monastic robes to him. My wish was that Ngawang Jigme would come to study at Kopan, but his parents and grandfather wanted him to follow the Nyingma tradition and I had difficulty trying to convince them. I went back to Lawudo in 1998 to attend the nyungne and paid a visit to Lama Zangpo at Genupa, where he showed me a very blessed stone with the handprints of his ancestor Chatang Chöying Rangdrol. His father Lama Ngawang had recently passed away, and Lama Zangpo finally agreed to send Ngawang Jigme to Kopan the following year because that particular year was not auspicious for entering a monastery.

The next year, Lhagpa's cousin Ngawang Labsum, who is the tulku of Lama Ngodrub (Lama Ngodrub was the middle son of the Thangme Lama Dondrub), visited the family at Genupa. When Ngawang Labsum offered to take Ngawang Jigme with him to Penor Rinpoche's monastery in South India and look after him, the parents agreed to let him take the boy. A couple of weeks after joining Penor Rinpoche's monastery, the boy fell down and injured his head very badly. I sent some Kopan monks from our hostel in Sera to take care of him and sponsored all the medical expenses. Ngawang Jigme's parents were unable to make the long journey to South India, and the boy stayed in a hospital in Mysore with his elder brother and the Kopan monks. He was operated on three or four times, but his condition did not improve. He was finally brought to Kathmandu, where he passed away in a hospital on October 27, 1999. My sister has built a chörten at Tesho in memory of Ngawang Jigme, and I pray that he will come back again in a new body and have the opportunity to practice the Dharma.

My mother was able to be reborn as a human in a Buddhist family and meet the Dharma because she had been a nun in her previous life and had kept pure morality. Having such a clear memory of his previous life was due to having recited Chenrezig's mantra so many times. She is just one example of how someone who has no intellectual training and cannot even read one sentence of the scriptures can actually practice Dharma. She was able to abandon the negative actions of killing, stealing, and so forth, and her everyday life activities—eating, walking, sitting, sleeping, or working—became pure Dharma actions. These normal activities became the path to enlightenment because they were done with compassion for others and with devotion. In this way, she was able to accumulate infinite merit.

## Conclusions

Just like my mother, most of the older generation of Sherpas do not have an intellectual education, but their lives are extremely rich and meaningful because of their great devotion and compassion. (Some of them, however, externally seem to be very devoted but have no compassion at all.) By making offerings to the lama and Chenrezig, and continuously reciting the six-syllable mantra even while walking on the road or working in the fields, they accumulate a great amount of merit and plant the seeds of enlightenment.

On the other hand, although in the West there is great material development and most people receive a high standard of intellectual education, very few of them have the good fortune to meet the Dharma and to develop devotion toward the Three Jewels, which are more precious than any wish-granting jewel. People do not know what is right and wrong and what should be developed or avoided. Their present wealth and material comfort is the result of previous good deeds, but since they have no opportunity to collect merit for their future lives, their stock of merit is diminishing day by day. If their attitude is not one of compassion for others but only of seeking happiness in this life, their wealth becomes the cause of creating negative karma leading them to a low rebirth.

The main difference between "primitive" or uncultured people, such as Sherpas, and those who belong to a highly developed, wealthy society with technological and scientific achievements is that Sherpas and other simple people have faith in a perfect object. Among wrong, average, and good medicines, they choose faith as the best medicine. When a person is falling from a cliff and sees various ropes hanging down, that person has to grab the right one in order to be pulled. In the same way, even blind faith toward the unmistakable, correct object has "skies" of benefits. Faith and devotion toward the Three Jewels leads to a good rebirth, wealth, liberation from cyclic existence, and full enlightenment. Thus, I rejoice very much in the lives of the "primitive" Sherpas or the Tibetan beggars who, thanks to the great compassion of His Holiness the Dalai Lama, the real emanation of Chenrezig, continuously chant *Om mani padme hum.*

These days the young Sherpas are more interested in climbing mountains than in listening to the Dharma. The person who climbs very steep and dangerous mountains is considered very brave. One renounces even one's life just to get a reputation and hear the empty words, "such and such a person climbed Mount Everest." Maybe the person doesn't die in an avalanche or a fall, makes it to the top, and is able to return safely. The person may receive some material profit and his or her name may appear in the papers, and people will talk about it for a few years. But what is the use of all this? There is no benefit for that person in that life or in future lives. How does it benefit their mental peace and their ability to free beings from suffering? All these hardships are meaningless. They cannot compare with the advantages of listening to just one hour of the Buddha's explanations on how to eliminate the negative emotions, which are the root of suffering. The really brave person, the real hero, is the one who can control, or climb on top of, negative emotions.

Since the first meditation course in 1971, I have taught the Kopan courses almost every year, although for the last twelve years or so I have only been able to teach a few days of each course. The first and second courses were taught in the old Nepali house. The third and fourth courses took place in the gompa, but afterward there were so many students that they could not fit in the prayer hall. The fifth, sixth, and seventh courses took place between the hill and the gompa, in a large tent made with bamboo poles and with hay and grass mats full of fleas on the floor. People had to sleep there at night because there were not enough rooms. In those days I used to teach about detachment and renunciation, and then the students would eat under the two large trees, while the smell from the toilets (labeled "Sam" and "Sara" respectively) arose around them. In November 1975 we moved the tent to the south side of the hill. The monks dug the earth, put roofing sheets on bamboo poles, and covered the sides with very cheap cloth. For many years the courses took place in that tent, until in 1991 a new gompa was built on the spot where the old house had been. Now, the Kopan course has become a luxurious "ten-star," or even a "fifteen-star," course!

54. Sherpas dancing in front of Lawudo Gompa

In the early days I used to teach very much about suffering. When I taught, the minds of the people became dark, like the sun going down. Then Lama Yeshe would come to teach, and everything would become light, like sunshine. Again I would teach, and everything would become dark. Like this we taught the courses. So, in those days Kopan was very primitive and there were many hardships, but we were extremely fortunate. Those were very meaningful times.

I am now the head of an organization comprised of over 130 Dharma centers—teaching and retreat centers, monasteries, nunneries, hospices, clinics, and schools—in different countries. I travel around the world quite often, teaching courses and leading retreats.[332] Occasionally, I find time to visit Lawudo for a few days. Then I really enjoy myself by relaxing in my cave, eating Sherpa food, listening to the local gossip, and joking with my sister and Ashang Ngawang Yonten.

According to our beliefs or perceptions, there is a truly existent Lawudo, which in fact does not exist at all as it appears or as we believe. Lawudo is a merely labeled phenomenon. In previous times, the villagers used to keep radishes inside the cave, and it eventually became known as Labudo. *Labu* means radish and *do* means stone. Other people have called it Rawudo because during the night the wild goats, the *ra,* would sleep there. So, on the basis of what occurred in the cave, people labeled it with thought and a name. That is how Lawudo came into existence. Then, because a lama, who was also merely labeled, practiced merely labeled meditation in that merely labeled cave, he became known as the Lawudo Lama, which is just another label. Lawudo and the Lawudo Lama appear to exist from their own side, but that is just the perception of our deluded mind. We believe they are truly existent, but their true existence cannot be perceived by the enlightened mind of the Buddha.

So now, when you look for the real nature of Lawudo and the Lawudo Lama, you might feel that they almost do not exist!

> *It is assumed that a person reincarnates,*
> *But when one looks for such a person,*
> *It cannot be found, neither in the five aggregates, the sense spheres,*
> *　nor the elements.*
> *Who, then, will reincarnate?*
>
> —Nagarjuna, *Mulamadhyamakakarika,* 16:2

# Epilogue

THE LAWUDO LAMA Thubten Zopa Rinpoche is now based in the United States of America, from where he takes care of his numerous students, Dharma centers, and projects. For a large part of the year he travels around the world giving teachings, and he also finds time to engage in private retreats in order to recharge his energy.

Besides providing the opportunity for young Sherpas to be educated in a monastic environment and spreading the Dharma in the West, Lama Zopa Rinpoche is very interested in reviving Buddhism in Mongolia. But his most outstanding project is the construction in India of a huge statue of the future Buddha, Maitreya, the Loving One. In Lama Zopa's own words, "The purpose of building a statue of Maitreya, who is the embodiment of the loving-kindness of all buddhas, is to increase peace, happiness, and prosperity, and for sentient beings to develop bodhichitta and universal responsibility, and to practice kindness, forgiveness, and rejoicing in the good deeds of themselves and others." In accordance with the late Lama Yeshe's wishes, the statue was to be erected in Bodh Gaya, but after many years of delays caused by difficulties in obtaining land, the original plan had to be abandoned. It will now be built in Kushinagar, the sacred place in northern India where Sakyamuni Buddha passed into nirvana and where the future Buddha Maitreya will be born.

## The Relatives of the Lawudo Lama Kunzang Yeshe

Karma Tenzin, the grandson of the Lawudo Lama Kunzang Yeshe, was totally dedicated to the Dharma and did not mind leading a simple life without material comfort. In 1960 he married Serkyimi, a girl from Chubarma in Shorong, but his wife was not happy and one day she went away, leaving their two small children, aged six and two, with their father.

When Diu Rinpoche's monastery in Chubarma burned down and the lama moved to Pangboche, Karma Tenzin would spend the summer months in Thangme and Pangboche and the winters in Bouddha with

Diu Rinpoche, taking one of his sons with him. He did not have enough money to rent a room and used to stay in the house of a Tamang family in a corner under the stairs. Sometimes he would go to collect firewood in the Shivapuri Mountain and sell it in Bouddha. Karma Tenzin sent his eldest son Sangye Yeshe to Mindroling Monastery. His second son Tenzin Dorje wanted to go to school to learn English and other subjects and then find a good job, but his father insisted that he also join Mindroling Monastery.

In 1984, when he was fifty-eight years old, Karma Tenzin became very sick, and his friends sent a message to the boys to come back and take care of their father. Shortly after Tenzin Dorje's arrival, Karma Tenzin died in Bir Hospital in Kathmandu. The boy had no money for the cremation and the funeral rites, but Lama Zopa's brother Sangye and the members of the Sherpa Gompa in Bouddha collected money and managed to arrange a decent funeral.

Karma Tenzin's sons sold most of their father's books to a distant relative from Namche and stayed in Kathmandu looking for jobs. After some difficult years, Sangye Yeshe found a job as cook in the monastery of Paltul Jampel Lodro Rinpoche in Bouddha, and Tenzin Dorje began to work for a trekking company. He sold one of the fields at Thangteng but kept the ruins of the old house at Thangme Gompa. Only recently he sold it to the monastery.

The Lawudo Lama's granddaughter Pemba Dekyi lives in Thangme. Her husband Pasang Namgyal, who built the gompa, kitchen, and retreat houses at Lawudo, passed away in 2000. Their eldest son Rithar Tsering, born in Lawudo in 1956, and their youngest son Lhakpa work for a trekking company in Kathmandu.

### Lama Zopa's Family

Lozang, the son of Aku Ayulha from Phag-ri, lives in Darjeeling, and Ngawang Samten, the daughter of Aku Ngawang Gedun, at Lawudo. After Ngawang Gedun's death, his wife married Aku Ngawang Jigme. Ngawang Jigme spent many years in Simigaon near Rolwaling. He later moved to the hermitage above Beding and became a widely respected lama. He passed away in October 2003.

Ashang Pasang and his wife now live in a nice, comfortable house that their children built for them not far from Kopan. Their son Pemba, who in 1982 became the cook for Lama Yeshe and Lama Zopa, later became a monk and is now the director of a Dharma center in Hong Kong. His younger brother Nyima Tashi also became a monk and is the attendant of Kusho Mangde's tulku. Ashang Trinle, who had been a monk for many years, married and lives near Khari Khola. He has four children, one of them a nun in the Kopan nunnery. Ashang Yonten lives in his little hut in Thangme Gompa and very seldom goes to Lawudo. Lama Zopa's niece Thubten Drolkar, who spent her childhood at Lawudo, became a nun in 1992 at the Kopan nunnery and is now known as Thubten Zangmo.

55. Ani Ngawang Samten serving *sen* in the Lawudo kitchen (courtesy of Ani Ngawang Zangmo)

Lama Zopa's brother Sangye became quite well off by engaging in various business and trekking ventures. He lives in his nice house in Chuchepati, not far from Bouddha, with his wife Nyima. His eldest son Pemba married a Nepali girl of Chetri caste and is now a pilot working for Yeti Airways. His second son Pasang and eldest daughter Yangchen have married Khumbu Sherpas and live in the United States. The youngest daughter Drolkar is studying in Kathmandu.

Lama Zopa's sister Ngawang Samten continues to preside over the Lawudo kitchen, surrounded by her dearest friends, the Lawudo cows. She supervises the shopping and cooking activities, cutting of firewood and grass for the cows, the planting and collection of potatoes, and so forth. And although age has made her less strong and energetic, she still prefers the hard, rough life of Khumbu to the noisy and polluted, although in some ways easier, life of the Kathmandu Valley.

### The Charog Lamas

After many years studying under the guidance of Trulzhig Rinpoche, the tulku of the Thangme Lama Dondrub, Ngawang Tsedrub Tenpe Gyaltsen, is now in full charge of the Thangme Gompa. He has enlarged and repaired the temple and courtyard to accommodate the growing number of Sherpas and tourists who come every year to attend the Mani Rimdu celebrations. There are now over thirty monks and a few married lamas at the gompa, besides an increasing number of young boy-monks who are pursuing basic Buddhist studies under the guidance of senior monks.

Lama Zangpo, the son of Lama Dondrub's youngest son (Lama Ngawang) and father of the late reincarnation of Lama Zopa's mother, lives with his family at Genupa. He takes care of the cave where his ancestor Chatang Chöying Rangdrol meditated, paints thangkas, and makes statues and masks for the Mani Rimdu. He is a kind person and a very skillful artist.

Kusho Mangde spent his last years in his hermitage at Charog with his son and daughter. His son Sonam Zangpo had married the daughter of the Jasa Lama Ngawang Sherab. The couple did not have children and Kusho Mangde worried that the family lineage would become extinct. Sonam Zangpo then took Sonam from Pare as his second wife, and soon two children were born to them.

In 1989, Kusho Mangde decided to bestow the complete transmission of his Dharma lineage to his son Sonam Zangpo, his daughter Pema Chöden, and grandson Tenzin Trinle. They made preparations and set up all the offerings and tormas for the rituals to begin early the next day, but during the night a cat crept inside the shrine room and ate the tormas. Kusho Mangde again made all the preparations for the empowerments; this time there were no further obstacles. When he was to give the empowerments of the Dharma protectors, he sent Sonam Zangpo to borrow various ritual clothes and implements from Thangme Gompa and told him to come back to Charog straight away because those implements were very powerful. On the way back, however, Sonam Zangpo stopped in Tramo to drink chang with a friend and went then to Tesho and continued to drink. His wife came down from Charog to get him, but he refused to go back and kept on drinking. He passed away that very night, and his youngest son also died the following week. Thus, the young Tenzin Trinle became the heir of the Charog Lamas' lineage.

A few years before his death in January 1992, Kusho Mangde had commissioned a silver chörten where his ashes were to be enshrined. His daughter then requested him, "Father, please do not come back as a tulku because the holder of your lineage is Tenzin Trinle," but we do not know Kusho Mangde's reply.

In early 1995, while on her way from Genupa to Lawudo, Lama Zopa's sister met a lady from Tramoteng struggling with her little son Lhagpa Tenzin. The boy was screaming at the top of his voice, saying that he wanted to go to "his house" at Charog. The mother told Ngawang Samten that when their house was damaged by the recent heavy snowfall, Lhagpa Tenzin had said, "Amala, you don't have to worry about this old, broken house. I have a big house up there at Charog, below a big cliff and surrounded by large boulders. My house has a gompa and two prayer wheels, and my daughter Pema Chöden lives there."

Soon after, Lhagpa Tenzin's father passed away, and Ngawang Samten offered to take the boy and his sister Lhagpa Butri to Lawudo, so that the mother could work as a porter in expeditions without having to worry about the young children. At Lawudo, Lhagpa Tenzin kept talking about "his house" at Charog. He spent the day making clay "tsog offerings" and pretending he was reading scriptures and chanting the Vajra Guru mantra. When Lama Ngawang Tsultrim of Tolu Gompa, one of the closest disciples of Kusho Mangde, came to Lawudo, Lhagpa Tenzin recognized him immediately. Later, Lhagpa Tenzin wanted to write to Lama Zopa saying that he was the Charog Lama and wanted to go to Kopan to study, become a great lama, and teach Westerners.

Trulzhig Rinpoche recognized Lhagpa Tenzin as the tulku of Kusho Mangde and gave him the name Ngawang Rigzin Tenzin Gyatso. In 1996, Ngawang Rigzin joined Kopan Monastery, and his sister entered the Khachö Gakyil nunnery. Ngawang Rigzin is now studying in Sera Monastery and later, if he wishes, he may receive the lineage of his predecessor from the disciples of his previous life. Meanwhile, Ani Pema Chöden and Tenzin Trinle live a secluded life at Charog, totally dedicated to meditation and ritual practices.

## Other Khumbu Gompas and Lamas

The Kyabrog Gompa is now under the leadership of Ngawang Tsultrim, a very intelligent and energetic young man. The Dzamtra Hermitage near Mingbo has been abandoned for many years, and the local people report that it is haunted by srindi, or ghosts, and that all kinds of strange things happen there. The Akar Cave Hermitage is likewise deserted, except for Ngawang Tagten, an old nun from Khumjung, who still remembers the visit of the previous Lawudo Lama to his ailing friend Au Yeshe.

Some of the Khari monks and nuns who came from Tibet in 1959 have already passed away, but in the last twelve years a large number of young Tibetan nuns have joined the nunnery. The third Khari Rinpoche Tenzin Yonten is studying in Sera Monastery. In 2003 he took a year off from his studies in order to build a new, larger prayer hall in the Tramo Nunnery.

Around 1974, Gen Lama Tenzin Tsultrim moved to a small hermitage above Khumde, where he built the Nyungne Lhakhang. He performed many nyungnes and gave empowerments from all traditions of Tibetan Buddhism. Gradually, many young monks arrived from Tibet, and the hermitage became a busy place. Gen Lama passed away in 1993 and stayed twenty-four days in thugdam, but he refused to manifest again as a tulku in this world and has now departed for other realms. Tenzin Zangpo and his wife Chöden, who had both been ordained monastics in Tramo, are now in charge of the hermitage.

Because of the increasing number of trekkers and mountaineering expeditions, the Tengboche Monastery is well known all over the world. The Tengboche Lama is doing a great work for the development of the monastery and of the whole region. At Tengboche, the Mani Rimdu festivities now take place during the ninth Tibetan month, at the height of the trekking season, when many foreigners are able to enjoy it.

Around 1989, a small hydroelectric plant was constructed at Tengboche with sponsorship from foreign organizations. But shortly after electricity had been installed in the monastery, an electric heater was inadvertently left on in the office, which happened to be full of paper to print mantras for a new prayer wheel. Soon the whole monastery was ablaze, and although no one was hurt, many old texts and Mani Rimdu costumes from Tibet were lost.[333] The gompa was promptly rebuilt with Sherpa and foreign donations, and consecrated by Trulzhig Rinpoche.

For many years, only a few elderly nuns were left at the Deboche nunnery. Among those, Ani Ngawang Pemo, who has been in retreat at Deboche for more than forty years, provides a strong spiritual inspiration to the whole area. Recently, some new young Tibetan nuns from Kham have joined the nunnery.

Diu Rinpoche passed away in 1989 in Pangboche. His tulku Ngawang

Jangchub Rigzin was born in Gyantse in 1991. After spending a few years in Thubten Chöling, he is now studying in Zang Zang Tulku's Lhundub Chöling Gompa in Budanilkanta, Kathmandu, where he was enthroned by Trulzhig Rinpoche on October 13, 2000. The spiritual needs of the Pangboche Sherpas are taken care of by Geshe Urgyen Dorje, who runs a lodge, gives teachings, and leads yearly nyungnes at the Namkha Dzong Hermitage above Dingboche.

After three years in Pemkar, Gomchen Gampa-la moved to Lukla and stayed for a while in the luxurious hotel of one of his benefactors until his sponsor Au Dorje offered him a small plot of land right above the airstrip. Although the place was very damp, Gomchen-la liked it, and in 1983 the villagers and some Khari nuns built a small hut for him. But soon after moving to the new house, he became quite sick and passed away. He stayed seven days in thugdam, and his body was cremated at a nice spot above Lukla. When the purkhang was opened a few days later, no relics or special signs could be found. Trulzhig Rinpoche was consulted, and the answer was that since the people in Lukla were always gambling, drinking, and fighting, the environment was too polluted for relics to manifest. Gelong Tsultrim Yeshe and Ani Donma Pande molded *tsatsas* with Gomchen-la's bones and ashes and built three chörtens at the spot where the cremation had taken place. Gomchen-la's tulku Ngawang Rigzin Tenpa was born in Pangboche the following year, and is now studying in the monastery of His Holiness Penor Rinpoche.

As for the Maratika Lama Ngawang Chöphel Gyatso, he took monastic vows in 1990 after his wife passed away. He did extensive work to develop the Maratika Cave until his death in 1997. His tulku Tenzin Chögyal was born in the iron dragon year (2000) in Sikkim and officially recognized by Trulzhig Rinpoche in January 2003. Ngawang Chöphel's son Lopön Karma Wangchug is now in charge of the monastery at Maratika.

## Khumbu, Present and Future

The old Khumbu has now become part of the realm of reminiscences. The opening of the country to trekkers and mountaineering expeditions in 1950, the creation of schools, the closure of the traditional trade with Tibet in the early sixties, and finally the transformation of Khumbu into the Sagarmatha National Park in 1975 brought about deep changes in Sherpa society. Thousands of trekkers and mountain climbers visit Khumbu every year, bringing with them new ideas and lifestyles.[334] Sherpa economy is now based on the tourist and trekking business instead of the traditional trade and husbandry.

One the most amazing traits of the Sherpa mind is its resilience and adaptability to changes. Although a large number of Khumbu Sherpas are working or studying in Kathmandu and the West, their social and religious identity has not been lost, and has in fact become even stronger. The families make even more lavish contributions to the Mani Rimdu and Dumche, sponsor the construction of temples, prayer wheels, and stupas in the Kathmandu Valley, and have repaired the mani walls, chörtens, and so forth in Khumbu. There is now a new generation of well-educated Sherpas who were born and grew up in Kathmandu and have lost contact with their ancestral Khumbu homeland, but they proudly consider themselves Sherpas and Buddhists, and follow most of the cultural and religious practices of their parents. On the other hand, they refuse to accept certain old beliefs that they see as superstitions and instead try to introduce more rational and practical behavior to Sherpa society. Many of them have received a high education in foreign institutions, and after obtaining their Ph.D.s, are now contributing extensively to the development of Khumbu.

These people want to open a restaurant atop Everest, Sir !

56. *The Kathmandu Post*, Saturday, May 18, 2002 (Rajesh K.C.)

With the help of the Austrian group Eco Himal, a small hydro power plant was constructed near Thangme and began functioning in 1995. It is managed by a Sherpa company (Khumbu Bijuli Company) and provides electricity to Namche, Khumjung, Khumde, Shangboche, Phurte, Samshing, Tesho, Mende, Lawudo, Tramo, Zamte, Thangme, Thangteng, Yulhajung, and Kyabrog Gompa.[335]

Electricity has brought about a wide range of changes in Sherpa life, some positive and some that tend to be negative. Thanks to it, the use of firewood for cooking and heating has been reduced considerably, although locals and tourists alike cannot resist the pleasure of sitting around a warm fireplace or stove during the cold evenings. To make the traditional butter tea, most Sherpas do not use the wooden dongmo anymore but an electric mixer instead. With less smoke produced by wood and yak dung, respiratory diseases and eye problems of Sherpa women have decreased. Electric light allows school children to do their homework in the evening and monks to recite the scriptures at night. Hot showers, sauna, bakeries, pizzerias, laundry, a cinema hall, computers, Internet, email, fax, phone, and photocopy are now common in Namche. On the negative side, electricity makes it easier to spend the nights gambling, playing in pool bars, watching videos and satellite television, listening to pop music, and dancing in discos. Noise pollution is becoming a problem in Namche and even in Lawudo, where electricity is being used (or rather misused) to blast Tibetan religious music all over the mountain.

Some other positive developments have taken place in Khumbu. In Namche there is a health post, dental clinic, and Tibetan medical center, as well as bank, money changers, bookshops, running water, two mineral water bottling plants, a Sagarmatha Pollution Control Center, about fifty lodges, and numerous shops. Now it is possible to buy practically everything in Namche, although at a much higher price than in Kathmandu.

Thanks to the efforts of the Sagarmatha National Park, extensive reforestation and wildlife conservation programs have been successfully introduced, and a large number of young trees are now growing above Namche and other areas. The population of wild goats and *danphe* birds has increased noticeably, but also the predators. During the spring of 2003, a group of two adult and two young snow leopards killed four cows around Lawudo in broad daylight, and similar incidents have been reported from the Thangme and Thangteng areas.

As a sad reminder of the impermanent nature of all phenomena, most of the Khumbu caves and hermitages are now empty and in ruins. With the opening of a luxurious hotel in Mende, tourists make impromptu appearances at Lawudo, Charog, and Genupa, thus disturbing religious practices and retreats. In exchange, tourists' visits result usually in large monetary reward for a nice smile and cup of tea.

Jomo Langma, Ama Dablam, Khumbilha, Tawoche, Tamserku, Gangtega, Kabsale, and their snowbound companions are still there, silent witnesses of these times of degeneration. Less than a hundred years ago, their slopes were adorned by spiritual seekers, strong-minded, dedicated practitioners who strove to attain buddhahood in one single lifetime. Now, in the twenty-first century, the quest for buddhahood has been replaced by the struggle toward the mountain peaks and the search for material prosperity. But hope for a spiritual revival is becoming stronger every day.

Increasing numbers of Sherpa youngsters are now joining the monasteries and nunneries. Others, who are not inclined to monastic life, are beginning to question the reasons why so many foreigners from affluent countries are becoming Buddhists and practicing meditation. Young Sherpas want to know the real meaning of their own religious tradition and not just the cultural aspects that they learned from their parents.

The Lawudo Cave is still there, open to serious practitioners who want to develop their meditational experiences.

The dakinis also (we hope), waiting to bestow their help.

And the yeti, of course!

# Long-Life Prayer for the
# Lawudo Lama Thubten Zopa Rinpoche

From a mass of wish-granting clouds—
The wisdom of the conquerors of the three roots, such as
    Amitayus—
A rain of jewels bestows the magnificence of fortune and
    happiness.
May the supremely virtuous brightness of wisdom spread
    everywhere.

Holder of the saffron robes of the three vows, the ornament of
    the Buddha's doctrine [Thubten],
Wearing the armor of enduring [Zopa] the hardships
Of striving in the practice of the infinite ocean of tantras,
Victor over the four maras, may your feet remain steadily firm
    [in this world].

With wonderful skillful deeds
You lead fortunate disciples on the sublime path to liberation,
Acting in accordance with the lives of innumerable holy beings.
Auspicious golden sun, may you shine forever.

*Colophon:*

This prayer for the long life and accomplishment of the deeds of the precious reincarnation of the wisdom knowledge-holder of the Khumbu Snow Wall was written by Dela Longchen Yeshe Dorje [Dephug Rinpoche] because of the insistent requests of Lama Karma Tenzin, the holder of the family lineage.

# Appendix I: Chronology of Events

15TH CENTURY: The first Khampas migrate to Khumbu (tentative).

17TH CENTURY: Sangwa Dorje and his brothers found the first Sherpa gompas; Terdag Lingpa founds Mindroling Monastery.

18TH CENTURY: Khumbu becomes part of the Nepal state; introduction of the potato; birth of Jamyang Chökyi Rigzin; Lama Tenpa Sangye is the head of Thangme Gompa; Kunzang Yeshe's ancestors come to Khumbu.

19TH CENTURY:

EARLY YEARS: Founding of Drag-ri Gompa, Charog, Genupa, and Jasa hermitages, Beding Gompa; Thangme Lamas Tulku Ngawang Dorje and Chatang Chöying Rangdrol.

1831: Founding of the Kangyur Lhakhang and beginning of Dumche at Khumjung.

1850: Birth of Lama Gulo and Serwa Lama Karma.

1852: Birth of Serkong Dorje Chang Ngawang Tsultrim Donden.

1853: Birth of Togden Shakya Shri.

1857: Death of Gyurme Urgyen Tenphel of Dza Rongphu.

1865: Birth of the Lawudo Lama Kunzang Yeshe (approximate); death of Chatang Chöying Rangdrol; his son Ngawang Trinle Lhundrub assumes the leadership of Thangme Gompa.

1867: Birth of Dzatul Ngawang Tenzin Norbu.

1877: Birth of Tripön Ngawang Padma Chögyal.

1886: Birth of Ani Karzang.

1890: Birth of the Khari Lama Lozang Tsultrim.

1892: Birth of Wangyal.

1894: Birth of Kunnu Lama Tenzin Gyaltsen and Aku Ayulha.

1895: Death of Ngawang Trinle Lhundrub; his son Kunzang Dechen Gyalpo assumes the leadership of Thangme Gompa.

1899: Birth of Drakar Taso Kagyu Tenzin Norbu.

20TH CENTURY:

1901:  Founding of Dza Rongphu Monastery; birth of Kuye Tenzin Chökyi Nyima and Trijang Rinpoche.

1902:  Kunzang Yeshe receives teachings from Trulzhig Kunzang Thongdrol at Rongphu.

1903:  Beginning of the Mani Rildrub practice at Rongphu; birth of Ling Rinpoche.

1904:  Birth of Diu Rinpoche.

1905:  Birth of Ngawang Sherab Zangpo (Kusho Mangde), Zong Rinpoche, and Au Palden; the Dzamtra Lama builds a mani tunchur at Namche.

1907:  Birth of Nyima Yangchen.

1909:  Birth of Pasang Puthar; founding of the Kangyur Lhakhang and beginning of the Dumche at Namche; Artsa Lama visits Khumbu and Kunzang Yeshe goes on pilgrimage with him.

1910:  Birth of H. H. Dilgo Khyentse Rinpoche.

1912:  Kunzang Yeshe returns from his pilgrimage.

1913:  Birth of Gen Lama Tenzin Tsultrim.

1914:  Dzatul Ngawang Tenzin Norbu asks the Sherpas to build a monastery in Khumbu; birth of Serkong Tsenshab Rinpoche and Lama Zopa's aunt Dawa Butri.

1915:  Death of Kunzang Dechen Gyalpo; the Kusho Tulku becomes the head of Thangme Gompa.

1916:  Kunzang Yeshe moves to Lawudo (approximate).

1919:  Birth of the second Serkong Dorje Chang and Ashang Pasang Dorje; death of Shakya Shri; Dzatul Ngawang Tenzin Norbu consecrates Tengboche Monastery.

1920:  Birth of Geshe Rabten and Aku Ngawang Jigme; beginning of the Mani Rimdu in Tengboche and Thangme.

1921:  First Everest mountaineering expedition.

1922:  Birth of Ngawang Chöphel Gyatso and Ashang Ngawang Trinle; death of Trulzhig Kunzang Thongdrol.

1923:  Kusho Tulku and Kusho Mangde leave for Shorong; Lama Tsering Dondrub assumes the leadership of Thangme Gompa.

1924:  Birth of Trulzhig Ngawang Chökyi Lodro; Lama Dondrub rebuilds Thangme Gompa.

1925:  Building of Chiwang Gompa and Deboche Nunnery begins.

1926:  Birth of Karma Tenzin, Ashang Ngawang Yonten, and Kirti Tsenshab Rinpoche; death of Nulu, Lama Zopa's maternal grandfather.

1927:   Birth of Pemba Dekyi and Au Dargye.

1928:   Consecration of Deboche Nunnery.

1929:   Consecration of Chiwang Gompa.

1930:   Birth of Drubthob Rinpoche Yeshe Namdag; Lama Wangyal builds a house at Lawudo.

1931:   Birth of Kochag Drogon Pema Wangchug; death of Serwa Lama Karma; Kusho Tulku and Kusho Mangde leave Chiwang Gompa.

1933:   Death of the Thirteenth Dalai Lama.

1934:   Great earthquake; death of Lama Gulo and destruction of Tengboche Gompa; Kusho Tulku and Kusho Mangde settle in Toloka.

1935:   Birth of the Fourteenth Dalai Lama, Lama Thubten Yeshe, Tengboche Lama Ngawang Tenzin Zangpo, and Kochag Drogon Ngawang Pema Rigzin.

1936:   Death of Kusho Tulku and Lama Wangyal.

1937:   Birth of Kusho Tulku Ngawang Lozang Yeshe Gyatso; Kusho Mangde begins the construction of Tolu Gompa; death of Dromo Geshe Ngawang Kalzang.

1938:   Death of Lama Wangyal's wife Peni; enthronement of the Kusho Tulku.

1939:   Birth of Geleg Rinpoche; death of Lama Serwa Sangye Tenpa.

1940:   Death of Dzatul Ngawang Tenzin Norbu; enthronement of the Tengboche Tulku.

1941:   Birth of the two tulkus of Ngawang Tenzin Norbu; death of the Drogonpa Tenzin Dorje.

1942:   Birth of Phurbu Butri (Kami Drolma), Lama Zopa's sister.

1943:   Death of Tsamchi; Kunzang Yeshe visits Au Yeshe in Khumjung.

1944:   Birth of Ani Pema Chöden; death of Au Yeshe; Ngawang Chöphel moves to Lawudo.

1945:   Birth of Dawa Chötar, the second Lawudo Lama (Thubten Zopa Rinpoche).

1946:   Death of the Lawudo Lama Kunzang Yeshe and Thangme Lama Tenzin.

1948:   Death of Pasang Puthar; birth of Pemba Chötar or Sangye.

1949:   Dawa Chötar is recognized as the tulku of the Lawudo Lama.

1950:   The Tengboche Lama cuts Dawa Chötar's hair and names him Gyaltsen Zangpo; he begins his studies at Thangme Gompa; building of Tragshingto Gompa; Nepal opens to foreign visitors; first mountaineering expedition arrives in Khumbu.

1951:   Gyaltsen Zangpo continues his studies in Rolwaling.

1952:   Tom Weir meets Gyaltsen Zangpo in Rolwaling.

1953:   Everest climbed for the first time by Tenzin Norgyay Sherpa and Edmund Hillary.

1954:   Last visit to Pangboche by the Drogon lamas (Pema Wangchug and Ngawang Pema Rigzin).

1955:   Death of the Charog Gelong Ngawang Samten and Sanyer Ani Ngawang Drolma.

1956:   Birth of Rita Tsering, eldest son of Pemba Dekyi and Pasang Namgyal; death of Urgyen, Aunt Dawa Butri's husband; Dawa Butri dies six months later.

1957:   Gyaltsen Zangpo goes to Tibet; death of Lama Dondrub; birth of Thangme Rinpoche.

1958:   Death of Ani Karzang, Lama Zopa's sister Ang Chökyi, Khumtul Karma Geleg Zangpo, and Tripon Pema Chögyal.

1959:   Gyaltsen Zangpo becomes the novice monk Thubten Zopa; escapes to India and settles in Buxa; Tibetan refugees arrive in Khumbu; Trulzhig Rinpoche stays in Thangme Gompa and Diu Rinpoche in Lawudo; Pemba Dekyi marries Pasang Namgyal and leaves Lawudo; birth of the Khumtul Ngawang Tenzin Jigdral; death of Kagyu Tenzin Norbu.

1961:   Thubten Zopa meets Ling Rinpoche in Darjeeling; studies with Gen Yeshe; Karma Tenzin leaves for Shorong and marries Serkyimi; birth of his son Sangye Yeshe; birth of Aku Ngawang Gedun's daughter Ngawang Samten; Sir Edmund Hillary builds the Khumjung School; Frida Bedi starts the Young Lamas Home School.

1962:   Thubten Zopa attends the Young Lamas Home School in Delhi; birth of Lama Serwa Geleg Gyatso Rinpoche; founding of Samtenling Gompa in Bouddhanath.

1963:   Thubten Zopa attends the Young Lamas Home School in Dalhousie; studies with Lama Thubten Yeshe; the Khari Lama builds Tramo Gompa; Sir Edmund Hillary builds the Thangme and Pangboche schools.

1964:   Gen Lozang Gyatso leaves Buxa and Lama Zopa moves to Lama Yeshe's house; Sir Edmund Hillary builds the Lukla airstrip and the Namche, Chaurikharka, and Junbesi schools; the Chinese confiscate Sherpa houses in Tibet.

1965:   Birth of Karma Tenzin's son Tenzin Dorje; death of Aku Ayulha; beginning of the weekly market in Namche; closure of the Young Lamas School.

1966: Sir Edmund Hillary builds the Khumde Hospital.

1967: Lama Yeshe and Lama Zopa meet Zina Rachevsky in Darjeeling; Kami Drolma takes novice vows and becomes Ani Ngawang Samten.

1968: Ashang Ngawang Yonten takes gelong vows; Zina takes novice vows; Lama Zopa returns to Nepal, meets Max Mathews; consecration of Thubten Chöling Monastery; death of Thangme Lama Ngodrub.

1969: His Holiness Dilgo Khyentse Rinpoche gives the transmission of the Kangyur in Bouddha; Lama Zopa meets his family, returns to Khumbu, and takes possession of the cave and property of the Lawudo Lama Kunzang Yeshe; begins to rebuild the Lawudo houses.

1970: Death of the Khari Lama and birth of his tulku; work on the Lawudo Gompa begins; Lama Yeshe and Lama Zopa move to Kopan; Ann McNeil and Max Mathews take monastic vows.

1971: Lama Zopa takes gelong vows; gives the First Kopan Meditation Course; the Mount Everest Centre starts to function; death of Aku Ngawang Gedun, Lama Zopa's maternal grandmother Nyima Chökyi, and Kuye Lama Tenzin Chökyi Nyima.

1972: Reconsecration of the Bouddha stupa and blessing of the Kopan land; Second Kopan Meditation Course in March; consecration of the Lawudo Gompa and official beginning of Mount Everest Center; Zina goes into retreat; Max Mathews moves to Kopan; Gen Tashi and Gen Wangyal teach the Lawudo monks; Lama Zopa prepares the first version of *The Wish-Fulfilling Golden Sun;* consecration of the new Kopan Gompa; Third Kopan Course in November; construction of the airstrip at Shangboche.

1973: Lama Zopa receives *Lama Chöpa* teachings from Ling Rinpoche in Bodh Gaya; Fourth Meditation Course in March; Lama Lhundrub Rigsel and Lama Pasang join Mount Everest Center; Zina's death; Fifth Kopan Course in November.

1974: Lama Zopa's mother takes monastic vows together with a large group of Westerners; Sixth Meditation Course in March; last visit of Gen Lozang Gyatso; the Mount Everest Center monks settle in Kopan; Lama Zopa meets Kunnu Lama; Seventh Meditation Course in November.

1975: Gomchen Gampa-la visits Kopan; Eighth Kopan Meditation Course in November; creation of the Sagarmatha National Park.

1976: Death of the second Khari Lama; Lama Zopa performs Tara fire offering at Lawudo.

1977: Death of Kunnu Lama; recitation of 100 million mani mantras at Lawudo; Serkong Rinpoche gives the empowerments of the *Precious Source* in Kopan.

1978: First Lawudo Chenrezig Group Retreat; Kusho Mangde returns to Charog.

1979: Second Lawudo Chenrezig Group Retreat; building of a new kitchen starts at Lawudo; Diu Rinpoche teaches in Kopan; Tseringma Mountain is climbed for the first time; death of Serkong Dorje Chang.

1980: Third Chenrezig Group Retreat; birth of the third Serkong Dorje Chang; Ngawang Chöphel builds the Chime Tagten Chöling Monastery in Maratika.

1981: Fourth Chenrezig Group Retreat with Lama Yeshe; death of Trijang Rinpoche.

1982: First Dharma Celebration; Amala and Ngawang Samten visit India; Aunt Lhamo arrives from Darjeeling; birth of Trijang Rinpoche's tulku.

1983: Death of twenty-eight Sherpas in a bus accident; deaths of Serkong Rinpoche, Ling Rinpoche, and Gomchen-la; Amala comes to Kopan; hydroelectric system installed in Namche.

1984: Death of Lama Thubten Yeshe, Zong Rinpoche, and Karma Tenzin; birth of the tulkus of Serkong Rinpoche and Gomchen-la.

1985: Second Dharma Celebration; birth of Lama Yeshe's tulku Tenzin Ösel and Charog Tenzin Trinle; a sudden lake outburst destroys all bridges and changes the landscape in Khumbu and Pharag.

1986: H. H. the Dalai Lama gives Kalachakra empowerment in Bodh Gaya; deaths of Geshe Rabten and Aunt Lhamo; Lama Zopa visits Tibet; Panchen Lama visits Nepal.

1987: Lama Zopa visits Tibet and meets the Panchen Lama; birth of Geshe Rabten's tulku.

1989: Tengboche Monastery is destroyed by fire; death of Diu Rinpoche; deaths of Charog Sonam Zangpo, his first wife, and his second child.

1990: Lama Zopa attends the nyungne at Lawudo; Ngawang Chöphel takes monastic vows.

1991: Deaths of H. H. Dilgo Khyentse Rinpoche and Lama Zopa's mother; birth of her reincarnation.

1992: Death of Kusho Mangde and birth of his tulku; Beding chörten destroyed by floods.

1993: Death of Gen Lama; Trulzhig Rinpoche consecrates the new Tengboche Gompa; Lama Zopa consecrates a kani in Lukla and a chörten at Samshing.

1994: Enthronement of Amala's reincarnation in Kopan.

1995: Death of Mrs. Cohen, Lama Zopa's sponsor; beginning of Dumche in Lukla; hydro power project inaugurated at Hungo, near Thangme.

1996: Enthronement of Charog Lama's tulku in Kopan.

1997: Deaths of Genupa Lama Ngawang and Maratika Lama Ngawang Chöphel Gyatso.

1998: Lama Zopa visits Lawudo.

1999: Deaths of Ngawang Jigme and Kyabrog Lama Tenzin.

2000: Building of a chörten at Tesho in memory of Ngawang Jigme and a prayer wheel at Lawudo; death of Au Palden.

2002: A large, luxurious hotel is built in Mende.

2003: Death of Aku Ngawang Jigme; rebuilding of the Khari Gompa in Tramo begins; electricity reaches Lawudo.

# Appendix II: The Four Original Sherpa Clans

A CLAN IS A GROUP OF PEOPLE related by patrilinear descent. The Tibetan term for clan is *ru*, meaning "bone," which according to the scriptures is the part of the body transmitted by the father. The mother transmits the *sha*, the flesh, or the *trag*, the blood. The rules governing clans are very strict among Sherpas, and sexual relations between members of the same clan are strictly prohibited.

The four original Sherpa clans are the Minyagpa, Lama, Thimmipa, and Chagpa (pronounced "chawa"). The Minyagpa and Lama clans later split into subclans. About two centuries after the first migration of people from Tibet, a new wave of Tibetan immigrants gave rise to new clans, such as the Shangkhug, Lhugpa, and so forth. Finally, the Tibetans who settled in Khumbu during the nineteenth and twentieth centuries became known to the Sherpas as "Khampas," even though most of them were originally from the area of Tsang.[336]

1. The Minyagpa *(mi nyag pa)*

   During the eleventh and twelfth centuries there was a kingdom known as Minyag, Tangut, or Hsi Hsia, in the region of present-day Kansu and Ch'ing-Hai provinces of China. In 1226 or 1227, Minyag was conquered by Genghis Khan, and a large part of the population fled southeast to the Domed, or Dokham, region of eastern Tibet, west of Dartsedo and east of Tao.[337]

   The ancestor of the Minyagpa was Gergyal, a leader of the *Dong* lineage who settled in the Zalmogang area of Dökham; the upper part of Zalmogang is known as Minyag Rimang and the lower part as Tsamorong. Gergyal had five sons who settled over the Zalmogang area. Four generations after Gergyal, his descendant Michen Dragpa settled in Khumbu. Michen Dragpa's grandson Michen Tsunchung Tashi, a disciple of Lama Sangwa Dorje, settled in Tragthobug in Shorong. His descendants split into the Benasa *(be gnas sa)*, Yulgongma *(yul gong ma)*, Tragtho *(brags mtho, grags mtho)*, Goleg *('go? legs)*, and Magenche *(ma rgan che)* subclans. The Minyagpas are known nowadays as the Gartsa *(mgar rtsa)* clan.

2.  The Lama *(bla ma)*
    a) The Lama Serwa *(bla ma ser ba)*
    Tsuglha Gyalpo and his wife Palmo Tsun settled in the Serta area of Kham. Of their four children, one had a beautiful body and a face that was white like a conch shell, and they named him Ser Dunglha Dagpo, Divine Conch Shell Lord of Serta. The four sons of Tsuglha Gyalpo were inclined to religion, and their clan became known as the Lama clan. Dunglha Dagpo's son was the treasure discoverer Nyang-ral Nyima Özer (1124–92).
    Many generations later, Nyima Özer's descendant Ser Dungyal set- tled in Khumbu. His son Phagtse was a disciple of Lama Sangwa Dorje and settled in Senge Phug in Shorong. His son Dorje Zangpo built the gompa at Junbesi. In the early twentieth century, his descendants Karma Dondrub and Sangye Tenpa sponsored the construction of Tengboche Monastery and Chiwang Gompa respectively.
    b) The Lama Gonpa *(bla ma dgon pa)*
    They came from Khams Lhodrag Dra Nga and Khams Zhamo Dul- dum, and settled in Shorong.

3.  The Thimmipa *(thim mi pa)*
    Yural Phogo and Gya Kyema settled in the Uni Gang area of Zalmo- gang. One of Yural's ancestors had been endowed with miraculous powers: at night he remained absorbed in meditation contemplating the clear-light nature of the mind, and during the day he could disap- pear or vanish *(thim)* into the cliffs. Thus, his descendants became known as the Thimmipas. Yural Phogo's son Zangpo Tashi settled in Latö Tratse Dzong. Zangpo Tashi's grandsons Phachen, Phuchen, and Dzomrab settled in Khumbu. Their descendants gave rise to the Zalaka *(za la sga)*, Gobarma *(sgo bar ma)*, Khampache *(khams pa che)*, and Lhabushingtog *(lha bu shing tog)* subclans. Nowadays the thimmipa are known as Pladorje.

4.  The Chagpa *(lcags pa)* or Chawa
    They came from Chagmodrag or Khams Nyedong. Samdrub Darpo's son Dongkha Ringmo settled in Latö with his son Sangye Paljor, a dis- ciple of Terton Ratna Lingpa (1403–79). Sangye Paljor's son Dudjom

Dorje and his companion Gyagarba Chenpo are said to be the first Khumbu settlers. Zilnon Dorje, son of Sangye Paljor's brother Palchen Dorje, settled in Pikye in Shorong. Their descendants split into the Lhugpa *(lhug pa)* and Nawa *(rna ba)* subclans.

The settlers that arrived in Khumbu during the eighteenth and early nineteenth centuries belong to the Chuserwa *(chu ser? ba)*, Mendewa *(sman sde ba)*, Shangkhug *(shang khug)*, Sherwa *(sher ba)*, Jongdongpa *(ljong sdong pa)*, and Murmin Tso *(mur min rtso)* clans.

# Appendix III: The Lineage of Lama Sangwa Dorje and Dzatul Ngawang Tenzin Norbu[338]

1. Translator Tsang Legdrub (*lo tsa ba gtsang legs grub*, ninth century). During the time of the Tibetan king Trisong Detsen, the translators Legdrub and Vairochana went to India to receive dzogchen teachings from Shri Singha. On the way back, Legdrub was killed by border guards.

2. Yudra Nyingpo (*g.yu sgra snying po*, ninth century). Born in Gyalmo Tsawarong in Kham, he became a student of the exiled master Vairochana and taught dzogchen to King Trisong Detsen at Samye. He became one of the twenty-five foremost disciples of Guru Rinpoche, one of the 108 translators of that period, and one of the main lineage holders of the mind category *(sems sde)* of dzogchen teachings.

3. Terton Samten Lingpa (*gter ston bsam gtan gling pa*, fourteenth century). Known also as Jangling Terton *(byang gling gter ston)*, he was prophesied in the *Padma Kathang* as the tulku of Yudra Nyingpo. Born in Kongpo, he is credited with the discovery of many termas.

4. Rigzin Tagsham Nuden Dorje (*rig 'dzin stags sham nus ldan rdo rje*, b. 1682). Also known as Samten Lingpa, he was born in Dome Parsho into a family of nomads and discovered various termas.

5. Ngagchang Sangwa Dorje (*sngags 'chang gsang ba rdo rje*, seventeenth century). Born in Khumbu, he contributed greatly to the religious life of the Sherpas.

6. Lochen Dharmashri (*lo chen dharma shri*, 1654–1717). Born in Dranang Dargye Chöling, he was the son of Rigzin Trinle Lhundrub and the younger brother of Rigzin Terdag Lingpa. He was decapitated by the Dzungkar Mongols.

7. Tenzin Daö Dorje (*bstan 'dzin zla 'od rdo rje*, eighteenth century). Born in Kongpo, he built a monastery in Pemakö and opened many hidden places.

8. Gyurme Urgyen Tendar (*'gyur med o rgyan bstan dar,* eighteenth century). Born in Domed, he was ordained as a monk by Minling Trichen Trinle Namgyal. He meditated at Rongphu and taught extensively in the Kharta and Phadrug areas. He was a teacher of Trulzhig Kunzang Thongdrol.

9. Gyurme Urgyen Tenphel (*'gyur med o rgyan bstan 'phel,* nineteenth century). Born in Kharta, he was recognized as the tulku of Urgyen Tendar. His parents wanted him to marry, but he escaped to Mindroling and received lay vows from Trichen Sangye Kunga. Some years later, he returned to Kharta, where he rebuilt two gompas and married. Afterward he renounced family life and went to meditate at Rongphu. He passed away in Phadrug in a fire female snake year (1857?).

10. Ngawang Tenzin Norbu (*ngag dbang bstan 'dzin nor bu,* 1867–1940). He built the Do-ngag Zungjug Ling Monastery and became the main teacher of the Khumbu Sherpas.

11. Two boys were recognized as tulkus of Ngawang Tenzin Norbu:

    1) Ngawang Rigzin Kunzang Chökyi Gyaltsen (*ngag dbang rig 'dzin kun bzang chos kyi rgyal mtshan,* b. 1941). Born in Lhasa on July 15, 1941, to Gedun Özer and Dechen Pemo, he was found by Trulzhig Rinpoche and officially recognized by the Regent Tagtra Rinpoche as the reincarnation of Ngawang Tenzin Norbu. In 1959 he escaped to Nepal and India and spent a few years in Darjeeling. He went to Dharamsala as one of twelve young lamas and three geshes who were studying English under the direct supervision of the Private Office of His Holiness the Dalai Lama. He was then sent to Switzerland as the leader of the first group of Tibetan refugees and spent thirty-one years in that country. After a number of years in Holland and Australia, he is now the representative of His Holiness the Dalai Lama in Japan.

    2) a) Khumbu Tulku (Khumtul) Karma Geleg Zangpo (*khum sprul karma dge legs bzang po,* 1940–58). Born in Milingbo in Khumbu into the Zalaka clan, he studied in Chiwang and Rongphu under the guidance of Trulzhig Rinpoche. After a few years in Phadrug, he passed away in Zurtso Chongma.

    b) Ngawang Tenzin Jigdral Wangchug Chökyi Gyaltsen (*ngag dbang bstan 'dzin 'jigs bral dbang phyug chos kyi rgyal mtshan,* b. 1959). Born on May 25, 1959, in Chagmiteng (between Tengboche and Pangboche) of Tibetan parents, he was recognized by Trulzhig Rinpoche and enthroned at Chiwang Gompa in 1964. He studied for ten years at Mindroling Monastery in India and two years in Manali with Khenpo Thubten. At eighteen he returned to Nepal to study with Dudjom Rinpoche and Dilgo Khyentse Rinpoche. He has a monastery in Pharping and two Dharma centers in Taiwan, where he spends most of his time.

# Appendix IV: The Thangme or Charog Lamas

[A note on abbreviations: T means "tulku"; M means "married to."]

## Clan: lhug pa

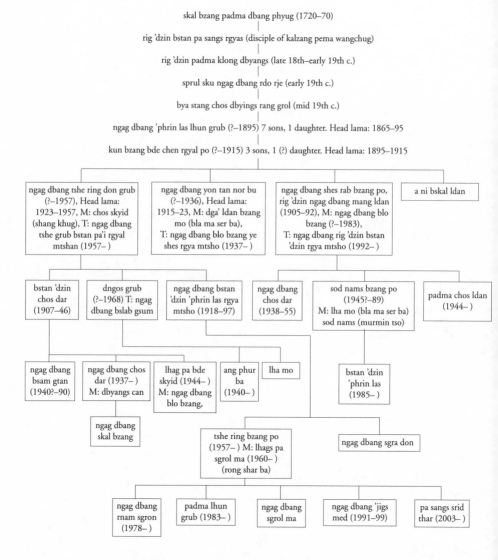

skal bzang padma dbang phyug (1720–70)

rig 'dzin bstan pa sangs rgyas (disciple of kalzang pema wangchug)

rig 'dzin padma klong dbyangs (late 18th–early 19th c.)

sprul sku ngag dbang rdo rje (early 19th c.)

bya stang chos dbyings rang grol (mid 19th c.)

ngag dbang 'phrin las lhun grub (?–1895) 7 sons, 1 daughter. Head lama: 1865–95

kun bzang bde chen rgyal po (?–1915) 3 sons, 1 (?) daughter. Head lama: 1895–1915

ngag dbang tshe ring don grub (?–1957), Head lama: 1923–1957, M: chos skyid (shang khug), T: ngag dbang tshe grub bstan pa'i rgyal mtshan (1957– )

ngag dbang yon tan nor bu (?–1936), Head lama: 1915–23, M: dga' ldan bzang mo (bla ma ser ba), T: ngag dbang blo bzang ye shes rgya mtsho (1937– )

ngag dbang shes rab bzang po, rig 'dzin ngag dbang mang ldan (1905–92), M: ngag dbang blo bzang (?–1983), T: ngag dbang rig 'dzin bstan 'dzin rgya mtsho (1992– )

a ni bskal ldan

bstan 'dzin chos dar (1907–46)

dngos grub (?–1968) T: ngag dbang bslab gsum

ngag dbang bstan 'dzin 'phrin las rgya mtsho (1918–97)

ngag dbang chos dar (1938–55)

sod nams bzang po (1945?–89) M: lha mo (bla ma ser ba) sod nams (murmin tso)

padma chos ldan (1944– )

ngag dbang bsam gtan (1940?–90)

ngag dbang chos dar (1937– ) M: dbyangs can

lhag pa bde skyid (1944– ) M: ngag dbang blo bzang,

ang phur ba (1940– )

lha mo

bstan 'dzin 'phrin las (1985– )

ngag dbang skal bzang

tshe ring bzang po (1957– ) M: lhags pa sgrol ma (1960– ) (rong shar ba)

ngag dbang sgra don

ngag dbang rnam sgron (1978– )

padma lhun grub (1983– )

ngag dbang sgrol ma

ngag dbang 'jigs med (1991–99)

pa sangs srid thar (2003– )

# Appendix V: Genealogy of the Lawudo Lama Kunzang Yeshe

Three families originated from a common ancestor from Sakya who settled in Khumbu:

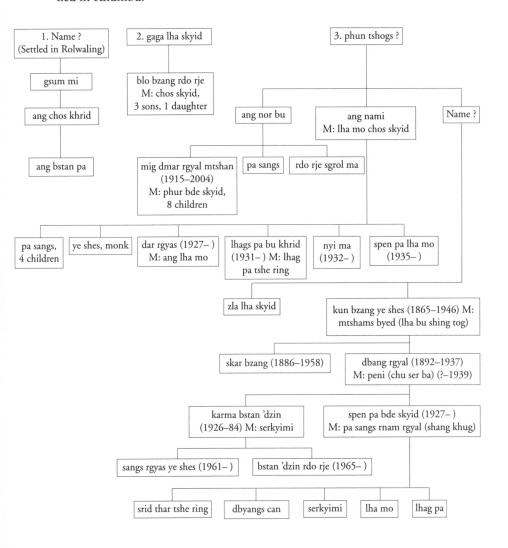

# Appendix VI: Genealogy of the Lawudo Lama Thubten Zopa Rinpoche

Family name: mtsho ba grong gsar

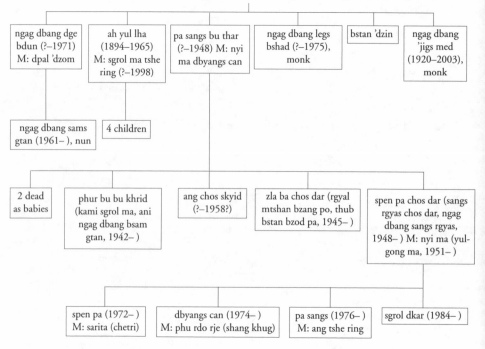

ang zla ba or zla pha che
(Went to Khumbu with his sister ani sgrol ma. Married a lady from Thangme, shang khug clan.)

| | | | | | |
|---|---|---|---|---|---|
| ngag dbang dge bdun (?–1971) M: dpal 'dzom | ah yul lha (1894–1965) M: sgrol ma tshe ring (?–1998) | pa sangs bu thar (?–1948) M: nyi ma dbyangs can | ngag dbang legs bshad (?–1975), monk | bstan 'dzin | ngag dbang 'jigs med (1920–2003), monk |

ngag dbang sams gtan (1961– ), nun | 4 children

2 dead as babies | phur bu bu khrid (kami sgrol ma, ani ngag dbang bsam gtan, 1942– ) | ang chos skyid (?–1958?) | zla ba chos dar (rgyal mtshan bzang po, thub bstan bzod pa, 1945– ) | spen pa chos dar (sangs rgyas chos dar, ngag dbang sangs rgyas, 1948– ) M: nyi ma (yul-gong ma, 1951– )

spen pa (1972– ) M: sarita (chetri) | dbyangs can (1974– ) M: phu rdo rje (shang khug) | pa sangs (1976– ) M: ang tshe ring | sgrol dkar (1984– )

# Family of Lama Zopa's Mother

## Clan: shang khug

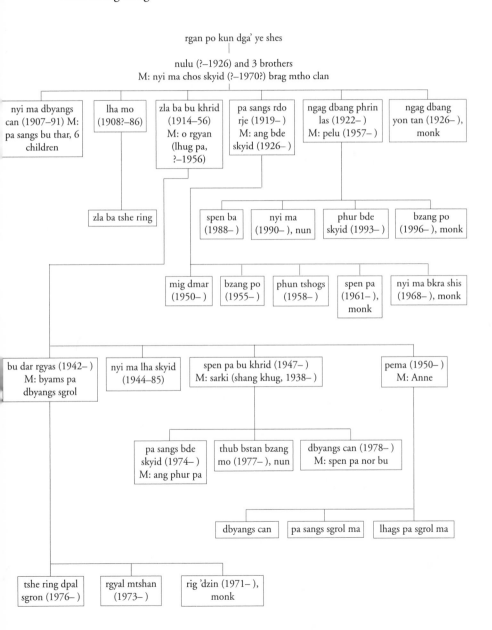

rgan po kun dga' ye shes

nulu (?–1926) and 3 brothers
M: nyi ma chos skyid (?–1970?) brag mtho clan

| nyi ma dbyangs can (1907–91) M: pa sangs bu thar, 6 children | lha mo (1908?–86) | zla ba bu khrid (1914–56) M: o rgyan (lhug pa, ?–1956) | pa sangs rdo rje (1919– ) M: ang bde skyid (1926– ) | ngag dbang phrin las (1922– ) M: pelu (1957– ) | ngag dbang yon tan (1926– ), monk |

zla ba tshe ring

| spen ba (1988– ) | nyi ma (1990– ), nun | phur bde skyid (1993– ) | bzang po (1996– ), monk |

| mig dmar (1950– ) | bzang po (1955– ) | phun tshogs (1958– ) | spen pa (1961– ), monk | nyi ma bkra shis (1968– ), monk |

| bu dar rgyas (1942– ) M: byams pa dbyangs sgrol | nyi ma lha skyid (1944–85) | spen pa bu khrid (1947– ) M: sarki (shang khug, 1938– ) | pema (1950– ) M: Anne |

| pa sangs bde skyid (1974– ) M: ang phur pa | thub bstan bzang mo (1977– ), nun | dbyangs can (1978– ) M: spen pa nor bu |

| dbyangs can | pa sangs sgrol ma | lhags pa sgrol ma |

| tshe ring dpal sgron (1976– ) | rgyal mtshan (1973– ) | rig 'dzin (1971– ), monk |

# List of Abbreviations

BT    *Byang gter*

DCH   *'Dran mchog kun bzang ye shes kyi rnam thar thog mtha' bar
      gsum dad pa'i phreng ba*

DTH   *Dus mthar chos smra ba'i btsun pa ngag dbang bstan 'dzin nor
      bu'i rnam thar 'chi med bdud rtsi'i rol mtsho*

JT    *'Jig rten chags tshad mdo tsam brjod pa'i sgo nas pha mes kyi
      byung rabs gsal dag khungs ldan rim par bkod pa*

KHB   *Ko bo bya btang chos dar ram ngag dbang nor bu bzang por 'bod
      pas rang snang 'khrul pa tshul bzhin brjod pa mu ti ka'i phreng ba*

MG    *Mi la'i mgur 'bum*

SCH   *Shar pa'i chos byung sngon med tshangs pa'i dbyu gu*

# Notes

## Introduction

1. Dowman (1973), chap. 3, p. 50: "The Consequences of Offering Circumambulation and Prayers." Translation of *Mchod rten chen po bya rung kha shor gyi lo rgyus thos pas grol ba (The Legend of the Great Stupa called "Permission to Do What Is Proper," entitled Liberating by Hearing)*, a rediscovered treasure *(gter ma)* of Ngagchang Shakya Zangpo *(sngags 'chang shakya bzang po*, early sixteenth century). On termas, cf. note 7 below.

2. *'Dran mchog kun bzang ye shes kyi rnam thar thog mtha' bar gsum dad pa'i 'phreng ba*, henceforth cited as DCH.

3. The dissolution process at the time of death consists of the gradual loss of the ability to manifest the five elements, five aggregates (form, feeling, perception, compounded phenomena, and consciousness), five wisdoms, five sense organs, and five objects of the senses. Cf. Lati Rinbochay and Hopkins (1979) and Tenzin Gyatso (1997).

4. For the meaning of tulkus and enthronement, see Lodro Thaye (1997).

5. For the "secret life" of the Sixth Dalai Lama see Aris (1988), Lhatsun Ngawang Dorje's *Secret Biography of Tsangyang Gyatso (Tshangs dbyangs rgya mtsho'i gsang rnam)* (2000), and Rispoli (1999).

6. Cf. Sangye Tenzin and Macdonald (1971), *An Historical Account of [Our] Ancestors from a Pure Clear Source, in Accordance with the Creation of the World as Told in the Sutras ('Jig rten chags tshad mdo tsam brjod pa'i sgo nas mes kyi byung rabs gsal dag khungs ldan rim par bkod pa)*, ff.15b and 16a/b; henceforth cited as JT. The Sherpa scholar Sangye Tenzin *(shar pa sangs rgyas bstan 'dzin*, 1924–90) was born at Tragthobug *(brag mtho sbug)* in Solu, or Shorong *(gshongs rong)*. In 1959 he built the Shedrub Zungdrel Ling *(bshad sgrub zung 'brel gling)* Monastery at Serlog, near his birthplace.

   I. S. Chemjong (1967, p. 8) says: "After the conquest of all the Kirat land of Eastern Himalayan region, King Maw Rong Hang divided his country into four provinces…The land lied [*sic*] between Kathmandu valley and river Dud Koshi was called Khombuwan. The Limbuwan State was called from river Dud Koshi in the west to river Mechi in the east. The district of Khampajong was included in Limbuwan State." Thus, it seems that the whole area between Gampa Dzong in Tibet and the Dudh Kosi, which has its source in Khumbu, was known as Khombu. Cf. also Macdonald (1987c).

7. Termas *(gter ma)*, or treasures, are religious texts or sacred objects concealed by Padmasambhava and his consort Yeshe Tsogyal *(ye shes mtsho rgyal)* in various parts of the world, particularly in Tibet and the Himalayan regions, and revealed by the reincarnations of Padmasambhava's disciples that were prophesized as *ter-tons (gter ston)*, or treasure discoverers. Termas can be concealed in the earth, rocks, water, trees, clouds, and so forth *(sa gter,* earth termas), or in the inner expanse of the mind *(dgong gter,* mind termas).

Five great terma cycles have been discovered: The Eastern Terma comprises the texts discovered by Pema Ledreltsal *(padma las 'brel rtsal,* 1291–1315) and Sangye Lingpa *(sangs rgyas gling pa,* 1340–96). The Southern Terma includes those discov-ered by Nyang-ral Nyima Özer *(nyang ral nyi ma 'od zer,* 1124–92), Guru Chöwang *(gu ru chos kyi dbang phyug,* 1212–70), and Pema Lingpa *(padma gling pa,* 1450–1521). The Western Terma was discovered by Rigzin Garwang Dorje *(rig 'dzin gar dbang rdo rje,* 1640–85), the Northern Terma by Rigzin Godem-chen *(rig 'dzin dngos grub rgyal mtshan rgod kyi ldem 'phru can,* 1337–1408), and the Cen-tral Terma by Rigzin Terdag Lingpa *(rig 'dzin gter bdag gling pa,* 1646–1714). Cf. Thondup (1986) and Ehrhard (1993, p. 15, n. 1).

8. Pema Lingpa's *Guidebook to the Hidden Valleys of Dremoshong and Khenpalung (Sbas yul 'bras mo gshongs dang mkhan pa lung gi gnas yig),* chap. 2, f.2b, mentions "four great, supremely hidden valleys: Lapchi Snow Wall *(la phyi gang[s] gi ra ba)* in the west, Nöjin Snow Wall *(gnod sbyin gang[s] gi ra ba)* in the north, Tsari Snow Wall *(tsa ri gang[s] gi ra ba)* in the east, and Baryul Snow Wall *(bar yul gang[s] gi ra ba)* in the south. Chapter 3, f.4b mentions four "small countries," four "similar countries," four "smaller countries," and "numberless great and blessed mountains, castles, and caves. The most special among them are the four hidden countries: Dremoshong *(sbras mo gshongs),* Dromalung *(gro ma lung),* Khenpalung *(mkhan pa lung),* and Rongmo Teng *(rong mo steng)."*

In his *Seven Plains and Ridges of the Seven Hidden Countries (Sbas yul bdun gyi thang sgang bdun ma),* Rigzin Godem mentions seven hidden valleys *(sbas yul):* the Valley of Rice *('bras mo ljongs),* the Happy Valley Endowed with Bliss *(bde ldan skyid mo lung),* the Hidden Lotus Park *(sbas pa padma'i tshal),* the Playground of the Dakinis *(rol ba mkha' 'gro'i gling),* the Valley of Artemisia in Gyal *(rgyal gyi mkhan pa lung),* the Central Palace of the Gods *(lha'i pho brang sdings),* and the Wheat Basin *(gro mo khud).* Lists of *beyuls,* or secret valleys, are found in the *Padma Kathang (O rgyan guru padma 'byung gnas kyi skyes rabs rnam par thar pa rgyas par bkod pa),* a terma of Urgyen Lingpa *(o rgyan gling pa,* 1323–60), and in various other texts. Cf. also Diemberger (1997, p. 322, nn. 19, 20).

Dzatul Ngawang Tenzin Norbu *(rdza rong phu sprul sku ngag dbang bstan 'dzin nor bu,* 1867–1940) in his *Pleasant Sound of the Summer Drum: A Guidebook to Rongphu (Rong phu rdza yi gangs kyi gnas yig dad pa'i gdong ldan dga' skyed dbyar gyi rnga sgra)*, f.4b, quotes the *Self-Arisen, Self-Manifested Eight Pronouncements (Bka' brgyad rang byung rang shar)* from the Northern Treasure (henceforth referred to as BT) as saying that there are eleven beyul in the Himalayan Range, from Tise (*ti se*, Kailash) in the west to Kongpo (*kong po*) in the east.

9. The Lotus Array (*padma bkod*) is situated in southeast Tibet near the Namchag Barwa Mountain (*gnam lcags 'bar ba*, 7,756 m), in the region where the Yarlung Tsangpo (*yar klung gtsang po*) makes a great bend before it descends toward the plains as the Brahmaputra River. For details about Beyul Pemakö, see the *Guidebook to the Sacred Place of Pemakö (Padma bkod kyi gnas kyi lam yig)* discovered by Rigzin Jatson Nyingpo (*rig 'dzin 'ja' tshon snying po*, 1585–1656) at Kongpo Buchu (*kong po bu chu)*, and the *Guidebook to the Hidden Valley of Pemakö (Sbas yul padma bkod pa'i gnas yig)* discovered by Dudul Dorje (*bdud 'dul rdo rje*, 1615–72) in Pubo (*spu bo*). The outer Pemakö was opened by Gampo Urgyen Drodul Lingpa (*sgam po o rgyan 'gro 'dul gling pa*, b. 1757), Rigzin Dorje Thogme (*rig 'dzin rdo rje thogs med*, 1746–97), and Chöling Garwang Chime Dorje (*chos gling gar dbang 'chi med rdo rje*, b. 1763). At the beginning of the twentieth century, about a thousand Tibetan families who were fleeing the war between the Chinese and Tibetans settled in Pemakö. Cf. Ehrhard (1999, pp. 228–39) and Bernbaum (2001).

10. The Happy Valley Endowed with Bliss (*bde ldan skyid mo lung*) is situated in Nepal at the source of the Buri Gandaki. The Half-Moon Shaped Heavenly Gate (*gnam sgo zla gam*) is also situated in Nepal, in the Langtang (*glang 'phrang*) range. Cf. Ehrhard (1997) and Bernbaum (2001).

11. f.470a/b.

12. *Phag mo'i zab khrid don gsal sgron ma*, BT: gnas ni shri ri lho nub na / khum bu gang[s] gyi ra ba zhes / zla ba phyed du phyin pa na / sbas pa'i yul mchog de nyid yod / dge byed rnams kyi sna drangs nas / phyi na khri khrag gsum gyi grong khyer chags.

13. *The Great Catalogue of Prophecies (Lung bstan bskul byang chen mo)* is one of the twenty-five sections of the *Thugs sgrub* cycle of the BT: khum bu'i rong sgo la gter yod / de thon bas bod khams la lo bdun gyi bde skyid 'byung....

14. *Snyan brgyud sde drug gi tho byang lung bstan rin po che'i lde'u mig*, found in vol. *om*, f.6b, of the *Kun bzang dgongs pa zang thal* cycle, BT: bud dang khum bu gnya' nang dang / skyid grong lho yi rong bdun gyi / kha mi bdun dang gting mi bdun / las can de yi 'khor du 'dus / sbas yul nges par rnyed pa'i dus / bka' bzhin sgrub pa'i 'khor bdun yod.

15. See Terton Ratna Lingpa's *Terjung Chenmo (ratna gling pa*, or *rin chen dpal bzang po*, 1403–78) entitled *Ghu ru ratna gling pa'i gter 'byung chen mo gsal ba'i sgron ma dang rnam thar bcas kyi gsung pod*, f.30b, where he mentions the Khumbu Snow Wall (*khum bu gang ra*) as one of the four hidden countries.

16. Cf. *The Marvelous Treasury: A Guidebook to the Hidden Valley of Dremojong and Explanation of Its Benefits (Sbas yul 'bras mo ljongs kyi gnas yig phan yon dang bcas pa ngo mtshar gter mdzod*), written by Lhatsun Gyurme Jigdral (*lha btsun 'gyur*

*med 'jigs bral),* and the above-mentioned Pema Lingpa's *Guidebook.* See also Rigzin Godem's *Secret Catalog of the Vajra Sun Guidebook (Rdo rje nyi ma'i gnas yig gsang ba'i dkar chag).* Rigzin Godem was the first to open Beyul Dremojong. In the seventeenth century, Lhatsun Namkha Jigme *(lha btsun nam mkha 'jigs med,* 1597–ca. 1650) opened the Lhari Ösel Nyingpo *(lha ri 'od gsal snying po)* area in northern Sikkim, as well as the inner part of the White Cliff of the Auspicious Plain *(brag dkar bkra shis gdengs).* In 1717, Ngagdag Sempa Chenpo *(ngag bdag sems dpa' chen po)* revealed the wish-fulfilling vase at the Cave of Great Bliss *(bde chen phug).*

17.  *Sbas yul mkhan pa lung gi gnas yig mthong ba don ldan,* f.21. Published by J. Reinhard in *Kailash,* vol. 6, n. 1, 1978. There are at least two hidden valleys with the same name, one near Bhutan and another in the valleys east of Khumbu. The northern gate of Khenpalung was first opened by Rigzin Godem and reopened by Rigzin Nyida Longsal *(rig 'dzin nyi zla klong gsal,* d. 1695). For a detailed study of Khenpalung, see Ehrhard (1997, pp. 335–36), Diemberger (1992, 1993, 1997), Reinhard (1978), and Bernbaum (2001).

18.  *Sbas yul mkhan pa ljongs kyi gnas yig padma gling pa'i gter ma,* from the *Klong gsal gsang ba snying bcud* cycle.

19.  According to the Tengboche Lama (Tenzin Zangbu, 2000), Kyikha Ratho came through the Amphu Labtsa pass *(am[?] phu lab rtse / la rtsa,* 5,780 m) into Dingboche *(sding po ched)* in Khumbu. From there he went to Dun Lhatso and Monzo *(sman rdzong)* in the Pharag *(pha rag,* or *bar skabs)* region, where he planned to build his residence. Padmasambhava caused his mind to worry about being swept away by floods, and so Kyikha Ratho moved farther south to Dolaghat near Kathmandu, where he died from the heat.

20.  Cf. Reinhard (1978) and Diemberger (1992, 1997). The most important pilgrimage sites in this region are the Lion Cave *(seng ge phug)* and the Crystal Cave *(shel gyi phug)* in the Barun Valley, about one day's walk from the Makalu Base Camp.

21.  Paltul Rinpoche *(rdza dpal sprul o rgyan 'jigs med chos kyi dbang po,* 1808–87) says: "Geographically speaking, the central region is generally said to be the Vajra Seat at Bodh Gaya in India, at the centre of Jambudvipa, the Southern Continent. The thousand buddhas of the Good Kalpa all attain enlightenment there. Even in the universal destruction at the end of the kalpa, the four elements cannot harm it, and it remains there as if suspended in space." Cf. *The Words of My Perfect Teacher (Kun bzang bla ma'i zhal lung),* 1994, p. 23. The reason is that this particular place does not come into existence through the power of the karma and delusions of ordinary sentient beings.

  The Bodhi Tree that gave shelter to Siddhartha Gautama, the buddha of the present time, grows near Uruvilva or Uruvela (present-day Uvel), six miles south of Gaya. After the Buddha's parinirvana, Bodh Gaya became a famous seat of learning. In the third century B.C., the emperor Ashoka built a small shrine next to the Bodhi Tree. A larger temple was later erected, on top of which Nagarjuna (second century A.D.) placed a stupa containing the relics of Shakyamuni Buddha.

After the Moghul invasion, the place fell into oblivion and was afterward taken over by Hindu priests. As the first British (and probably the first European), Dr. Francis Buchanan visited Bodh Gaya on December 9, 1811. The main temple was restored in 1870 by Sir Alexander Cunningham. Cf. Allen, 2002. Bodh Gaya is now a thriving pilgrimage place for Buddhists of all traditions and countries.

22. *Gnas chen brag phug ma ra ti ka 'am ha las bshad kyi gnas bshad mdor bsdus.* It has been published by his son, Lopön Karma Wangchug Sherpa *(slob dpon karma dbang phyug shar pa),* together with a short guide to Maratika composed by Chatral Rinpoche Sangye Dorje *(bya bral sangs rgyas rdo rje,* b. 1913) entitled *The Melodious Pleasing Tambura ('Chi med tshe'i gnas mchog brag phug ma ra ti ka'i nges mdzod dbyangs can dgyes pa'i tambu ra).* See also chapter 4, pp. 282–84, of the *Padma Kathang.*

 There are actually two caves at Halesi. In the lower cave, known as the Cave of the Demon *(bdud kyi phug),* Padmasambhava is said to have killed a demon. The upper cave is the main place of pilgrimage for both Hindus and Buddhists. It contains a stone vase with the water of life and many self-created images and syllables. For the local Hindu population, the place is sacred to Shiva and is known as Mahadevsthan. Hindus come for pilgrimage to the cave on the special days of Shivaratri (February–March), Ram Navami (March–April), Tij (August–September) and Bala Chaturdasi (November–December). Cf. Macdonald (1985) and Buffetrille (1994).

23. See *Guide to the Holy Place Known as Godavari or Lapchi Snow Wall (Gsang lam sgrub pa'i gnas chen nyer bzhi'i ya gyal gau da wa ri 'am 'brog la phyi gangs kyi ra ba'i sngon byung gi tshul las brtsams pa'i gtam gyi rab tu byed pa nyung ngu rnam gsal),* by Drigung Tenzin Chökyi Lodro *('bri gung bstan 'dzin chos kyi blo gros,* 1868–1906), translated into English by Toni Huber (1997). Cf. also Aufschnaiter (1976), Fillibeck (1988), and Chan (1994). For Milarepa and Lapchi, see the *Collected Songs of Milarepa (Mi la mgur 'bum),* henceforth quoted as MG, and Chang (1977).

24. Beyul Rolwaling is mentioned in at least two works of Rigzin Godem-chen, *The Seven Plains* (see above, note 8) and the *General Catalogue of the Hidden Valleys (Sbas yul spyi'i them byang).* In the latter, f.8a, the Playground of the Dakinis in Khumbu is mentioned as a hidden valley that is easy to find and can be easily kept by skillful means *(khum bu'i mkha' 'gro gling btsal sla / 'dzin pa thabs la mkhas na zin no).* The *phur bu'i sgrub khang* is mentioned in *The Abbreviated Chronicle (O rgyan padmas gsungs pa'i bka' thang bdus pa),* a terma of Urgyen Lingpa.

 Tseringma, or the Deep Blue Queen Mountain *(gangs thon thing rgyal mo),* is a triangular mountain with two peaks. Hindus associate the southern peak with the goddess Gauri and the northern one with Shankar, or Shiva. At an altitude of 3,600 to 5,000 meters, the Rolwaling Valley runs in an east–west direction and is surrounded by high snow mountains on every side. It is accessible from Tibet via the Menlung La *(sman klung la,* 5,600 m) and from Khumbu via the Tashi

Labtsa (*bkra shis la rtsa / lab rtse*, 5,700 m), but the easiest approach is from the west. Because of its high altitude and very harsh weather, Rolwaling used to be an empty valley where only wandering yogis came to practice meditation. In the eighteenth century, two Tibetans from Kyirong *(skyid grong)* settled in the valley. Soon some Khumbu Sherpas arrived, and nowadays there are about fifty families living in the area. Down the valley is the winter settlement called Ramding *(ra sdings)*, and up the valley is Na *(gna' ?)*, the principal summer settlement (4,200 m). For more details on Rolwaling, see Weir (1955), Sacherer (1975, 1977), and Sætreng (1995).

25. Pema Lingpa's *Guidebook* (chap. 3, f.4b) mentions Tökyi Tsibri Dzong *(stod kyi rtsib ri rdzong)* as one of the four countries similar *(yul 'dra)* to the main hidden countries. For Milarepa's visit, see MG (p. 321) and Chang (1977, pp. 157–58). The Drukpa Kagyu *('brug pa bka' rgyud)* lama Gotsangpa Gonpo Pal *(rgod tshang pa mgon po dpal*, 1189–1258) built the Vultures' Nest *(rgod tshang)* Hermitage perched on a sheer cliff at the southeastern corner of the mountain. During the lifetime of his disciple Yang Gonpa *(yang dgon pa*, 1213–58), many monasteries and hermitages were built in that region. Tripön Pema Chögyal *(khrid dpon padma chos rgyal*, 1876–1958) set up eleven hermitages in Tsibri (see note 227 below). In 1870, Lama Senge Dragpa *(seng ge grags pa)* founded Samling *(bsam gling)* Gompa. Chuzang Samten Yangtse *(chu bzang bsam gtan yang rtse)* was a Gelug hermitage associated with Shelkar Chöde *(shel dkar chos sde)* Monastery. Cf. Aziz (1978), Chan (1994), and sKal ldan/Diemberger (1996).

26. In f.4a, Dzatul Rinpoche quotes *The Self-Arisen, Self-Manifested Eight Pronouncements (Bka' brgyad rang byung rang shar)*, BT, where Rongphu or Rongbu *(gang gi rong bu 'khyil ba rdza yi gangs)* is mentioned as one of the eight principal snow mountains of Tibet, the others being the King of Snow Mountains (Kailash, *gangs ri'i rgyal po ti se)*, the General Pomra Snow Mountain *(gangs ri dmag dpon spom ra)*, the Snow Mountain of the God Yarlha Shampo *(yar lha sham po lha yi gangs)*, Yaksha Gangwa Zangpo Snow Mountain *(gangs ba bzang po gnod sbyin gangs)*, Tsen Tago Trampa Snow Mountain *(rta sgo bkram pa btsan gyi gangs)*, and White Naga Bule Snow Mountain *(bu le dkar po klu yi gangs)*. Dzatul Rinpoche quotes extensively from the works of Chatang Shakya Palzang *(bya stang shakya dpal bzang)*, a Drukpa Kagyu married lama who spent some time in Rongphu. According to him, the valley is shaped like a white conch shell curled to the right (usually conch shells are curled to the left; those curled to the right are said to be the shells of special beings or bodhisattvas), and contains self-arisen representations of the buddhas' body, speech, mind, qualities, and activities. The Rongphu Valley is about one mile wide and twenty miles long, at an average altitude of 5,000 meters. Cf. Howard-Bury (1991, pp. 83–84), Noël (1989, p. 136), Ruttledge (1937, p. 77), A. W. Macdonald (1987a), and Chan (1994). For details about Ngawang Tenzin Norbu (1867–1940), see chapter 9.

27. According to the *Pleasant Sound of the Summer Drum,* the first lamas who came to

meditate at Rongphu were Padmasambhava's disciples Namkhai Nyingpo *(nam mkha'i snying po)*, Nyamdrel Lui Gyaltsen *(nyam 'brel klu'i rgyal mtsan)*, Nanam Tsultrim Jungne *(sna nam tshul khrims 'byung gnas)*, and others. The "door" to Rongphu was opened by Thutob Namgyal *(mthu stobs rnam rgyal)*, a disciple of Rigzin Godem-chen's son Sechog Namgyal Gonpo *(sras mchog rnam rgyal mgon po, 1398–1423)*. Afterward came Namgyal Zangpo *(rnam rgyal bzang po)*, who belonged to the early lineage of the Kuye Labrang in Kharta *(sku e/ye bla brang,* see note 175 below) and was able to subdue Sharlungdrag *(shar lung brag)*, the spirit *(btsan)* guardian of the place. After receiving teachings from Namgyal Zangpo, Sharlungdrag promised to protect the Dharma practitioners who came to Rongphu. Namgyal Zangpo then took the oath to remain in Padmasambhava's cave until attaining enlightenment; he survived on water and by extracting the essence of stones. He left his footprints on the rocks and finally attained enlightenment.

28. *Sbas yul mkhan pa lung gi nub sgo'i sde mig*, BT, f.26, published by Reinhard (1978).

29. Howard-Bury (1991, p. 83) mentions: "The legend was that from this valley [Rongphu] there used to be a pass over into the Khombu valley, but the high lama who lived here forbade the use of it, as it disturbed the meditations of the recluses and hermits." And further (pp. 150–51), when he climbed to the top of the ridge between Mount Everest and Makalu with the Sherpa Ang Tenzin: "To the South-west of us across the nevé, there appeared to be another easy pass which seemed to lead round to the South of Mount Everest, and Ang Tenze, who came from the Khombu Valley, said…that if we crossed this pass, we should eventually descend into the Khombu Valley. He also told me that there were stories that once upon a time there was a pass from the Khombu Valley into the Kama Valley, and that this was probably the pass in question, but that it had been disused for a great number of years. To support his theory we found on the way down a kind of shelter built of stones and some pieces of juniper hidden under a big rock. This would have been too high up for any yak herds to camp, as it was above the grazing pastures, and seemed to prove that the spot might have been used as a halting-place for smugglers or people fleeing from the law before they crossed these passes." I have heard a similar story from local Sherpas.

30. Erma *(g.yer ma)*, also called timur, prickly ash bark, or Guinea pepper *(Zanthoxylum armatum)*, is a small tree found in the eastern Himalayas. Its fruits are small berries with antiseptic, carminative, and digestive properties. According to Lama Zopa Rinpoche, erma can cure even cancer when taken in strong doses.

31. For the flora and fauna of the Everest region, cf. Mingma Norbu (1986), Brower (1991), Jefferies (1991), Stevens (1996), and Lhakpa Norbu (1999).

32. One of the first occasions of contact between Westerners and the yeti took place in 1889 in Sikkim, when Major L. A. Waddell saw large footprints in the snow that seemed to belong to a very large primate-type creature. Coleman (1989, p. 33ff.) quotes the Belgian zoologist B. Heuvelmans, *Sur la piste des bêtes ignorées* (1955), where he gives a detailed history of encounters with yetis or their footprints up to

1955. In 1957, 1958, and 1959, the American millionaire Tom Slick financed various yeti expeditions to East Nepal. During one of those, P. Byrne took the thumb and phalanx of the yeti hand that was kept in Pangboche *(spang po ched)* and substituted them with human ones. When the bones were examined by scientists, the analysis of their skin indicated that they were not human, but they could not identify to which kind of animal they belonged (Coleman, 1989, p. 90). For more information on the yeti, see Hutchison (1989), Messner (2000), and Ortner (1999).

33. Regarding whether yetis are just spirits or whether they have a gross body, Coleman quotes again Heuvelmans: "In 1954, Stonor of the London Zoo and others went to Khumbu in search of the yeti. They met Sherpa Pasang Nyima of Namche, who said he had seen a yeti and gave a detailed description. Stonor asked him: 'Is the yeti a flesh-and-blood animal, or is it a spirit?' To which the Sherpa replied with disarming logic: 'How could it have been a spirit since we saw its footprints after it had run away?'" (Coleman, 1989, pp. 41–42).

34. On July 12, 1974, Lhagpa Drolma of Khumjung *(khum ljongs/gshongs/'byung)* was tending a herd of yaks at Maccherma when she heard a whistle. Suddenly she was grabbed from behind and flung into the river. She then saw a *chugti (phyugs dre)* killing some of her animals. When the chugti went away, she managed to get back home and inform her family. The police from Namche went to investigate and filed a report. Cf. Hutchison (1989, pp. 166–67) and Thubten Lama (1999, p. 55).

35. One of the traits of yeti behavior is that they like to copy human activities. To get rid of the yetis that were eating their cattle and crops, the villagers of Tarnga *(rta rnga)* in the Thangme Valley (other Sherpas set the story at Pangboche) decided to play a trick on the yetis. They went to the top of the mountain bringing with them large containers filled with strong alcoholic drink *(arak)*. They drank some arak and pretended to fight among themselves with large Nepali knives known as *khukuris*. Meanwhile, the yetis were watching them, hidden in the crags of the cliffs. After some time the villagers went home and left the *arak* containers and the *khukuris* behind. At night, the yetis came down from the cliffs, drank the strong liquor, and, grabbing the knives, killed each other. And so the Sherpa people got rid of yetis for some time. The bodies of the dead yetis, however, could never be found.

36. This section is based on SCH, JT, Macdonald (1987a–c), Ortner (1989, 1990, 1999), Tenzin Zangbu and Klatzel (2000), and personal communication from Khumbu Sherpas. See also Lhakpa Norbu (1999) and *History and Culture of the Sherpas (sherpaharu ko itihas ra samskrit)*, written in Nepali by Acharya Ngawang Özer Sherpa (2002).

37. The story of the hunter Gonpo Dorje *(khyi ra ba mgon po rdo rje)* is a typical case of mixing historical facts with religious and folk stories. Gonpo Dorje could have been a member of the *khyi ra ba bdun* family from Lapchi, a native of Kyirong *(skyid rong)*, or a member of the ancient Kirat or Kiranti tribe. The Kirantis (who can be divided into Limbus and Rais) live in eastern Nepal and

had an independent kingdom until the Gorkha conquest in 1768. Cf. Shrestha and Singh (1987) and Chemjong (1966, 1967). The story of Kyirawa Gonpo Dorje could have evolved from a family of Kiranti Rais who came into Khumbu through the Amphu Labtsa Pass and settled in Dingboche. This, however, seems to have happened about a hundred years after the first Khampa immigrants settled in Khumbu. Later, the Kirantis moved south and returned to their home country. Cf. Ortner (1989, p. 26) and Tenzin Zangbu (2000).

The religious ingredient refers to the well-known story of Milarepa's meeting with Kyirawa Gonpo Dorje, which took place in Nyishang Gurta *(gnyi shang 'gur rta)*. Nyishang has been identified as Manang in western Nepal, but most available records point to a cave situated near Bhaktapur in the Kathmandu Valley; it is known as Sarasvati sthan to the locals. Thus, the story does not relate to the Khumbu area. Cf. MG (p. 430 ff.), Chang (1977, p. 275 ff.), and Decleer.

38. According to the *Clear Mirror (Rgyal rabs gsal ba'i me long)* and the *Mani Kabum (Mani bka' 'bum)*, the first humans of Tibet were known as the six tribes of Tibetan children *(bod kyi mi bu gdung drug)*: Se *(bse)*, Dong *(ldong)*, Mu *(dmu)*, Tong *(stong)*, Be *(dbas)*, and Da *(zla)*. Cf. bSod nams Gyaltsen (1996), JT (f.13b), and Tarthang Tulku (1986, pp. 114–15). Under the leadership of Gergyal, the people of the Dong tribe settled in Minyag Rimang *(mi nyag ri mang)*, the upper part of the Zalmogang *(zal mo sgang)* Range in Kham. Their descendants later migrated to southern Tibet and Khumbu.

39. Cf. SCH. It is not known with certainty why those Khampa chieftains decided to leave their homeland, but we know that during the thirteenth and fourteenth centuries the kings of Ling *(gling)*, a region adjacent to Minyag-Zalmogang, became very powerful and aggressive. On the other hand, the Mongols were leading incursions into Amdo *(a mdo)* and Kham, and the people of Zalmogang were living in constant fear. With the collapse of the Phagmo Drukpa dynasty in 1434, Tibet entered into a hundred years of fierce power struggles between the Gelug leaders of U *(dbus)* and the Kagyu rulers of Tsang *(gtsang)*. The majority of the Khampa population followed the Nyingma, Kagyu, or Sakya traditions, and had to endure the attacks of the Gelugpas, who were backed by the powerful Mongol tribes. Many monks were killed, and monasteries were badly damaged or totally destroyed during that period. Cf. Shakabpa (1984).

40. The four Khampa clans settled at Tinkye *(gting skyes)*, Tashi Dzong *(bkra shis rdzong)*, Dingri Langkor *(ding ri glang skor)*, Phadrug *(pha 'drug)*, Kharta *(mkhar rta)*, Rongshar *(rong shar)*, and other areas. Donkha Ringmo *(ldong kha ring mo)* and Sangye Paljor *(sangs rgyas dpal 'byor)* spent some time in Chung Riboche in Northern Latö with Thangtong Gyalpo *(thang stong rgyal po brtson 'grus bzang po, 1361–1464)*, who belonged to the Ladong Karpo *(lha ldong dkar po)* tribe of Minyag. It is said that when Donkha Ringmo passed away, Sangye Paljor built a three-storied chörten in his memory at Chung Riboche *(cung ri bo che)* that was consecrated by Thangtong Gyalpo himself. Cf. SCH (f.6a/b). The ancestors of the

first Sikkimese ruler Puntsog Namgyal (*phun tshogs rnam rgyal,* seventeenth century) were also originally from Minyag, as were the rulers of Northern Latö *(byang la stod).* Cf. sKal ldan/Diemberger (1996).

41. Taking advantage of the unstable situation in Tibet, the powerful Newar king Yaksha Malla (1428–82) invaded Tibet and reached Shelkar Dzong. Although the Nepali invasion did not last long, houses and temples were looted, crops were destroyed, and people had to flee for their lives to high and almost inaccessible mountain caves (there is a large cave above Zamte in Khumbu where it is said that Tibetans took shelter when escaping a war with the Nepali army). Then, in 1533 Sultan Sa'id Khan of Kashgar and General Muhammed Haidar Dughlat invaded Tibet from the west. The Muslim invasion once again caused great turmoil in the Latö area. Cf. Oppitz (1974). For the Tibeto-Nepali wars, see Uprety (1980).

42. The SCH (f.7a) says that Gyagarba Chenpo *(rgya gar ba chen po),* the "Great Indian," was the son of Guru Chogden *(guru mchog ldan),* from the lineage of the terton Guru Chöwang *(chos kyi dbang phyug,* 1212–70) of Lhodrag *(lho brag).* Guru Chogden could be identified as Chogden Gonpo *(mchog ldan mgon po,* 1497–1530), but according to known sources, Chogden Gonpo's son was called Gyalse Tenpe Jungne *(rgyal sras bstan pa'i 'byung gnas),* and his life does not seem to have been related to Sherpa history (F. K. Ehrhard, personal communication). The text does not mention his actual name, but the name "Gyagarba Chenpo" refers to Drubthob Gyergompa *(grub thob gyer sgom pa)* and his descendants. Gyergompa, a member of the Licchavi tribe in northern India, was carried by a *dremo,* or female yeti, to the Kharta area of Latö, where he founded the Kuye Labrang. See also note 176 below.

Gyergompa built another temple at a place where there is a three-story high boulder shaped like a ritual vase that was made by female spirits and dakinis; he named it Bumkhang Labrang *(bum khang bla brang).* The present Kusho Bumkhang Jamyang Zangpo lives near Bungamati in the Kathmandu Valley (personal communication from the Kuye and Bumkhang families).

43. There are no historical records stating the year when the first Khampas came into Khumbu. Although Oppitz (1974) has given 1533 as a possible date, some Sherpas believe that the first immigrants arrived in Khumbu at a much earlier date, while others think that the migration took place much later (see Lhakpa Norbu, 1999). Regarding the route they followed, the easiest and most direct road crosses the Nangpa La *(snang pa'i la)* near Cho Oyu (*jo bo u yug,* 8,153 m) and leads into the valley of the Nangpe Tsangpo, or Bhote Kosi. In that case, one could argue that they would have settled in that valley instead of proceeding as far as Pangboche. In fact, there is much evidence pointing to the Nangpe Tsangpo Valley as the first area to be permanently populated (Lhakpa Norbu, 1999). The aforementioned pass east of Jomo Langma *(jo mo glang ma)* is another possible route, and again, there is the possibility of their having crossed the Menlung La into

Rolwaling and then into Khumbu through the Tashi Labtsa. Or, as some suggest, they could have come through the Rongshar Valley into Shorong and then up to Khumbu.

44. The Dilbu Dingma Cave *(dril bu sding ma phug)* is situated near Satarma across the Nangpe Tsangpo, near Namche. A large chörten and a long row of carved *mani* stones were erected near the spot where Phachen had landed. Phachen's footprint can still be seen on the northern ridge above Phurte.

45. According to the SCH (f.3a), 200 years after Dudjom Dorje and Gyagarba Chenpo a new wave of Khampa immigrants came into Khumbu. Among them were Sangwa Dorje *(gsang ba rdo rje)*, Serpa Dungyal *(ser pa dung rgyal)*, Minyagpa Michen Dragpa *(mi nyag pa mi chen grags pa)*, and others. Serpa Dungyal and Michen Dragpa settled in the Pangboche area. This new migration may have been related to a severe famine that hit Southern Latö *(la stod lho)* in the seventeenth century. Cf. sKal ldan/Diemberger (1996, p. 126).

46. Cf. the autobiography of Dzatul Ngawang Tenzin Norbu entitled *Playful Ocean of Immortal Nectar (Dus mthar chos smra ba'i btsun pa ngag dbang bstan 'dzin nor bu'i rnam thar 'chi med bdud rtsi'i rol mtsho)*, quoted henceforth as DTH, ff.16–18a, and SCH (ff.3, 4). See also appendix II. It seems that there is another, more ancient source of the story, but I have been unable to locate it. According to Tenzin Zangbu (2000), Buddha Tsenchen *(buddha mtshan can)* was born in Khumbu two generations after Phachen, while the SCH mentions that he was born in Tibet. Ehrhard (1997, p. 340) quotes the *Dwangs shel 'phrul gyi me long* as saying that Sangwa Dorje, Samye Karchen Kunga Dragpa *(bsam yas dkar chen kun dga' grags pa)*, and Yolmowa Shakya Zangpo *(yol mo ba shakya bzang po,* early sixteenth century) were the "field of offerings" of the king of Gungthang, Kunzang Nyida Dragpa *(kun bzang nyi zla grags pa,* 1514–60).

47. For the Drogon lamas, see chapter 7 and note 108.

48. Tobden Pawo Tenzin Norbu *(stobs ldan dpa' bo bstan 'dzin nor bu,* 1598–1644) was the reincarnation of Tulku Namkha Gyajin *(sprul sku nam mkha' brgya byin,* sixteenth century). For the lineage of the Yolmo tulkus, cf. Ehrhard, forthcoming.

49. At the Sky Castle *(nam mkha' rdzong)* above Dingboche, he obtained attainments related to the body. In a cave on the Wild Horse Mountain *(rta rgod gangs ri'i sgrub phug)* in Khumbu he achieved speech attainments. In a hut on the lower slopes of that same mountain he achieved mind attainments, good qualities at the Lion Cave *(seng ge phug)* on the higher slopes of Tawoche *(rta bo che,* 6,367 m) Mountain in Khumbu (Sherpas identify this cave with Senge Phug in Shorong), and beneficial activities at the Treasure Cave *(gter phug)* close to Pangboche. He meditated also in the Gyachog Valley, the White *Ah* Cave *(a dkar phug)* above Khumjung, and in various other hermitages of Khumbu, Shorong, and Tibet. He visited Khenpalung three times and stayed for a long time at Mani Gang and Thongdroling *(mthong grol gling)* in the Rongphu Valley. Cf. DTH (f.16b).

50. According to a printed sheet distributed at Rimejung *(ri smad ljongs)* Gompa,

seven thieves once stole the Buddha image. They wanted to take it to Tibet, but when they reached a place called Childo Phug just across the Tibetan border, the statue became so heavy that they were unable to lift it. Then the face of the Buddha began to sweat and said that it wanted to go back and stay at Tulo Gomila (the village below Rimejung). The thieves brought the statue back and built a temple at that place. The pamphlet does not mention Khenpa Dorje. Probably the present Rimejung Gompa was built at the spot where Khenpa Dorje had built some kind of small temple or hermitage.

51. See Ortner (1989, pp. 87–89) for the full story. In those days the Kathmandu Valley was ruled by the Malla dynasty, while the rest of the country was divided into the twenty-four and the twenty-two principalities (Chaubis and Bais), independent hill states ruled by descendants of Hindu families from India. Among those, the kingdom of Makwanpur was ruled by a king of the Sena dynasty who also had control over the eastern kingdom of Vijaypur, populated by Kirantis. Cf. I. S. Chemjong (1966, 1967).

52. In the seventeenth century, Tibet continued to be troubled by sectarian violence and had to endure the invasions of the Gorkha king Ram Shah, the Newar king of Kathmandu Pratap Malla (reigned 1641–74), and the Ladakhi king Senge Namgyal (*seng ge rnam rgyal,* reigned 1590–1620). Although a member of the reformed Gelug order founded by Tsongkhapa (*tsong kha pa,* 1357–1419), the Fifth Dalai Lama Ngawang Lozang Gyatso (*ngag dbang blo bzang rgya mtsho,* 1617–82) was also a follower of the Nyingma tradition, and monasteries of this lineage flourished during his reign. Thus, in 1632 Rigzin Ngag-ki Wangpo (*rig 'dzin ngag gi dbang po,* 1581–1639) built the Thubten Dorje Drag (*thub bstan rdo rje brag)* Monastery in Central Tibet as a center for the study and practice of the Northern Treasure. Some years later, Rigzin Terdag Lingpa Gyurme Dorje (*rig 'dzin gter bdag gling pa, 'gyur med rdo rje,* 1646–1714) built Mindroling (*smin sgrol gling)* Monastery for the study and practice of the *Heart Drop (snying thig)* teachings.

After the Fifth Dalai Lama's death, sectarian conflict flared high again in Tibet. The persecution of the Nyingma tradition reached its peak in 1717, when the Dzungkar Mongol Lozang Puntsog (*blo bzang phun tshogs)* of Drepung Gomang (*'bras spungs sgo mang)* incited the destruction of up to 500 of the best Nyingma monasteries. His followers killed four great Nyingma lamas: Rigzin Chenpo Pema Trinle (*rig 'dzin chen po padma 'phrin las,* 1640–1718) of Dorje Drag; Terdag Lingpa's brother Lochen Dharmashri (*lo chen dharma shri,* 1654–1717); the throneholder of Mindroling, Pema Gyurme Gyatso (*padma 'gyur med rgya mtsho,* 1635–1717); and Konchog Chödrag (*dkon mchog chos grags)* of Namgyaling (*rnam rgyal gling)* Monastery in Tsang. Nyingma practitioners were persecuted, and texts and images were systematically burnt and destroyed. Only after Polhane Sonam Tobgye (*pho lha nas bsod nams stobs rgyas,* 1689–1747) took control of the government in 1728 were the Nyingmapas allowed to rebuild their monasteries. Cf. Smith (1969) and Petech (1972).

53.  Cf. Ortner (1989, p. 92).

54.  According to Fürer-Haimendorf (1984), potato cultivation spread in eastern Nepal from the gardens of the Europeans in Darjeeling and the British Embassy in Kathmandu. In 1848, Joseph Hooker found potatoes in the region of Yangma west of Kangchenjunga and remarked that they had been recently introduced. In 1774–75, George Bogle made a journey to Bhutan and Lhasa and apparently planted potatoes at many places on the way, as desired by the British Governor General of India Warren Hastings. Cf. Markham (1989, p. 19). Ortner (1989, p. 158) mentions that according to her Sherpa informants, the first potatoes came from the garden of the British resident in Sikkim. See also Stevens (1996).

   The Sherpas have become real experts and can prepare up to thirteen different potato dishes: (1) *dog-dog:* grated potatoes mixed with buckwheat flour, made into balls, and cooked in soup with pickled vegetables *(shotse);* (2) boiled potatoes; (3) *sen:* mashed potatoes mixed with millet or barley tsampa and cooked into a thick porridge; (4) *kur:* potato pancakes; (5) *shagpa:* potato stew *(shagpa* literally means "sliced" and refers to the sliced potatoes that are its main ingredient); (6) *kyu thugpa:* porridge made with potatoes, corn, and sour milk; (7) dried potatoes with popcorn; (8) fried potatoes with *chiura* (dried flattened rice); (9) potato curry with vegetables; (10) potato momos (dumplings stuffed with potato); (11) *rildog:* mashed potatoes; (12) *rilthug:* mashed potatoes in soup with sour, rotten cheese *(somar);* (13) french fries for the tourists.

55.  The establishment of the tea industry in 1856 brought the need to improve the road and railway systems connecting Calcutta with Darjeeling, Gangtok, and Kalimpong. That opened new possibilities of work for the Sherpas and for the population of east Nepal as a whole. Cf. Ortner (1989, pp. 105–8).

56.  Tibet and Nepal actually fought a war in 1855–56 because of border disputes, a problem about debased Nepali coins current in Tibet, and the maltreatment of Nepalis by the Tibetans. Another quarrel took place in 1883 because of a fight with a Newar merchant in Lhasa. During 1886–89 there was a great deal of tension over the issue of their borders, but the problems were solved without actual war. Cf. Uprety (1980).

57.  The only records available are the prayers to the lineage lamas of various ritual texts. It seems that Rigzin Tenpa Sangye *(rig 'dzin bstan pa sangs rgyas)* was a disciple of Kelzang Pema Wangchug *(bskal bzang padma dbang phyug),* who spent long periods of time in Drakar Taso *(brag dkar rta so);* he was probably the fifth Rigzin Chenpo (1720–70) of Thubten Dorje Drag Monastery in Central Tibet.

58.  Rigzin Pema Longyang *(rig 'dzin padma klong yangs)* is mentioned by the Phortse *(pho rtse)* Lama Kagyu Chökyi Rigzin *(bka' brgyud chos kyi rig 'dzin)* as the lama to whom he offered his hair. See SCH, f.29b. A statue of Rigzin Pema Longyang is found in Pangboche Gompa.

59.  According to his descendant Lama Zangpo of Genupa *(dga' phug pa),* he was one of his blood ancestors and is credited with the rebuilding or enlarging of the Thangme Gompa. But according to the Tengboche Lama, Tulku Ngawang Dorje

was a fully ordained monk from the Shangkhug clan and disciple of a Yolmo lama. Other informants say that he came from Tibet. His remains are enshrined in a copper chörten and kept in Thangme Gompa.

60. Chatang Chöying Rangdrol *(bya stang chos dbyings rang grol)* was either the son or grandson of Tulku Ngawang Dorje. From Chökyi Wangchug of the White Cliff Horse Tooth Hermitage *(brag dkar rta so chos kyi dbang phyug, 1775–1837)*, one of Milarepa's caves, he received the main lineages of the Nyingma tradition. He meditated in Pangthog Shingsa in the Arun Valley near Khenpalung and in Yolmo Senge Phug, Milarepa's Lion Cave, where he performed one set of preliminaries. The platform made of stones where he used to sit and teach, and his footprint on a nearby rock, can still be seen at Genupa. Traditionally, the relics of the lamas of that family are enshrined in a chörten or in a statue alternatively. About one century later, when his descendant Lama Zangpo wanted to repair the old statue of Chatang Chöying Rangdrol, he found inside many relics and a stone with his handprint from which nectar flows when touched with devotion. According to Ani Pema Chöden, Chatang Chöying Rangdrol was one of the four "Rangdrol": Shabkar Tsodrug Rangdrol, Tsele Natsog Rangdrol, Zurchen Chöying Rangdrol, and Chatang Chöying Rangdrol.

61. Drakar Taso Chökyi Wangchug was born in Kyirong and recognized as the tulku of Yeshe Chödag *(ye shes chos grags, 1705–72)*. He studied with Rigzin Trinle Dudjom *(rig 'dzin 'phrin las bdud 'joms, 1726–89)* of Yolmo in Nepal and with Rigzin Tsewang Norbu of Kathog *(ka thog rig 'dzin tshe dbang nor bu, 1698–1755)*. His autobiography mentions that in 1825 Chatang Chöying Rangdrol helped in the renovation of the shrine of Rigzin Tsewang Norbu in Ribo Palbar *(ri bo dpal 'bar)* together with Rongshar Shung Lama Trinle *(rong shar gzhung bla ma 'phrin las)* and Rongshar Shung Lama Tsewang Dondrub *(rong shar gzhung bla ma tshe dbang don grub)*. His *Collected Letters* includes some correspondence with Chatang Chöying Rangdrol. Cf. Ehrhard, forthcoming.

62. According to Fürer-Haimendorf (1964), he was the head of Thangme Gompa from 1865 until his death in 1895. He had seven sons and at least one daughter, Ani Kyipal.

63. According to Ortner (1989), the Khumjung Gompa was built in 1831. The DTH mentions that it was built by the Tragtho *(brag mtho)* family.

64. Rigzin Chökyi Gyaltsen *(rig 'dzin chos kyi rgyal mtshan)* is mentioned in the lineage of the *Self-Created and Self-Luminous Primordial Purity (Bka' dag rang byung rang shar)*, BT: Chatang Kalzang Rabgye *(bya stang bskal bzang rab rgyas)* →Rigzin Chökyi Gyaltsen *(rig 'dzin chos kyi rgyal mtshan)* →Kagyu Chökyi Lodro *(bka' brgyud chos kyi blo gros)* →Kagyu Tenzin Rangdrol *(bka' brgyud bstan 'dzin rang grol)* →Ngawang Norbu Zangpo *(ngag dbang nor bu bzang po, bla ma dgu lo, 1850–1934)*. And in the *Excellent Secret Slaying of the Ego (Gcod gsang ba rmad 'byung)*, BT: Kalzang Rabgye →Chökyi Gyaltsen →Dreltse Donden *('brel tshad don ldan 'jam dyangs chos kyi rigs 'dzin)* →Chökyi Lodro. There is a statue of

Umdze *(dbu mdzad)* Chökyi Gyaltsen in Pangboche Gompa, with a moustache and a large hat.

65. Dreltse Donden Jamyang Chökyi Rigzin was born in a fire-bird year (probably 1777) in Upper Khumbu. He studied with Rigzin Chökyi Gyaltsen until he was twenty-five. During those years he received the empowerments, oral transmissions, and commentaries of all the lineages that his teacher held. Cf. his *Heart Nectar Benefiting Others: The Little Happy Songs of Experience of Jamyang Chökyi Rigzin ('Jam dbyangs chos kyi rig 'dzin nyams shar dga' glu chung gzhan phan snying gi bdud rtsi),* ff.78b, 79a/b and SCH (f.25b). According to the local folklore, he flew from Lukla *(lug la,* the Pass of the Sheep) in Pharag to Tsibri, carrying an iron staff and a ritual dagger in his hands. During his travels in Tibet, Dreltse Donden became the teacher of the royal family of Sikkim. In KHB, f.7b, Lama Gulo mentions that when he himself was in his mother's womb, his elder brother was very sick, and his parents called for Dreltse Donden. The lama came to perform rituals at their house and told the parents that the sick boy would die but the baby in the womb should be well cared for and kept clean because he would benefit many beings.

The rock with Dreltse Donden's footprints is still there among the potato fields, but it is completely covered with grass and bushes, and no one seems to know where the footprints are. Lama Ngawang Lozang *(ngag dbang blo bzang),* the owner of Yeti Lodge in Lukla, is currently in charge of the religious activities in Lukla and has repaired the Tashi Chöding *(bkra shis chos ldings)* or Lukla Gompa.

66. Cf. the "Song of Milarepa's Meeting with the Five Sisters of Long Life" *(tshe ring mched lnga),* MG (pp. 479–80) and Chang (1977, pp. 322–23).

67. This description belongs to the *Wish-Granting Cow (Yid bzhin 'dod 'jo)* composed by Dzatul Ngawang Tenzin Norbu. Slightly different descriptions of the Five Sisters can be found in *The Precious Source of Ritual Practices of the Ocean of Mind-Bound Deities (Yi dam rgya mtsho'i sgrub thabs rin chen 'byung gnas),* also known as the *Rinjung Gyatsa, the Hundred [Rituals] Source of Jewels,* compiled by Jetsun Taranatha Kunga Nyingpo *(rje btsun ta ra na tha kun dga' snying po,* 1575–1635), and in the *Heart Drop of the Great Expanse* cycle *(Klong chen snying thig)* revealed by Jigme Lingpa *(jigs med gling pa,* 1729–98). The *Rinjung Gyatsa* mentions Miyo Lozangma *(mi g.yo blo bzang ma),* or Immutable Good Mind Lady, instead of Langzangma. All the other sources consulted agree on the name Langzangma.

68. Cf. Nebesky-Wojkowitz (1996) and Aufschnaiter (1976). In Milarepa's songs we find the five dakinis also mentioned under different names relating to their specific abodes. Cf. MG (pp. 457, 520) and Chang (1977, p. 360).

69. Cf. Norbu (1995) and Nebesky-Wojkowitz (1996).

70. *Yul lha rnams kyi mchod sprin gser gyi 'phreng ba.* Composed by a Sherpa lama, probably Buddha Tsenchen.

71. The ritual texts associated with Zurra Rakye *(zur rva ra skyes)* were discovered in 1923 by Reting Terton Sangye Wangdu *(rva sgreng gter ston sangs rgyas dbang dus),*

a disciple of Ngawang Tenzin Norbu. Cf. Diemberger (1992, 1993, 1997), Chan (1994), and sKal ldan/Diemberger (1996).

72. The mountain is known as Three Bodies White Mountain (*sku gsum gangs dkar mo*, 6,369 m), Three Bodies and Five Peaks *(sku gsum rtse lnga)*, or Three Bends Mountain *(gug gsum)*. Sherpas perform rituals on that mountain during the third, fourth, and ninth months of the lunar year. See also Funke (1982).

## Part One

73. Lay tantric practitioners are known as *ngagpas (sngags pa)*, which literally means "one versed in mantra." Ngagpa lamas pass their own lineage of practices and teachings to their blood descendants, usually the eldest son, although in some families the youngest son becomes the lineage holder. Ngagpas tend to marry within their own group of married lamas and form a kind of religious aristocracy. Gompas populated by married lamas are called *serkyim (ser khyim)* or "yellow households." All the Khumbu lamas were ngagpas until the beginning of the twentieth century. For the ngagpa tradition, cf. Snellgrove (1957, pp. 201, 220–21).

74. The great grandfather of Kunzang Yeshe was a disciple of the Holder of the Throne of Sakya *(sa skya khri 'dzin)*. The name "Four Corners" refers to the four *labrang (bla brang)*, or residences, of married lamas situated near Sakya Monastery. According to Ralo Rinpoche (b. 1934), who comes originally from that area, the four labrang are Lama Shara, Kochag Drogon, Tanag Yangchog, and Thabsang Labrang (cf. Chan, 1994, pp. 889, 900). While still in Tibet, Ralo Rinpoche heard that married lamas from a labrang at Yalung *(g.ya lung)* near Sakya had migrated to Khumbu some time before, but I have not been able to find any more information on this matter.

75. His Holiness the Fourteenth Dalai Lama explains thus the system of the Nyingma tradition: "In the early translation school of the Nyingma, a system of nine *yanas* (vehicles) is taught. Three of these—the paths of the shravaka, pratyekabuddha, and bodhisattva—constitute the sutra tradition, while the tantric tradition consists of six levels—the three outer tantras [kriya, upa, and yoga] and the three inner tantras [mahayoga, anuyoga, and atiyoga]. The tradition of dzogchen, or atiyoga, is considered to be the pinnacle of these nine yanas. The other, lower, yanas are said to be philosophical systems that depend on an ordinary consciousness, and so the path is based on that ordinary consciousness. Here the distinction being made is between ordinary mind—*sem*—and pure awareness—*rigpa*. The ninth yana, the most majestic, is beyond ordinary consciousness, for its path is based on *rigpa*, not on the ordinary mind." See Tenzin Gyatso (2000, p. 47).

76. *Hum!* In the northwest of the land of Oddiyana, / In the heart of a lotus flower, / Endowed with the most marvelous attainments / You are renowned as the Lotus Born, / Surrounded by a retinue of many dakinis. / Following in your footsteps,

I will become accomplished. / Please come and bestow your blessings. / *Guru Pema Siddhi Hum!*

"As Guru Rinpoche said: 'When a disciple calls upon me with devotion and the yearning song of the seven-line prayer, I shall come at once from Sangdogpalri [*zangs mdog dpal ri*, the Copper-Colored Mountain], like a mother who cannot resist the call of her child.'" Cf. Khyentse Rinpoche (1995, p. 31).

77. *Bsam pa lhun grub ma*, BT.

78. Kagyu Chökyi Lodro *(bka' brgyud chos kyi blo gros)* was a disciple of Dreltse Donden Jamyang Chökyi Rigzin (see above, n. 64). A small chörten containing his ashes *(sku gdung)* is kept at Pangboche Gompa.

79. The Tibetan term is *darchog (dar lcog)*, which Karmay (1993) translates as "the cloth [attached to] the pinnacle or turret." These are pieces of cloth of the five colors associated with the five astrological elements (yellow for metal, red for fire, green for wood, white for water, and blue for space) printed with various astrological and religious symbols. Originally the real meaning and purpose of the flags was to purify the different elements and astrological forces by utilizing the wind element as the main vehicle. With the introduction of Buddhism in Tibet, mantras and images of deities were added, and the so-called "prayer flags" became a skillful method to benefit beings. It is said in the scriptures that the mantras and deities printed on them can bestow blessings and even liberation from cyclic existence on every being that sees them, touches them, or even breathes the air that has come in contact with them.

According to Karmay (1993), the original spelling was *klong rta* or "space horse," one of the four basic elements in Tibetan astrology, the other three being vital force *(srog)*, body *(lus)*, and power and prosperity *(dbang thang)*. Later the spelling was changed to *rlung rta*, "wind horse." The syllable *rta* refers to the excellent horse *(rta mchog)* that is adorned with the wish-granting jewel or with the Three Jewels (Buddha, Dharma, Sangha). The horse is traditionally associated with the wind, or air, element and is a symbol of speed. In this context, it relates to the speedy transformation of the negative aspects of the elements into positive forces. Whatever the spelling may be, the *lungta* is a kind of protective energy tied to a person's life force bringing about well-being, prosperity, and good fortune.

The flags printed with the *lungta* depict in the center a horse adorned with flaming jewels, symbolizing space, surrounded by a garuda or eagle (fire), a dragon (water), a tiger (wood or air), and a lion (earth).

80. The syllables of the six expanses, or spheres *(klong drug yig ge)*, purify the beings of the six realms (gods, demigods, humans, animals, hungry ghosts, and hell beings). Explanation about the six syllables can be found in the mind category *(sems sde)* and space category *(klong sde)* of dzogchen tantras. The particular boulders mentioned here were washed away or covered by the river during the great flood of 1985.

81. For the Tibetan practice of burning fragrant plants and substances together with grains, sugar, milk, etc., as a purifying ritual, see Norbu (1995, pp. 109–12).

82. *Ka dag rang 'byung rang shar,* BT.

83. *Gsang ba rmad 'byung gi gcod,* BT. The practice of *chöd,* or slaying the concept of ego-grasping, was introduced by Machig Labdron *(ma gcig lab sgron,* 1055–1143), a Tibetan female practitioner and disciple of the Indian Phadampa Sangye. The chöd practice is based on the Prajnaparamita scriptures that explain the emptiness of self and phenomena. The ritual involves melodious chanting and the use of a large hand drum, a thighbone trumpet, and a small bell.

84. Kagyu Tenzin Rangdrol *(bka' brgyud bstan 'dzin rang grol)* was a disciple of Kagyu Chökyi Lodro. In his autobiography (*Kho bo bya stang chos dar ram ngag dbang nor bu bzang por 'bod pas rang snang 'khrul pa tshul bzhin brjod pa mu ti ka'i phreng ba,* henceforth quoted as KHB), f.19b, Chatang Chötar, or Lama Gulo, (1850–1934) mentions that after receiving the *Unobstructed Primordial Mind* from him, in the monkey year 1884–85 he began a three-year retreat. Further (f.36a/b) he mentions that when Kagyu Rangdrol passed away, Gembu Tsepel *(rgan po tshe dpal)* from Namche offered a chörten to enshrine his relics.

85. *Rdzogs chen dgongs pa zang thal,* BT, five vols. Regarding the meaning of *zangthal,* or unobstructed, Ricard (1994, p. 271, n. 42) quotes Taglung Tshetrul Pema Wangyal *(stag lung tshe sprul padma dbang rgyal):* "*Zangthal* can be explained as *zang kha ma thal du 'byung. Zang kha ma* is the natural condition, the unmodified simplicity of the primordial nature *(ma bcos pa'i gdod ma'i gnas lugs). Thal du 'byung* literally means 'to reduce to dust,' and refers to the annihilation of deluded thoughts. Thus, *zangthal* could be translated as 'pristine simplicity that crushes delusion into dust.'"

86. *Rlung phag mo zab rgya,* BT.

87. Urgyen Chöphel *(ras chen 'gro mgon o rgyan chos 'phel)* was a Sherpa "Khampa" lama who spent long periods of time at Lapchi and Rongphu. He was probably from Drogon Gompa in Kochag (see below). In KHB (f.6b) Lama Gulo mentions that around 1883 he received the *Easy Gradual Path (Lam rim bde lam)* from Urgyen Chöphel, "the heart son of Urgyen Tenphel, the reincarnation of Yudra Nyingpo" (*o rgyan bstan 'phel,* the immediately previous embodiment of Dzatul Ngawang Tenzin Norbu; see appendix III). Lama Gulo also mentions (ff.34b, 35a) that when Drogon Urgyen Chöphel passed away at Khumjung Hermitage, there were many auspicious signs, and that he built a chörten in his memory.

88. *Rdzogs chen ati zab don snying po,* a terma of Rigzin Terdag Lingpa. A commentary to it was written by his daughter Jetsun Mingyur Paldron (*rje btsun mi 'gyur dpal sgron,* 1699–1769). Published in the *Rinchen Terdzö,* vol. 58 *(si),* and as the *Ati Zab Don sNying po* cycle, by Kocchen sprul sku, Dehradun, 1977.

89. *Explanation of the Stages of the Path of the Great Vehicle Called the Holy Dharma Wish-Fulfilling Jewel (Dam chos yid bzhin gyi nor bu thar pa rin po che'i rgyan zhes bya ba theg pa chen po'i lam rim gyi bzhad pa),* written by Gampopa Sonam Rinchen *(sgam po pa bsod nams rin chen,* 1079–1153), one of the two foremost disciples of Milarepa. Gampopa learned the teachings on the gradual path from the Kadampa followers of Atisha (982–1054).

90. The teachings of the *Heart Drop of the Dakinis (Mkha' 'gro snying thig)* were given by Padmasambhava to Yeshe Tsogyal at the Great Gathering Cave of the Dakinis at Tidro *(gzho stod ti sgro brag dkar mkha' 'gro'i tshogs khang chen mo)* in Drigung *('bri gung),* Central Tibet. The teaching was hidden as a terma in Danglha Tramodrag *(ldang lha khra mo brag)* and its revelation entrusted to Princess Pemasal *(padma gsal),* daughter of King Trisong Detsen. It was revealed by Pema Ledreltsal *(padma las 'brel rtsal,* 1231–59). Later, the Omniscient Longchen Rabjampa *(kun mkhyen klong chen rab 'byams pa,* 1308–63), who was the reincarnation of both Princess Pemasal and Pema Ledreltsal, received the oral transmission of the text from Sho Gyalse Legpa *(zho'i rgyal sras legs pa,* 1290–1367) and the actual transmission from Padmasambhava and Yeshe Tsogyal in a vision. Cf. Thondup (1999).

91. Guru yoga *(bla ma rnal 'byor)* is a practice directed to merging one's mind with the mind of the teacher. It is not clear which particular transmission Kunzang Yeshe received on this occasion.

92. The preliminary practices are mental and physical exercises aimed at building a solid foundation for advanced practices. To begin with, the practitioners reflect upon the great value of this precious human body, impermanence and death, the sufferings of cyclic existence, and the law of cause and effect. These reflections are followed by the practice of full-length prostrations while reciting the prayer for taking refuge in the Three Jewels, the recitation of the purificatory mantra of the deity Vajrasattva, the symbolic offering of oneself and the universe *(mandala),* and unifying one's mind with the mind of one's spiritual master *(bla ma rnal 'byor).* Each of these practices has to be repeated at least 110,000 times. The order of the practices varies according to different tantric systems.

93. Sherpa weddings wisely take place in stages. After the formal engagement takes place, the boy visits the girl and lives with her at her parents' home. Months, or even years later, the final marriage ceremony takes place, and the girl moves to her husband's home together with any children that have been born.

94. In good weather, the journey from Thangme to Kyatrag and back takes four nights and five days on foot. Animals are better able to negotiate the snows of the Nangpa La during the dry seasons (April–May and October–November). The Sherpas used to take to Tibet items such as rice, corn, millet, butter, chilies, rock sugar and brown sugar, dried sliced potatoes from Khumbu, vegetable dyes, spices, medicinal herbs, and flowers from the Himalayas, cotton cloth, needles, and so forth. Nepali paper was in great demand for printing religious books in the Rongphu, Tsibri, and Shelkar monasteries, while the *zobgyos (mdzo bskyod),* the crossbreed between a yak and a cow that could be bred only in Nepal, were greatly prized as beasts of burden. Besides salt and wool to make clothes, blankets, and bags, the Sherpas used to take back to Khumbu items such as sheepskins, hides, woolen cloth, carpets, Chinese silk, hats, boots, aprons for the womenfolk, religious books and instruments, dried mutton, and tsampa. Cf. Fürer-Haimendorf (1964, 1975).

The most important trading commodity was salt from the lakes of the pastures *(byang thang)*. In autumn, the nomads would go to the lakes to buy salt from those people who had the monopoly of digging it out. The salt was then carried by yaks and sheep to Chung Riwoche in Northern Latö, the first trading town south of the pastures. Most of it was sold at Chung Riwoche, while the rest was taken to Kyatrag for trade with the Sherpas.

95.  *Ri bo bsang mchod.* The Sherpas use a text from the *Life Accomplishment of Knowledge-Holders (Rig 'dzin srog sgrub)* cycle discovered by Lhatsun Namkha Jigme (*lha btsun nam mkha' 'jigs med,* 1597–ca. 1650).

96.  There are five *jobos,* or lords, in that part of the Himalayas: Jobo Rabzang (*jo bo ra bzang,* 6,666 m), Jobo Uyug or Cho Oyu (*jo bo u yug,* 8,153 m), Jobo Lonpo (*jo bo blon po,* 7,660 m, Makalu range), Jobo Garu *(jo bo sga ru? dkar po?)* or Menlungtse (*sman klung rtse,* 7,181 m), and Jobo Bamung-ri (*Ba men? ri,* Bamare or Kukuraja, 5,927 m). Cf. Chan (1994, p. 261).

97.  *Nyungne (smyung gnas)* literally means "abiding in little," or abiding in retreat. It is a two-day lower tantra *(kriya)* practice related to Chenrezig *(spyan ras gzigs),* the Great Compassionate One. The nyungne practice started with Bhikshuni Lakshminkara *(dge slong ma dpal mo),* an Indian princess who had a direct vision of Chenrezig. Cf. Zopa Rinpoche (1979), Seventh Dalai Lama Kelsang Gyatso (1995), and Yeshe Gyaltsen (1998).

98.  *'Phags pa shes rab kyi pha rol tu phyin pa brgyad stong pa (Ashtasahasrika prajnaparamita sutra),* a Mahayana sutra written in 8,000 verses, or *slokas,* a *sloka* being a unit of thirty-two syllables. It is an anonymous work that, according to Conze (1973), could have been composed between 50 A.D. and 700 A.D. The teachings of the Perfection of Wisdom were discovered by Arya Nagarjuna and contain detailed explanations about the concept of emptiness *(shunyata).* This particular text was translated into Tibetan in around 850 A.D. and again in 1020. It was revised in 1030, 1075, and 1500. It was translated into English by Conze (1973).

99.  Popularly known as *Many Sutras (Mdo mang)* or *Condensed Scriptures (Gsungs btus),* it is a compilation of various sutras and mantras. The full name is *The Garland of Wish-Granting Jewels: A Useful Extract of the Essence of the Ocean of Sutra and Tantra Scriptures (Mdo rgyud gsung rab rgya mtsho'i snying po gces pa'i btus pa 'dod 'byung nor bu'i phreng ba).*

100. The full name is the *Stainless Royal Tantra: A Text of Atonement Restoring All Degenerated Commitments (Dam tshig thams cad kyi nyams chag skong ba'i lung bshags pa thams cad kyi rgyud dri ma med pa'i rgyal po).* It was translated into Tibetan from the original Sanskrit by Vimalamitra and Nyag Jnanakumara (*gnyags jnanakumara,* eighth century). It was later concealed as a terma and subsequently discovered by Sangye Lingpa (*sangs rgyas gling pa,* 1340–96).

101. *Chanting the Names of the Buddha: The Precious Garland of the Confession of Oaths (Sangs rgyas mtshan brjod mna' bshags rin chen 'phreng ba).* This text is probably a terma, but not much is known about it.

102. *Kurim (sku rim)* and *zhabten (zhabs brtan)* are general names given to the ritual ceremonies performed for curing sickness and averting obstacles. According to Trulzhig Rinpoche, the three types of kurim are *Twenty-One Praises to Tara (Sgrol ma nyer gcig)*, the ritual of the Lion-Faced Dakini *(seng ge ldong ma)*, and White Umbrella *(sdugs dkar)*. According to other informants, they are the *Sutra of the Three Heaps (Phung po gsum pa'i mdo)*, commonly known as the *Confession Prayer of the Thirty-Five Buddhas, Twenty-One Praises to Tara,* and long-life rituals. Again, sometimes the three kurim refer to the *Essence of Wisdom Sutra (Shes rab snying po'i mdo)* and the rituals of White Umbrella and the Lion-Faced Dakini.

103. The DCH has *bshags smon* only, without further details. This could be a text named *Bshags pa smon lam rnams bzhug pa'i dbus phyogs lags so*, found at Lawudo among the texts of Lama Kunzang Yeshe. It is volume *kha,* but I have not identified to which cycle it belongs.

104. The *Bardo Thödrol (bar do thos grol)*, from the *Peaceful and Wrathful Deities: The Self Liberated Mind Cycle (Zhi khro dgongs pa rang grol)* discovered by Karma Lingpa (*karma gling pa,* b. 1326). It was translated into English as the *Tibetan Book of the Dead* by Kazi Dawa Samdrub *(zla ba bsams grub)* in 1927, as well as by Fremantle and Trungpa (1975) and Thurman (1993), among others.

105. The prayer wheel is still at Thangme Gompa, at the upper end of the long mani wall.

106. "In the future, on the tenth day of every month, I, Padmasambhava, will come riding upon the rays of the sun." Cf. *The Garland of the Gandharvas' Song: The Biography of the Tibetan Lady Yeshe Tsogyal (Bod kyi jo mo ye shes mtsho rgyal gyi mdzad tshul rnam par thar pa gab pa mngon byung rgyud mangs dri za'i glu phreng)*, discovered by Namkhai Nyingpo *(nam mkha'i snying po)*, chap. 7, f.95b. See also the translation by Tarthang Tulku (sNying po, 1983, p. 152). Padmasambhava was born in the month of the monkey, which according to the astrological system of the *Kalachakra Tantra* corresponds to the fifth lunar month of the Tibetan calendar. But according to the system of *The Condensed Thought of the Lama (Bla ma dgongs 'dus* or *dgongs 'dus chen mo)*, a terma of Sangye Lingpa, the monkey month corresponds to the sixth lunar month.

107. Every year eight different families have to shoulder the total cost of the Dumche celebrations, which includes the offering of food, drink, and large balls of cooked rice (now replaced by about a half kilogram of uncooked rice) to the whole population. A religious officer is responsible for organizing the festival, the administration of funds, upkeep of the temple, and appointing the sponsors.

In the Thangme area the Dumche takes place from the 10th to the 13th of the fifth month. In the evening of the 10th, the sponsors and monks perform an incense and serkyem offering ceremony at the shrine of Gonpo Maning behind Thangme Gompa, and set long tree branches with attached prayer flags behind the shrine. On the 11th, the monks and lamas perform the Phurba ritual from Ratna Lingpa's tradition. In the evening the Thangme Lama and a few monks perform ritual dances, followed by the throwing away of the torma imbued with negative forces *(log phar or gtor rgyab)* and a fire offering ritual. On the 12th the monks perform the rituals of the *Great Compassionate One Liberating All Migrators* (*Thugs rje chen po 'gro ba kun grol*, BT) and the *Lineage of Knowledge-Holders* (*Rig 'dzin gdung sgrub*, BT). A large tsog offering takes place in the evening. On the 13th the ritual of the *Wrathful [Guru] Mind Practice* (*Thugs sgrub drag po rtsal*, BT) takes place, followed by the official appointment of sponsors for the following year and large offerings to the monks and nuns.

Nowadays the Dumche takes place in Pangboche, Thangme, Khumjung, Namche, Rimejung, and Lukla. The Rimejung Dumche takes place only when there are enough sponsors; otherwise, the people from Pharag join the Thangme Dumche. The Lukla Dumche, which was started in 1995, takes place from the seventh to the tenth of the fourth month. During the Dumche, Ralpa Dorje's twisted iron rod is displayed at Thangme and the image of Shakyamuni Buddha and the seven grains at Rimejung. See also Jerstad (1969).

An outstanding feature of the Dumche celebrations is the huge quantities of chang and arak that the Sherpas are able to ingest. Everyone gets drunk to some degree during the Dumche, and the people say jokingly that most Sherpa babies are born nine months after the Dumche festival.

108. Ratna Lingpa *(ratna gling pa rin chen dpal bzang po,* 1403–78) had three sons. Tsewang Dragpa *(tshe dbang grags pa)* went to Kham and Ngawang Dragpa *(ngag dbang grags pa)* settled in Dingri. The third son, Thaye Dragpa *(mtha' yas grags pa),* decided to perform a divination to find out where he could benefit sentient beings and threw a cymbal *(rol mo)* into the sky. The cymbal landed in Kochag Drozhig *(ko lcag 'gro gzhig),* a village under Sakya jurisdiction near Shelkar. It is said that since that time, all the stones in that area are shaped like cymbals. Thaye Dragpa built a temple on the mountainside above the village *('gro mgon bla brang),* and his descendants became known as the Drogon lamas, or Drogonpas. Often they were invited by the head of the Sakya school to assist him in controlling the female spirits *('bag mo)* kept at Sakya.

The last Drogonpas to visit Pangboche in 1954 or 1955 were Pema Wangchug *(padma dbang phyug,* 1931–1980 or 1981) and his brother Ngawang Pema Rigzin *(ngag dbang padma rig 'dzin,* 1935?–2001). After 1959, when the Drogon lamas escaped to India, the Sherpas asked Trulzhig Rinpoche, and later the Tengboche Lama, to perform the opening and sealing of the box of the Gonpo Sungjonma *(mgon po gsung byon ma).* Now the connection between the Drogonpas and the Sherpas seems to be lost. The Kochag Drogon Gompa was destroyed in 1959 and has not been rebuilt because all its members live in India and Nepal.

Regarding the lineage of the Drogon lamas, Drogon Jigdral Zangpo and his son Norbu Wangyal *(nor bu dbang rgyal)* were teacher and disciple respectively of Lama Sangwa Dorje. Dudjom Rinpoche (1991) mentions that the lineage of Ratna Lingpa passed from Tsewang Dragpa to Ngawang Dragpa, to his son

Ngawang Norbu, to Norbu Yongdrag, and to Gyalse Norbu Wangyal. Jamyang Chökyi Rigzin in his autobiography (f.108) mentions Drogonpa Dudul Wangdag Trinle *(bdud 'dul dbang drag 'phrin las)*. The KHB, f.8b, mentions that in 1850 the Drogonpa Kyabje Palden Rithar *(skyabs rje dpal ldan srid thar)* visited the newborn son of Nyima Dondrub *(nyi ma don grub)* and Dawa Yangchen *(zla ba dbyangs can)* in Khumjung. He predicted that the boy would have many obstacles until he was nine, but afterward he would become very beneficial for the Dharma and sentient beings. Eventually, the boy became known as "Lama Nine Years" *(bla ma dgu lo)* and built the Tengboche Monastery. Drogonpas Tenzin Dorje *(bstan 'dzin rdo rje,* d. 1941 or 1942) and Lama Palden *(bla ma dpal ldan)* are mentioned in DTH. Tenzin Dorje's son was Pema Wangchug, who worked in the Tibetan Refugee Center in Sonada near Darjeeling. Since all his nine children were quite young when he died, the lineage passed to his brother Ngawang Pema. The next lineage holder will be one of Pema Wangchug's sons, either the eldest Wangchen Geleg or Tsultrim Dorje *(tshul khrims rdo rje),* also known as Buchung, now a monk at Ka-nying Shedrup Ling Monastery *(bka' rnying bshad sgrub gling)* in Bouddha, Nepal.

109. *Tshe sgrub lcags sdong ma,* BT.

110. *rta mgrin gsang sgrub.* Hayagriva is a wrathful aspect of Chenrezig. The lineage comes from Kyergangpa Chökyi Senge *(dbon ston skyer sgang pa chos kyi seng ge,* twelfth century), who received the *Secret Hayagriva* empowerment and teachings directly from Padmasambhava in a dream. He also received the transmission from Nyemowa Sangye Wangchen *(snye mo ba sangs rgyas dbang chen),* who had discovered those teachings as a terma. Cf. Roerich (1996, p. 737ff.) and Thondup (1986, p. 261). Kyergangpa's Hayagriva is also widely practiced in the Gelug tradition.

111. *Bka' rdzogs pa chen po dkon mchog spyi 'dus,* a terma of Rigzin Jatson Nyingpo or Letro Lingpa *(rig 'dzin 'ja' tshon snying po, las 'phro gling pa,* 1585–1656). It contains the practices of the peaceful and wrathful aspects of Guru Rinpoche and of the Lion-Faced Dakini.

112. The Guru Rinpoche stone was situated near the edge of the cliff along the trail from Zamte to Thangme. On August 5, 1985, at around two o'clock in the afternoon, a huge flood of mud and rocks caused by a lake outburst above Langmoche and Dzamtra rushed down from the valley above Thangteng and swept everything away. Fourteen bridges between Thangme and Jubing in Shorong were washed away, the hydroelectric project that was being built at Tramo was completely destroyed, houses and trees were carried away or buried under the mud, and the whole landscape of the Thangme and Pharag valleys was changed. Most Sherpas were celebrating a festival in their gompas or were in the summer settlements with the cattle; thus, only two people lost their lives. The mountainside below Zamte was washed away, but the Guru Rinpoche stone and the mani wall next to it stood undamaged, just at the edge of the cliff. It was dangerous to walk around them, and so a few years later, Lama Zopa's sister Ngawang Samten organized

the transfer of all the carved stones, including the extremely heavy Guru Rinpoche stone, to a safer spot on the new path above Zamte.

113. *Byang gter sgrub skor rnam gsum.* These refer to the outer practice of *The Great Compassionate One Liberating Migrators (Thugs rje chen po 'gro ba kun grol)*, the inner practice of *The Lineage of the Knowledge-Holders (Rig 'dzin gdung sgrub)*, and the secret practice of the *Wrathful [Guru] Mind Practice (Thugs sgrub drag po rtsal)*.

114. *O rgyan padmas gsungs pa'i gsol 'debs le'u bdun ma*, BT, is a prayer to Guru Rinpoche containing his life story, lineage of transmission, and levels of his teachings. It was concealed by Prince Mutri Tsangpo *(mu khri btsan po)* and discovered by Zangpo Dragpa *(bzang po grags pa*, fourteenth century). It was later rearranged by Rigzin Godem-chen. Cf. Blondeau (1980) and Ricard (1994, p. 25, n. 48).

115. *Zhi khro nges don snying po*, discovered by Jatson Nyingpo in Kongpo. It is a text based on the *Sgyu 'phrul dra ba gsang ba snying po (Guhyagarbhamayajalatantra)*, the main mahayoga tantra, related to the forty-two peaceful and fifty-eight wrathful deities.

116. *Rdzogs chen ye shes mthong grol*, discovered by Pema Tsewang Gyalpo or Tennyi Lingpa *(padma tshe dbang rgyal po, bstan gnyis gling pa*, 1480–1535).

117. *Tshe rta zung 'brel 'chi med dpal gter*, a longevity practice that combines the deities Amitayus *(tshe dpag med)* and Hayagriva *(rta mgrin)*. It was concealed by Padmasambhava in the Magnificent Secret Cave *(zil chen gsang phug)* at Tsari and discovered by Thangtong Gyalpo at Chimpu *(mchims phu)* near Samye *(bsam yas)*. Cf. Dargyay (1979, p. 154) and Gyatso (1980).

118. Cf. KHB (ff.33a/b, 34a/b) and Fürer-Haimendorf (1964).

119. Kunzang Dechen Gyalpo was the head of Thangme Gompa from 1895 to 1915. He married Dekyi Lhamo and had at least three sons and a daughter. When his father Ngawang Trinle Lhundrub went to Jasa *('ja' sa)* in Shorong to perform the Shitro ritual for guiding the dying Jasa Lama Ratna Tsewang through the bardo, Kunzang Dechen Gyalpo and his wife went with him. Ratna Tsewang gave a khatag to the young couple and asked them whether he could "borrow their house." He was later reborn as the second son of Kunzang Dechen Gyalpo, the Kusho Tulku Ngawang Yonten Norbu.

120. Lama Gulo mentions the Dzamtra Lama as one of his teachers. The name of the place is spelled as *rdzam mkhrang* in KHB and *'dzam 'phrang* in DTH.

121. *Tshe sgrub rdo rje 'phreng ba*, discovered by Pema Lingpa.

122. The *Mani Kabum (Mani bka' 'bum)* is attributed to the Tibetan king Songtsen Gampo *(srong btsan sgam po*, 617–50). It contains an account of historical events of ancient Tibet and teachings about Chenrezig. It is usually assembled into two volumes and divided into three cycles: the *Cycle of Sutras (Mdo skor)*, the *Cycle of Attainments (Sgrub skor)*, and the *Cycle of Precepts (Zhal gdams kyi skor)*. The *Mani Kabum* was concealed under the feet of the Hayagriva image and inside the right thigh of the image of Naga Kubera in the main temple *(gtsug lag khang)* of Lhasa. Padmasambhava revealed the texts to King Trisong Detsen and concealed them

again. One part of the texts were rediscovered by Drubthob Ngodrub (*grub thob dngos grub,* twelfth century), another by Nyang-ral Nyima Özer (*nyang ral nyi ma 'od zer,* 1124–1192 or 1204), and yet another by Shakya Zangpo or Shakya Öd (*shakya bzang po).* Cf. Kapstein (2000, p. 145ff.).

123. *srung brgya'i tsa kra,* from the *Lama Gongdu* cycle *(Bla ma dgongs 'dus),* discovered by Sangye Lingpa in 1364.

124. The DTH (f.267b) mentions the great mahamudra practitioner *(phyag chen pa)* Mipham Tashi Chögyal *(mi pham bkra shis chos rgyal)* as a Sherpa disciple of Trulzhig Kunzang Thongdrol who lived in Khumbu and went often to Rongphu to receive teachings.

125. The *Mi la'i mgur 'bum,* composed by Tsang Nyon Heruka (*gtsang smyon he ru ka,* 1452–1507), contains the life and songs of Milarepa. Milarepa's life has been translated into English by Kazi Dawa Samdup (1928) and Lhalungpa (1979). Chang (1977) has translated Milarepa's songs. Regarding the different editions of this work, see Smith (2001). Another version of Milarepa's life and songs was compiled by his twelve great disciples, another by Shije Repa (14th to 15th century), and yet another by Lhatsun Rinchen Namgyal (1473–1557). Cf. Lhalungpa (1979, p. xxx).

126. *Lam mchog rin po che'i phreng ba,* by Gampopa Sonam Rinchen. It is a very short text of the gradual path type.

127. *Bka' rgyud gser phreng,* a collection of biographies of Kagyu masters. There are various texts with the same name. Cf. Smith (2001).

128. *phur grub bstan 'dzin* is mentioned in SCH (f. 25a) as a realized Sherpa lama from Drag-ri *(brag ri)* Gompa. In KHB, f.22a, Lama Gulo mentions Phurdrub Tenzin as one of his teachers. He passed away sometime after Kagyu Rangdrol (KHB, f. 36b).

129. *Rat gling chos 'khor.* Published as the *Collected Rediscovered Teachings of Ratna Lingpa (Chos rgyal ratna gling pa'i gter chos)* by Taklung Tsetrul Pema Wangyal, vols. 1–19, Darjeeling, 1977–79.

130. *Zur skor tshe sgrub gsangs 'dus,* a terma of Ratna Lingpa.

131. *Rta mgrin lcags ral can,* discovered by Pema Lingpa in Gedo *(gad mdo)* in Lhodrag in 1483. Cf. Aris (1988, p. 48).

132. *Phyag rdor dregs pa kun 'dul,* a terma of Pema Lingpa.

133. *Naro mkha' spyod ma.* This particular tradition stemming from Naropa (11th century) is widely practiced in the Kagyu, Sakya, and Gelug traditions.

134. The Sherpa lamas Sangye Tenzin *(sangs rgyas bstan 'dzin),* Rinchen Dorje *(rin chen rdo rje),* and Lama Ngodrub *(dngos grub)* of Charog are mentioned in KHB (ff.21b and 22a), but I was unable to obtain more information about them.

135. Information about Yonten Gyatso is very scant. The Charog Lama Kusho Mangde told me that when he took teachings from Yonten Gyatso, the lama was 140 years old (I was unable to clarify how old Kusho Mangde was at that time). Kusho Mangde added that when Yonten Gyatso was thirty years old, he was invited to preside over the enthronement of the Tibetan king Shenphen Shedrag (no indication

about who that king was or the area ruled by him), which took place during the rule of Jang Bahadur Rana in Nepal (who assumed office in 1846). Khenpo Trinle Chöphel, the Gelug abbot of Chubar Gompa in Lapchi, remembers the story of a very old Nyingma practitioner who lived near Tagshang *(stag tshang?)* and who one day disappeared. It was not clear whether he had attained the rainbow body or had been killed by robbers. According to Trulzhig Rinpoche, he was a disciple of Dza Paltul Rinpoche, and after Yonten Gyatso's death or disappearance, his wife, Ani Jomo-la, a disciple of Shakya Shri, went to stay in Rongphu.

136. The Rongshar or Drin Valley is situated east of the Lapchi Range and north of Tseringma Mountain and Rolwaling. The Excellent Cave *(kun bzang phug)*, also known as Kunzang Tse, where according to oral tradition Guru Rinpoche subdued the Five Sisters of Long Life (there seem to be no scriptural references to that episode), is situated northwest of Tagshang, near a village called Zagalung *(za ga lung)*. At the beginning of the twentieth century a Gelug lama from Kham called Kunzang Chökyi Gyaltsen also stayed in that hermitage. His second tulku Kuntse Rinpoche Thubten Gyaltsen belongs to Sera Me Monastery.

137. The *Seven Great Treasuries (Mdzod chen bdun)* are *The Precious Wish-Fulfilling Treasury (Yid bzhin rin po che'i mdzod)*, a survey of all the Mahayana doctrines; *The Precious Treasury of Instructions (Man ngag rin po che'i mdzod)*, about the dzogchen doctrine; *The Precious Treasury of the Sphere of Reality (Chos dbyings rin po che'i mdzod)*, an exposition of the categories of dzogchen *(sems sde, klong sde,* and *man ngag sde); The Precious Treasury of Doctrinal Views (Grub mtha' mdzod)*, an explanation of philosophical tenets; *The Precious Treasury of the Supreme Path (Thegs mchog mdzod)*, which explains various practices, including the *thögal* practices; *The Precious Treasury of Words and Meaning (Tshig don mdzod)*, which explains the crucial points of practice; and *The Precious Treasury of the Way of Abiding (Gnas lugs mdzod)*, which explains the ultimate meaning of dzogchen.

Longchen Rabjam (1308–63) was a great Nyingma meditator, scholar, and treasure discoverer, and is considered to be an emanation of Mañjushri, the bodhisattva of wisdom. Born in Tödrong *(stod grong)* in Central Tibet, he is considered to be an incarnation of Princess Pemasal, the daughter of King Trisong Detsen who had been entrusted by Padmasambhava with the transmission of the *Heart Drop* teachings, and of Pema Ledreltsal. His main hermitage was at Gangri Tökar *(gangs ri thod dkar)*, a holy mountain situated on the left bank of the lower Kyichu River, southwest of Lhasa. Cf. Thondup (1989, 1999, pp. 109–17) and Smith (2001, pp. 33–35). See also the *Biography of the Omniscient Longchen Rabjam (Kun mkhyen klong chen rab 'byams kyi rnam thar)* composed by Sonam Chödrub *(bsod nams chos sgrub)*, and the *Biography of the Omniscient Drime Ozer Meaningful to Behold (Kun mkhyen dri med 'od zer gyi rnam thar mthong ba don ldan)* by Chödrag Zangpo *(chos grags bzang po)*, published in 1993 (by the *si khron mi rigs dpe skrun khang)*.

138. The full name is *The Profound and Extensive Practical Commentary on the Preliminaries of the Heart Drop, Called the Words of My Perfect Teacher (Rdzogs pa chen*

*po klong chen snying thig gi sngon 'gro'i khrid yig kun bzang bla ma'i zhal lung),* written by Paltul Rinpoche Urgyen Jigme Chökyi Wangpo *(dpal sprul o rgyan 'jigs med chos kyi dbang po,* 1808–87), also known as Palge Tulku *(dpal dge sprul sku).* Paltul Rinpoche was born in Kham and became extremely learned, but led an itinerant life without caring about property or home. Cf. *O rgyan 'jigs med chos kyi dbang po'i rnam thar dad pa'i gsos sman bdud rtsi'i bum bcud,* by Khenpo Kunzang Palden *(mkhan po kun bzang dpal ldan,* 1870–1940), vol. *kha* of Paltul Rinpoche's *Collected Works* (pp. 353–481), and Thondup (1999, pp. 201–10).

139. *Klong chen gtor bu.* The 1901 Lhasa edition was sponsored by Trulzhig Kunzang Thongdrol. Cf. Smith (2001, p.35).

140. According to DCH, Dorje Chang Pema Kunzang Gyatso was from Kham and was related to Mindroling Monastery. Ngawang Chöphel added that he was a disciple of Shakya Shri, but his name is not included among Shakya Shri's close disciples. Lama Gulo (KHB, f.32b) calls him "the tulku from Kham" *(khams sprul)* but does not give more details.

141. *Rnying ma rgyud 'bum,* compiled by Ratna Lingpa. When Buton Rinpoche *(bu ston rin chen grub,* 1290–1364) supervised the editions of the Kangyur *(Bka' 'gyur)* and the Tengyur *(Bstan 'gyur)* that were to be printed at Narthang *(snar thang)* Monastery in Tsang, he excluded most of the Nyingma tantras from the Kangyur as not being the authentic words of the Buddha. The Nyingma scholars felt then the need to collect and print the texts that had been rejected by Buton and were in danger of getting lost. Ratna Lingpa was able to receive the oral transmission of all the Nyingma tantras from Me Gomten Zangpo *(mes sgom gtan bzang po)* and compiled them into a single collection. In 1686, Terdag Lingpa compiled an enlarged edition *(Sgrub thabs 'dod 'jo'i bum bzang),* and later Jigme Lingpa *('jigs med gling pa,* 1729–98) added twenty-five volumes to Terdag Lingpa's edition and wrote a catalogue, or table of contents. Cf. Dargyay (1979, pp. 145–46) and Smith (2001, pp. 22, 239).

142. *gza' rgod dug gi spu gri.* This is another name for Rahula *(gza' mchog chen po ra hu la),* an important protector of the Nyingma school.

143. Trulzhig Kunzang Thongdrol Dorje *('khrul zhig kun bzang mthong grol rdo rje,* d. 1922) was also known as Drubwang Do-ngag Lingpa *(sgrub dbang mdo sngags gling pa)* and Shri Gyalse *(shri rgyal sras).* In the latter part of his life he took a young consort who later became the mother of his reincarnation, the present Trulzhig Rinpoche Ngawang Chökyi Lodro *(ngag dbang chos kyi blo gros,* b. 1924). He passed away on the fifth day of the ninth month of the water dog year (1922) (DTH, f.292b). Cf. *The Wonderful Chariot of Devotion: The Biography of the Holder of the Treasury of Extremely Secret Doctrine, Trulzhig Guyang Heruka Kunzang Thongdrol Dorje (Yang gsang bstan pa'i mdzod 'dzin 'khrul zhig gu yang he ru ka kun bzang mthong grol rdo rje'i rnam par thar pa ngo mtshar dad pa'i shing rta),* composed by Ngawang Tenzin Norbu. For Chingkarwa Donyo Dorje *(phying dkar ba rig 'dzin don yod rdo rje),* cf. Ricard (1994).

144. The *jo bo thugs rje chen po yig ge drug pa* is a cycle of practices related to the four-armed aspect of the Great Compassionate One. Jamyang Khyentse Wangpo received this practice from Thangtong Gyalpo and his tulkus Tsultrim Zangpo *(tshul khrims bzang po)* and Chartulwa *(phyar thul ba)* in a vision. Cf. Dargyay (1979, p. 153ff.).

145. Probably the *Glorious Blazing Wisdom (Rje btsun ras pa chen pa la brten pai bla ma'i rnal 'byor tshogs mchod dang bcas pa ye she dpal 'bar)* composed by Jamgon Kongtrul.

146.*Sgrol ma'i zab thig*, a mind terma *(dgongs gter)* of Chogyur Lingpa.

147. Shakya Shri, also known as Pawo Rigsal Thogme *(dpa' bo rig rtsal thogs med)* and Rigzin Jalu Dorje Tsal *(rig 'dzin 'ja' lus rdo rje rtsal)*, was born near Chamdo *(chab mdo)* in Khams in the water female ox year, 1853. He studied with the sixth Khamtrul Rinpoche Tenpe Nyima *(khams sprul bstan pa'i nyi ma,* 1849–1907), Nangchen Tsognyi Rinpoche *(tshogs gnyis rin po che)*, Drugon Lama Chenpel *(gru dgon bla ma mchan dpal)*, Adzom Drukpa *(a 'dzom 'brug pa,* 1842–1924), Pema Ösel Do-ngag Lingpa *(padma od gsal mdo sngags gling pa,* or *'jam dbyangs mkhyen brtse'i dbang po)*, Jamgon Kongtrul *('jam mgon kong sprul)*, and other masters. He spent many years in retreat in different caves where, to prevent himself from falling asleep, he would tie his hair to a notch in the cave. After having a vision of a dakini, he renounced his monastic vows and took a consort. Around 1890 he visited Lapchi and stayed in Milarepa's caves, such as Rechen *(ras chen)* and Crystal Cave Bamboo Castle *(shel phug chu shing rdzong)*. In 1906, when he was in Tsari, he had a vision of a dakini asking him to repair the Swayambhu Stupa in the Kathmandu Valley. He then returned to Lapchi and, after collecting donations, sent his disciple Tsewang Jigme *(tshe dbang 'jigs med)* to Nepal to undertake the restoration work, which was completed in 1918. Shakya Shri passed away on the nineteenth day of the fifth month of the earth sheep year, 1919. Cf. *The Garland of Flowers: The Biography of the Venerable Master, the Great Vajra-Holder Shakya Shri Gyana (Rje btsun bla ma rdo rje 'chang chen po sha kya shri jnana'i rnam thar me tog phreng ba)*, composed by Situ Chökyi Gyatso *(shar ka thog si tu pa chos kyi rgya mtsho,* 1880–1925). The story of Shakya Shri's levitation is in f.47a. Cf. also Crook and Low (1997).

148. *'Chi med thugs thig gi tshe yum candali'i gdams skor.* Sections *nyi, thi,* and *di* of Shakya Shri's *Collected Works,* composed at Tsari during the earth bird year, 1909. It is a longevity practice received by Jamyang Khyentse Wangpo from Padmasambhava's consort Mandarava in a pure vision *(dag snang)*. Cf. Thondup (1986, p. 91). Shakya Shri wrote the ritual texts of the practice.

149. *Rtsa gsum spyi 'dus.* Earth terma of Jamyang Khyentse Wangpo, discovered at Terlung Pema Shelri *(gter klung padma shel ri)*. Cf. Dargyay (1979, p. 286).

150. The *Longchen Nyingthig (Klong chen snying thig)* cycle is a mind treasure of Rigzin Jigme Lingpa discovered in 1757 at the Bouddhnath Stupa in Nepal in a vision. Jigme Lingpa is considered to be an emanation of Vimalamitra, Trisong Detsen, Longchen Rabjam, Ngari Panchen Pema Wangyal *(mnga' ris pan chen padma*

*dbang rgyal,* 1487–1542), and many other great masters. Jigme Lingpa reincarnated as Jamyang Khyentse Wangpo (his body emanation), Paltul Rinpoche (speech emanation), and Do Khyentse Yeshe Dorje (*mdo mkhyen brtse ye shes rdo rje,* 1800–59) as his mind emanation. Cf. Dargyay (1979, pp. 186–90), Gyatso (1998), and Thondup (1999, pp. 118–35).

151. *The Gathering of Knowledge Holders (Rig 'dzin 'dus pa)* is the Father *(yab ka)* section and *The Queen of Great Bliss (Bde chen rgyal mo)* the Mother section *(yum kha)* of the *Longchen Nyingthig.*

152. Cutting through *(khregs gcod)* is related to the primordial purity *(ka dag)* and refers to cutting through the solidity of mental concepts and the belief in the concrete reality of phenomena. Leap over *(thod rgal)* refers to spontaneous appearance *(lhun grub)* and consists on meditating directly upon the highest reality. These teachings are only found in the dzogchen path. Cf. Ricard (1994, p. 554) and H. H. the Dalai Lama (Tenzin Gyatso, 2000, p. 32).

153. Differentiating between samsara and nirvana *('khor 'das ru shan)* is a special method of meditating on the view of the dzogchen path.

154. *Skyabs rje rang 'byung lags mchog* is mentioned in KHB, f.21a. The Cave of Subduing Evil Beings *(bdud 'dul phug)* at Lapchi is one of the four widely known caves of Milarepa, where he subdued demons and evil beings, performed miracles, and spent six months in isolation after a heavy snowfall had blocked all paths. Cf. MG (pp. 214ff., 223, 718), Chang (1977, pp. 23ff., 30, 570), and Huber (1997).

155. Chakrasamvara *('khor lo sdom pa* or *'khor lo bde mchog)* is a deity belonging to the *maha-anuttara,* or highest tantra of the New Translation schools. There are three lineages of this particular deity stemming from the Indian mahasiddhas Luyipa, Ghantapa, and Krishnacharya. Cf. Templeman (1983, 1989).

156. For a short biographical sketch of Artsa Lama Namgyal Palden *(a rtsa bla ma rnam rgyal dpal ldan)* see the biography of Shakya Shri (f.63b). Artsa Lama was credited with great powers, such as being able to break guns in half and tie spears in knots. According to his biographer, he built a wall in Bodh Gaya around the main temple with more than 10,000 Buddha images and a shrine at the left side of the main temple. (I have not found any evidence of those images.) Artsa Lama was also known as Rigzin Dewe Dorje *(rig 'dzin bde ba'i rdo rje)* and Rigzin Ngag-ki Wangpo *(rig 'dzin sngags kyi dbang po).* In a handwritten copy of the *Unobstructed Primordial Mind* belonging to the Lawudo Lama, the lineage lamas are given as follows: Khyentse Wangpo →Drodul Natsog Rangdrol *('gro 'dul sna tshogs rang grol),* a disciple of Shabkar Tsogdrul Rangdrol *(zhabs dkar tshogs drug rang grol,* 1781–1851) →Rigzin Jalü Dorje *(rig 'dzin 'ja' lus rdo rje,* or Shakya Shri) →Rigzin Dewe Dorje *(rig 'dzin bde ba'i rdo rje)* →*tsawe* lama (Lama Gulo).

157. The original *chayig (bca' yig)* handwritten by the Dzamdra Lama and dated in the fourth month of the earth bird year (1909) is still kept at the gompa by Ang Gyaltsen (Paldorje clan), the eighty-two-year-old (in 2001) manager of the Namche

Kangyur Lhakhang. It contains a long list of about fifty-seven sponsors, some of them from Shorong, Rongshar, and Nyanam, but mostly from Namche. Later, Lama Gulo composed a longer, elaborate chayig (cf. Ngawang Odzer, 2002, 236–50). The Dzamtra Lama invested a large amount of money with the Namche traders, and the profits were used for sponsoring the annual reading of the Kangyur. The first caretaker of the temple was Lama Tenzin Zangpo. Years later, a second prayer wheel containing the Vajra Guru mantra was sponsored by Gaga Zumpa, a Sherpa who made his fortune in Darjeeling, and constructed under the guidance of Au Palden, a benefactor of the Lawudo Lama.

158. From the *Zanglingma (Slob dpon padma'i rnam thar bka' thang zangs gling ma)*, compiled by Yeshe Tsogyal and discovered by Nyang-ral Nyima Özer (*nyang ral nyi ma'i 'od zer*, 1124–92). There seem to be two versions of this text. The original version is said to contain a chapter with a large number of prophecies related to the Latö area and the Nepal Himalayas. According to some Sherpa lamas, at some point in the early twentieth century the Tibetan government decided to eliminate those prophecies from the official version. Thus, the text now available does not contain any of them. It has been translated into English as *Advice from the Lotus-Born* by Erik Pema Kunzang (Rangjung Yeshe Publications, 1994). Special signs have occurred when high lamas meditated at the Maratika Cave, such as water or milk flowing from various spots.

159. The Cool Grove (Sitavana or *bsil ba'i tshal*) Cemetery is one of the eight cremation grounds or cemeteries mentioned in the tantras as places where the dakas and dakinis gather, and where tantric practices become very powerful. In the Nyingma tradition, the names for the eight cemeteries are given as follows: Cool Grove *(bsil ba'i tshal)* in the east; Perfected in Body *(sku la rdzogs)* in the south; Lotus Mound *(padma brtsegs)* in the west; Lanka Mound *(lan ka brtsegs)* in the north; Spontaneously Accomplished Mound *(lhun grub brtsegs)* in the southeast; Display of Great Secret *(gsang chen rol pa)* in the southwest; Pervasive Great Joy *(he chen brdal ba)* in the northwest; and World Mound *('jigs rten brtsegs)* in the northeast. In the tantras of the New Translation schools the names are given differently.

160. When Padmasambhava and Mandarava returned from Maratika to Zahor, the king seized Padmasambhava and gave orders to burn him alive in a secluded valley, while Mandarava was thrown into a pit full of thorns and scorpions. After a few days, the king himself went to inspect the pyre, but he found instead a beautiful lake and Padmasambhava sitting upon a lotus in the middle of the waters. The king paid homage to the Precious Guru, and the lake became known as the Lotus Lake, or Tso Pema *(mtsho padma)* for the Tibetans.

161. The Indian master Phadampa Sangye spent twenty years (from 1097 to 1117) at Langkor *(glang skor)* near Dingri. Cf. Aziz (1980) and Roerich (1996). His present reincarnation lives in Nepal.

162. *Yang gsang bla na med pa rdzogs pa chen po rgyal thabs spyi blugs gi dbang.*

163. *Thugs rje chen po 'khor ba dong sprugs,* an earth terma of Chogyur Lingpa discovered

at Khandro Bumzong *(mkha' 'gro 'bum rdzong)*. Cf. Dargyay (1979, pp. 190–97).

164. *guru bde ba chen po,* a mind terma of Shakya Sri discovered at the Crystal Cave Bamboo Castle.

165. According to *The Great Tibetan-Chinese Dictionary (Bod rgya tshig mdzod chen mo),* Zapulung *(zab bu lung)* is in the Shang district of Tsang province and is one of Padmasambhava's hidden valleys. Pema Lingpa mentions Zambulung of Shang as one of the four "small countries" (see note 8). I have no information about the Zapulung lama mentioned in the DCH.

166. *Lan kar gshegs pa'i mdo,* taught by Shakyamuni Buddha to Ravana, the lord of Lanka, on top of Kailash.

167. *'Phags pa thar pa chen po phyogs su rgyas pa 'gyod tshangs kyis sdig sbyangs te sangs rgyas su grub par rnam par bkod pa zhes bya ba theg pa chen po'i mdo.*

168. Cf. *Bsam gtan ngal gso,* f.3b, the second part of the *Ngal gso 'kor gsum* trilogy. Translated by Guenther in *Kindly Bent to Ease Us,* vol. 2, *Meditation,* p. 49.

169. The *Abhisamayalankara (Mngon rtogs rgyan)* is one of the five scriptures given by Maitreya to the Indian master Asanga in Tushita pure land, the other being the *Sutralamkara (Mdo sde rgyan), Madhyantavibhanga (Dbus mtha' rnam 'byed), Dharmadharmatavibhanga (Chos dang chos nyid rnam 'byed),* and *Uttaratantra (Rgyud bla ma).*

170. Cf. Nebesky-Wojkowitz (1996).

171. The *'ja' sa ri khrod* (sometimes wrongly pronounced as "Chalsa" or "Jalsa") is near Salleri, the administrative town of the Solu Khumbu district. It was founded by Pema Sang-ngag Tenzin *(padma gsang sngags bstan 'dzin)* of the Lama Serwa clan in the early nineteenth century on a hill on top of which he had seen many rainbows. His son Ratna Tsewang *(ratna tshe dbang),* the immediate previous embodiment of Kusho Tulku Ngawang Yonten Norbu *(ngag dbang yon tan nor bu,* d. 1936), was the tulku of Pema Gyalpo from Yolmo, himself the tulku of Domarba Migyur Dorje *(rdo dmar zhabs drung mi 'gyur rdo rje,* d. 1675) of Yolmo Langthang. After the 1934 earthquake, Ratna Tsewang's son Karma Donden enlarged the temple and named it Samtenling Gompa. Karma Donden's son Ngawang Sherab had many Sherpa and Tamang disciples. His son Lama Babu started a school at Jasa and has done outstanding work for the Solu people. Cf. SCH (ff.34a/b, 35a) and Tashi Tsering (1999).

172. Jo bo dpal ldan Atisha (Dipamkara Shri Jnana, 982–1054) was a Bengali master who revived Buddhism in Tibet. His disciples became known as the Kadampas *(bka' gdams pa).*

173. Ngawang Sherab Zangpo *(ngag dbang shes rab bzang po)* or Rigzin Ngawang Mangde *(rig 'dzin ngag dbang mang ldan)* was also a special child. While he was in the womb, his mother dreamt often of Tibetan gompas, and he himself as a small child used to dream about large Tibetan houses and temples. The lamas concluded that he was the reincarnation of a Khampa lama, but he was never formally enthroned as a tulku. After his father's death, Kusho Tulku took care of his

education and Kusho Mangde became his brother's attendant. He took monastic vows in Rongphu and spent three years in Tengboche Monastery learning the Mani Rimdu rituals. He spent another three years at Thubten Dorje Drag and Mindroling monasteries and studied astrology with Lama Tsewang Gyurme of Jang Dorshang, near Chung Riboche.

174. This refers to the tripods made of three human heads that support the skullcups used in tantric rituals. The quotation is supposed to be in the *Zanglingma,* but I haven't been able to find it, even though many elder Sherpas affirm having seen it.

175. Cf. MG (p. 237) and Chang (1977, p. 49).

176. Kuye Labrang *(sku e,* or *ye, bla brang)* is situated in Upper Kharta *(mkhar rta stod),* across the river from Shode village, below a cliff with a self-arisen syllable *Eh.* It was built by Drubthob Gyergompa (see above, note 42). Namgyal Zangpo *(rnam rgyal bzang po)* belonged to the early lineage of Kuye (see above, note 27). Later, the lineage came from Pema Wangyal *(padma dbang rgyal)* →Pema Chögyal *(padma chos rgyal)* →Pema Wangchug Gyalpo *(padma dbang phyug rgyal po)* →Pema Dargye *(padma dar rgyas)* →Gyurme Trinle Namgyal *('gyur med 'phrin las rnam rgyal),* who was the root lama of Ngawang Tenzin Norbu. Cf. CY (ff.154–55). In 1959 Gyurme Trinle Namgyal's son Tenzin Chökyi Nyima *(bstan 'dzin chos kyi nyi ma,* 1901–71) and his three sons escaped to Panthog Shingsa in Nepal, where the lama had many followers, taking with them the Kangyur and Tengyur and some valuable statues. Tenzin Chökyi Nyima's successor as the holder of the lineage was his elder son Tsering Dorje *(tshe ring rdo rje),* but he died soon after his father. The present, thirty-fifty lineage holder, is Tsering Dorje's son Urgyen *(o rgyan),* who has been recognized as the tulku of Tenzin Chökyi Nyima (personal communication from Tenzin Chökyi Nyima's son Dorje-la). See also Diemberger (1992, 1993, 1997).

177. Situated in the Drachi *(gvra phyi)* Valley in Central Tibet, Urgyen Mindroling *(o rgyan smin grol gling)* Monastery was founded in 1677 by Terdag Lingpa on the site of an earlier small temple built by Lume Tsultrim Sherab *(klu med tshul khrims shes rab,* 950–1025). Terdag Lingpa, a speech emanation of the great translator Vairochana, was born in Dranang *(grva nang)* as the son of the great Nyingma master Rigzin Trinle Lhundrub *(rig 'dzin 'phrin las lhun grub,* 1611–62). He became a disciple and later a teacher of the Fifth Dalai Lama. Mindroling was destroyed during the Dzungar Mongol invasion in 1718 and restored with the help of Po-lhane. It was one of the largest Tibetan monasteries in terms of size and housed about 300 monks as well as some married lamas. The monastery was destroyed again in recent times during the Cultural Revolution and has been partially rebuilt. A new Mindroling Monastery has been constructed in Clement Town, India. The present throne-holder is H. H. Kunzang Wangyal *(kun bzang dbang rgyal,* b. 1930), who is also the current head of the Nyingma school. Cf. Dargyay (1979), Tenpe Dronme *(bstan pa'i sgron me)* (1992), and Chan (1994).

178. Cf. Ruttledge (1937, p. 77). With the 1921 British Everest Reconnaissance Expedition led by C. K. Howard-Bury, a steady flow of mountaineering expeditions began to arrive into the previously peaceful Rongphu Valley. From 1922 until 1947, there were six British Everest expeditions and two solo attempts to climb Mount Everest from the Rongphu side. After 1950, the Everest expeditions took place from the Nepali side instead. Cf. Unsworth (1989) and Howard-Bury (1991). The Rongphu Monastery and hermitages were destroyed during the Chinese Cultural Revolution. Monks, nuns, and ngagpas took refuge in Nepal and India. Trulzhig Rinpoche, who succeeded Ngawang Tenzin Norbu as the head of Dongag Zungjug Ling *(mdo sngags zung 'jug gling)*, built the Thubten Chöling Monastery in Shorong.

179. The following account is an almost literal translation of the DTH (f.253ff.). Lama Karma (1850–1931) of the Lama Serwa clan was the eldest brother of Sangye Tenpa, who later sponsored the building of Chiwang *(spyi dbang)* Gompa in Shorong. After the completion of Tengboche Monastery, he stayed at the monastery and kept a herd of cows and dzomos to supply the monks with butter and milk. Gen Sherab Tsepel *(rgan shes rab tshe phel)* of the Goleg clan was also from Shorong. After marrying a lady from Namche, he moved to Khumbu and became a trader. In 1895 he was nominated *gembu (rgan po)*, or headman, of Namche, but due to some political problems he was forced to leave Khumbu. He then settled in Lhasa and paid frequent visits to the Rongphu Sangye. He pledged support for Tengboche Monastery and later for the Deboche *(sde po ched)* Nunnery as well. Jampa *(byams pa)* of the Tragtho clan was the younger brother of Kunzang, another main sponsor of Tengboche, who married a daughter of Lama Karma. Kunzang's son Nyima Dondrub was a sponsor and disciple of the Lawudo Lama Yeshe. Cf. also Ortner (1989).

180. They obtained the *Precious Treasury of Discovered Scriptures (Rin chen gter mdzod)*, a collection of tantric practices in sixty-three volumes compiled by Jamgon Kongtrul *('jam mgon kong sprul blo gros mtha' yas,* 1813–99), which could only be printed at Tsurphu in Central Tibet or in Palpung *(dpal spungs)* in Kham. They also bought the twenty-one volumes of the collected works of the Fifth Dalai Lama, the medical treatises available at the Chagpori Medical College in Lhasa, and the thirty volumes of the *Collection of Nyingma Tantras.* Lama Karma's brother Sangye Tenpa sponsored the printing of the Kangyur and the Tengyur and donated the paper. In total, they were able to obtain four hundred and thirty-one volumes of scriptures, seventy-one statues, and four chörtens (cf. DTH, f.265b). For the *Precious Treasury,* cf. Smith (1970, 2001).

181. Dzogchenpa Urgyen Tenzin *(rdzogs chen pa o rgyan bstan 'dzin)* was a disciple of Togden Shakya Shri and Ngawang Tenzin Norbu, who had given him the name Guyang Repa *(gu yangs ras pa)* and called him a "yogi of the highest vehicle, a worthy disciple." During the Ronphu Sangye's journey to Khumbu, Urgyen Tenzin offered service to the lama with his body, speech, and mind.

182. *Gzhi gsum cho ga.* These are the rituals of confession *(gso sbyong),* rains retreat *(dbyar gnas),* and end of rains retreat *(dgag dbye),* which monastic communities have to perform regularly.

183. The full name of the Tengboche *chayig* is the *All Clear Mirror: Regulations of the Dharma Island of the Supreme Vehicle of Secret Mantra, which is in East Khumbu, Adjacent to Rolwaling* (*Shar khum bu rol ba gling gi 'dab 'brel gsang sngags theg mchog chos gling gi bca' yig kun gsal me long).* An addendum was written by the sponsors on the eighth day of the tenth month of the earth sheep year, 1919 (cf. Ortner, 1989).

184. *Thugs rje chen po bde gshegs kun 'dus,* a terma of Terdag Lingpa retrieved from Shaug Tago *(sha 'ug stag sgo)* in Mon on the twenty-ninth of the sixth month of the year 1680. Cf. Dargyay (1979, p. 179) and Tenpe Dronme (1992).

185. *Gu ru drag dmar,* a practice related to the wrathful aspect of Padmasambhava discovered by Terdag Lingpa at Okar Drag *(o dkar brag)* on the fifteenth day of the eleventh month, 1676. Cf. Tenpe Dronme (1992).

186. *Tshe sgrub* (or *'chi med*) *yang snying kun 'dus,* retrieved by Terdag Lingpa on the tenth day of the fifth month of the water hare year (1663) at Samye Yamalung *(bsam yas g.ya' ma lung).* Cf. Tenpe Dronme (1992).

187. *Bstan pa skyongs pa'i dam can chen po rnams kyi 'phrin las dngos grub kyi rol mtsho,* a collection of fulfillment rituals for various protectors composed by Terdag Lingpa.

188. In 1903, the Rongphu Sangye introduced the practice of blessing small pills with the mantra of Chenrezig *(mani ril grub),* based on the ritual of the *Embodiment of All the Blissful Ones.* Later the ritual was enhanced with elaborate dances, some of which were created by Ngawang Tenzin Norbu himself.

189. *rtsa gsum chos 'khor.* The three roots are the lama (the root of blessings), the meditational deity (the root of accomplishments), and the dakini (the root of enlightened activities).

190. The practice of walking clockwise around holy objects or persons is mentioned in the Vedas and Laws of Manu. The Sanskrit term *pradakshina* literally means "going toward the south," because practitioners imagine that they are facing east toward the entrance of the deities' residence so that the right hand corresponds to the south. Cf. Simpson (1976, pp. 75–86). The Tibetan term is *bskor ba,* circuit, circle, or to go in a circle.

191. Story told by Lama Lhagpa Dorje of Thangteng. He asserts that it is true and that he himself saw the hole in Kalden's belly.

192. *Ma mgon lcam dral,* Ekajati, or *ral gcig ma,* is represented with one hair tuft, one eye, one tooth, and one breast. She is the special protectress of dzogchen practitioners.

193. The Nyingma practices are classified into three categories: root practices (lama, yidam, and dakini), branch practices related to various activities, and essential practices (cycles related to Guru Rinpoche, the dzogchen system, and the practices related to the Great Compassionate One). Ratna Lingpa discovered a text of the *Peaceful and Wrathful Guru (Bla ma zhi drag),* a collection of practices related to the *Secret Great Compassionate One (Thugs rje gsang 'dus),* and the *Sun of Clear*

*Expanse of the Great Perfection (Rdzogs chen klong gsal nyi ma).* Cf. Dargyay (1979, pp. 69–70) and Thondup (1986, p. 116).

194. *Chos nyid mngon sum,* the first of the four visions, or stages of realization, of thö-gal. The other three are developing the experiences *(nyams gong 'phel),* increasing awareness to its full measure *(rig pa tshad phebs),* and the exhaustion of all phenomena into the sphere of reality *(chos nyid zad pa).* Cf. Ricard (1994, p. 599).

195. In Thangme the Mani Rimdu schedule is as follows: 30th of the Tibetan third month: offering ritual to the local gods, consecration of the ground, and offerings to the guardian kings of the four directions; the monks start to draw the sand mandala of the deity. From the 5th to the 9th: the ritual of the *Embodiment of All the Blissful Ones* is performed; the mantra of the deity is recited continuously day and night without break. 9th: rehearsal of the dances. 10th: torma empowerment, blessing of the people, and distribution of mani pills and blessed water. 11th: dances with costumes and masks. 12th: fire-offering ceremony and destruction of the sand mandala. 13th: the colored sand of the mandala is taken in procession to the river and thrown into the water.

There are fifteen dances or "acts" in the Mani Rimdu, each one lasting twenty minutes: (1) *rol 'cham,* "cymbals' dance"; (2) *gser skyems,* offering the "golden drink" to the deities of the *Embodiment of All the Blissful Ones*; (3) *ging pa* (ancient Tibetan deities); (4) *rdo rje gro lod,* the wrathful aspect of Guru Rinpoche; (5) *rnga 'cham,* the dance of the drums; (6) *mi tshe ring,* the long-life man, is a comic act with an actor personifying a Chinese-looking old man; (7) *dur bdag,* the lords of the cemeteries, wearing skeletonlike costumes and masks; (8) *chos skyong,* the eight Dharma protectors; (9) *gnas srung,* or Sharlungdrag, the local protector of Dza Rongphu; (10) *mkha' 'gro,* the five dakinis that symbolize the five elements; (11) *rtogs ldan,* literally "the realized one," is another comic act performed by an actor characterized as an Indian holy man and his attendant; (12) *lhag ma,* the "left-overs" or remainder of the tsog offering; (13) *gri 'cham,* the sword dance; (14) *zor 'cham,* the magic weapon dance; (15) *log 'cham,* the "return dance," in which all the dancers return and dance together. For a comprehensive study of the Mani Rimdu, see Kohn (2001). Cf. also Jerstad (1969), Fantin (1976), and Tenzin Zangbu (2000).

196. Ngawang Tsering Dondrub (*ngag dbang tshe ring don grub,* d. 1957) became the head of Thangme Gompa in 1923. He built a new, much larger temple, with a spacious courtyard where the Mani Rimdu dances could be performed. Lama Dondrub had three sons. The eldest, Lama Tenzin, died in February 1946 (Lama Tenzin's eldest son Ngawang Samten became a monk and later took care of the tulku of Lama Dondrub). Lama Ngodrub, the second son, took care of the Thangme Gompa until the tulku of his father was able to assume the responsibility. He passed away around 1968. His reincarnation, Ngawang Labsum (*ngag dbang bslab gsum),* was born in Rolwaling. Lama Dondrub's third son, Lama Ngawang Tenzin Trinle Gyatso, inherited the house at Genupa.

197. According to Kusho Mangde, to begin with the lamas and Sangye Tenpa went to Kathmandu, where Sangye Tenpa had many acquaintances, to request permission from Prime Minister Chandra Shumsher Rana (who ruled from 1901 to 1929) to build the gompa. At the Singha Darbar Palace, the Sherpas were taken into the presence of the prime minister, who sat on an elaborately ornamented armchair while his attendants held a parasol above his head, fanned him, and stood at his side holding a tray with a glass of water. Sangye Tenpa presented the offerings they had brought and a letter requesting permission and assistance to build the new monastery. Chandra Shumsher was particularly pleased to meet a reincarnated lama from the kingdom of Nepal itself. Permission to build the monastery was granted, and the prime minister donated the sum of 500 rupees for building expenses. The Sherpa lamas were very happy and returned to Shorong, but not before spending a few weeks visiting different offices in Kathmandu while trying to get hold of the 500 rupees. Kusho Tulku and Kusho Mangde went to Tibet to find the best Sherpa carpenter, who was working in Tibet at that time, arranged the printing of the Kangyur and Tengyur in Tibet, and supervised all the construction work. For Chiwang Gompa, see Snellgrove (1957), SCH (ff.32, 33a), and Ortner (1989, 1999).

198. Upon entering the monastery, each monk received a new set of robes; every month they were given four *pati* (about eight kilograms) of tsampa and a supply of butter, tea, salt, and chilies.

199. Gelong Ngawang Samten *(dge slong ngag dbang bsam gtan)* belonged to a very poor family from Mende *(sman sde/sdings)*. His father died when he was very young, and he had to take care of his aged mother. When his mother died, he tried to carry the corpse to the cremation place, but he was not strong enough, and the corpse fell down on the way. At that time he developed great renunciation toward worldly life and decided to become a hermit. He stayed for twenty years at a cave in Charog until his death in the late 1950s. His tulku, Tenzin Dorje Rinpoche, born around 1960, became a monk at Kopan Gompa. After a few years working as the manager of Tushita Retreat Center in Dharamsala, he gave back his vows and now lives in Germany.

200. She belonged to the Murmin Tso clan, was scarred by smallpox, and was renowned for her pills. The husband of her elder sister was a relative of Lama Zopa Rinpoche. She passed away around 1955 or 1956 and has reincarnated twice. The first reincarnation was a girl born at Tomde *(dom sde)*, between Tramo and Zamte, but she died when she was only five years old. The present reincarnation, Phurba Yangchen, was born in 1986 in Tramo as the daughter of Ang Chödar (Khampa) and Ang Chökyi. She is studying in a Kathmandu school.

201. He was a Tibetan disciple of the Rongphu Sangye known as Lama Ralchagpa because he had very long hair *(ral)*. He stayed with his attendant Ani Drolma in a large cave, inside of which he built a hut. The water supply was a long way down the mountain, but after a while a large spring appeared in the cave itself and two

more springs a little way below. The Khang sar bar dgongs sdod kyi phug hermitage is mentioned in DTH (f.351b).

202. Situated a couple of miles east of Kathmandu, the Great Stupa of Bouddha, or Bouddhanath, is one of the largest stupas in the world. According to the Newar tradition, it was built in the fifth century A.D. by the Licchavi king Manadeva as a penance for having unwittingly killed his father. According to *The Legend of the Great Stupa* (see above, note 1), the stupa contains the relics of the previous Buddha Kashyapa and was built by a poultry woman who obtained permission from the king to build a stupa as large as the ground that her sari could cover. She then unthreaded the sari's fabric and was able to cover a large tract of ground with the threads. Although the people complained about the size of the stupa, the king told them that he had already given his word, and there was no question of going back on it. Therefore, Tibetans call it *jarung khashor (bya rung kha shor)*, the meaning of which can be given as "permitted to build because it was promised." Cf. Dowman (1973, 1981, 2002) and Ehrhard (1990).

203. Cf. Sever (1993).

204. Situated on the banks of the Bagmati River, Pashupatinath is the holiest Hindu shrine in Nepal, dedicated to Lord Shiva in his aspect as Pashupati, the Lord of Animals. The whole area is one of the twenty-four holy places associated with Shiva and Parvati for Hindus, or Chakrasamvara and Vajravarahi for Buddhists. Hindus believe that dying or being cremated at Pashupatinath purifies all sins and ensures rebirth in a pure land. Cf. Dowman (1981) and *Nepala-mahatmya of the Skandapurana,* translated by J. Acharya (1992, 1, p. 13ff.).

205. The Helpful Enclosure (*skyobs rva,* pronounced as "Kyabrog" by the local people) Gompa is situated at Chagnyapa, near Thangteng. The original temple containing a large Guru Rinpoche clay statue had been built by Lama Tenzin Dragpa, also known as Rolpa Dorje, of the Lhabushingtog clan, at nearby Dragpur. Rolpa Dorje (not to be identified with Lama Sangwa Dorje's brother, according to the locals) was a highly accomplished practitioner. One day, a fire broke out in the house and everyone ran away. When they returned to see the damage, they could not find the statue. Some time later, a girl who was collecting wood heard a bell in the forest and found the statue farther up the mountain. When the villagers tried to take it back to the lama's house, the statue spoke and said it did not want to go back and that a gompa should be built at that very spot. Rolpa Dorje then built a new temple at that place to house the statue. His descendant Lama Lhagpa was the head of Kyabrog Gompa during the time of the Lawudo Lama Kunzang Yeshe. He passed away in the early 1960s and was succeeded by his son Lama Tenzin (1919–97), who wrote a history of the gompa and the lineage of his ancestors. Lama Tenzin's son Ang Tsering took charge of the gompa, but he died in October 2000 and was succeeded by his own son Ngawang Tsultrim.

206. Cf. DTH (f.408b).

207. After Kusho Tulku's death, Kusho Mangde traveled to Tibet, where he offered 2,000 butter lamps at the Gyantse *(rgyal rtse)* Chörten on behalf of his brother and paid a visit to the Rongphu Sangye. Before returning to Toloka, he performed elaborate rituals for Kusho Tulku at Charog and undertook some repairs in the shrine room. The construction of the Tolu, or Toloka, Gompa began in the ox year (1937) at a beautiful spot above a lake chosen by Kusho Tulku himself and took three years to complete. Kusho Mangde worked very hard to get donations for the building and traveled many times to Tibet to obtain a complete set of the Kangyur and Tengyur. The new gompa was named Tharling *(thar gling)* Gompa, the Island of Liberation, by the Rongphu Sangye. Kusho Mangde married Ngawang Lozang from Namche and had two sons and four daughters. The eldest son became a monk in Tashi Lhunpo *(bkra shis lhun po)* and died young, and the second son, Sonam Zangpo, was a monk in Thangme for some years. Three of his daughters also died young. The surviving daughter, Pema Chöden, offered her hair to Jamyang Khyentse Chökyi Lodro *( 'jam dbyangs mkhyen brtse chos kyi blo gros,* 1896–1959) in Bodh Gaya and stayed at home taking care of her parents.

208. Shortly before his death, Kusho Tulku offered a scarf to his consort Ganden Zangmo, which was regarded as a sign that he was to be reborn as her son. Ganden Zangmo then married Lama Ngawang Rangdrol of the Goleg clan. Their first son, born in the fire ox year (1937), was recognized by both Kusho Mangde and Ngawang Tenzin Norbu as the reincarnation of Kusho Tulku.

Around 1946, the tulku was taken to Tibet to continue his education under Trulzhig Rinpoche and Napta Rinpoche Kunzang Namgyal *(nab khra rin po che kun bzang rnam rgyal)* at Shing Ri Gompa, near Dingri. In 1953 he went back to Khumbu to perform the preliminary practices and receive teachings from the Thangme Lama Dondrub and Gelong Ngawang Samten of Charog. In 1959 he married a lady from Toloka and had one son and five daughters. His son Ngawang Jigdral Yeshe Loden *(ngag dbang 'jigs bral ye shes blo ldan)* is the tulku of Lama Ngawang Lodro *(ngag dbang blo gros)* of Kyirong Sang-ngag Chöling Monastery. Kusho Tulku lives in Kumari Gal near Bouddha.

209. The tulku of Lama Gulo was born in Namche as the son of Pasang Namgyal *(khams pa)* and Palzim Dekyi *(shang khug).* He was enthroned in 1940 at Tengboche and studied in Tibet with masters of the Nyingma, Kagyu, and Sakya traditions. Cf. DTH (f.457a) and Tenzin Zangbu (2000).

210. Trulzhig Rinpoche Ngawang Chökyi Lodro *( ngag dbang chos kyi blo gros,* b. 1924) was born in Taglung Dzong, between Gyantse and Khampa Dzong, on the tenth day of the ninth month of the wood mouse year, 1924. His father was Tenzin Chödar *(bstan 'dzin chos dar),* a disciple of the Rongphu Sangye from Parshing Chölung Gompa *(par shing chos lung)* in Phadrug, and his mother was Jamyang Dechen Yeshe Chödron *( 'jams dbyangs bde chen ye shes chos sgron),* the consort of Kunzang Yeshe Thongdrol. In 1926, the child was recognized as the reincarnation of Trulzhig Kunzang Thongdrol and taken to Rongphu. Trulzhig Rinpoche

studied at Rongphu and Mindroling. In 1940 he was appointed abbot of Rong-phu Monastery and spent most of his time teaching and traveling extensively. In 1951 he visited the Kathmandu Valley and afterward spent three years in Samye. In 1959 he left Tibet and stayed in Thangme for two years before moving to Shorong, where he built a new monastery, Thubten Do-ngag Chöling *(thub bstan mdo sngags chos gling)*, that was consecrated in 1968. Cf. Aziz (1978) and Tashi Tsering (1999). He is the thirtieth in a lineage of incarnations that includes Ananda *(kun dga' bo)*, Aryadeva (2nd century A.D.), Drubchen Nagpopa *(grub chen nag po spyod pa)*, Thumi Sambhota (*thu mi sam bho ta*, 7th century), Shantarakshita (*mkhan chen zhi ba 'tsho*, 9th century), Lochen Vairochana (*lo chen vairocana*, 9th century), Lhalung Palgyi Dorje (*lha lung dpal gyi rdo rje*, 9th century), Rongzom Pandita (*rong zom pandita*, 11th century), Phamthing Jigme Dragpa (*pham mthing 'jigs med grags pa*, 10th? century), Jobo Dipankara Atisha (*jo bo di pam ka ra*, 982–1054), Rechung Dorje Drag (*ras chung rdo rje grags*, b. 1084), Sakya Pandita (1182–1251), Drubchen Melong Dorje (*grub chen me long rdo rje*, 1243–1303), Drime Özer (*dri med 'od zer, klong chen rab 'jams*, 1308–63), Jonang Kunga Nyingpo *(jo nang kun dga' snying po)*, Terchen Gyurme Dorje (*gter chen 'gyur med rdo rje*, 1634–1714), Guyang Lodetsal or Rigzin Donyo Dorje (*gu yangs blo bde rtsal*, or *rig 'dzin don yod rdo rje)*, and Kunzang Thongdrol Dorje, among others. Cf. *The Bathing Place of Devotion: A Series of Lives of Wagindra Dharmamati Joined Together as a Requesting Prayer (Ngag dbang chos kyi blo gros kyi skyes rabs dang rnam thar gsol 'debs su btags pa dad pa'i 'jug ngogs)* composed by Trulzhig Rin-poche. See also Tashi Tsering (1999).

When I asked Trulzhig Rinpoche himself about his name, he replied that he has the following names: Ngawang Gyurme Chökyi Lodro, Ngawang Do-ngag Tenzin Norbu, Gyalse Shenphen Thaye, Ngawang Kalden Palzang, Rigzin Tse-wang Norbu Pal, Tenzin Dorje, Kalon Jampa Tsal, Dorje Wangchug Tsal, Gyalse Drime Lodro, Natsog Rangdrol, Ngawang Lozang Do-ngag Tenzin, Kunzang Trinle Drodul Tsal, and many more....

211. Story told by Pemba Gyaltsen. Years later, four sons of Pemba Gyaltsen (Thubten Sherab, Thubten Thabke, Thubten Tsering, and Thubten Tharchin) and a nephew of Ang Pasang (Thubten Tenzin) became monks at Lawudo Gompa.

212. Ngawang Chöphel Gyatso *(ngag dbang chos 'phel rgya mtsho)* was born on the tenth day of the fourth month of the water dog year 1922 as the fifth son of Tser-ing Dorje of the Zalaka clan and Pasang Kyima. After receiving teachings from the Rongphu Sangye, Lama Drukpa Rinpoche Ngawang Palzin (*ngag dbang dpal 'dzin* or *shes rab rdo rje*, d. 1941), and other masters, he spent one year at the Pemkar Her-mitage in Pharag performing the preliminary practices. Afterward, he spent another year in retreat at the Sengdong Cave in Kulung before receiving teachings from Au Yeshe Dorje. Cf. *The Brief Autobiography of the Maratika Lama Ngawang Chöphel Gyatso, A Truthful Account without Exaggeration or Underestimation (Brag phug ma ra ti ka'i bla ma ngag dbang chos 'phel rgya mtsho'i rnam thar mdor bsdud*

*pa sgro skur bral ba'i bden gtam)*, published by Buffetrille (1994) and Karma Wangchug (2000).

213. In the dzogchen system, the highest realization is known as the inseparability of appearances and emptiness *(snang stong)* according to mahayoga, of bliss and emptiness *(bde stong)* according to anuyoga, and of awareness and emptiness *(rig stong)* according to atiyoga. Clarity and emptiness *(gsal stong)* refers to the body of a buddha, and sound and emptiness *(grags stong)* to the speech of a buddha. Personal communication from Changling *(byang gling)* Tulku.

214. The *Bzang po spyod pa'i smon lam gyi rgyal po* (*Bhadracaryapranidhanaraja* in Sanskrit) is included in a collection of sutras known as the *Avatamsaka Sutra (Snyan gong gi rgyan 'phal po che mdo)* and is sometimes translated as *The King of Prayers*.

215. The *Bodhicharyavatara (Byang chub sems dpa'i spyod pa la 'jug pa)*, composed by the Indian master Shantideva (685–763), is the most popular scripture of Mahayana Indian Buddhism. It contains detailed explanations on how to practice the six perfections, or *paramitas*.

216. Information provided by Lama Lhagpa of Thangteng, who heard it directly from Kusho Mangde. However, he does not remember clearly whether the Lawudo Lama gave the name of both parents or only of his mother. Lama Zopa's mother confirmed that Lama Zopa was born about two months before the Lawudo Lama passed away.

217. The three postures *(sku gsum gyi 'dug stangs)* are the lion posture of the dharmakaya, the elephant posture of the sambhogakaya, and the sage posture of the nirmanakaya. They are related to the pith instructions *(man ngag sde)* class of atiyoga.

218. Jamgon Kongtul Lodro Thaye (*'jam mgon kong sprul blo gros mtha' yas*, 1813–99) was one of the most important scholars and representatives of the *rime (ris med)*, or nonsectarian, movement of the nineteenth century. His literary work comprises about ninety volumes. Cf. Smith (1970, 2001).

219. The primordial ground *(thog ma'i gzhi)* is also called the Youthful Vase Body *(gzhon nu bum sku)*. Some dzogchen tantras explain four different ways of dying or dissolving the physical elements. The first is called "the way of the dakinis": having purified even the subtlest defilements of the winds and mind that obscure the ultimate reality, one attains the exhaustion of phenomena into the inner ultimate expanse *(nang dbyings)*, and thereby the external body dissolves into pure energy. This is the fourth vision, or stage, of the thögal practice. At that moment, the ultimate reality of intrinsic awareness that was based in the body becomes unified with the natural absolute expanse of reality *(rang bzhin chos kyi dbyings)*, just as the space inside a vase merges with the outer space when the vase breaks. Cf. Thondup (1989). Sometimes, even though they have the capacity to dissolve their physical form into what is called the rainbow body, practitioners choose to leave a gross body behind. This is known as the state of a knowledge-holder with residues *(rnam smin rig 'dzin)*. Cf. Jigme Lingpa's *Treasury of Good Qualities (Yon tan rin po che'i mdzod)*.

220. In the *Treasury of Good Qualities (Yon tan rin po che'i mdzod)* Jigme Lingpa talks about death with a display of five signs of accomplishment: lights, sounds, images of deities appearing in the bones, relics *(gdung)*, and earthquakes. Cf. Thondup (1989).

221. In the *Treasury of Words and Meaning* (ff.297a/b, 298a) Longchen Rabjampa explains that relics *(gdung)* are indestructible and can be of various colors. White ones are the size of peas, and colored ones can be like a pea or a mustard seed. There is another type of relic, called *ringsel (ring bsrel)*, which is white, can be destroyed, and can be as small as a sesame seed or a tiny atom. They can also multiply by themselves. See also Thondup (1989).

## Part Two

222. *Sems nyid ngal gso* (f.55a/b), first part of the *ngal gso 'kor gsum* trilogy.

223. Among those who spent time at the Lawudo Cave were Diu Rinpoche, the Sengdrag Lama Pema Chökyi Gyaltsen, Kusho Donyo from Zang Zang Lhadrag, Gomchen Gampa-la, Geshe Urgyen Dorje, Kyetsang Rinpoche, Gelong Jamyang Puntsog and Gelong Wangchug from Khari Gompa, and Lama Zopa's uncle Ngawang Yonten.

224. His ancestor was a learned lama who taught writing at Tsogo *(mtsho sgo)*, a town two days' walk east of Shelkar in the lower valley of the Phung Chu, and became known as the "secretary of Tsogo" *(mtsho sgo'i drung yig)*. Ang Dawa's father settled in Nechung *(gnas chung)* in the Shartö *(shar stod)* area south of Dingri, where some of his relatives live at present.

225. The eight freedoms refer to freedom from being born in the eight states without leisure to practice the spiritual path. The ten endowments (or "richnesses," as Lama Zopa likes to translate the term) refer to the beneficial circumstances needed for practicing Dharma. Cf. *A Letter to a Friend (Bshes pa'i spring yig, Suhrllekha)* by Nagarjuna, and Paltul Rinpoche (Rinpoche, 1994, pp. 19–37).

226. When a baby is due, Sherpa parents prepare a large quantity of chang and store it in large wooden containers. After the baby's birth, they invite a lama to perform the naming ceremony on an auspicious day. The lama does the *Ribo Sangcho* ritual, and some prayer flags are set on the roof of the house. Another prayer flag on a long pole adorned with juniper branches on the top is set at the right side of the door if the baby is a boy and at the left if it is a girl. The chang containers are opened on this occasion; the first cup is offered to the buddhas and local protectors, while the rest is served to the relatives and friends who come to congratulate the parents.

227. Kagyu Rinpoche Tenzin Norbu *(bka' brgyud rin po che bstan 'dzin nor bu, 1899–1959)* was the fourth tulku of Drakar Taso Chökyi Wangchug. He had been a married lama, but when his pregnant wife and the baby died, he developed a

strong sense of renunciation and became a monk at Mindroling Monastery. He studied with Togden Shakya Shri, Tripön Pema Chögyal, and Karmapa Khakhyab Dorje (*karma pa mkha' khyab rdo rje*, 1871–1922) among others. Cf. *Gdan rabs lo rgyus drang srong dga' ba'i dal gtam gyi kha skong* in his *Collected Works*. His tulku, Karma Drubgyu Tenpai Gyaltsen Trinle Kunkhyab Palzangpo (*karma grub brgyud bstan pa'i rgyal mtshan 'phrin las kun khyab dpal bzang po*, b. 1961), was born in the Tsum area of Nepal and lives in Swayambhu in the Kathmandu Valley.

228. Tripön Ngawang Pema Chögyal (*khrid dpon ngag dbang padma chos rgyal*, 1877–1958) was born in Ladakh. He traveled to Tsari and Kham, where he met Shakya Shri and became one of his foremost disciples. After Shakya Shri's death, Pema Chögyal engaged in long retreats at Tsibri and Lapchi and later established eleven hermitages. Between 1934 and 1958 he compiled an anthology called the *Tsibri Parma: The Collected Instructional Material on the Practice of the Teachings of the Kargyu (dkar brgyud) and Dzogchen (rdzogs chen) Traditions (Dkar rnying gi skyes chen du ma'i phyag rdzogs kyi gdams ngag gnas bsdus nyer mkho rin po che'i gter mdzod rtsibs ri'i par ma)* and founded a printing house, the Nerang Parkhang *(gnas rang phar khang)*, with about 10,000 woodblocks of rare Buddhist manuscripts from Bhutan, Sikkim, Ladakh, and other areas. His tulku, known as Se Rinpoche *(sras rin po che)*, was born in Manali, India, as the son of Shakya Shri's son Awo Rinpoche. Cf. Crook and Low (1997).

229. *The Quintessential Drop, Wisdom Liberating by Seeing (Yang tig ye shes mthong grol)*, the *Three Cycles of Rituals*, the *Profound Seal of [Dorje] Phagmo, Phur ba*, and other empowerments from the Northern Treasure.

230. Rain depends on the *nagas (klu)*, a type of being that is half snake and half human and is endowed with great powers. For the ability to control rain, hail, and so on, see the story of Ngagpa Yeshe Dorje (*The Rainmaker*, Woolf and Blanc, 1994).

231. At the beginning of his term, the *nyerpa (gnyer pa)* is entrusted with certain amount of money. Through business and trade, he has to ensure that the next year there will be a profit that can be used for the Mani Rimdu. If he has losses instead of profit, he has to repay the gompa with his own money.

232. Shri Negi Lama Tenzin Gyaltsen (*bstan 'dzin rgyal mtshan*, 1894–1977), known as the Kunnu Lama, was born in the Kinnaur, or Kunnu, region of Himachal Pradesh in northern India. Although he belonged to the Drukpa Kagyu school, he studied with masters from all the different traditions and became a great scholar. Later in his life he returned to India and spent a number of years in Varanasi. He became renowned as a master of bodhichitta and gave teachings to His Holiness the Dalai Lama. His most important work is a short text called *The Precious Lamp, a Praise of Bodhichitta (Byang chub sems kyi bstod pa rin chen sgron ma)*, published by Negi and Vaid (1986). The English translation by Gareth Sparham has been published under the title *Vast as the Heavens, Deep as the Sea*. Cf. Khunu Rinpoche (1999), G. C. Negi, and a short anonymous Tibetan biography.

233. Cf. Weir (1955, p. 51). The Scottish mountaineer Tom Weir visited Rolwaling in early November 1952 with George Roger, Douglas Scott, and Tom MacKinnon. He took some interesting photographs of Lama Zopa and his uncles, which he kindly made available for the present book.

234. If the boulders and earth blocking Tso Rolpa ever give way, the flood will completely submerge the valley. To prevent that from happening, the local Sherpas perform many rituals and offer prayers to Padmasambhava and Tseringma. Since 1998 there has been a joint project of the governments of Nepal and the Netherlands to drain the water of the lake, thus reducing the risk of lake outburst flooding. A canal was opened in June 2000, but it is still not sufficient. Previously, a project of the Nepali government and the World Bank had installed nineteen early warning sirens in the Rolwaling villages to warn the villagers in case of danger (cf. Surendra Phuyal in the *Kathmandu Post,* June 8, 2000). However, the villagers say that since those projects began, a few people have died suddenly without any sickness, and they attribute the deaths to the anger of the local gods.

235. The Sang-ngag Chöling *(gsang sngags chos gling),* or Beding, Gompa was built on the advice of the Rongphu Sangye. The first Rolwaling Gompa was built at Na *(gna'?),* sponsored by the father of Ngawang Yonten of the Lhugpa clan and consecrated by Chatang Chöying Rangdrol in the mid-nineteenth century.

236. Ngawang Tharpa, or Ang Phurba (Murmin Tso clan), later was appointed ritual master in the gompa, but he did not like the job and escaped to Khumbu. After being a monk in Thangme for about eight years, he left for Sikkim. He enrolled in the army and spent almost four years in Gangtok before returning to Nepal. He works part time on trekking expeditions. His wife is a half sister of the Thangme Rinpoche, and his son Thubten Jinpa is a monk in Kopan Monastery. Ngawang Özer is still in Rolwaling.

237. *'Phags pa shes rab kyi pha rol tu phyin pa rdo rje gcod pa,* or in Sanskrit *Vajracchedika-prajnaparamita.* Cf. Conze (1988).

238. According to the highest philosophical view of the Prasangika Madhyamaka system, all phenomena exist by depending upon other phenomena and therefore lack an independent nature or intrinsic reality. Cf. Tsongkhapa's *Essence of Eloquent Speech (Drang nges rnam 'byed legs bshad snying po).*

239. Gelong Pasang (Shangkhug clan) was from Yulhajung *(yul lha ljong),* near Thangteng. He had been a monk in Chiwang and Tengboche; later, the Rongphu Sangye asked him to teach in Rolwaling. He sponsored the carving of mani stones next to the chörten below the gompa. The carving was done by one Lama Dondrub from Thangme, and he charged one *mohar* (fifty *paisa*) for each syllable, so that the cost of carving the seven syllables *(Om ma ni pad me hum hrih)* on a stone amounted to three rupees and fifty paisa. Years later, Diu Rinpoche visited Rolwaling and offered a set of the *Rinchen Terdzö.* Consequently, Gelong Pasang built the Terdzö Lhakhang *(gter mdzod lha khang)* above the old gompa to house the volumes. He passed away around 1975. As a small child, a Rolwaling boy called

Dawa Tenzin (Kyirong Khampa clan) insisted that his real name was Ngawang Pasang; he was later acknowledged as the tulku of Gelong Pasang. Due to some "political" problems among the families, he could not be submitted to the test of identifying the possessions of his predecessor and was never officially recognized as the tulku. He spent a few years in Kopan Gompa and is now a freelance mountaineer and trekking guide.

240. The chörten was destroyed during the Dumche celebrations in the early nineties by floods caused by a break in the Ripumo glacier. In 1979 a joint Nepali-American expedition with the Sherpa Pertemba as *sardar* climbed Tseringma for the first time, and shortly after that, there was a series of landslides and floods. The Rolwaling elders had tried to prevent the climbing of Tseringma, but they did not succeed, and the natural disasters that ensued are attributed to having defiled the goddess. Cf. Fisher (1990).

241. According to the *Treasure of Phenomenology (Abhidharmakosha)* of Vasubandhu (4th century), the center of this universe is known as Mount Meru and is surrounded by four great continents in the four cardinal directions. The bodies of the humans inhabiting the other three continents are said to be different from ours.

I haven't been able to clarify to which expedition those events relate. The first Rolwaling expedition took place in 1951 (Shipton, Hillary, and others), followed by three expeditions in 1952 (Tom Weir, Murray, and Shipton) and one in 1955 (Merseyside). The Swiss geologist Toni Hagen also visited Rolwaling when Lama Zopa was there.

242. The new building was sponsored by Ngawang Yonten of the Lhugpa clan (the father of the present Thangme Rinpoche), Umdze Pemba Puthar, and Au Summi (Sakya Khampa), who was the village headman. The famous artist Khapa Kalden from Khumjung came with three attendants to paint the walls. On their way back to Khumjung they were caught in a blizzard at the Tashi Labtsa, and one of them died. The gompa was renovated again in 2002.

243. The hill was originally known as the Queen Mountain *(rgyal mo ri)* after the queen *(rgyal mo)* of the dakinis, Dorje Yudronma *(rdo rje gyu sgron ma)*. Situ Chökyi Rinchen *(si tu chos kyi rin chen,* d. 1402) changed its name to Drolma Mountain *(sgrol ma ri)*. He then built a palace that resembled a bowl of white crystal turned upside down on top of the hill, and the mountain became known as Shelkar *(shel dkar)*, the White Crystal. The monastery was founded in 1385 by the translator Dragpa Gyaltsen *(grags pa rgyal mtshan,* 1352–1405) with the support of Situ Chökyi Rinchen. The abbots belonged to the Sakya and Bodongpa *(bo dong pa)* traditions until the seventeenth century, when the Fifth Dalai Lama transformed it into a Gelug monastery. Cf. sKal ldan/Diemberger (1996, pp. 49, 72–76), Diemberger and Guntram (1999, pp. 35–37), and Roerich (1996, p. 788).

244. Tashi Lhunpo Monastery was founded in 1447 by Gedun Drubpa *(dge 'dun grub pa,* 1391–1474), the nephew and disciple of Tsongkhapa who was later designated as the First Dalai Lama. The Fifth Dalai Lama recognized the abbot of Tashi Lhunpo,

Chökyi Gyaltsen (*chos kyi rgyal mtshan,* 1570–1662), as an emanation of the Buddha Amitabha, and gave him the title of Panchen (great scholar) Lama. There are two colleges, or *dratsang (gra tshang),* in Tashi Lhunpo, the Ngagpa *(sngags pa)* Dratsang and the Tsenyi *(mtshan nyid)* Dratsang. Cf. Phurchog Ngawang Jampa (1989).

Some Sherpa monks from Tashi Lhunpo became very learned and influential, such as Kachen Ang Nyima from Tramoteng, who became the teacher of the Seventh Panchen Lama Lozang Trinle Lhundrub Chökyi Gyaltsen (*blo bzang 'phrin las lhun 'grub chos kyi rgyal mtshan,* 1938–89). In 1959 there were about fifteen Sherpa monks at Tashi Lhunpo: Drongpa Ngodrub and his brother Ang Dorje (Lhugpa clan), three brothers from the Shugma Gembu family (Shangkhug clan), and Drongpa Sangye from Thangme; Tenzin, Ang Phurba and his brother Ang Nyima, Puntsog, Gyaltsen (Khumde), Gyaltsen (Solu), Ang Tenpa, Ang Karma, Ang Kyipa, Ang Tamdin (Changma, Solu), and Tenzin Norbu. Sangye Tenpa of the Lama clan from Paphlu offered to their khamtsen the wooden planks *(glegs shing)* for the volumes of the Kangyur and Tengyur, made of *akaro* wood. Personal communication from Gelong Ang Dorje (Lhugpa clan).

245. Phag-ri is mentioned in the *Padma Kathang* (p. 589). Jomolhari *(jo mo lha ri,* 7,314 m) is the abode of Palden Hari Dorje *(dpal ldan ha ri rdo rje),* one of the Twelve Tenma Goddesses *(bstan ma bcu gnyis)* subdued by Padmasambhava. She holds an arrow in her right hand and a vessel with jewels in her left and rides on a deer. She is flanked by two mountains said to be her ministers: Jobo Gendun *(jo bo dge 'dun)* and Jobo Ramding *(jo bo ram sdings).* Guru Rinpoche meditated at the Karleb Drag Phug *(dkar leb brag phug)* Cave near Phag-ri, and Yeshe Tsogyal at another cave nearby. Cf. Chan (1994) and Lodro Chötar (1996).

246. See Williamson (1987), Taring (1986), Maraini (1993: "…But the village is horrible. It must certainly be one of the filthiest places in the world."), Knight (1992), and Bell (1987: "At Phagri the walls of the houses are made of clods of earth and the floors are sunk a couple of feet below the ground level for the sake of warmth."). All my Phag-ri informants agree that not only is Phag-ri *not* dirty, but it is even cleaner than Lhasa.

247. The Pomdatsang *(spom mda' tshang)* and Tsangdutsang *(tshang khrug tshang)* families had houses in all the important trading towns of Tibet. The oldest and most important family in Phag-ri was the Zerpön family *(gzer dpon),* who owned three old houses with about 250 rooms each. The mahasiddha Drukpa Kunleg ( *'brug pa kun legs,* 1455–1529) stayed in one of those houses while on his way to Bhutan. He slept with one of the servant girls and left in the early morning riding on the rays of the sun. His stove and walking stick were still there in 1959. Later the Chinese confiscated the houses and gave the family only three rooms to live in. There were at least seven good schools at Phag-ri ( *bzo khang, khang skyid, nyi chung, don 'dus, lha khang 'og ma,* and others) where both boys and girls received an education.

248. Yamantaka *(rdo rje 'jigs byed)* is a highest tantra deity widely practiced in the Gelug tradition in the aspects of Solitary Yamantaka *(dpa' bo gcig pa)* or Thirteen-Deity.

249. Dromo Geshe Ngawang Kalzang (*gro mo dge shes ngag dbang skal bzang*, d. 1937) was a monk from Sera Monastery who spent about twelve years meditating in various caves in south Tibet. No one knew he was there until a herdsman found him in a very remote cave. People developed great faith in him and requested him to take care of the Dungkar (*dung dkar*), or White Conch, Monastery in the Dromo Valley. He became well known for his great powers and compassion. He passed away in Dungkar in 1937 and remained in thugdam for a few weeks. His tulku, Jigme Ngawang Kalzang (*'jigs med ngag dbang skal bzang*), was born in Gangtok, Sikkim. He studied in Sera Monastery and became a geshe in 1959. After being imprisoned by the Chinese, he was released in 1961 because of his being an Indian national. He was director of the Tibet House in Delhi for some years before moving to the U.S., where he passed away in 2001. Cf. Govinda (1977).

250. The oracle in Dungkar used to be possessed by the local protector Tashi Öbar (*bkra shis 'od 'bar*), the worldly spirit known as Gyachen (*rgyal chen*), or his acolytes Namkha Barzin (*nam mkha' 'bar 'dzin*), Khache Marpo (*kha che dmar po*), Genyen Jingkarwa (*dge bsnyen phying dkar ba*), and Pawo Trobar (*dpa' bo khro 'bar*). Cf. Nebesky-Wojkowitz (1996, p. 432). On that occasion the oracle had come to Phag-ri and was possessed by Gyachen.

251. Receiving offerings of food from benefactors and not being able to perform proper rituals on their behalf causes spiritual or mental pollution. Cf. Rinpoche (1994, pp. 173–74).

252. Situated on a small hill near Phag-ri, the Richung Pote (*ri chung spo te*) Monastery was built by Geshe Palden Tendar (*dpal ldan bstan dar*) from Ganden Shartse Monastery, who later offered it to Ganden Monastery. The next abbot was Geshe Ngawang Palden (*ngag dbang dpal ldan*), followed by Zong Rinpoche (1905–84), who stayed three years. When Lama Zopa was in Phag-ri, the abbot was Mili Khentul Donyö Palden (*mi li mkhan sprul don yod dpal ldan*), who built two new monasteries at Phag-ri, Dragtogang (*brag rtog sgang*) and Samdrub Chöling (*bsam 'grub chos gling*), on older foundations of temples built by Thangtong Gyalpo. Cf. Lodro Chötar (1996).

253. The Wild Rose Dharma Island of the Great Vehicle (*se ra theg chen chos gling*) was founded in 1419 by Jamchen Chöje Shakya Yeshe (*byams chen chos rje shakya ye shes*, 1379–1449), a disciple of Tsongkhapa, at the foot of a hill north of Lhasa. There are three colleges in Sera, Je (*byes*), Me (*smad*), and Ngagpa (*sngags pa*). The Sera Je college was founded by Kunkhyen Lodro Rinchen Senge (*kun mkhyen blo gros rin chen seng ge*), who belonged to a family of Nyingma practitioners from Northern Latö in Tsang. The main deity propitiated by the Sera Je monks is Hayagriva (*rta mgrin*), which is in fact a Nyingma deity. Before 1959 there were 5,000 monks in Sera Monastery, residing in different hostels according to their respective countries. Cf. Shakabpa (1984) and Phurchog Ngawang Jampa (1989, pp. 47–71).

254. If a monk was wealthy enough to make offerings to the monasteries, he was exempted from work and had enough time to study. Those who were poor had to work for their teachers and the community without learning practically anything.

255. The *yul lha,* or country god, Tashi Öbar *(bkra shis od 'bar)* was originally an Indian god brought from India to Shelkar by Pang Lotsawa Lodro Tenpa (*dpang lo tsa ba blo gros brtan pa,* 1276–1342). He is the protector of Shelkar, Tashi Lhunpo, and Dungkar monasteries and is particularly connected with the followers of Bodong Chogle Namgyal (*bo dong phyogs las rnam rgyal,* 1375–1451). Cf. sKal ldan/Diemberger (1996, pp. 125–28), Diemberger and others (1997, p. 22), and Nebesky-Wojkowitz (1996, pp. 174–75).

256. The story of Namkha Barzin is as follows. In the late 1920s or early 1930s, a Mongolian man came to Dungkar Monastery seeking ordination as a monk. He was old and poor, and the monk in charge told him that beggars were not admitted in the monastery and threw him out. The Mongolian Namkha Barzin was very hurt but begged to be allowed to stay because he had nowhere to go. He had come all the way from Mongolia enduring much hardship in order to become a monk, but instead he was abused and thrown out. At the gate of the monastery he met four monks and again asked for help, but they beat him and chased him out. Then Namkha Barzin cursed the five monks and told them that within one year they would all be dead. Sometime later Namkha Barzin was found dead on top of the pass near Pema Chöling *(padma chos gling).* The nomads threw his body into the river, where it got stuck for a few days among the rocks, and the herders nearby amused themselves by throwing stones at the corpse. Finally, the body was carried away by the water and disappeared.

A few months later, the herders and their yaks died one by one of a terrible disease and looked as if they had been attacked by demons. The monk who had first mistreated Namkha Barzin caught the same disease and died. Then a monk fell into a trance and began to make weird noises, while holding his hand with four fingers outstretched. Dromo Geshe thought that it was the spirit of a dead person trying to communicate. Sometime later another monk died in a similar way, and Dromo Geshe inquired whether they had been connected with any crime against anyone who had died recently. Somebody then remembered Namkha Barzin and his curse. Dromo Geshe was able to turn Namkha Barzin into a protecting spirit *(dam can,* literally "one having taken oath") under the command of the spirit Dorje Shugden. His oracle was established at Dungkar Monastery in the hope that he would be pacified and spare the other three monks, but they also died shortly thereafter. After that, Namkha Barzin gave advice through the medium, and he was consulted for any important matters concerning the monastery. Later, a shrine was built on the pass where he had died, and everyone would stop to do a short prayer at that place. Those who did not would invariably meet with an accident. Cf. Pemba (1957).

Namkha Barzin is said to be a wild tsen *(btsan)* spirit. He is depicted as standing on top of a decaying corpse, red in color, with one face, two hands, three eyes,
and a ferocious expression. Cf. Nebesky-Wojkowitz (1996, pp. 143–44).

257. Composed by Rendawa Shonu Lodro (*red mda' ba gzhon nu blo gros,* 1349–1412)
in praise of Tsongkhapa, it begins "Mig me tse we..." and is therefore known as
the *Migtsema* prayer. Here follows one translation:

Avalokiteshvara, great treasure of universal love.

Mañjushri, powerful one of stainless knowledge.

Vajrapani, destroyer of the multitude of maras.

Tsongkhapa, crown ornament of the learned ones of the Snow Land.

Lozang Dragpa, at your feet I make requests.

258. *Byang chub lam gyi rim pa'i dmar khrid myur lam gyi sngon 'gro'i ngag 'don gyi rim
pa khyer bde bklag chog bskal bzang mgrin rgyan,* composed by Dvagpo Jampel
Lhundrub *(dvags po 'jam dpal lhun grub).* The abbreviated name *jorchö ('byor chos)*
means "preparation" and refers to the fact that this text is a preparatory practice
for understanding the essential points of the gradual path.

259. The Tremo *(dre? mo)* La is about three hours walk southeast of Phag-ri. Drugkye
Dzong *('brug rgyal rdzong),* the Bhutanese Victory Fort, was built in 1647 by Shab-
drung Ngawang Namgyal to commemorate his victory over the Tibetans. It was
burned and completely destroyed in 1951. Kyerchu *(skyer chu)* Lhakhang was built
by the Tibetan king Songtsen Gampo in the seventh century to subjugate the border regions. Cf. Pommaret (1991). The Kyerchu Lhakhang is mentioned in the
*Padma Kathang* (p. 552) in connection with Padmasambhava.

260. The Buxa Fort where the Tibetans stayed is situated near the India-Bhutan border at an altitude of 867 m, on a low hill surrounded by higher ones. The high
mountain behind seems to be called Peachokum or Pichakonum or Peachakam,
according to Mr. Bogle, who passed through Buxa Duar in 1774 on his way to
Tibet. Cf. Markham (1989, pp. 16–17). In 1930 the British drove away the
Bhutanese and the fort became a prison. *Duar* is a Sanskrit word meaning
"entrance" and refers to the fort's location at the foot or entrance of the Himalayas.

261. Pretas are described as having a very large stomach, a narrow throat, thin legs that
cannot support their weight, and dry mouths that emit flames. They are always
suffering from hunger and thirst but are unable to find any food or drink. Humans
can help them by offering food and water blessed with a particular mantra *(Om
utshikshta pandita ashibaya svaha).*

262. Geleg *(dge legs)* Rinpoche (or "Gehlek," as his name is now sometimes spelled), was
born in 1939 and recognized as the tulku of an abbot of the Upper Tantric College. He studied for fourteen years in Drepung Monastery. After escaping to India
he stayed for a while in Buxa and was one of the first lamas to attend the School
for Young Tulkus in Delhi. Later he gave back his vows and stayed in Delhi for
many years. He now lives in the U.S.

263. *Dura (bsdus grva).*

264. Geshe Tamdin Rabten (*rta mgrin rab brtan*, 1920–86) was born in Trehor, Kham. He studied for about twenty years in Sera Monastery, and after escaping to India was sent to Buxa to teach the monks. In 1963 he became a geshe and went to Dharamsala as a debating partner *(mtshan zhabs)* of His Holiness the Dalai Lama. He stayed in retreat in a small house above McLeod Ganj and came down only when he had to help His Holiness. In 1975 he was appointed abbot of the Tibetan Monastic Institute in Rikon, Switzerland. In 1976 he began a traditional program of Gelug studies for Westerners, and the following year he founded Tharpa Chöling Center of Higher Tibetan Studies in Mont-Pélèrin (now called Rabten Chöling). His tulku Tenzin Rabgye was born in 1987 in Dharamsala as the grandson of the famous Dr. Lozang Drolma from Kyirong.

265. Yongzin Ling Rinpoche Thubten Lungtog Namgyal Trinle (*yong 'dzin gling rin po che thub bstan lung rtogs rnam rgyal 'phrin las*, 1903–83) was born at Yabphu, northwest of Lhasa, and recognized as the sixth incarnation of the Ling lamas, many of whom had been tutors of the Dalai Lamas. At ten he entered the Loseling *(blo gsal gling)* College of Drepung Monastery. In 1936 he was appointed abbot of the Upper Tantric College and in 1940 became the junior tutor of His Holiness the Fourteenth Dalai Lama; some time later he became the senior tutor. In 1959 he escaped with His Holiness and settled in Dharamsala. In 1965 he became the ninety-seventh Holder of the Throne of Ganden, the Ganden Tripa *(dga' ldan khri pa)*, or head of the Gelug tradition. Cf. Tenzin Gyatso (1988).

In November 1960 Ling Rinpoche became sick and went to various Indian hospitals for treatment, but his condition did not improve. In 1961 he went to Darjeeling to receive treatment from Dr. Hunter, a Westerner, and a Tibetan doctor. Information about his visit to Darjeeling was kindly given by his secretary Thubten Tsering ("T.T.-la").

266. Trijang Rinpoche Lozang Yeshe Tenzin Gyatso (*khri byang rin po che blo bzang ye shes bstan 'dzin rgya mtsho*, 1901–81) belonged to the Shartse College of Ganden Monastery. Cf. his autobiography, *Skyabs rje khri byang rdo rje 'chang mchog gi mdzad rnam snying bsdud zur 'don*. His tulku Tenzin Lozang Yeshe Gyatso was born in Dalhousie in 1982.

267. *Zab lam bla ma mchod pa bde stong dbyer med*, composed by the first Panchen Lama Lozang Chökyi Gyaltsen.

268. There are different techniques for developing bodhichitta. One of them includes developing love, compassion, the wish to liberate sentient beings from suffering, and giving rise to bodhichitta.

269. Born and educated in England, she became a Theravadan nun, but later married an Indian and moved with him to India. She became a follower of Gandhi and fought against the British during the independence struggle, being imprisoned for a while. She had three children, one of whom became a famous film actor (Kabir Bedi). One of her children went to school with the son of Pandit Nehru, and she became quite close to that family. She did some very important work for the

exiled Tibetan community. Later, she was ordained as a nun by His Holiness Karmapa, whereas her husband became a Hindu holy man and psychic healer. Frida Bedi, also known as Sister Khechog Palmo, was a close friend of the owners of the Oberoi Hotel in Delhi, where she passed away on May 2, 1977. Cf. Cooke (1992, pp. 317–26) and personal communication from Ven. Tenzin Palmo.

270. Among the Nyingma tulkus were Chogling Rinpoche, Tarthang Tulku, Chime Rinpoche, Tulku Pema, Urgyen Tobgyal, Kochen Tulku, Ringu Tulku (Nyingma-Kagyu), Bagan Tulku Pema Tenzin, Bairo Tulku, Bhaka Tulku, and Amdo Rinpoche. Among the Sakyas were Sherab Gyaltsen Amipa, Chiwang Tulku and his brother Drubthob Tulku, and Khorchag Rinpoche. Among the Karma Kagyu tulkus were Trungpa Rinpoche, Akhong Rinpoche and his brother Yeshe Losel, Chökyi Nyima Rinpoche, Jampa Gyaltsen Mutuktsang (nephew of the Sixteenth Karmapa), and others. The Drukpa Kagyu tulkus were Dorzong Rinpoche and Chögyal Rinpoche. The Gelug tulkus at the school were Sharpa Tulku, Gala Rinpoche(?), Geleg Rinpoche, Rala Tulku, Langon Tulku, Thubten Zopa Rinpoche, and many others. During the last term two Bonpo lamas from Simla were also in attendance. In total there were about fifteen Kagyu, twelve Nyingma, ten Sakya, and many Gelug tulkus. An English girl who later became Ani Tenzin Palmo taught the tulkus English for a while.

271. *Tshad ma rnam 'grel (Pramanavarttika)*, composed by the Indian pandit Dharmakirti (7th century).

272. After becoming a geshe *lharampa* (the highest scholastic degree in the Gelug system), Kyorpon Rinpoche decided to go into the mountains to meditate. He took with him the *Lamrim Chenmo* of Tsongkhapa and went to look for a cave at Lhunpo Tse, a very high mountain in the Pembo region near Lhasa. While he was walking up the mountain, some stones began to fall as if someone were throwing them. Kyorpon Rinpoche walked in the direction from where the stones were coming and reached a cave where there was a skeleton sitting straight in meditation posture. When Kyorpon Rinpoche sat down and offered a mandala, the skeleton collapsed. Then the lama decided to stay in that cave and his disciples settled in some other places close by.

273. Mrs. Rachel Levy was a distinguished archaeologist and expert in Eastern religions. Mrs. Cohen (1906–95) graduated from Oxford, married, and had four children. Before the Second World War she and her husband were followers of P. D. Ouspensky, one of the main disciples of Gurdjieff. In the 1960s they met the Maharishi Mahesh Yogi and began to practice Transcendental Meditation. In 1976 they met Lama Zopa and Lama Yeshe in England and became Buddhists. Cf. Harris in *Mandala*, May/June 1995, p. 29.

274. Lama Thubten Yeshe was born in 1935 in Shinga Khang, a small hamlet in the Tölung *(stod lung)* area of Central Tibet, and was considered to be the reincarnation of the abbess of a nearby Nyingma nunnery. He joined Sera Je College and became extremely learned. He had a deep realization of bodhichitta and a

profound wish to benefit living beings extensively. For details about his life, see Adele Hulse, forthcoming.

275. *Necklace of the Fortunate Ones (Dbu ma la 'jug pa'i spyi don skal bzang mgul rgyan)*, by Sera Jetsun Chökyi Gyaltsen (*rje btsun chos kyi rgyal mtshan*, 1469–1544). Gelug monks study the commentaries written by the lamas of their own monastery and their own college; very few of them study the original Indian texts.

276. Samtenling Monastery was founded by the Mongolian Lama Guru Deva in 1962 with forty monks from the original Tashi Samtenling *(bkra shis bsam gtan gling)* Monastery, founded by Tsechogling Kachen Yeshe Gyaltsen (*tshe mchog gling yong 'dzin pandita dka' chen ye shes rgyal mtshan*, 1713–93) at the hermitage of Milarepa's disciple Repa Zhiwe Öd *(ras pa zhi ba'i 'od)* in Kyirong.

277. In the mid-nineteenth century, the Chinese master Tai Fo Shi came to Bouddha on a pilgrimage and married a Tamang lady. In 1853 he acted as interpreter during the peace negotiations between the invading Chinese army and the Nepali government, and in 1859 the Nepali government appointed him caretaker of the stupa as a reward for his services. In 1880 he was succeeded by his son Buddhavajra (Sangye Dorje), followed by Punyevajra (Sonam Dorje, 1886–1982) in 1922. Nowadays, the main priest performing rituals at the stupa is Gyani Bazra. Cf. Dowman (2002).

278. His predecessor, Ngawang Tsultrim Donden (*ngag dbang tshul khrims don ldan*, 1852–1918), the son of a Lhasa government official (*yab gzhis g.yu thog* family), had been a very learned geshe and tantric yogi from Ganden Monastery. The Thirteenth Dalai Lama gave him official permission to take a consort and remain as the head of his monastery in Tsethang, something unusual in the Gelug tradition. Serkong Dorje Chang lived with his family in Tsethang and continued to give teachings and empowerments to the monks in Ganden. The reincarnation of Tsechogling Kachen Yeshe Gyaltsen, said to be an emanation of Milarepa, also gave back his vows and married, but was not allowed to remain as head of his monastery.

Ngawang Tsultrim Donden had two sons. The eldest joined Drepung Monastery, while the youngest, Tsenshab Serkong Rinpoche, joined Ganden. The second Serkong Dorje Chang Thubten Tsultrim Ngawang Donden (*gser kong rdo rje 'chang thub bstan tshul khrims ngag dbang don ldan*, 1919–79) was also born in Lhasa. The present Serkong Dorje Chang Tenzin Ngawang Tsultrim Donden *(bstan 'dzin ngag dbang tshul khrims don ldan)* was born in Kollegal, South India, in 1980 and is now studying in Ganden Monastery. Oral communication from Serkong Rinpoche's attendant Ngawang-la. Cf. also *The Biography of Ngawang Tsultrim Donden (Ngag dbang tshul khrims don ldan gyi nam thar)* written by Lozang Palden Tenzin Yargye (*blo bzang dpal ldan bstan 'dzin yar rgyas*, 1927–96).

279. Drubthob Rinpoche Yeshe Namdag (*grub thob rin po che ye shes rnam dag*, b. 1930) is the reincarnation of a Nyingma practitioner who spent twelve years in a hermitage near Lhasa. Shortly before his death, in the middle of winter, he offered a fresh peach to his future parents and told them to eat one half each as an auspicious connection. He then predicted that in his next life he would follow the

Gelug tradition. Drubthob Rinpoche was born in Lhasa and joined Drepung Loseling College. When he escaped to Nepal, he was offered an old Tamang monastery in Swayambhu (the tulku of the previous lama of that monastery is a monk at Kopan Gompa). He has built another monastery in Pharping and has many disciples in the Newar community.

280. The name of that area is Kapan. It is the site of an ancient Licchavi settlement called Kampring grama pradesha or Kampilamba. No archaeological excavations have taken place so far at Kapan, but they would probably yield some interesting results about local palaces, temples, and stupas. Cf. Tiwari (2001, pp. 103–4).

281. The Tibetan astrological system, based on the Chinese system, consists of a cycle of twelve animals combined with four elements, male and female, resulting in a sixty-year cycle. Every year in the month of Marg (around January), the Tamang community takes the image of Ajima, or Pukka Siddhi, in procession around the stupa, but in the bird year the celebrations are much more elaborate. In previous times many auspicious events would take place during the bird years, such as small white pills springing from the dome of the stupa. Once, when he was young, Gyani Bazra Lama was directed in a dream to go to a hole on the southern side of the stupa. The next morning he went there and found milky water flowing from the hole. He collected some in a bottle and found that the water was sometimes clear and sometimes milky. According to him, there is now too much pollution around the stupa and such things do not happen any more.

282. Dilgo Khyentse Rinpoche Tashi Paljor (*dil mgo mkhyen brtse rin po che bkra shis dpal 'byor*, 1910–91) was born in Denkhok in Kham and recognized as the mind incarnation of Jamyang Khyentse Wangpo. He studied in Shechen (*zhe chen*) Monastery with Shechen Gyaltsab Gyurme Pema Namgyal (*zhe chen rgyal tshab 'gyur med padma rnam rgyal*, 1871–1926), and between the ages of fifteen and twenty-eight spent most of his time in retreat in isolated places. After escaping to India, he taught the royal family in Bhutan, and in 1982 built Shechen Tennyi Dargyeling (*zhe chen bstan gnyis dar rgyas gling*) Monastery in Bouddha. He had many Western disciples and became a teacher to His Holiness the Dalai Lama. Cf. Ricard (1996) and Tashi Tsering (1999).

283. In 1964, Sir Edmund Hillary built the Lukla airstrip in order to bring building materials for the schools and hospital he was building in Khumbu. In 1970 he built another airstrip and hospital in Paphlu in Shorong.

284. He built paths and bridges, and after buying back thousands of mani stones that the local Rais had used for building houses and pig stalls, he arranged them into a long mani wall. He even managed to have the headmen sign documents stipulating that those who hunted, cut trees, or took away the mani stones would have to pay a large fine. Cf. Buffetrille (1994b) and Karma Wangchug (2000).

285. Diu Rinpoche Ying-rig Jangchub Wangpo (*bde phug rin po che dbyings rig byang chub dbang po*, 1904–89), an emanation of the translator Kawa Paltseg (*ka ba dpal brtsegs*, 9th century), was born in Dephug (*bde phug*) in Northern Latö. He studied

Tibetan medicine at Mugulung with a doctor from the Chagpori Medical College of Lhasa and became a well-known doctor. His main teachers were Dzatul Ngawang Tenzin Norbu and the Fifteenth Karmapa Khakhyab Dorje (*mkha' khyab rdo rje*, 1871–1922), who was a native of Shelkar. He studied the Gelug tradition teachings in Ngamring *(ngam ring)* Monastery and received the *Unobstructed Primordial Mind* from Lama Gulo at Tengboche.

Diu Rinpoche received full ordination and the name Jampa Jampel Wangchug *(byams pa 'jams dpal dbang phyug)* from Khenpo Jampel Tashi in Sakya Monastery. Khamtra Rinpoche gave him the name Dela Longchen Yeshe Dorje *(bde la klong chen ye shes rdo rje)*, and in his monastery near Ngamring he was known as Lozang Dorje *(blo bzang rdo rje)*. He became expert in the *Kalachakra Tantra* and many high lamas requested teachings from him, but he always remained extremely humble. When his gompa in Chubarma burned down, he moved to the Terphug Chökor Yangtse *(gter phug chos 'khor yangs rtse)* Hermitage above Pangboche, where he spent his last twenty-five years until his death in 1989.

286. *Theg pa chen po'i blo sbyong khrid yig bdud rtsi snying po,* also known as *Blo sbyong chen mo,* is a commentary in 416 pages related to the practice of thought transformation. Kachen Yeshe Gyaltsen was the tutor of the Eighth Dalai Lama Jampel Gyatso *('jam dpal rgya mtsho,* 1758–1804).

287. Known as the Khadgayogini or Ugra Tara shrine, the Gum Baha, or Padmagiri Dharmadhatu Mahavihara, above Sankhu is one of the oldest Buddhist sites of the Kathmandu Valley. The *Gopalarajavamsavali* mentions that King Manadeva (5th century) retired to Gum Baha to perform religious practices and that due to the power of his practice, a small stupa arose spontaneously next to the Vajra-yogini shrine. Padmasambhava also meditated at Sankhu, where he met his consort Shakyadevi and concealed some termas. The present temple was built by King Pratap Malla in the seventeenth century. Cf. Dowman (1981) and Locke (1985).

288. Sir Edmund Hillary built a hospital in Khumde in 1966, where two New Zealand or Canadian doctors take care of patients. They started to give iodine to the Sherpas, and now there are fewer people with thyroid deficiency, which causes goiter and cretinism. They also introduced eye surgery and contraceptives. Sir Hillary created the Himalayan Trust to help the Sherpas with different projects and is extremely loved and respected by the locals. Cf. Fisher (1990) and Hillary (2000).

289. Au Palden was the grandson of a nomad from Purang *(pu rangs)* who settled in Namche. One of his cousins from Darjeeling wanted to build a large prayer wheel next to the gompa at Namche, so Au Palden built it for him. He worked as the Namche postmaster for a while. He used to name children, perform rituals, and read scriptures, and became known as Chenrezig Palden and a kind of legendary personality in Namche. Au Palden died in 2000 at the age of ninety-six.

290. Two sons of Migmar Gyaltsen from Kyisa *(skyid sa)* (Thubten Ngodrub and Dawa Tenpa), three sons of Lama Lhagpa Dorje from Thangteng (Ngawang Norbu, Norbu Lamzang, and Thubten Geleg), the son of Migmar (Murmin Tso clan) of

Thangme (Thubten Samphel), the son of Nyima Rithar of Tramo (Tsultrim Norbu), the son of Nyima Chötar of Kyongma (Lhagpa Gyalo or Thubten Tenzin), Summi's son Thubten Dorje, Ang Chöti's sons Ngawang Namgyal and Thubten Palden, four sons of Pemba Gyaltsen from Dunde in Pharag, Tragtho Ngawang Khenzin, the son of Kami Tenpa of Mende, and Thubten Monlam (Dzarog) were among the first to join the Lawudo school.

291. The Chinese allowed only the salt trade to continue, but they controlled everything and paid very low prices. According to Lhagpa Dorje, a Khampa trader from Namche, in about 1964 the Chinese confiscated the houses of the Khumbu traders in Dingri and Kyatrag, and told them that the land belonged to the Chinese but that the Sherpas could take the stones and the wood. The Chinese offered to buy their houses, but if a house were worth 10,000 rupees, the Chinese would give only 2,000. The Sherpas demanded full payment, and when the Chinese refused, they did not accept any money at all. The Sherpas continued to trade in Tibet for another six to ten years. At the beginning, the Chinese would give them a large amount of money to buy goods in Nepal and India and bring them to Tibet, but afterward they paid them very badly, alleging that the goods were very damaged or were of poor quality. The Chinese allowed neither bargaining nor the barter system, and changed the basis of trade from volume to weight. The economy of Khumbu was severely affected by these changes. Lhagpa Dorje, his father Dawa Tsering, and his grandfather Yulha Gyaltsen were very wealthy traders who had a large house in Dingri Gangar and a warehouse in Kyatrag. Dawa Tsering and Yulha Gyaltsen were benefactors of the Lawudo Lama Kunzang Yeshe. Cf. also Fürer-Haimendorf (1984) and Fisher (1990).

292. The Khari Lama Lozang Tsultrim (*blo bzang tshul khrims*, 1890–1970) was born in Phadrug *(pha drug)* in Latö. When he was about twenty years old, he received the empowerment, oral transmission, and commentaries of Guhyasamaja, Yamantaka, and Chakrasamvara from Lingka Kangyur Rinpoche Ngawang Lozang Tsultrim Gyaltsen *(gling ka bka' 'gyur rin po che ngag dbang blo bzang tshul khrims rgyal mtshan)*. At the same time he studied philosophical, lamrim, and thought training texts. After working for one year in Sera Monastery, he returned to Shelkar and went into retreat in a hermitage above the monastery. Following the advice of the Fourth Tsibri Chuzang Rinpoche Lozang Sangye Tenpe Dronme (*blo bzang sangs rgyas bstan pa'i sgron me*, 1892–1956), he went to meditate at Lapchi in one of Milarepa's caves and did a three-year retreat on Yamantaka. He also took teachings from Zalung Kunzang Chöje of the Zagalung Hermitage at Rongshar and from Dzatul Ngawang Tenzin Norbu. In 1940, when he was about fifty years old, he was requested by the villagers to rebuild the Khari *(mkha' ri)* Gompa above Drongkha *(grong kha)* in Phadrug. In 1959 there were 115 nuns and 25 monks in his monastery.

293. One of the monks who escaped with the Khari Lama was the unofficial tulku of Lingka Rinpoche. After meditating in the Golchag cave above Thangteng and in

Pharag, he spent many years meditating in the mountains above Dharamsala and became well known as Gen Lamrimpa (d. 2003).

294. The *Great Gradual Path to Enlightenment (Lam rim chen mo)*, is the most important work of Tsongkhapa. It contains a detailed explanation of the stages of the path to enlightenment.

295. Ngawang Tsedrub Tenpe Gyaltsen *(ngag dbang tshe grub bstan pa'i rgyal mtshan)* was born in Rolwaling on the twenty-second day of the ninth Tibetan month of the bird year (1957) as the son of Ngawang Yonten (Lhugpa clan) and Ang Chökyi. At six, he was recognized by Trulzhig Rinpoche as the tulku of Lama Dondrub and enthroned in Thangme. He spent eighteen years with Trulzhig Rinpoche and received the transmission of the Charog lamas' lineage from Kusho Mangde in Toloka. In 1989 he gave up his monastic vows and married a daughter of Lama Tenzin of Kyabrog. He now has three daughters and one son, and continues as the head of Thangme Gompa. The wife of Lama Dondrub has also reincarnated as a boy in Thangme.

296. *The Good Nectar Vase: A Commentary to the Thirty-Seven Practices of the Buddhas' Children Uniting the Scriptural and Oral Instructions (Rgyal sras lag len so bdun ma'i 'grel ba gzhung dang gdams ngag zung 'jug bdud rtsi'i bum bzang).*

297. There are many stories about water flowing from very blessed statues. I have witnessed water flowing from a self-created image of Tara in Pharping while a Tibetan lady disciple of Lama Zopa was praying in front of it.

298. "This perfection of wisdom makes the spot of earth where it is into a true shrine for beings—worthy of being worshipped and adored—into a shelter for beings who come to it, a refuge, a place of rest and final relief." Conze (1973, pp. 104–5).

299. *Byang chub lam kyi rim pa la blo sbyong ba la thog mar blo sbyong chos kyi sgo 'byed*, written by Chengawa Lodro Gyaltsen *(spyan snga ba blo gros rgyal mtshan, 1402–72)*, a disciple of Tsongkhapa and author of many teachings on thought training. Lama Zopa gave teachings on that text in 1990, that were later published by Wisdom Publications as *The Door to Satisfaction*.

300. For the benefits of constructing and turning prayer wheels, cf. Lama Zopa in *Mandala*, July/August 1995, and Ladner (2000).

301. Gen Lama Tenzin Tsultrim was born in Gyamo Tsawarong in Kham. He studied in Ngor Monastery in Tsang with Dampa Rinpoche and became expert in all the Sakya rituals. He stayed one year at Tramo as the head lama. Cf. *Ngor bla ma bstan 'dzin tshul khrims kyi rnam par thar pa dad gsum gsol 'debs*, written by Geshe Oti Vajra (Pangboche Geshe Urgyen Dorje).

302. The "Equilibrium Meditation" consists of visualizing in front of us a helping friend, a disturbing enemy, and a stranger. Then, we reflect on the fact that the labels "friend," "enemy," and "stranger" are caused by our own greed, hatred, and ignorance and that there is no valid reason for being attached to one's friends, hating one's enemies, or feeling indifferent toward strangers.

303. *The Sixty-Four Offerings to Kalarupa*. Kalarupa *(las kyi gshin rje)* is one of the main protectors of the Gelug tradition.

304. The story about the White Cliff and so forth was told to me recently by Sonam Puntsog and Ngawang Sherab, the nephews of Gelong Pasang. During my stays in Lawudo I had heard the rumors about termas, but no one could (or wanted) to tell me the full story.

305. Gomchen Gampa-la Ngawang Norbu was born in Gampa Dzong (gam pa rdzong), near Sakya. In his youth he studied medicine, married, and had a son. He used to drink much chang and engage in fights, and one day he killed his wife by making a mistake in the medicines (or while he was drunk, no one really knows). To purify his karma he became a monk in Rongphu and burnt his ring finger as a light offering. After studying the Dharma with Dragtho Rinpoche, he gave up all his possessions and went to practice chöd at the cemeteries around Tsibri. Later he went to Gyachu in Phadrug and built many bridges over the Dzakar River. He used to say that he was an emanation of Thangtong Gyalpo, who had dedicated his life to building bridges all over Tibet. After escaping to Khumbu, he meditated in Tandar, Phortse, Pangboche, Genupa, Lawudo, and the Akar Hermitage. He gave long-life empowerments and taught the practice of the Great Compassionate One. He had achieved control over the channels and energies of his body and, even though he was old and quite bulky, was able to walk extremely fast.

306. It seems that one night there was a very heavy storm and the stupa was hit by lightning. In the morning, smoke could be seen coming from the top of the stupa. Many people came from Kathmandu to help, but it took about nine hours to extinguish the fire. The wooden structure at the top was completely burned. When people climbed to the top to inspect the damage, they discovered that the wooden axis of the stupa, the srog shing or life tree, was rotten and eaten by insects, so they changed its upper part. On the uppermost part they found nine copper chests filled with gold, silver, precious stones, texts, statues, and a pot with water. After the renovation they installed twenty-one steel chests filled with precious objects, including the original nine copper chests. A few years later the top of the stupa fell down and the supporting bamboo frame was replaced by iron bars. In the year of the pig 1971–72, many great lamas, such as His Holiness Karmapa, Dilgo Khyentse Rinpoche, Trulzhig Rinpoche, and many others, performed the re-consecration. Oral communication from Lama Gyani Bazra.

307. Serkong Rinpoche Ngawang Lozang Thubten Tobjor (ngag dbang blo bzang thub bstan stobs 'byor, 1914–83) was born in southern Tibet. He began to give teachings to the Ganden monks when he was still a baby in his mother's lap. Later, he joined Ganden Jangtse Monastery and studied with masters from all the four traditions. In 1948 he was appointed as debate partner to His Holiness the Dalai Lama. In India, Serkong Rinpoche settled in Dharamsala and traveled extensively in Nepal and Spiti in Himachal Pradesh. He visited the West twice. He passed away in Kyipar in Spiti and was reborn in 1984 in a nearby village. His tulku, Tenzin

Thubten Ngawang Lozang *(bstan 'dzin thub bstan ngag dbang blo bzang)*, is now studying in Ganden Monastery in South India. Cf. *Wisdom* magazine (1984) and www.berzinarchives.com.

308. Milarepa's Stomach Cave *(grod pa phug)* is situated about ten kilometers from Nyanang. In the seventeenth century the lama of Drakar Taso, Ngogton Karma Lozang *(rngog ston karma blo bzang)*, established a Kagyu monastery next to the cave. A few years later, the Kagyu practitioners were expelled and the monastery was transformed into the Gelug Ganden Pelgyeling *(dga' ldan 'phel rgyas gling)* Monastery. Cf. Huber (1997, p. 272).

309. The first Dodrubchen Jigme Trinle Özer *(rdo grub chen 'jigs med phrin las 'od zer*, 1745–1821) was a disciple of Jigme Lingpa. His mind treasures, including the practice of Milarepa, are collected under the title *The Excellent Path of Supreme Joy, the Holy Teachings (Dam chos bde chen lam mchog)*. Cf. Thondup (1999).

310. *Datura solanacea* is an aphrodisiac also known as Jimson weed.

311. The eight worldly concerns are desiring the pleasures of the six senses and to be free from the unpleasant; wishing to hear sweet words and not to hear unpleasant words or sounds; craving to acquire material things and to avoid losing or not obtaining material things; craving for personal praise and to avoid slander and criticism.

312. The Second Khari Lama Tenzin Özer *(bstan 'dzin 'od zer*, 1970–76) was born at Tramo. Lama Zopa advised the parents to bring the boy to Kopan, but they preferred to take him to Pelgyeling Gompa. The boy died a few months later, in September 1976. The Third Khari Rinpoche Tenzin Yonten *(bstan 'dzin yon tan)* was born in Dzampu *(rdza phu)* in Phadrug around 1980 and recognized by His Holiness the Dalai Lama in 1986. He is now studying in Sera Me Monastery in South India.

313. Tenzin Norbu (Chuserwa clan) later disrobed and now lives in Switzerland. Tenzin Dorje (Lhabushingtog clan) worked for a while in Tushita Retreat Center in Dharamsala. He also disrobed and now lives in Münich, Germany. Geleg Gyatso (Lama Serwa clan) was born in Paphlu in 1962. He was recognized as the tulku of Togden Ngawang Tsultrim *(rtogs ldan ngag dbang tshul khrims)*, a monk who used to play the part of the togden during the Mani Rimdu festival and had been involved in the founding of Shedrub Tharling Monastery *(bshad sgrub thar gling)* at Tragshingto *(brag shing thog)*, about five hours' walk east of Junbesi.(Cf. Mülich, 1996). The boy had been enthroned at Tragshingto, but his father did not want him to become a monk and sent him to a school instead. In 1972, after his father died in a mountaineering expedition in Manaslu, his mother took him to Kopan. Known in the monastery as Lama Babu, Geleg Gyatso has done outstanding work for Kopan Gompa.

314. A French boy called Edouard has been recognized by His Holiness Sakya Trizin as the reincarnation of Zina. Zina's children Rhea and Alex live in the U.S.

315. Susan Lee (Jampa Chözom) from England and Helly Pelaez (Jampa Chökyi or

Jamyang Wangmo) from Spain were ordained in May 1973. Nick Ribush (Thubten Donyo) and Marie Obst (Yeshe Khadro) from Australia, Marcel Bertels (Thubten Palgye, Holland), Gareth Sparham (Thubten Thardo) and Nicole Lajeunesse (Thubten Chödron) from Canada, Feather Meston (Thubten Wangmo), Spring Livingstone (Thubten Chökyi), Jim Dougherty (Thubten Pende), Linda Grossman (Thubten Pemo), and Ursula Bernis (Thubten Chösang) from the U.S., were ordained in Bodh Gaya with Amala. Piero Cerri (Thubten Donyo), Claudio Cipullo (Jampa Thogme), and Luca Corona from Italy, Steve Malasky (Thubten Samten, U.S.), Peter Kedge (England), and others were ordained shortly after.

316. The text is probably the *Bshes gnyen dam pa tshul bzhin bsten tshul bsdus don skal bzang snying gi bdud rtsi,* 14 folios, in vol. 2 of the *Collected Works* of Ngawang Tenzin Norbu. Lama Zopa translated and taught part of this text in Dharamsala in 1990.

317. Geshe Urgyen Dorje, or Oti Vajra, began his studies at Kochag Drogon Labrang with the Drogonpa Lama Tenzin Dorje. Afterward, he studied in Kham in a Sakya monastery and received teachings from masters of all the traditions. After leaving Tibet, he received teachings from Trulzhig Rinpoche and other great lamas.

318. *Request to the Sublime Great Compassionate One ('Phags pa thugs rje chen po'i gsol 'debs),* composed by Dzatul Ngawang Tenzin Norbu when he was fifteen years old. Cf. Seventh Dalai Lama (1995, pp. 48–51). It was translated with the help of a Tibetan (Lozang Gyaltsen) and Nick Ribush.

319. *Thugs rje chen po'i sgrub thabs kyi don rnam par bshad pa bya ba'i rgyud kyi don gsal mkhas pa'i dga' ston,* a text of 338 pages contained in volume *nya* of Yeshe Gyaltsen's *Collected Works.*

320. The *Yi dam rgya mtsho'i sgrub thabs rin chen 'byung gnas,* compiled by Jetsun Taranatha Kunga Nyingpo, is a collection of empowerments of 305 deities. For an abbreviated translation of *The Precious Source,* see Jampa Chökyi (1985).

321. Zong Rinpoche Lozang Tsondru Thubten Gyaltsen (*blo bzang brtson 'grus thub bstan rgyal mtshan,* 1905–84) was born in Kham and studied in Ganden Monastery and the Upper Tantric College. After escaping to India in 1959, Rinpoche spent a few years at Buxa until His Holiness the Dalai Lama appointed him principal at the Central Institute of Higher Tibetan Studies in Sarnath. Later, he moved to the new Ganden Monastery in South India and traveled to the West on a few occasions. Cf. Zasep (1984).

322. The last talk of Lama Yeshe, called *Bodhicitta: The Perfection of Dharma,* was published in *Wisdom,* n. 2, 1984, and *Mandala,* July/August 1996. It is available at www.lamayeshe.com.

323. For Lama Zopa's comments on Lama Yeshe, see also *Wisdom,* n. 2, 1984.

324. His Holiness the present Sakya Trizin, Ngawang Kunga Thegchen Palbar Trinle Samphel Wangi Gyalpo *(ngag dbang kun dga' theg chen dpal 'bar 'phrin las bsam 'phel dbang gi rgyal po),* was born in the Drolma Phodrang in Sakya on September 7, 1945. After leaving Tibet, he established the Sakya College in Rajpur near

Dehradun as the main seat of the Sakya tradition in exile. His Holiness has two sons and a large number of Western disciples.

325. Kirti Tsenshab Rinpoche Lozang Jigme Damchö *(blo bzang 'jigs med dam chos)* was born in 1926 in Amdo and was recognized as the reincarnation of the abbot of Kirti Gompa. He studied in Kirti Gompa and left Tibet at the end of 1959. After some time in Buxa, he became a teacher at the Tibetan Children's Village in Dharamsala. In 1970 he left the school and spent the next thirteen years in the mountains above McLeod Ganj. Afterward he moved to a small house next to the residence of Ling Rinpoche. In 1989 he moved to the new Kirti Monastery in Dharamsala and has been teaching Tibetans and Westerners in India and abroad. Rinpoche is an expert, realized practitioner of the *Kalachakra Tantra.*

326. For details about Lama Ösel, see Mackenzie (1995).

327. In spite of many difficulties, Ngawang Chöphel built the Chime Tagten Chöling *('chi med rtag brtan cho gling)* Monastery at the request of Trulzhig Rinpoche, Dilgo Khyentse Rinpoche, and Dudjom Rinpoche. For information on the *tagdrol,* cf. Tenzin Gyatso (2000, p. 231, n. 17)

328. Lama Zopa visited the birthplace and family of Lama Yeshe in Tölung Shinga Khang, where he gave teachings and a Chenrezig empowerment. He spent two weeks in Amdo and visited the Lhamo Latso, Samye, Drag Yerpa, Nenang, and other interesting places.

329. *Byang sham bha lar skye ba'i smon lam,* composed by Panchen Lozang Palden Yeshe *(blo bzang dpal ldan ye shes,* 1737–80).

330. The Spring of Enlightenment *(byang chub chu mig)* is situated near Daman, about seventy kilometers south of Kathmandu.

331. From a speech by His Holiness the Dalai Lama at the fourth general body meeting of the Tibetan Women's Association, April 1, 1994.

332. For the activities of Lama Zopa Rinpoche and the Foundation for the Preservation of the Mahayana Tradition (FPMT), see www.fpmt.org. Lama Zopa's educational activities include the Universal Education program of studies based on teaching loving-kindness as the essence of all religious traditions. Rinpoche is also very keen on having large statues, thangkas, and stupas in all his centers all over the world. His social projects include the running of schools for poor children, hospices for the terminally ill, a leprosy project, soup kitchens, clinics, and so forth.

333. Cf. Tenzin Zangbu (2000) and Ortner (1999).

334. For the present situation of Khumbu and the impact of tourism and development in Sherpa society, see Fisher (1990), Stevens (1996), Ortner (1999), and Luger (2000).

335. Cf. Rachbauer, D. (editor), 2001.

336. This section is based on the JT, f.13bff. See also Ngawang Özer (2002).

337. Cf. Shakabpa (1984) and Tarthang Tulku (1986).

338. Cf. DTH, ff.6b–44b.

# Bibliography

## Western-Language Works

Acharya, Jayaraj, trans. *The Nepala-mahatmya of the Skandapurana: Legends on the Sacred Places and Deities of Nepal.* Jaipur: Nirala Publications, 1992.

Allen, Charles. *The Buddha and the Sahibs.* London: John Murray, 2002.

Aris, Michael. *Hidden Treasures and Secret Lives.* Shimla: Indian Institute of Advanced Study, 1988.

Aufschnaiter, Peter. "Lands and Places of Milarepa." *East and West* (new series), 26, pt. 1–2 (1976): 175–90.

Aziz, Barbara Nimri. *Tibetan Frontier Families.* Delhi: Vikas Publishing House, 1978.

____. "The Work of Pha-dam-pa Sangs-rGyas as Revealed in Ding-ri Folklore." In *Tibetan Studies in Honor of Hugh Richardson.* Ed. by M. Aris and Aung San Suu Kyi, pp. 21–27. Delhi: Vikas Publishing House, 1980.

Bell, Sir Charles. *Portrait of a Dalai Lama.* London: Wisdom Publications, 1987 (1946).

Bernbaum, Edwin. *The Way to Shambhala.* Boulder and London: Shambhala, 2001 (1981).

Blondeau, Anne Marie. "Analysis of the Biographies of Padmasambhava according to Tibetan Tradition: Classification of Sources." In *Tibetan Studies in Honor of Hugh Richardson.* Ed. by M. Aris and Aung San Suu Kyi. Delhi: Vikas Publishing House, 1980.

____. "Bya-rung kha-shor, legende fondatrice du Bouddhisme Tibetain." In *Tibetan Studies.* Ed. by Per Kvaerne, vol. 1, pp. 31–48. Oslo: Institute for Comparative Research in Human Culture, 1994.

Bourdillon, Jennifer. *Visit to the Sherpas.* London: Collins, 1956.

Brower, Barbara. *Sherpa of Khumbu.* Delhi: Oxford India Paperbacks, 1991.

Buffetrille, Katia. "Les grottes de Halase-Maratika (Nepal oriental): un lieu saint pour les hindouistes at les bouddhistes." Institut Francais de Pondicherry, 1994a.

_____. "Revitalisation d'un lieu saint bouddhique: Les grottes de Halashe-Maratika, Nepal Oriental (district de Khotang)." In *Tibetan Studies: Proceedings of the Sixth Seminar of the International Association for Tibetan Studies, Fagernes 1992*. Oslo: Institute for Comparative Research in Human Culture, 1994.

Bruce, C. G. *The Assault on Mount Everest.* London: Edward Arnold & Co., 1923.

Chan, Victor. *Tibet Handbook.* Chico, Calif.: Moon Publications, 1994.

Chang, Garma C. C. *The Hundred Thousand Songs of Milarepa.* Boulder and London: Shambhala, 1977.

Chemjong, Iman Singh. *History and Culture of the Kirat People,* Part I. Phedim, 1966.

_____. *History and Culture of the Kirat People,* Part II. Kathmandu, 1967.

Chökyi, Jampa. *The Precious Source of Attainment of the Ocean of Mind-Bound Deities.* Kathmandu: Enlightened Experience Celebration II, 1985.

Coleman, Loren. *Tom Slick and the Search for the Yeti.* Boston and London: Faber and Faber, 1989.

Colony, Merry, and Teresa Bianca. "A Kalachakra Master: Bringing Internal and External Harmony." *Mandala* (September/December 1998): 60ff.

Conze, Edward. *The Perfection of Wisdom in Eight Thousand Lines and Its Verse Summary.* Bolinas, Calif.: Four Seasons Foundation, 1973.

_____. *Buddhist Wisdom Books. The Diamond and the Heart Sutra.* London: Unwin Paperbacks, 1988 (1958).

Cooke de Herrera, Nancy. *Beyond Gurus.* New Delhi: Rupa, 1992.

Crook, John, and James Low. *The Yogins of Ladakh.* Delhi: Motilal Banarsidas, 1997.

Dargyay, Eva M. *The Rise of Esoteric Buddhism in Tibet.* Delhi: Motilal Banarsidas, 1979.

Dawa Samdup, Kazi. *Tibet's Great Yogi Milarepa.* London: Oxford University Press, 1928.

Decleer, Hubert. *The Milarepa Caves of Nyishang and Bhaktapur, and other Himalayan Studies and Tales.* Unpublished collection of essays by students of the School for International Training, Kathmandu.

Diemberger, Hildegard. "Lovanga [Lo 'bang pa?] Lama and Lhaven [Lha Bon]: Historical Background, Syncretism and Social Relevance of Religious Traditions among the Khumbo (East Nepal)." In *Tibetan Studies: Proceedings of the Fifth Seminar of the International Association for Tibetan Studies, Narita, 1989*, vol. 2, pp. 421–31. Narita Japan: Naritan Shingshoji, 1992.

_____. "Gangla Tshechu, Beyul Khenbalung: Pilgrimage to Hidden Valleys, Sacred Mountains and Springs of Life Water in Southern Tibet and Eastern Nepal." In *Anthropology of Tibet and the Himalayas*. Ed. by C. Ramble and M. Brauen, pp. 60–72. Zürich: Ethnological Museum of the University of Zürich, 1993.

_____. "Beyul Khenbalung, the Hidden Valley of the Artemisia." In *Mandala and Landscape*. Ed. by A. W. Macdonald. Delhi: D. K. Printworld, 1997.

Diemberger, Hildegard and Hazod Guntram. "Machig Zhama's Recovery: Traces of Ancient History and Myth in the South Tibetan Landscape of Kharta and Phadrug." In *Sacred Spaces and Powerful Places in Tibetan Culture*. Ed. by Toni Huber, pp. 34–51. Dharamsala, India: Library of Tibetan Works and Archives, 1999.

Diemberger, Hildegard, P. Wangdu, M. Kornfeld, and C. Jahoda. *Feast of Miracles*. Italy: Porong Pema Chöding Editions, 1997.

Dowman, Keith. *The Legend of the Great Stupa*. Berkeley: Tibetan Nyingma Meditation Center, 1973.

_____. "A Buddhist Guide to the Power Places of the Kathmandu Valley." *Kailash* VIII, no. 3, pp. 204–87. Kathmandu: Ratna Pustak Bhandar, 1981.

_____. *The Flight of the Garuda*. Boston: Wisdom Publications, 1994.

_____. *The Great Stupa of Boudhanath*. New Delhi: Robin Books, 2002.

Dudjom Rinpoche, Jikdrel Yeshe Dorje. *The Nyingma School of Tibetan Buddhism: Its Fundamentals and History*, 2 vols. Trans. by Gyurme Dorje and Matthew Kapstein. Boston: Wisdom Publications, 1991.

Ehrhard, Franz-Karl. "The Stupa of Bodhnath: A Preliminary Analysis of the Written Sources." *Ancient Nepal Journal of the Department of Archaeology* (Kathmandu), 120 (October–November 1990): 1–9.

_____. *Views of the Bodhnath Stupa*. Kathmandu: Erhard, 1991.

_____. "Two Documents on Tibetan Ritual Literature and Spiritual Genealogy." *Journal of the Nepal Research Center* 9 (Kathmandu) (1993): 77–100.

_____. "A 'Hidden Land' in the Tibetan-Nepalese Borderlands." In *Mandala and Landscape*. Ed. by A. W. Macdonald, pp. 335–64 Delhi: D.K. Printworld, 1997.

_____. "Political and Ritual Aspects of the Search for Himalayan Sacred Lands." In *Sacred Spaces and Powerful Places in Tibetan Culture*. Ed. by T. Huber, pp. 240–57. Dharamsala, India: LTWA, 1999.

_____. "A Forgotten Incarnation Lineage: The Yol-mo-ba sPrul sKus (16th to 18th centuries)." In *The Pandita and the Siddha: Tibetan Studies in Honor of E. Gene Smith*, ed. by Ramon Prats (in press).

Fantin, Mario. *Sherpa Himalaya Nepal.* New Delhi: The English Bookstore, 1974.

____. *Mani Rimdu Nepal.* New Delhi: The English Bookstore, 1976.

Fillibeck, E. de Rossi. "Two Tibetan Guidebooks to Tise and Lapchi," *Monumenta Tibetica Historica,* Abteilung 1, Bund 4. Bonn: 1988.

Fisher, J. E. *Sherpas.* Delhi: Oxford University Press, 1990.

Freemantle, Francesca and Chögyam Trungpa. *The Tibetan Book of the Dead.* Berkeley: Shambhala, 1975.

Funke, F. W. *Religiöses Leben der sherpa, Khumbu himal.* Innsbruck: Universitätsverlag Wagner, 1982.

Fürer-Haimendorf, Christoph von. *The Sherpas of Nepal.* London: John Murray, 1964.

____. *Himalayan Traders.* New York: St. Martin's Press, 1975.

____. *The Sherpas Transformed.* Delhi: Sterling, 1984.

Govinda, Anagarika. *The Way of the White Clouds.* Delhi: B. I. Publications, 1977 (1960).

Guenther, Herbert V. *Kindly Bent to Ease Us: Part Two, Meditation.* Emeryville, Calif.: Dharma Publishing, 1976.

Gyatso, Janet. "The Teachings of Thang-sTong rGyal-po." In *Tibetan Studies in Honor of Hugh Richardson.* Ed. by M. Aris and Ang Sang Suu Kyi. Delhi: Vikas Publishing House, 1980.

____. *Apparitions of the Self.* Princeton, N.J.: Princeton University Press, 1998.

Harris, Bridget. "Lama Zopa's English Mother Dies." *Mandala* (May/June 1995): 29.

Hillary, Sir Edmund. *View from the Summit.* London: Corgi Books, 2000.

Howard-Bury, C. K. *Mount Everest, the Reconnaissance, 1921.* New Delhi: SBW Publishers, 1991 (1922).

Huber, Toni. "A Guide to the La-Phyi Mandala." In *Mandala and Landscape.* Ed. by A. W. Macdonald. Delhi: D.K. Printworld, 1997.

Hutchison, Robert A. *In the Tracks of the Yeti.* London: Macdonald & Co., 1989.

Jefferies, Margaret. *Sagarmatha, Mother of the Universe.* Seattle: The Mountaineers, 1991.

Jerstad, Luther G. *Mani Rimdu, Sherpa Dance-Drama.* Calcutta: Oxford and IBH, 1969.

sKal ldan rgya mtsho, ngag dbang. *Shel dkar chos 'byung. History of the "White Crystal."* Transl. by Wangdu, Pasang, and Hildegard Diemberger. Wien: Verlag der Österreichischen Akademie der Wissenschaften, 1996.

Kapstein, Matthew. *The Tibetan Assimilation of Buddhism*. New York: Oxford University Press, 2000.

Karma Wangchug Sherpa, Lopon. *The Guide to Maratika*. Kathmandu: Lopon Karma Wangchug Sherpa, 2000.

Karmay, Samten G. "The Wind Horse and the Well-Being of Man." In *Anthropology of Tibet and the Himalayas*. Ed. by C. Ramble and M. Brauen, pp. 150ff. Zurich: Ethnological Museum of the University of Zürich, 1993.

Khunu Rinpoche. *Vast as the Heavens, Deep as the Sea*. Trans. by Gareth Sparham. Boston: Wisdom Publications, 1999.

Khyentse Rinpoche, Dilgo. *The Wish-Fulfilling Jewel*. Kathmandu and Delhi: Shechen Publications, 1995; Boston: Shambhala, 1988.

_____. *The Heart Treasure of the Enlightened Ones*. Boston and London: Shambhala, 1992.

Knight, G. E. O. *Intimate Glimpses of Mysterious Tibet and Neighbouring Countries*. Delhi: Asian Educational Services, 1992 (1930).

Kohn, Richard J. *Lord of the Dance*. Albany, N.Y.: State University of New York Press, 2001.

Ladner, Lorne. *Wheel of Great Compassion*. Boston: Wisdom Publications, 2000.

Lang-Simons, Lois. *The Presence of Tibet*. London: The Cresset Press, 1963.

Lati Rinbochay and Jeffrey Hopkins. *Death, Intermediate State and Rebirth in Tibetan Buddhism*. London: Rider, 1979.

Lhakpa Norbu Sherpa. *Human Impacts on High-Altitude Forest Structures in the Nangpa and Hinku, Sagarmatha and Makalu-Barun National Park, Nepal*. Doctoral thesis, University of Washington, Seattle, 1999.

Lhalungpa, Losang P. *The Life of Milarepa*. London: Granada Publishing, 1979.

Locke, John K. *Buddhist Monasteries of Nepal*. Kathmandu: Sahayogi Press, 1985.

Lodro Thaye, Jamgon Kongtrul. *Enthronement*. Trans. and intro. by Ngawang Zangpo. Ithaca, N.Y.: Snow Lion, 1997.

Luger, Kurt. *Kids of Khumbu*. Kathmandu: Mandala Book Point, 2000.

Macdonald, A. W. "Points of View of Halashe, a Holy Place in East Nepal." *Tibet Journal* 10, no. 3 (1985): 3–13.

_____. "The Lama and the General." In *Essays on the Ethnology of Nepal and South Asia*, vol. 2, pp. 1–10. Kathmandu: Ratna Pustak Bhandar, 1987.

_____. "The Writing of Buddhist History in the Sherpa Area of Nepal." In *Essays on the Ethnology of Nepal and South Asia,* vol. 2, pp. 54–66. Kathmandu: Ratna Pustak Bhandar, 1987.

_____. "The Coming of Buddhism to the Sherpa Area of Nepal." In *Essays on the Ethnology of Nepal and South Asia,* vol. 2, pp. 67–74. Kathmandu: Ratna Pustak Bhandar, 1987.

Mackenzie, Vicki. *Reincarnation: The Boy Lama.* Boston: Wisdom Publications, 1995 (1988).

Maraini, Fosco. *Secret Tibet.* Delhi: Book Faith India, 1993.

Markham, Clements R. *Narratives of the Mission of George Bogle to Tibet and of the Journey of Thomas Manning to Lhasa.* Kathmandu: Tiwari's Pilgrims Book House, 1989 (1876).

Messner, Reinhold. *My Quest for the Yeti.* London: Macmillan, 2000.

Mingma Norbu Sherpa. *Visitors' Guide to the Birds and Animals of Sagarmatha National Park.* Nepal, 1986.

Nebesky-Wojkowitz, Rene de. *Oracles and Demons of Tibet.* Kathmandu: Book Faith India, 1996 (1975).

Negi, G. C. *A Page in the Life of a Great Buddhist Savant.* Kinnaur.

Ngag dbang bstan 'dzin 'jigs bral. *Birth Series History of Dzatul Rinpoche: A Lineage of Devotional Luminaries.* Trans. of *Rdza sprul ngag dbang bstan 'dzin 'jigs bral gyi skyes rabs rag bdus dad pa'i snang 'byed.* Published by Dzatul Rinpoche, Pharping, Nepal.

Noël, Captain J. B. L. *Through Tibet to Everest.* London: Hodder and Stoughton, 1989 (1927).

Norbu, Namkhai. *Drung, Deu and Bon.* Dharamsala: LTWA, 1995.

sNying po, Nam mkha'i. *Mother of Knowledge: The Enlightenment of Ye-shes mTshorgyal.* Oral translation by Tarthang Tulku. Berkeley: Dharma Publishing, 1983.

Oppitz, M. "Myths and Facts: Reconsidering Some Data Concerning the Clan History of the Sherpa." *Kailash* 2, nos. 1–2, pp. 128ff. Kathmandu: Ratna Pustak Bhandar, 1974.

Ortner, Sherry B. "Sherpa Purity." *American Anthropologist* 75, no. 1 (February 1973): 49–63.

_____. *High Religion.* Delhi: Motilal Banarsidas, 1989.

_____. *Patterns of History: Cultural Schemas in the Foundings of Sherpa Religious Institutions.* Palo Alto, Calif.: Stanford University Press, 1990.

_____. *Life and Death on Mt. Everest.* Delhi: Oxford University Press, 1999.

Pabongka Rinpoche. *Liberation in the Palm of Your Hand: A Concise Discourse on the Path to Enlightenment.* Trans. of *Rnam grol lag bcangs* by Michael Richards. Boston: Wisdom Publications, 1997.

Pemba, Tsewang Yeshe. *Young Days in Tibet.* London: Jonathan Cape, 1957.

Petech, L. "China and Tibet in the Early XVIII Century." In *Monographies du T'oung Pao*, vol. 1. Leiden: E. J. Brill, 1972.

Pommaret, Francoise. *Bhutan.* Geneva: Editions Olizane S.A., 1991.

Rachbauer, Dieter, ed. *Energy from the Roof of the World.* Salzburg: Eco Himal, 2001.

Reinhard, Johan. "Khembalung: The Hidden Valley." *Kailash* 6, no. 1, 5–35. Kathmandu: Ratna Pustak Bhandar, 1978.

Reynolds, John M. *The Golden Letters.* Ithaca, N.Y.: Snow Lion, 1996.

Ricard, Matthieu. *The Life of Shabkar.* Kathmandu: Shechen Publications, 1994.

____. *Journy to Enlightenment.* New York: Apeture, 1996.

Rinpoche, Paltul. *The Words of My Perfect Teacher.* Trans. by Padmakara Translation Group. New Delhi: Harper Collins India, 1994.

Rispoli, Enrica, trans. *La biografia segreta del Sesto Dalai Lama (1683–1706[1746]).* Milano: Luni Editrice, 1999.

Roerich, George N. *The Blue Annals.* Delhi: Motilal Banarsidas, 1996 (1949).

Ruttledge, Hugh. *Everest, the Unfinished Adventure.* London: Hodder and Stoughton, 1937.

Sacherer, Janice. "The Sherpas of Rolwaling: A Hundred Years of Economic Change." In *Reserches sur l'ecology et la geologie de l'Himalaya Central*, pp. 289–93. Paris: Centre National de la Reserche Scientifique, 1977.

____. "Sherpas of the Rolwaling Valley: Human Adaptation to a Harsh Mountain Environment." *Objects et Mondes, La Revue du Musee de l'Homme*, tome XIV, fasc. 4 (hiver 1975) (Paris): 317–24.

Saetreng, Sigmund K. "Mother Earth's Treasures and Their Revealers." In *Biblioteca Himalayica*, series 3, vol. 8. Kathmandu: EMR Publishing House, 1995.

Seventh Dalai Lama, Losang Kälsang Gyatso. *Nyung nä: The Means of Achievement of the Eleven-Faced Great Compassionate One, Avalokiteshvara.* Comp. and trans. by Lama Thubten Zopa Rinpoche and George Churinoff. Boston: Wisdom Publications, 1995.

Sever, Adrian. *Nepal under the Ranas.* Delhi: Oxford and IBH, 1993.

Shah, Rishikesh. "Ancient and Medieval Nepal." *Kailash* 15, nos. 1–2 (1989).

Shakabpa, Tsepon W. D. *Tibet: A Political History.* New York: Potala Publications, 1984.

Shrestha, D. B., and C. B. Singh, *Ethnic Groups of Nepal and Their Ways of Living.* Kathmandu: Himalayan Book Sellers, 1987.

Simpson, William. *The Buddhist Prayer Wheel.* Lucknow: Oriental Reprinter, 1976.

Smith, Gene E. "Auto-Biographical Reminiscences of Ngag-dbang-dpal-bzang, Late Abbot of Katog Monastery." In *Ngagyur Nyingmay Sungrab.* Gangtok: Sonam T. Kazi, 1969.

_____. "'Jam mgon Kong sprul and the Nonsectarian Movement." In *Kongtrul's Encyclopaedia of Indo-Tibetan Culture,* pp. 1–87. New Delhi: International Academy of Indian Culture, 1970.

_____. Preface to *Rdzogs pa chen po dgons pa zan thal and Ka dag ran byun ran sar.* 5 vols. Smanrtsis shesrig spendzod, vols. 60–64. Leh: S.W. Tashigangpa, 1973.

_____. *Among Tibetan Texts.* Boston: Wisdom Publications, 2001.

Snellgrove, David L. *Buddhist Himalaya.* Oxford: Cassirer, 1957.

_____. *Himalayan Pilgrimage.* Boston: Shambhala, 1989.

bSod nams rgyal mtshan, Sa skya pa bla ma dam pa. *The Clear Mirror.* Translated by Taylor McComas and Lama Choedak Yuthok. Ithaca, N.Y.: Snow Lion, 1996.

Stevens, Stanley F. *Claiming the High Ground.* Delhi: Motilal Banarsidas, 1996 (1993).

Taring, Rinchen Dolma. *Daughter of Tibet.* Delhi: Rupa, 1986 (1970).

Tarthang Tulku. *Ancient Tibet.* Emeryville, Calif.: Dharma Publishing, 1986.

Tashi Tsering, Lopon. *Ngagyur Nyingmapas of Nepal.* Published by Lopon Tashi Tsering (Hom Bahadur Lama), Kathmandu, 1999.

Templeman, David. *The Seven Instruction Lineages.* Dharamsala: LTWA, 1983.

_____. *Taranatha's Life of Krsnacarya/Kanha.* Dharamsala: LTWA, 1989.

Tenzin Gyatso, the Fourteenth Dalai Lama. *Sleeping, Dreaming, and Dying.* Boston: Wisdom Publications, 1997.

_____. *Dzogchen.* Ithaca, N.Y.: Snow Lion, 2000.

Tenzin Zangbu, Ngawang, and Frances Klatzel. *Stories and Customs of the Sherpas.* Kathmandu: Mera Publications, 2000 (1985).

Thondup, Tulku. *Hidden Teachings of Tibet.* London: Wisdom Publications, 1986.

_____. *Buddha Mind.* Ithaca, N.Y.: Snow Lion, 1989.

_____. *Masters of Meditation and Miracles.* Boston and London: Shambhala, 1999.

Thubten Lama Sherpa. *The Sherpas and Sharkhumbu.* Kathmandu: Sherpa Art Center, 1999.

Thurman, Robert. *The Tibetan Book of the Dead.* NewYork: Bantam, 1993.

Tilman, H. W. *The Seven-Mountain Travel Books.* London: Diadem Books; Seattle: The Mountaineers, 1983.

Tiwari, Sudarshan Raj. *The Ancient Settlements of the Kathmandu Valley.* Kathmandu: Centre for Nepal and Asian Studies, Tribhuvan University, 2001.

Unsworth, Walt. *Everest.* Delhi: Harper Collins India, 1989.

Uprety, Prem R. *Nepal-Tibet Relations 1850–1930.* Kathmandu: Puga Nara, 1980.

Weir, Tom. *East of Kathmandu.* London: Oliver and Boyd, 1955.

Williamson, Margaret D. *Memoirs of a Political Officer's Wife in Tibet, Sikkim and Bhutan.* London: Wisdom Publications, 1987.

Woolf, Marsha, and Karen Blanc. *The Rainmaker.* Boston: Sigo Press, 1994.

Yeshe Gyaltsen, Tsechogling Yongdzin. *The Complete Ritual of the Fasting Retreat (smyung gnas).* Trans. by Gelongma Jampa Chökyi. Published by Michael Foo, Singapore, 1998.

Yeshe Tsogyal. *The Lotus Born.* Trans. by Erik Pema Kunzang. Boston: Sham-bhala, 1993.

Zasep Tulku and M. Willson. *Kyabje Song Rinpoche: A Biography.* London: Wisdom Publications, 1984.

Zopa Rinpoche, Lama Thubten. *Meditation Course Notes: 1972–1985.* Multiple volumes. Kathmandu: Kopan Monastery, 1972–85.

____. *Chenrezig Group Retreat.* Nepal: Lawudo Gompa, 1979.

____. *The Door to Satisfaction.* Boston: Wisdom Publications, 1994.

____. "The Power of Prayer Wheels." *Mandala* (July/August 1995).

____. *Teachings from the Vajrasattva Retreat.* Boston: Lama Yeshe Wisdom Archives, 2000.

## Nepali Works

Ngawang Özer Sherpa, Acharya. *Sherpako Itihas ra Samskriti.* Sunsari, Dharan: Yampu Sherpa Chichog, Nepal Sherpa Society, District Work Committee, 2002.

## Tibetan Works

Chatral Sangye Dorje (bya bral sangs rgyas rdo rje, b. 1913). *'Chi med tshe'i gnas mchog brag phug ma ra ti ka'i nges mdzod dbyangs can dgyes pa'i tambu ra.* Composed in the fire tiger year, 1986. Published by Lopon Karma Wangcchu Sherpa, Kathmandu, 2000.

Chödrag Zangpo (chos grags bzang po). *Kun mkhyen dri med 'od zer gyi rnam thar mthong ba don ldan.* Si khron mi rigs dpe skrun khang, 1993.

Chökyi Gyatso, Shar Kathog Situpa (chos kyi rgya mtsho, shar ka thog si tu pa, 1880–1925). *Rje btsun bla ma rdo rje 'chang chen po sha kya shri jnana'i rnam thar me tog phreng ba.* In the *Collected Works of Rig 'dzin Grub dban Sa kya sri (grub dbang shakya shri gyana'i gsung 'bum),* vol. *ka,* ff. 17–230. Published by Sherab Gyaltsen, Palace Monastery, Gangtok, Sikkim, 1980. Reprint by Khenpo Shedrub and Lama Trinley Namgyal, Kathmandu.

Dudul Dorje (bdud 'dul rdo rje, 1615–72). *Sbas yul padma bkod pa'i gnas yig.*

Jampa Jampel Wangchug, Diu Rinpoche (byams pa 'jams dpal dbang phyug, bde phug rin po che, 1904–89). *'Dren mchog ngag dbang nor bu bzang por rnam thar gsol 'debs dad gsum nor bu'i phreng ba.*

Jampel Lhundrub ('jam dpal lhun grub, dvags po rin po che). *Byang chub lam gyi rim pa'i dmar khrid myur lam gyi sngon 'gro'i ngag don gyi rim pa khyer bde bklag chog bskal bzang mgrin rgyan.* Shes rig dpar khang, Dharamsala.

Jamyang Chökyi Rigzin ('jam dbyangs chos kyi rig 'dzin, b. 1777?). *'Jams dbyangs chos kyi rig 'dzin nyams shar ngag gi glu chung gzhan phan snying gi bdud rtsi.* Reel L8127–L894/12, National Archives, Kathmandu.

Jigme Lingpa ('jigs med gling pa, 1729–98). *Klong chen snying thig las/ bka' srung sman btsun mched lnga'i 'phrin las dpag bsam yangs 'du.*

_____. *Yon tan rin po che'i mdzod.*

Jonang Jetsun Taranatha Kunga Nyingpo (jo nang rje btsun ta ra na tha kun dga' snying po, 1575–1635). *Yi dam rgya mtsho'i sgrub thabs rin chen 'byung gnas. A collection of sadhanas for invoking the various tutelary deities of Lamaism,* vol. 15 *(ba)* of his *Collected Works.* Reproduced from a print from the blocks preserved at Bkra-shis-lhun-grub Chos-grwa by Chophel Legdan, 2 vols. New Delhi, 1974.

Kagyu Tenzin Norbu (dkar brgyud bstan 'dzin nor bu, 1899–1959). *Gdan rabs lo rgyus drang srong dga' ba'i dal gtam gyi kha skong. Sman rtsis shes rig spe mdzod,* vol. 142. Published by D. L. Tashigang, B.P.O Nemo, Leh, Ladakh, 1996.

*Khu nu bla ma rin po che'i rnam par thar pa nyid kyi zhal gsungs ma.* Anonymous.

Kongtul Pema Garwang (kong sprul padma gar dbang, 1813–99). *Zab mo'i gter dang gter ston grub thob ji ltar byon pa'i lo rgyus mdor bsdud bkod pa rin chen bai du rya'i phreng.* In *rin chen gter mdzod,* vol. *ka.*

Kunzang Palden, Khenpo (kun bzang dpal ldan, mkhan po, 1870–1940). *O rgyan 'jigs med chos kyi dbang po'i rnam thar dad pa'i gsos sman bdud rtsi'i bum bcud.* In *Dpal sprul gsung 'bum,* vol. *kha,* pp. 353–481.

Lhatsun Gyurme Jigdral (lha btsun 'gyur med 'jigs bral). *Sbas yul 'bras mo ljongs kyi gnas yi phan yon dang bcas pa ngo mtshar gter mdzod.*

Lhatsun Ngawang Dorje (lha btsun ngag dbang rdo rje). *Tshangs dbyangs rgya mtsho'i gsang rnam.* Bod ljongs mi dmangs dpe skrun khang, 2000.

Lodro Chötar (blo gros chos dar, dngos grub khang gsar). *Dbul po'i nor rdzas sam phal pa'i mthong tshul: Dkhong.* New Delhi, 1996.

Longchen Rabjam (klong chen rab 'byams, 1308–63). *Tshig don rin po che'i mdzod.*

———. *Sems nyid ngal gso.* Vol. 1 of the *rdzogs pa chen po ngal gso skor gsum* trilogy. A reproduction of the A-'dzom xylographic edition published by Pema Thinley for the Ven. Dodrupchen Rinpoche, Gangtok, 1987.

———. *Bsam gtan ngal gso.* Vol. 2 of the *rdzogs pa chen po ngal gso skor gsum* trilogy. A reproduction of the A-'dzom xylographic edition published by Pema Thinley for the Ven. Dodrupchen Rinpoche, Gangtok, 1987.

Lopon Karma Wangchug Sherpa (slob dpon karma dbang phyug shar pa). *Ma ra ti ka'i gnas bshad.* Kathmandu, 2000.

Lozang Palden Tenzin Yargye (blo bzang dpal ldan bstan 'dzin yar rgyas, 1927–96). *Ngag dbang tshul khrims don ldan gyi rnam thar (Gsang chen rig pa 'dzin pa'i chos kyi 'khor los bsgyur ba 'jam mgon snyan brgyud kyi bstan pa'i bdag po dga' ldan gser skong rdo rje 'chang chen po ngag dbang tshul khrims don ldan dpal bzang po'i gsang ba gsum gyi rnam par thar pa thub bstan gser ldan mdzes pa'i nor bu'i dga' rtsal).* Composed in 1975. In vol. 4 of his *Gsung 'bum,* pp. 399–604.

Lozang Yeshe Tenzin Gyatso (blo bzang ye shes bstan 'dzin rgya mtsho, khri byang). *Skyabs rje khri byang rdo rje 'chang mchog gi mdzad rnam snying bsdud zur 'don.*

Nagarjuna (second century). *Bshes pa'i spring yig,* (Skt. *Suhrllekha*).

Namkhe Nyingpo (nam mkha'i snying po). *Bod kyi jo mo ye shes mtsho rgyal gyi mdzad tshul rnam par thar pa gab pa mngon byung rgyud mangs dri za'i glu phreng.* Printed at Zangs mdog dpal ri, ka sbug (Kalimpong).

Ngagchang Sakya Zangpo (ngags 'chang shakya bzang po, sixteenth century). *Mchod rten chen po bya rung kha shor gyi lo rgyus thos pas grol ba.*

Ngawang Chöphel Gyatso (ngag dbang chos 'phel rgya mtsho, 1922–97). *Brag phug ma ra ti ka'i bla ma ngag dbang chos 'phel rgya mtsho'i rnam thar mdor bsdud pa sgro skur bral ba'i bden gtam.* In *Ma ra ti ka'i gnas bshad.* Published by Karma Wangchhu Sherpa, Kathmandu, 2000.

_____. *Gnas chen brag phug ma ra ti ka 'am ha las bshad kyi gnas bshad mdor bsdus.* In *Ma ra ti ka'i gnas bshad.* Published by Karma Wangchhu Sherpa, Kathmandu, 2000.

_____. *'Dran mchog kun bzang ye shes kyi rnam thar thog mtha' bar gsum dad pa'i phreng ba.*

Ngawang Dongag Tenzin Norbu Chokyi Lodro (ngag dbang mdo sngags bstan 'dzin nor bu, chos kyi blo gros, 'khrul zhig rin po che, b. 1924). *Kho bo wagindra dharma mati'i skyes rabs dang rnam thar gsol 'debs su btags pa dad pa'i 'jug ngogs.*

Ngawang Norbu Zangpo, Chatang Chötar, Lama Gulo (ngag dbang nor bu bzang po, or bya btang chos dar, or bla ma dgu lo, 1850–1934). *Kho bo bya btang chos dar ram ngag dbang nor bu bzang por 'bod pas rang snang 'khrul pa tshul bzhin brjod pa mu ti ka'i phreng ba.* Written in the water monkey year, 1932, in Tengboche Monastery.

Ngawang Tenzin Norbu, Dzatul (ngag dbang bstan 'dzin nor bu, rdza sprul, 1867–1940). *Yang gsang bstan pa'i mdzod 'dzin 'khrul zhig gu yang he ru ka kun bzang mthong grol rdo rje'i rnam par thar pa ngo mtshar dad pa'i shing rta.* Incomplete text from private collection of Ani Ngawang Chönyi.

_____. *Gcod yul nyon mongs zhi byed kyi bka' gter bla ma brgyud pa'i rnam thar byin rlabs gter mtsho.*

_____. *Dus mthar chos smra ba'i btsun pa ngag dbang bstan 'dzin nor bu'i rnam thar 'chi med bdud rtsi'i rol mtsho,* DTH.

_____. *Bstan srungs bkra shis tshe ring ma'i cho ga yid bzhin 'dod 'jo.* Vol. *ja* of his *Collected Works.* Printed at rdza rong phu. From the private collection of Lama Zopa Rinpoche.

_____. *Shar khum bu rol ba gling gi 'dab 'brel gsang sngags theg mchog chos gling gi bca' yig kun gsal me long.* Filmed at Thangme from the private collection of Ngawang Lemon by the Nepal-German Manuscript Preservation Project. In the National Archives, Kathmandu, Microfilm Section, reel L3884/l318/3.

_____. *Bshes gnyen dam pa tshul bzhin bsten tshul bsdus don skal bzang snying gi bdud rtsi.*

_____. *Rong phu rdza yi gangs kyi gnas yig dad pa'i gdong ldan dga' skyed dbyar gyi rnga sgra.* Written in the water-male monkey year (1932) at mdo sngags zung 'jug chos gling.

_____. *Rgyal sras lag len so bdun ma'i 'grel ba gzung dang gdam ngag zung 'jug bdud rtsi'i bum bzang,* 118 pp. Published in Nepal, 1970. Private collection of Lama Zopa Rinpoche.

Nyang Nyima Özer (nyang nyi ma 'od zer, 1124–92). *Slob dpon padma'i rnam thar zangs gling ma.* Si khron mi rigs dpe skrun khang, 1987.

\_\_\_\_\_. *Dbu ma rtsa ba shes rab* (Skt. *Mulamadhyamakakarika*).

Oti Vajra (o rgyan rdo rje). *Ngor bla ma bstan 'dzin tshul khrims kyi rnam par thar pa dad gsum gsol 'debs.* Written in the water bird year, 1993, Khumde, Nepal.

Pema Lingpa (padma gling pa, 1450–1521). *Klong gsal gsang ba snying bcud las / sbas yul mkhan pa ljongs kyi gnas yig.*

\_\_\_\_\_. *Sbas yul 'bras mo gshongs dang mkhan pa lung kyi gnas yig.*

Phurchog Ngawang Jampa (phur lcog ngag dbang byams pa). *Grva sa chen po bzhi dang rgyud pa stod med chags tshul pad dkar 'phreng ba.* Bod ljongs mi dmangs dpe skrun khang, mtsho sngon, 1989.

Rigzin Ngodrub Gyaltsen Gokyi Demdruchen (rig 'dzin dngos grub rgyal mtshan rgod kyi ldem 'phru can, 1337–1409). *Ka dag rang byung rang shar kyi gsol 'debs.* Reel L8233–1904/13, National Archives, Kathmandu.

\_\_\_\_\_. *Bka' brgyad rang byung rang shar.*

\_\_\_\_\_. *'Gro ba kun grol bla rgyud.*

\_\_\_\_\_. *Sngon 'gro gzer lnga / bla rgyud gsol 'debs.*

\_\_\_\_\_. *Gcod gsang ba rmad 'byung.*

\_\_\_\_\_. *Thugs sgrub kyi bla ma'i rnal byor dang rgyud 'debs.*

\_\_\_\_\_. *Rdo rje nyi ma'i gnas yig gsang ba'i dkar chag : A pilgrims guide to the hidden land of Sikkim.* Tashigang, Bhutan. Sonam Tobgyal, 1983. Reproduced from a print carved by rig 'dzin rtogs ldan dpa' bo.

\_\_\_\_\_. *Phag mo'i zab khrid don gsal sgron ma.*

\_\_\_\_\_. *Sbas yul mkhan pa lung gi gnas yig mthong ba don ldan.* Published by J. Reinhard in *Kailash* 6, no. 1. Kathmandu: Ratna Pustak Bhandar, 1978.

\_\_\_\_\_. *Sbas yul mkhan pa lung gi nub sgo'i sde mig.* Published by J. Reinhard in *Kailash* 6, no. 1. Kathmandu: Ratna Pustak Bhandar, 1978.

\_\_\_\_\_. *Sbas yul bdun gyi thang gang bdun ma.* In *Ma 'ongs lung bstan gsol ba'i sgron me sman rtsis shes rig spe dzod,* vols. 33 & 34, Leh, 1973.

\_\_\_\_\_. *Sbas yul spyi'i them byang.* In the *Byang gter lugs kyi rnam thar dang ma 'ongs lung bstan.*

\_\_\_\_\_. *Rdzogs chen zang thal gyi snyan brgyud sde drug gi tho byang.*

\_\_\_\_\_. *Rig 'dzin gdung sgrub kyi 'phrin las bklags chog mthong ba don ldan du dkod pa.* Shes rig dpar khang, Dharamsala, 1992.

_____. *Lung bstan bskul byang chen mo.*

Sans rgyas bstan 'jin (Sangye Tenzin), Car-pa'i Bla-ma (1924–90) and A. W. Macdonald. *Shar pa'i chos byung sngon med tshangs pa'i dbyu gu.* In *Documents pour l'etude de la religion at de l'organisation des sherpas.* Junbesi/Paris-Nanterre, 1971.

_____. *'Jig rten chags tshad mdo tsam brjod pa'i sgo nas pha mes kyi byung rabs gsal dag khungs ldan rim par bkod pa.* In *Documents pour l'étude de la religion et de l'organisation des sherpas.* Junbesi/Paris-Nanterre, 1971.

Sonam Chödrub (bsod nam chos grub). *Kun mkhyen klong chen rab 'byams kyi rnam thar.* Si khron mi rigs dpe skrun khang, 1993.

Tenpe Dronme (bstan pa'i sgron me). *O rgyan smin grol gling gi dkar chag.* Krung go'i bod kyi shes rig dpe skrun khang, zi ling, 1992.

Tenzin Chökyi Lodro (bstan 'dzin chos kyi blo gros, 'bri gung, 1868–1906). *Gsang lam sgrub pa'i gnas chen nyer bzhi'i ya gyal gau da wa ri'am 'brog la phyi gangs kyi ra ba'i sngon byung gi tshul las brtsams pa'i gtam gyi rab tu byed pa nyung du rnam gsal.* Published by Sherab Gyaltsen, Palace Monastery, Gangtok, 1983.

Tenzin Gyaltsen (bstan 'dzin rgyal mtshan, sri negi bla ma, 1894–1977). *Byang chub sems kyi bstod pa rin chen sgron ma.* Negi, Hukan Sain, and Tsewang Norbu Vaid, 1986.

Tenzin Gyatso (bstan 'dzin rgya mtsho), the Fourteenth Dalai Lama. *'Jam mgon rgyal tshab yongs 'dzin gling sprul rdo rje 'chang thub bstan lung rtogs rnam rgyal 'phrin las dpal bzang po'i zhal snga nas kyi thun mong ba'i mdzad pa rnam thar mdo tsam brjod pa nor bu'i do shal.* Dharamsala, 1988.

Tsangnyon Heruka (gtsang smyon he ru ka, 1452–1507). *Mi la'i mgur 'bum.* Reprinted from the 1980 Kokonor edition. Published by Sherab Gyaltsen, Gangtok, 1983.

Tsongkhapa Lozang Dragpa (tsong kha pa blo bzang grags pa, 1357–1419). *Lam rim chen mo.*

_____. *Drang nges rnam 'byed legs bshad snying po.*

Urgyen Lingpa (o rgyan gling pa, 1323–60). *O rgyan gu ru padma 'byung gnas kyi skyes rabs rnam par thar pa rgyas par bkod pa.* Si khron mi rigs dpe skrun khang, 1996.

Urgyen Jigme Chökyi Wangpo, Paltul Rinpoche (o rgyan 'jigs med chos kyi dbang po, dpal sprul rin po che, 1808–87). *Rdzogs pa chen po klong chen snying thig gi ngon 'gro'i khrid yig kun bzang bla ma'i zhal lung.*

Vasubhandu (fourth century). *Abhidharmakosha.*

Zhang Yisum, et al. *Bod rgya tshig mdzod chen mo.* Mi rigs dpe skrun khang, 1985.

# General Index

# Index of Persons and Deities

# Index of Places

# Index of Texts

# About the Author

JAMYANG WANGMO, also known as Jampa Chokyi, was born in Salamanca, Spain, in 1945. She has a degree in law from Granada University and completed two years of art studies in Madrid. In 1972 she attended the meditation course given by the Sherpa lama Thubten Zopa Rinpoche at Kopan Monastery, and in 1973 she took the vows of a novice nun, subsequently taking those of a fully ordained nun in 1987. Since 1973 she has spent long periods of time in retreat in and around Lawudo Gompa and thus has become well acquainted with Sherpa culture and religion.

Her teachers include H.H. the Fourteenth Dalai Lama and many high lamas of the Gelug, Sakya, Kagyu, and Nyingma traditions. She has translated a number of tantric sadhanas and teachings from the Tibetan into both English and Spanish, she writes articles for a Spanish Dharma magazine, and she paints traditional thangkas and Khumbu landscapes. She presently spends the winters in Bouddha in the Kathmandu Valley and the summers in her hermitage at Thangme Gompa in Khumbu.

# About Wisdom

Wisdom Publications, a nonprofit publisher, is dedicated to making available authentic Buddhist works for the benefit of all. We publish translations of the sutras and tantras, commentaries and teachings of past and contemporary Buddhist masters, and original works by the world's leading Buddhist scholars. We publish our titles with the appreciation of Buddhism as a living philosophy and with the special commitment to preserve and transmit important works from all the major Buddhist traditions.

To learn more about Wisdom, or to browse books online, visit our website at wisdompubs.org. You may request a copy of our mail-order catalog online or by writing to:

Wisdom Publications
199 Elm Street
Somerville, Massachusetts 02144 USA
Telephone: (617) 776-7416
Fax: (617) 776-7841
Email: info@wisdompubs.org
www.wisdompubs.org

*The Wisdom Trust*
As a nonprofit publisher, Wisdom is dedicated to the publication of fine Dharma books for the benefit of all sentient beings and dependent upon the kindness and generosity of sponsors in order to do so. If you would like to make a donation to Wisdom, please do so through our Somerville office. If you would like to sponsor the publication of a book, please write or email us at the address above.

Thank you.

Wisdom is a nonprofit, charitable 501(c)(3) organization affiliated with the Foundation for the Preservation of the Mahayana Tradition (FPMT).